CORPUS-BASED LANGUAGE STUDIES

Routledge Applied Linguistics is a series of comprehensive resource books, providing students and researchers with the support they need for advanced study in the core areas of English language and Applied Linguistics.

Each book in the series guides readers through three main sections, enabling them to explore and develop major themes within the discipline:

- Section A, Introduction, establishes the key terms and concepts and extends readers' techniques of analysis through practical application.
- Section B, Extension, brings together influential articles, sets them in context, and discusses their contribution to the field.
- Section C, Exploration, builds on knowledge gained in the first two sections, setting thoughtful tasks around further illustrative material. This enables readers to engage more actively with the subject matter and encourages them to develop their own research responses.

Throughout the book, topics are revisited, extended, interwoven and deconstructed, with the reader's understanding strengthened by tasks and follow-up questions.

Corpus-Based Language Studies:

- covers the major theoretical approaches to the use of corpus data
- adopts a 'how to' approach with exercises and cases, providing students with the knowledge and tools to undertake their own corpus-based research
- gathers together influential readings from key names in the discipline, including: Biber, Widdowson, Stubbs, Carter and McCarthy
- is supported by a website featuring long extracts for analysis by students, with commentary by the authors.

Written by experienced teachers and researchers in the field, *Corpus-Based Language Studies* is an essential resource for students and researchers of Applied Linguistics.

Tony McEnery is Professor of English Language and Linguistics and Head of the Department of Linguistics and English Language, Lancaster University, UK. **Richard Xiao** is a researcher at the Department of Linguistics and English Language, Lancaster University, UK. **Yukio Tono** is Professor at the Department of Languages and Cultures, Meikai University, Japan.

ROUTLEDGE APPLIED LINGUISTICS

SERIES EDITORS

Christopher N. Candlin is Senior Research Professor in the Department of Linguistics at Macquarie University, Australia and Professor of Applied Linguistics at the Open University, UK. At Macquarie, he has been Chair of the Department of Linguistics; established and was Executive Director of the National Centre for English Language Teaching and Research (NCELTR), and was foundation Director of the Centre for Language in Social Life (CLSL). He has written or edited over 150 publications and co-edits the *Journal of Applied Linguistics*. From 1996 to 2002 he was President of the International Association of Applied Linguistics (AILA). He has acted as a consultant in more than thirty-five countries and as external faculty assessor in thirty-six universities worldwide.

Ronald Carter is Professor of Modern English Language in the School of English Studies at the University of Nottingham. He has published extensively in applied linguistics, literary studies and language in education, and has written or edited over forty books and a hundred articles in these fields. He has given consultancies in the field of English language education, mainly in conjunction with the British Council, in over thirty countries worldwide, and is editor of the Routledge Interface series and advisory editor to the Routledge English Language Introduction series. He was recently elected a Fellow of the British Academy for Social Sciences and is currently UK Government Advisor for ESOL and Chair of the British Association for Applied Linguistics (BAAL).

TITLES IN THE SERIES

Intercultural Communication: An advanced resource book
Adrian Holliday, Martin Hyde and John Kullman, Canterbury Christ Church University College, UK

Translation: An advanced resource book
Basil Hatim, Heriot-Watt University, UK and The American University of Sharjah, UAE and Jeremy Munday, University of Surrey, Guildford, UK

Grammar and Context: An advanced resource book
Ann Hewings, Open University, UK and Martin Hewings, University of Birmingham, UK

Second Language Acquisition: An advanced resource book
Kees de Bot, Wander Lowie and Marjolijn Verspoor

Corpus-Based Language Studies: An advanced resource book
Tony McEnery, Richard Xiao and Yukio Tono

Corpus-Based Language Studies

An advanced resource book

Tony McEnery, Richard Xiao and Yukio Tono

Routledge
Taylor & Francis Group

LONDON AND NEW YORK

First published 2006
by Routledge
2 Park Square, Milton Park, Abingdon, Oxon OX14 4RN

Simultaneously published in the USA and Canada
by Routledge
270 Madison Ave, New York, NY10016

Reprinted 2007, 2008

Routledge is an imprint of the Taylor & Francis Group, an informa business

© 2006 Tony McEnery, Richard Xiao and Yukio Tono

Typeset in Akzidenz Grotesk, Minion and Novarese
by Keystroke, Jacaranda Lodge, Wolverhampton
Printed and bound in Great Britain by
TJ International Ltd, Padstow, Cornwall

British Library Cataloguing in Publication Data
A catalogue record for this book is available from the British Library

Library of Congress Cataloging in Publication Data
A catalog record for this book has been requested

ISBN10: 0–415–28622–0 (hbk)
ISBN10: 0–415–28623–9 (pbk)

ISBN13: 978–0–415–28622–0 (hbk)
ISBN13: 978–0–415–28623–7 (pbk)

Contents

Contents

Contents

Contents cross-referenced

Series editors' preface

The Routledge Applied Linguistics Series provides a comprehensive guide to a number of key areas in the field of applied linguistics. Applied linguistics is a rich, vibrant, diverse and essentially interdisciplinary field. It is now more important than ever that books in the field provide up-to-date maps of what is an ever-changing territory.

The books in this series are designed to give key insights into core areas of applied linguistics. The design of the books ensures, through key readings, that the history and development of a subject is recognized while, through key questions and tasks, integrating understandings of the topics, concepts and practices that make up its essentially interdisciplinary fabric. The pedagogic structure of each book ensures that readers are given opportunities to think, discuss, engage in tasks, draw on their own experience, reflect, research and to read and critically reread key documents.

Each book has three main sections, each made up of approximately ten units:

A: An **Introduction** section: in which the key terms and concepts which map the field of the subject are introduced, including introductory activities and reflective tasks, designed to establish key understandings, terminology, techniques of analysis and the skills appropriate to the theme and the discipline.

B: An **Extension** section: in which selected core readings are introduced (usually edited from the original) from existing key books and articles, together with annotations and commentary, where appropriate. Each reading is introduced, annotated and commented on in the context of the whole book, and research/follow-up questions and tasks are added to enable fuller understanding of both theory and practice. In some cases, readings are short and synoptic and incorporated within a more general exposition.

C: An **Exploration** section: in which further samples and illustrative materials are provided with an emphasis, where appropriate, on more open-ended, student-centred activities and tasks, designed to support readers and users in undertaking their own locally relevant research projects. Tasks are designed for work in groups or for individuals working on their own. They can be readily included in award courses in applied linguistics, or as topics for personal study and research.

The books also contain a glossary/glossarial index, which provides a guide to the main terms used in the book, and a detailed, thematically organized further-reading section, which lays the ground for further work in the discipline. There are also extensive bibliographies.

The target audience for the series is upper undergraduates and postgraduates on language, applied linguistics and communication studies programmes as well as teachers and researchers in professional development and distance-learning programmes. High-quality applied research resources are also much needed for teachers of EFL/ESL and foreign-language students at higher-education colleges and universities worldwide. The books in the Routledge Applied Linguistics series are aimed at the individual reader, the student in a group and at teachers building courses and seminar programmes.

We hope that the books in this series meet these needs and continue to provide support over many years.

The editors

Professor Christopher N. Candlin and Professor Ronald Carter are the series editors. Both have extensive experience of publishing titles in the fields relevant to this series. Between them they have written and edited over one hundred books and two hundred academic papers in the broad field of applied linguistics. Chris Candlin was president of AILA (International Association for Applied Linguistics) from 1996–2002 and Ron Carter is Chair of BAAL (British Association for Applied Linguistics) from 2003–2006.

Professor Christopher N. Candlin,
Senior Research Professor
Department of Linguistics,
Division of Linguistics and Psychology
Macquarie University
Sydney NSW 2109
Australia

and

Professor of Applied Linguistics	Professor Ronald Carter
Faculty of Education and Language Studies	School of English Studies University of Nottingham
The Open University	Nottingham NG7 2RD
Walton Hall	UK
Milton Keynes MK7 6AA	
UK	

Preface

The corpus-based approach to linguistic analysis and language teaching has come to prominence over the past two decades. This book seeks to bring readers up to date with the latest developments in corpus-based language studies. In comparison with the existing introductory books in corpus linguistics, *Corpus-Based Language Studies* is unique in a number of ways.

First, this is a book which covers the 'how to' as well as the 'why'. In approaching 'how to', we obviously have to focus on specific concordance packages and corpora which are currently available. However, our aim is to embrace a range of corpora and packages, hence hopefully offsetting any problems due to corpora being withdrawn or software radically changed. It is the 'how to' focus which in large part makes this book stand out from other available volumes. This book includes six case studies, each exploring a particular research question using specific tools. This is where the reader learns how to do corpus linguistics, as the process of investigating the data using the package(s) concerned is spelled out step by step, using text and screenshots. Thus by the end of each case study, a corpus has been introduced, the reader has learned how to use a retrieval package and some research questions have been explored. Readers are then encouraged to explore a related research question using the same corpus data, tools and techniques. As well as explaining 'how to', the book also addresses 'why'. While we may expect the reader to consult other books on corpus linguistics, we want this book, for two distinct reasons, to explore what one may do with corpus data and why one should want to do it. First, and obviously, if we want the reader to be able to 'become' a corpus linguist having read the book, we clearly have to explain the rationale for corpus-based studies, and to use case studies both to exemplify the worth of corpus linguistics as well as the features of the packages concerned. Second, we want this book to tie in much more closely with linguistic theory than previous books in corpus linguistics have done. Our goal is to engage research questions and theory with corpus linguistics with an increasing depth and intensity as the book progresses.

Second, this is a book which engages with a range of approaches to the use of corpus data, which makes it different from existing books in corpus linguistics, with each case study focusing on a major approach to the use of corpus data while paying little or no attention to other approaches. After reading this volume, readers are expected to understand when and how to combine these approaches with other methodologies.

Finally, this is a book which is more focused on multilingual corpus linguistics than available corpus books. While this volume is concerned mainly with English corpus linguistics, we also cover issues in multilingual corpus linguistics, and have one case study focusing on a language other than English.

We would like to take this opportunity to thank the following people who have generously offered their help to us while we were writing this book. We are obliged to the series editors, Professors Christopher N. Candlin and Ronald Carter, for their constructive suggestions and advice throughout the process. We also thank Professor Irma Taavitsainen from the University of Helsinki and Ms Austina Shih from the Language Training and Testing Centre, Taipei for reading and commenting on the whole manuscript. Louisa Semlyen, Julene Knox and Christy Kirkpatrick from Routledge equally deserve our thanks for their unfailing help and support. Finally, we thank all of the copyright holders for permitting us to use the excerpts in Section B of this volume.

Tony, Richard and Yukio
March 2005

Acknowledgements

Douglas Biber, 'Representativeness in corpus design', *Literary and Linguistic Computing*, 1993, 8(4), pp. 243–438, by permission of Oxford University Press.

Atkins, S., J. Clear and N. Ostler, 'Corpus design criteria', *Literary and Linguistic Computing*, 1992, 7(1), pp. 4–5, by permission of Oxford University Press.

Henry G. Widdowson, 'The limitations of linguistics applied', *Applied Linguistics*, 2000, 21(1): 6–10, by permission of Oxford University Press.

Michael Stubbs, 'Texts, corpora, and problems of interpretation: a response to Widdowson', *Applied Linguistics*, 2001 22(2), pp. 150–4, by permission of Oxford University Press.

Robert de Beaugrande, 'Large corpora and applied linguistics: H.G. Widdowson versus J. McH. Sinclair'. Reproduced by kind permission of the author.

Ramesh Krishnamurthy, 'Collocation: from silly ass to lexical sets', in Heffer and Sauntson (eds) *Words in Context: a tribute to John Sinclair on his retirement*, pp. 31–34 University of Birmingham. Reproduced by kind permission of Ramesh Krishnamurthy.

From A. Partington, 'Utterly content in each other's company', in *International Journal of Corpus Linguistics*, 2004, 9(1), pp. 145–149. With kind permission by John Benjamins Publishing Company, Amsterdam/Philadelphia (www.benjamins.com), and the Foundation of Language.

R. Carter and M. McCarthy, 'The English *get*-passive in spoken discourse', *English language and Linguistics* 3(1), pp. 54–57, © Cambridge University Press, 1999, reprinted with permission of the author and publisher.

R. Kreyer, 'Genitive and *of* construction in modern written English', *International Journal of Corpus Linguistics*, 2003, 8(2), pp. 200–204. With kind permission by John Benjamins Publishing Company, Amsterdam/Philadelphia (www.benjamins.com), and the Foundation of Language.

Douglas Biber, 'On the role of computational, statistical, and interpretive techniques in multidimensional analysis of register variation', *Text*, 1995, 15(3), pp. 342–349. Reproduced by kind permission of the author and Mouton de Gruyter.

K. Hyland, 'Talking to students: metadiscourse in introductory coursebooks', *English for Specific Purposes* 18(1), pp. 3–12, Copyright © 1999, with permission from Elsevier.

H. Lehmann, 'Zero subject relative constructions in American and British English', *New Frontiers in Corpus Research*, 2002, pp. 170–176. Reproduced by permission of Editions Rodopi B.V.

Y. Kachru, 'On definite reference in world Englishes', *World Englishes*, 2003, 22(4), pp. 497–510. Reproduced by permission of Blackwell Publishing.

B. Altenberg and S. Granger, 'Recent trends in cross-linguistic lexical studies', in B. Altenberg, and S. Granger (eds) *Lexis in Contrast*, 2002, pp. 14–21. With kind permission by John Benjamins Publishing Company, Amsterdam/Philadelphia (www.benjamins.com), and the Foundation of Language.

A. McEnery, Z. Xiao and L. Mo, 'Aspect marking in English and Chinese', *Literary and Linguistic Computing*, 2003, 18(4), pp. 368–376, by permission of Oxford University Press.

M. Kilpiö, 'On the forms and functions of the verb *be* from old to modern English', in M. Rissanen, M. Kytö and K. Heikkonen (eds) *English in Transition: Corpus-Based Studies in Linguistic Variation and Genre Styles*, 1997, pp. 105–111. Reproduced by permission of Mouton de Gruyter.

C. Mair, M. Hundt, G. Leech and N. Smith, 'Short-term diachronic shifts in part-of-speech frequencies', in *International Journal of Corpus Linguistics*, 2003, 7(2), pp. 252–257. With kind permission by John Benjamins Publishing Company, Amsterdam/Philadelphia (www.benjamins.com), and the Foundation of Language.

L. Gavioli and G. Aston, 'Enriching reality: language corpora in language pedagogy', *ELT* Journal, 2001, 55(3), pp. 238–241, by permission of Oxford University Press.

J. Thurston and C. Candlin, 'Concordancing and the teaching of the vocabulary of academic English', *English for Specific Purposes* 17(3), pp. 267–271, Copyright © 1998, with permission from Elsevier.

S. Conrad, 'The importance of corpus-based research for language teachers', *SYSTEM* 27(1), pp. 1–3, Copyright © 1999, with permission from Elsevier.

Every effort has been made to trace and contact copyright holders. The publishers would be pleased to hear from any copyright holders not acknowledged here so that this section may be amended at the earliest opportunity.

SECTION A
Introduction

The corpus-based approach to linguistic analysis and language teaching has come to prominence over the past two decades. This book seeks to bring readers up to date with the latest developments in corpus-based language studies. The book is intended as an advanced resource book. This means that, by reading this book, readers will not only become familiar with the basic approach of corpus linguistics, they will also learn how to *do* corpus linguistics through a series of case studies.

Section A of this book sets the scene for corpus-based language studies by focusing on the theoretical aspects of corpus linguistics and introducing key concepts in the field. This section is broken into ten units, each focusing on either a key concept in corpus linguistics or on a practical issue that may face the corpus-builder or user.

Unit A1 introduces corpus linguistics and answers questions such as 'What is a corpus?' and 'Why is a corpus-based approach important?' Unit A2 is concerned with such issues as representativeness, balance and sampling, while Units A3 and A4 discuss corpus mark-up and annotation respectively. In Unit A5 we introduce the multilingual dimension of corpus linguistics. Unit A6 seeks to raise readers' statistical awareness, an awareness which is essential in corpus-based language studies. Unit A7 introduces publicly available, well-known and influential corpora while Unit A8 considers the important decisions and practical issues one may face when constructing a corpus. Unit A9 deals with copyright issues in corpus-building. Finally, Unit A10 explores the use of corpora in language studies.

Unit A1
Corpus linguistics: the basics

A1.1 INTRODUCTION

This unit sets the scene by addressing some of the basics of corpus-based language studies. We will first briefly review the history of corpus linguistics (Unit A1.2). Then the term *corpus*, as used in modern linguistics, will be defined (Unit A1.3). Following this is an explanation of why corpus linguists use computers to manipulate and exploit language data (Unit A1.4). We will then compare the intuition-based approach and the corpus-based approach to language (Unit A1.5), which is followed by an explanation of why corpus linguistics is basically a methodology rather than an independent branch of linguistics (Unit A1.6). Finally, we will consider the corpus-based vs. corpus-driven debate (Unit A1.7).

A1.2 CORPUS LINGUISTICS: PAST AND PRESENT

Although the term *corpus linguistics* first appeared only in the early 1980s (cf. Leech 1992: 105), corpus-based language study has a substantial history. The corpus methodology dates back to the pre-Chomskyan period when it was used by field linguists such as Boas (1940) and linguists of the structuralist tradition, including Sapir, Newman, Bloomfield and Pike (see Biber and Finegan 1991: 207). Although linguists at that time would have used shoeboxes filled with paper slips rather than computers as a means of data storage, and the 'corpora' they used might have been simple collections of written or transcribed texts and thus not *representative* (see Unit A2), their methodology was essentially 'corpus-based' in the sense that it was empirical and based on observed data. As McEnery and Wilson (2001: 2–4) note, the basic corpus methodology was widespread in linguistics in the early twentieth century.

In the late 1950s, however, the corpus methodology was so severely criticized that it became marginalized, if not totally abandoned, in large part because of the alleged 'skewedness' of corpora (see Chomsky 1962; see McEnery and Wilson 2001: 5–13 for a more detailed discussion). Chomsky's criticism was undoubtedly true when it was made. At that time, the size of 'shoebox corpora' was generally very small, and those corpora were used primarily for the study of distinguishing features in phonetics (Ling 1999: 240), though a few linguists of this era, notably Jesperson (1909–1949) and Fries (1952), also used paper-based corpora to study grammar.

Using paper slips and human hands and eyes, it was virtually impossible to collate and analyse large bodies of language data. Consequently the corpora of the time could rarely avoid being 'skewed'.

But with developments in technology, and especially the development of ever more powerful computers offering ever increasing processing power and massive storage at relatively low cost, the exploitation of massive corpora became feasible. The marriage of corpora with computer technology rekindled interest in the corpus methodology. The first *modern corpus* (see Unit A1.3) of the English language, the Brown corpus (i.e. the Brown University Standard Corpus of Present-day American English, see Unit A7.4), was built in the early 1960s for American English. Since then, and increasingly so from the 1980s onwards, the number and size of corpora and corpus-based studies have increased dramatically (see Johansson 1991: 12). Nowadays, the corpus methodology enjoys widespread popularity. It has opened up or foregrounded many new areas of research. Much of the research presented in this book would not have been produced without corpora. Unsurprisingly, as we will see in Unit A10, corpora have revolutionized nearly all branches of linguistics.

A1.3 WHAT IS A CORPUS?

In modern linguistics, a corpus can be defined as a body of naturally occurring language, though strictly speaking:

> It should be added that computer corpora are rarely haphazard collections of textual material: They are generally assembled with particular purposes in mind, and are often assembled to be (informally speaking) *representative* of some language or text type.
>
> (Leech 1992: 116)

Sinclair (1996) echoes Leech's definition of *corpus*, as he also stresses the importance of *representativeness* (see Unit A2): 'A corpus is a collection of pieces of language that are selected and ordered according to explicit linguistic criteria in order to be used as a sample of the language.' The 'linguistic criteria', which are external to the texts themselves and dependent upon the intended use for the corpus (see Aston and Burnard 1998: 23; see Units A2 and B1 for further discussion), are used to select and put together these texts 'in a principled way' (Johansson 1998: 3). Thus a corpus is different from a random collection of texts or an archive whose components are unlikely to have been assembled with such goals in mind (Aston and Burnard 1998: 5; Leech and Fligelstone 1992: 120). Rather, the term *corpus* as used in modern linguistics can best be defined as a collection of sampled texts, written or spoken, in machine-readable form which may be annotated with various forms of linguistic information (see Unit A4 for a discussion of corpus annotation).

There are many ways to define a corpus (e.g. Francis 1992: 17; Atkins, Clear and Ostler 1992: 1), but there is an increasing consensus that a corpus is a collection of (1) *machine-readable* (2) *authentic* texts (including transcripts of spoken data) which is (3) *sampled* to be (4) *representative* of a particular language or language variety. While all scholars agree upon the first two qualities, there are differing opinions regarding what can be counted as representative. Also, the question of what sampling techniques should be used to achieve representativeness is contentious. While some scholars propose that a corpus must be defined in linguistic terms (e.g. the distribution of words or other patterns), it is our view that non-linguistic (or extralinguistic) parameters should be used as important definitional criteria also (see Units A2 and B1 for further discussion).

It has been argued that corpora like the Lancaster Corpus of Abuse (i.e. LCA; see McEnery, Baker and Hardie 2000: 46), which are built using extracts from large corpora to study a specific linguistic phenomenon, are not corpora in a real sense. Such an argument, nevertheless, is arguably misleading for a number of reasons. First, corpora of this kind certainly meet the four criteria of a corpus as discussed above. Second, not all corpora are *balanced*. Specialized corpora serve a different yet important purpose from balanced corpora (see Unit A7.3). If specialized corpora which are built using a different sampling technique from those for balanced corpora were discounted as 'non-corpora', then corpus linguistics would have contributed considerably less to language studies. Third, it is simply unreasonable to argue that a subcorpus, which contains part of a larger corpus, is not a corpus. In fact, some corpus tools helpfully allow users to define a subcorpus from a larger corpus. For example, SARA (Aston and Burnard 1998) allows users to define subcorpora from the British National Corpus (i.e. BNC, see Unit A7.2) using the selected parameters; Xaira, the XML-aware version of SARA (see Burnard and Todd 2003; see Unit A3.3 for a discussion of Extensible Mark-up Language), even allows users to define a subcorpus from a large corpus through a query. The new version of WordSmith Tools (version 4, see Scott 2003) now includes a WebGetter function to help users to build their corpora using web pages on the Internet which contain the specified search patterns. If carefully selected subcorpora do not merit the label 'corpus', then corpora (or subcorpora) built using the corpus tools outlined above would not be called corpora either. So while it may be appealing to define precisely what a corpus is, the criteria should not be applied with such zeal that terminology is used as a tool to exclude carefully composed collections of language data from corpus-based research. The term corpus, while useful, should always be viewed as a somewhat vague and inclusive term.

A1.4 WHY USE COMPUTERS TO STUDY LANGUAGE?

It is clear from the previous section that the essential qualities of a corpus include machine-readability, authenticity and representativeness. Authenticity will be discussed when we compare a corpus-based and intuition-based approach while representativeness, together with related issues such as balance and sampling, will be explored in Units A2 and B1. In this section, we will focus on machine-readability and explain why corpus linguists use computers to manipulate and exploit language data.

Machine-readability is a *de facto* attribute of modern corpora. Electronic corpora have advantages unavailable to their paper-based equivalents. The most obvious advantage of using a computer for language study is the speed of processing it affords and the ease with which it can manipulate data (e.g. searching, selecting, sorting and formatting). Computerized corpora can be processed and manipulated rapidly at minimal cost. Second, computers can process machine-readable data accurately and consistently (see Barnbrook 1996: 11; see also Unit A4.2). Third, computers can avoid human bias in an analysis, thus making the result more reliable. Finally, machine-readability allows further automatic processing to be performed on the corpus so that corpus texts can be enriched with various metadata and linguistic analyses (see Units A3 and A4). It is the use of computerized corpora, together with computer programs which facilitate linguistic analysis, that distinguishes modern machine-readable corpora from early 'drawer-cum-slip' corpora (Svartvik 1992: 9). Without computers, many of the corpus-based studies undertaken in the past twenty years would have been impossible. As Tognini-Bonelli (2000: 210) observes, the computer has affected the methodological frame of linguistic enquiry. Given the prominence of the computer in corpus linguistics, it is unsurprising that corpora are typically in fact computerized corpora, and 'computer corpus linguistics' (CCL) has been suggested as the improved name for corpus linguistics (CL) (Leech 1992: 106). However, CCL is not a term that is widely used, as most scholars assume that CL implies CCL.

A1.5 THE CORPUS-BASED APPROACH VS. THE INTUITION-BASED APPROACH

In principle, by using the intuition-based approach, researchers can invent purer examples instantly for analysis, because intuition is readily available and invented examples are free from language-external influences existing in naturally occurring language. However, intuition should be applied with caution (see Seuren 1998: 260–262). First, it is possible to be influenced by one's dialect or sociolect; what appears unacceptable to one speaker may be perfectly felicitous to another. Assuming that what we see in a corpus is largely grammatical and/or acceptable, the corpus at least provides evidence of what speakers believe to be acceptable utterances in their language, typically free of the overt judgement of others. Second, when one invents an example to support or disprove an argument, one is consciously monitoring one's language production. Therefore, even if one's intuition is correct, the utterance may not represent typical language use. The corpus-based approach, in contrast, draws upon authentic or real texts, though authenticity itself may be a cause of dispute (see Units A10.8 and B2). Finally, results based on introspection alone are difficult to verify as introspection is not observable. All of these disadvantages are circumvented by the corpus-based approach. Additional advantages of the corpus-based approach are that a corpus can find differences that intuition alone cannot perceive (see Francis, Hunston and Manning 1996; Chief, Hung, Chen, Tsai and Chang 2000), and a corpus can yield reliable quantitative data.

Broadly speaking, compared with the more traditional intuition-based approach, which rejected or largely ignored corpus data, the corpus-based approach can offer the linguist improved reliability because it does not go to the extreme of rejecting intuition while attaching importance to empirical data. The key to using corpus data is to find the balance between the use of corpus data and the use of one's intuition. As Leech (1991: 14) comments:

> Neither the corpus linguist of the 1950s, who rejected intuition, nor the general linguist of the 1960s, who rejected corpus data, was able to achieve the interaction of data coverage and the insight that characterise the many successful corpus analyses of recent years.

While the corpus-based approach has obvious advantages over a purely intuition-based approach, not all linguists accept the use of corpora, as we will see in Unit B2. Indeed, it must be accepted that not all research questions can be addressed by the corpus-based approach (see Unit A10.15). This in large part explains why the corpus-based approach and the intuition-based approach are not mutually exclusive. The two are complementary and must be so if as broad a range of research questions as possible are to be addressed by linguists (see McEnery and Wilson 2001: 19; Sinclair 2003: 8).

A1.6 CORPUS LINGUISTICS: A METHODOLOGY OR A THEORY?

We have, so far, assumed that corpus linguistics is a methodology rather than an independent branch of linguistics. This view, however, is not shared by all scholars. For example, it has been argued that corpus linguistics 'goes well beyond this methodological role' and has become an independent 'discipline' (Tognini-Bonelli 2001: 1). While we agree that corpus linguistics is 'really a domain of research' and 'has become a new research enterprise and a new philosophical approach to linguistic enquiry' (*ibid.*), we maintain that corpus linguistics is indeed a methodology rather than an independent branch of linguistics in the same sense as phonetics, syntax, semantics or pragmatics. These latter areas of linguistics describe, or explain, a certain aspect of language use. Corpus linguistics, in contrast, is not restricted to a particular aspect of language. Rather, it can be employed to explore almost any area of linguistic research (see Unit A10). Hence, syntax can be studied using a corpus-based or non-corpus-based approach; similarly, we have corpus semantics and non-corpus semantics.

As corpus linguistics is a whole system of methods and principles of how to apply corpora in language studies and teaching/learning, it certainly has a theoretical status. Yet theoretical status is not theory itself. The qualitative methodology used in social sciences also has a theoretical basis and a set of rules relating to, for example, how to conduct an interview, or how to design a questionnaire, yet it is still labelled as a methodology upon which theories may be built. The same is true of corpus linguistics.

Definitional confusion bedevils corpus linguistics. As we have seen with the term *corpus* itself, strict definitions often fail to hold when specific examples are considered. Similarly, with the methodology question, the attempt to construct corpus linguistics as anything other than a methodology ultimately fails. In fact, even those who have strongly argued that corpus linguistics is an independent branch of linguistics have frequently used the terms 'approach' and 'methodology' to describe corpus linguistics (e.g. Tognini-Bonelli 2001). Hence, as with the term *corpus* itself, our approach is to take the less rigid, indeed less limiting, position. Corpus linguistics should be considered as a methodology with a wide range of applications across many areas and theories of linguistics.

A1.7 CORPUS-BASED VS. CORPUS-DRIVEN APPROACHES

One further, notable, area where differences emerge between corpus linguists is with regard to the question of corpus-based and corpus-driven approaches. In the corpus-based approach, it is said that corpora are used mainly to 'expound, test or exemplify theories and descriptions that were formulated before large corpora became available to inform language study' (Tognini-Bonelli 2001: 65). Corpus-based linguists are accused of not being fully and strictly committed to corpus data as a whole as they have been said to discard inconvenient evidence (i.e. data not fitting the pre-corpus theory) by 'insulation', 'standardisation' and 'instantiation', typically by means of annotating a corpus (see Unit A4). In contrast, corpus-driven linguists are said to be strictly committed to 'the integrity of the data as a whole' (*ibid*.: 84) and therefore, in this latter approach, it is claimed that '[t]he theoretical statements are fully consistent with, and reflect directly, the evidence provided by the corpus' (*ibid*.: 85). However, the distinction between the corpus-based vs. corpus-driven approaches is overstated. In particular the latter approach is best viewed as an idealized extreme. There are four basic differences between the corpus-based vs. corpus-driven approaches: types of corpora used, attitudes towards existing theories and intuitions, focuses of research and paradigmatic claims. Let us discuss each in turn.

Regarding the type of corpus data used, there are three issues – representativeness, corpus size and annotation. Let us consider these in turn. According to corpus-driven linguists, there is no need to make any serious effort to achieve corpus balance and representativeness (see Unit A2) because the corpus is said to balance itself when it grows to be big enough as the corpus achieves so-called cumulative representativeness. This initial assumption of self-balancing via cumulative representativeness, nonetheless, is arguably unwarranted (see Unit A2.4). For example, one such cumulatively representative corpus is the corpus of Zimbabwean English that Louw (1991) used in his contrastive study of collocations in British English and Zimbabwean English. This study shows that the collocates of *wash* and *washing,* etc. in British English are *machine, powder* and *spin* whereas in Zimbabwean English the more likely collocates are *women, river, earth* and *stone.* The different collocational behaviours were attributed to the fact that the Zimbabwean corpus has a prominent element of literary texts such as Charles Mungoshi's novel *Waiting for the Rain,* 'where women washing in the river are a recurrent theme across the novel' (Tognini-Bonelli 2001: 88). One could therefore reasonably argue that this so-called cumulatively balanced corpus was skewed. Especially where whole texts are included, a practice corpus-driven linguists advocate, it is nearly unavoidable that a small number of texts may seriously affect, either by theme or in style, the balance of a corpus (see Units A2.5 and B1.4 for a further discussion of whole texts). Findings on the basis of such cumulatively representative corpora may not be generalizable beyond the corpora themselves as their representativeness is highly idiosyncratic.

The corpus-driven approach also argues for very large corpora. While it is true that the corpora used by corpus-driven linguists are very large (for example, the latest release of the Bank of English has grown to 524 million words as of early 2004), size is not all-important (see Unit A8.2), as Leech (1991: 8–29) notes (see also McCarthy and Carter 2001). Another problem for the corpus-driven approach relates to frequency. While it has been claimed that in the corpus-driven approach corpus evidence is exploited fully, in reality frequency may be used as a filter to allow the analyst to exclude some data from their analysis. For example, a researcher may set the minimum frequency of occurrence for a pattern which it must reach before it merits attention, e.g. it must occur at least twice – in separate documents (Tognini-Bonelli 2001: 89). Even with such a filter, a corpus-driven grammar would consist of thousands of patterns which would bewilder the learner. It is presumably to avoid such bewilderment that the patterns reported in the *Grammar Patterns* series (Francis, Hunston and Manning 1996, 1998), which are considered as the first results of the corpus-driven approach, are not even that exhaustive. Indeed, faced with the great number of concordances, corpus-driven linguists often analyse only the nth occurrence from a total of X instances. This is in reality currently the most practical way of exploring a very large unannotated corpus. Yet if a large corpus is reduced to a small dataset in this way, there is little advantage in using very large corpora to explore frequent features. It is also difficult to see how it can be claimed that the corpus data are exploited fully and the integrity of the data is respected in such cases. It appears, then, that the corpus-driven approach is not so different from the corpus-based approach – while the latter allegedly insulates theory from data or standardizes data to fit theory, the former filters the data via apparently scientific random sampling, though there is no guarantee that the corpus is not explored selectively to avoid inconvenient evidence.

The corpus-driven linguists have strong objections to corpus annotation. This is closely associated with the second difference between the two approaches – attitudes towards existing theories and intuitions. It is claimed that the corpus-driven linguists come to a corpus with no preconceived theory, with the aim of postulating linguistic categories entirely on the basis of corpus data, though corpus-driven linguists do concede that pre-corpus theories are insights cumulated over centuries which should not be discarded readily and that intuitions are essential in analysing data. This claim is a little surprising, as traditional categories such as nouns, verbs, prepositions, subjects, objects, clauses and passives are not uncommon in studies which identify themselves as corpus-driven. When these terms occur they are used without a definition and are accepted as given. Also, linguistic intuitions typically come as a result of accumulated education in preconceived theory. So applying intuitions when classifying concordances may simply be an implicit annotation process, which unconsciously makes use of preconceived theory. As implicit annotation is not open to scrutiny, it is to all intents and purposes unrecoverable and thus more unreliable than explicit annotation (see Unit A4.2). Corpus-based linguists do not have such a hostile attitude towards existing theory. The corpus-based approach typically has existing theory as a starting point and corrects and revises such theory in the light of corpus evidence. As part of this process, corpus annotation is common. Annotating a corpus, most notably through part-of-speech tagging (see Unit A4.4.1), inevitably involves developing a set of parts of speech on the basis of an existing theory, which is then tested and revised constantly to mirror the attested language use. In spite of the clear usefulness of outcomes of corpus annotation, which greatly facilitate corpus exploration, the process of annotation itself is also important. As Aarts (2002: 122) observes, as part of the annotation process the task of the linguist becomes 'to examine where the annotation fits the data and where it does not, and to make changes in the description and annotation scheme where it does not'. The claimed independence of preconception on the part of corpus-driven linguists is clearly an overstatement. A truly corpus-driven approach, if defined in this way, would require something such as someone who has never received any education related to language use and therefore is free from preconceived theory, for, as Sampson (2001: 135) observes, schooling also plays an important role in forming one's intuitions. Given that it is difficult to totally reject and dismiss preconceived theory, and intuitions are indeed called upon in corpus-driven linguistics, it is safe to conclude that there is no real difference between the corpus-driven demand to re-examine pre-corpus theories in the new framework and corpus-based linguists' practice of testing and revising such theories. Furthermore, if the so-called proven corpus-driven categories in corpus-driven linguistics, which are supposed to be already fully consistent with and directly reflect corpus evidence, also need refinement in the light of different corpus data, the original corpus data are arguably not representative enough. The endless refinement will result in inconsistent language descriptions which will place an unwelcome burden on the linguist or the learner. In this sense, the corpus-driven approach is no better than the corpus-based approach.

The third important difference between the corpus-driven and corpus-based approaches is their different research focuses. As the corpus-driven approach makes no distinction between lexis, syntax, pragmatics, semantics and discourse (because all of these are pre-corpus concepts and they combine to create meaning), the holistic approach provides, unsurprisingly, only one level of language description, namely, the functionally complete unit of meaning or language patterning. In studying patterning, corpus-driven linguists concede that while collocation can be easily identified in KWIC concordances of unannotated data, colligation is less obvious unless a corpus is grammatically tagged. Yet a tagged corpus is the last thing the corpus-driven linguists should turn to, as grammatical tagging is based on preconceived theory, and consequently results in a loss of information, in their view. To overcome this problem, Firth's definition of colligation is often applied in a loose sense – in spite of the claim that corpus-driven linguistics is deeply rooted in Firth's work – because studying colligation in Firth's original sense necessitates a tagged or even a parsed corpus. According to Firth (1968: 181), colligation refers to the relations between words at the grammatical level, i.e. the relations of 'word and sentence classes or of similar categories' instead of 'between words as such'. But nowadays the term colligation has been used to refer not only to significant co-occurrence of a word with grammatical classes or categories (e.g. Hoey 1997, 2000; Stubbs 2001c: 112) but also to significant co-occurrence of a word with grammatical words (e.g. Krishnamurthy 2000). The patterning with grammatical words, of course, can be observed and computed even using a raw corpus.

A final contrast one can note between the corpus-based and corpus-driven approaches is that the corpus-based approach is not as radical as the corpus-driven approach. The corpus-driven approach claims to be a new paradigm within which a whole language can be described. No such claim is entailed in the corpus-based approach. Yet as we will see in Unit A10, the corpus-based approach, as a methodology, has been applied in nearly all branches of linguistics.

The above discussion shows that the sharp distinction between the corpus-based vs. corpus-driven approaches to language studies is in reality fuzzy. As with the definition of what a corpus is and the theory vs. methodology distinction, we maintain a less rigid distinction between the two approaches. In our book, the term corpus-based is used in a broad sense, encompassing both corpus-based and corpus-driven approaches, as suggested by the title of this book.

Summary

This unit addressed some basic issues in corpus linguistics, including a brief review of the history of corpus linguistics, a definition of *corpus* as used in modern linguistics, a discussion of the advantages of using computers in language studies, a comparison of the intuition-based and the corpus-based approaches, an explanation of why corpus linguistics should be viewed as a methodology rather than an independent branch of linguistics, and finally a discussion of the debate over the corpus-based vs. corpus-driven linguistics.

LOOKING AHEAD

In this unit, we focused only on one salient feature of a modern corpus, namely, machine-readability. Other issues of corpus design (e.g. balance, representativeness, sampling and corpus size) will be discussed in Units A2 and A8, and further explored in Unit B1. Corpus processing (e.g. data capture, corpus mark-up and annotation) will be discussed in Units A3–A4 and A8. Using corpora in language studies will be introduced in Unit A10 and further discussed in Section B and explored in Section C of this book.

Unit A2
Representativeness, balance and sampling

A2.1 INTRODUCTION

We noted in Unit A1 that representativeness is an essential feature of a corpus. It is this feature that is typically used to distinguish a corpus from an archive (i.e. a random collection of texts). A corpus is designed to represent a particular language or language variety whereas an archive is not. Unless you are studying a dead language or highly specialized sub-language (see Unit A2.3 for further discussion), it is virtually impossible to analyse every extant utterance or sentence of a given language. Hence, sampling is unavoidable. Yet how can you be sure that the sample you are studying is representative of the language or language variety under consideration? The answer is that one must consider balance and sampling to ensure representativeness. Hence, this unit introduces the key concept of corpus representativeness as well as the related issues of balance and sampling. We will first explain what we mean by *representativeness* (Unit A2.2), followed by a discussion of the representativeness of general and specialized corpora (Unit A2.3). We will then move on to discuss corpus balance (Unit A2.4) and finally introduce sampling techniques (Unit A2.5).

A2.2 WHAT DOES REPRESENTATIVENESS MEAN IN CORPUS LINGUISTICS?

What does representativeness mean in corpus linguistics? According to Leech (1991: 27), a corpus is thought to be representative of the language variety it is supposed to represent if the findings based on its contents can be generalized to the said language variety. Biber (1993: 243) defines representativeness from the viewpoint of how this quality is achieved: 'Representativeness refers to the extent to which a sample includes the full range of variability in a population.' A corpus is essentially a *sample* of a language or language variety (i.e. *population*). Sampling is entailed in the compilation of virtually any corpus of a living language. In this respect, the representativeness of most corpora is to a great extent determined by two factors: the range of genres included in a corpus (i.e. *balance*, see Unit A2.4) and how the text chunks for each genre are selected (i.e. *sampling*, see Unit A2.5).

We noted in Unit A1.2 that the criteria used to select texts for a corpus are principally external. The external vs. internal criteria correspond to Biber's (1993: 243) situational vs. linguistic perspectives. External criteria are defined situationally irrespective of the distribution of linguistic features whereas internal criteria are defined linguistically, taking into account the distribution of such features. Biber refers to situationally defined text categories as *genres* or *registers* (see Unit A10.4), and linguistically defined text categories as *text types* (see Unit B1), though these terms are typically used interchangeably in the literature (e.g. Aston and Burnard 1998), and in this book.

Internal criteria have sometimes been proposed as a measure of corpus representativeness. Otlogetswe (2004), for example, argues that:

> The study of corpus word distributions would reveal whether words in a corpus are skewed towards certain varieties and whether in such instances it is accurate to say they are representative of the entire corpus. It would also reflect the stability of the design – whether overall representativeness is very sensitive to particular genres.

Similar views can be found elsewhere. For example, in a discussion of representativeness on the Corpora Mailing List, most discussants appeared to assume that a corpus should sufficiently represent particular words: 'A representative corpus should include the majority of the types in the language as recorded in a comprehensive dictionary' (Berber-Sardinha 1998). Such a decision would in turn entail a discussion of what should be counted as a word, e.g. whether one should count different forms of the same word as instances of the same type.

In our view, it is problematic, indeed it is circular, to use internal criteria like the distribution of words or grammatical features as the primary parameters for the selection of corpus data. A corpus is typically designed to study linguistic distributions. If the distribution of linguistic features is predetermined when the corpus is designed, there is no point in analysing such a corpus to discover naturally occurring linguistic feature distributions. The corpus has been skewed by design. As such, we generally agree with Sinclair (1995) when he says that the texts or parts of texts to be included in a corpus should be selected according to external criteria so that their linguistic characteristics are, initially at least, independent of the selection process. This view is also shared by many other scholars including Atkins, Clear and Ostler (1992: 5–6) and Biber (1993: 256). Yet once a corpus is created by using external criteria, the results of corpus analysis can be used as feedback to improve the representativeness of the corpus. In Biber's (1993: 256) words, 'the compilation of a representative corpus should proceed in a cyclical fashion'.

In addition to text selection criteria, Hunston (2002: 30) suggests that another aspect of representativeness is change over time. She claims that '[a]ny corpus that is not regularly updated rapidly becomes unrepresentative' (*ibid.*). The relevance of permanence in corpus design actually depends on how we view a corpus, i.e.

whether a corpus should be viewed as a static or dynamic language model. The static view typically applies to a *sample corpus* whereas a dynamic view applies to a *monitor corpus* (see Units A4.2 and A7.9 for further discussion). While monitor corpora following the dynamic language model are useful in tracking rapid language change such as the development and lifecycle of neologisms, they normally cover a relatively short span of time. Very long-term change can, of course, be studied using diachronic corpora such as the Helsinki Diachronic Corpus (see Units A7.7, A10.7 and B5.4), in which each component represents a specific time period. Static sample corpora, if resampled, may also allow the study of language change over time. Static sample corpora which apply the same *sampling frame* (see Unit A2.5) are particularly useful in this respect. Typical examples of this type of corpus are the Lancaster–Oslo–Bergen corpus (i.e. LOB) and the Freiburg–LOB corpus (i.e. FLOB), which represent British English in the early 1960s and the early 1990s respectively (see Unit A7.4). Another corpus following the same sampling frame is under construction on a project which is funded by the Leverhulme Trust and undertaken by Lancaster University. The corpus is designed as a match for LOB in the early 1930s. These three corpora are specifically constructed with the study of language change in mind. Diachronic corpora like the Helsinki corpus and the corpora of the LOB family are sample corpora of the static language model sort, yet they are all well suited for the study of language change.

A2.3 THE REPRESENTATIVENESS OF GENERAL AND SPECIALIZED CORPORA

There are two broad types of corpora in terms of the range of text categories represented in the corpus: *general* and *specialized* corpora. General corpora typically serve as a basis for an overall description of a language or language variety. The British National Corpus (BNC, see Unit A7.2), for example, is supposed to represent modern British English as a whole. In contrast, specialized corpora tend to be domain (e.g. medicine or law) or genre (e.g. newspaper text or academic prose) specific. For a general corpus, it is understandable that it should cover, proportionally, as many text types as possible so that the corpus is maximally representative of the language or language variety it is supposed to represent. Even a specialized corpus, e.g. one dealing with telephone calls to an operator service should be balanced by including within it a wide range of types of operator conversations (e.g. line fault, request for an engineer call-out, number check, etc.) between a range of operators and customers (see McEnery, Baker and Cheepen 2001) so that it can be claimed to represent this variety of language.

While both general and specialized corpora should be representative of a language or language variety, the representativeness of the two types of corpora are measured in different ways. The representativeness of a general corpus depends heavily on sampling from a broad range of genres (see Unit A2.4) whereas the representativeness of a specialized corpus, at the lexical level at least, can be measured by the degree of 'closure' (McEnery and Wilson 2001: 166) or 'saturation' (Belica 1996:

61–74) of the corpus. Closure/saturation for a particular linguistic feature (e.g. size of lexicon) of a variety of language (e.g. computer manuals) means that the feature appears to be finite or is subject to very limited variation beyond a certain point. To measure the saturation of a corpus, the corpus is first divided into segments of equal size based on its tokens. The corpus is said to be saturated at the lexical level if each addition of a new segment yields approximately the same number of new lexical items as the previous segment, i.e. when 'the curve of lexical growth has become asymptotic' (Teubert 1999), or is flattening out. The notion of saturation is claimed to be superior to such concepts as balance for its measurability (*ibid.*). It should be noted, however, that saturation is only concerned with lexical features. While it may be possible to adapt saturation to measure features other than lexical growth, there have been few attempts to do this to date (though see McEnery and Wilson 2001: 176–183 for a study of part-of-speech and sentence type closure).

A2.4 BALANCE

As noted in the previous section, the representativeness of a corpus, especially a general corpus, depends primarily upon how balanced the corpus is, in other words, the range of text categories included in the corpus. As with representativeness, the acceptable balance of a corpus is determined by its intended uses. Hence, a general corpus which contains both written and spoken data (e.g. the BNC, see Unit A7.2) is balanced; so are written corpora such as Brown and LOB (see Unit A7.4), and spoken corpora like CANCODE (see Unit A7.5); domain-specific corpora (e.g. the HKUST Computer Science Corpus, see Unit A7.3) can also claim to be balanced. A balanced corpus usually covers a wide range of text categories which are supposed to be representative of the language or language variety under consideration. These text categories are typically sampled proportionally (see Unit A2.5) for inclusion in a corpus so that 'it offers a manageably small scale model of the linguistic material which the corpus builders wish to study' (Atkins *et al.* 1992: 6).

While balance is often considered a *sine qua non* of corpus design, any claim of corpus balance is largely an act of faith rather than a statement of fact as, at present, there is no reliable scientific measure of corpus balance. Rather the notion relies heavily on intuition and best estimates. Nevertheless, one thing we can be certain of is that work in text typology – classifying and characterizing text categories – is highly relevant to any attempt to achieve corpus balance. Yet different ways of classifying and characterizing texts can produce different text typologies. The text typology proposed by Atkins *et al.* (1992) lists up to twenty-nine text attributes which are considered relevant in constructing a balanced corpus. All of the parameters are extra-linguistic variables, though the authors are aware that external criteria alone cannot achieve corpus balance: 'Controlling the "balance" of a corpus is something which may be undertaken only after the corpus (or at least an initial provisional corpus) has been built' (*ibid.*: 6). Yet while useful, such work is rarely the basis of corpus construction. A more typical approach to corpus balance is that corpus-builders – for good or ill – adopt an existing corpus model when building their own corpus, assuming that balance will be achieved from the adopted model.

For example, the British National Corpus (BNC) is generally accepted as being a balanced corpus. The BNC model has been followed in the construction of a number of corpora, for example, the American National Corpus, the Korean National Corpus, the Polish National Corpus and the Russian Reference Corpus (Sharoff 2003) (see Unit A7.2 for a description of these corpora). Given the importance of such a model, a closer look at the design criteria used in building the BNC may help to give us a general idea of what is assumed to be corpus balance.

The BNC contains approximately 100 million words, of which 90 per cent are written texts and 10 per cent are transcripts of spoken data. Written texts were selected using three criteria: 'domain', 'time' and 'medium'. Domain refers to the content type (i.e. subject field) of the text; time refers to the period of text production, while medium refers to the type of text publication such as books, periodicals or unpublished manuscripts. Table A2.1 summarizes the distribution of these criteria (see Aston and Burnard 1998: 29–30). The spoken data in the BNC was collected on the basis of two criteria: 'demographic' and 'context-governed'. The demographic component is composed of informal encounters recorded by 124 volunteer respondents selected by age group, sex, social class and geographical region, while the context-governed component consists of more formal encounters such as meetings, lectures and radio broadcasts recorded in four broad context categories. The two types of spoken data complement each other, as many contexts of speech may not have been covered if demographic sampling techniques alone were used in data collection. Table A2.2 summarizes the composition of the spoken BNC. Note that in the table, the first two columns apply to both demographic and context-governed components while the third column refers to the latter component alone.

As the BNC is designed to represent contemporary British English as a whole, the overall aim of using the above text selection criteria was to achieve a balanced

Table A2.1 Composition of the written BNC

Domain	%	Date	%	Medium	%
Imaginative	21.91	1960–74	2.26	Book	58.58
Arts	8.08	1975–93	89.23	Periodical	31.08
Belief and thought	3.40	Unclassified	8.49	Misc. published	4.38
Commerce/finance	7.93			Misc. unpublished	4.00
Leisure	11.13			To-be-spoken	1.52
Natural/pure science	4.18			Unclassified	0.40
Applied science	8.21				
Social science	14.80				
World affairs	18.39				
Unclassified	1.93				

Table A2.2 Composition of the spoken BNC

Region	%	Interaction type	%	Context-governed	%
South	45.61	Monologue	18.64	Educational/informative	20.56
Midlands	23.33	Dialogue	74.87	Business	21.47
North	25.43	Unclassified	6.48	Institutional	21.86
Unclassified	5.61			Leisure	23.71
				Unclassified	12.38

selection within each text category. Aston and Burnard's (1998: 28) summary of the design criteria of the BNC illustrates the notion of corpus balance very well:

> In selecting texts for inclusion in the corpus, account was taken of both production, by sampling a wide variety of distinct types of material, and reception, by selecting instances of those types which have a wide distribution. Thus, having chosen to sample such things as popular novels, or technical writing, best-seller lists and library circulation statistics were consulted to select particular examples of them.

Balance appears to be a more important issue for a static sample corpus than for a dynamic monitor corpus. As corpora of the latter type are updated frequently, it is usually 'impossible to maintain a corpus that also includes text of many different types, as some of them are just too expensive or time consuming to collect on a regular basis' (Hunston 2002: 30–31). The builders of monitor corpora appear to feel that balance has become less of a priority – sheer size seems to have become the basis of the corpus's authority, under the implicit and arguably unwarranted assumption that a corpus will in effect balance itself when it reaches a substantial size (see Units A1.7 and A7.9 for further discussion).

Like corpus representativeness, balance is an important issue for corpus creators, corpus users and readers of corpus-based studies alike. Representativeness links to research questions. The research question one has in mind when building (or thinking of using) a corpus defines representativeness. If one wants a corpus which is representative of general English, a corpus representative of newspapers will not do. If one wants a corpus representative of newspapers, a corpus representative of *The Times* will not do. Representativeness is a fluid concept. Corpus creators should not only make their corpora as balanced as possible for the language variety in question by including a great variety of relevant representative language samples, they must also document corpus design criteria explicitly and make the documentation available to corpus users so that the latter may make appropriate claims on the basis of such corpora and decide whether or not a given corpus will allow them to pursue a specific research question. Readers of corpus-based research should also interpret the results of corpus-based studies with caution and consider whether the corpus data used in a study were appropriate. With that said, however, we entirely agree with Atkins *et al.* (1992: 6), who comment that:

It would be short-sighted indeed to wait until one can scientifically balance a corpus before starting to use one, and hasty to dismiss the results of corpus analysis as 'unreliable' or 'irrelevant' because the corpus used cannot be proved to be 'balanced'.

A2.5 SAMPLING

Corpus representativeness and balance are closely associated with *sampling*. Given that we cannot exhaustively describe natural language, we need to sample it in order to achieve a balance and representativeness which match our research question. Having decided that sampling is inevitable, there are important decisions that must be made about how to sample so that the resulting corpus is as balanced and representative as practically possible.

As noted earlier in this unit, with few exceptions, a corpus – either a sample or monitor corpus – is typically a *sample* of a much larger *population*. A sample is assumed to be representative if what we find for the sample also holds for the general population (see Manning and Schütze 1999: 119). In the statistical sense, samples are scaled-down versions of a larger population (see Váradi 2000). The aim of sampling theory 'is to secure a sample which, subject to limitations of size, will reproduce the characteristics of the population, especially those of immediate interest, as closely as possible' (Yates 1965: 9).

In order to obtain a representative sample from a population, the first concern to be addressed is to define the *sampling unit* and the boundaries of the population. For written text, for example, a sampling unit may be a book, periodical or news-paper. The population is the assembly of all sampling units while the list of sampling units is referred to as a *sampling frame*. The population from which samples for the pioneering Brown corpus were drawn, for instance, was written English text published in the United States in 1961 while its sampling frame was a list of the collection of books and periodicals in the Brown University Library and the Providence Athenaeum. For the LOB corpus, the target population was all written English text published in the United Kingdom in 1961 while its sampling frame included the *British National Bibliography Cumulated Subject Index* 1960–1964 for books and *Willing's Press Guide* 1961 for periodicals.

In corpus design, a population can be defined in terms of language production, language reception or language as a product. The first two designs are basically demographically oriented as they use the demographic distribution (e.g. age, sex, social class) of the individuals who produce/receive language data to define the population while the last is organized around text category/genre of language data. As noted earlier, the Brown and LOB corpora were created using the criterion of language as a product while the BNC defines the population primarily on the basis of both language production and reception. However, it can be notoriously difficult to define a population or construct a sampling frame, particularly for spoken language, for which there are no ready-made sampling frames in the form of catalogues or bibliographies.

Once the target population and the sampling frame are defined, different sampling techniques can be applied to choose a sample which is as representative as possible of the population. A basic sampling method is *simple random sampling*. With this method, all sampling units within the sampling frame are numbered and the sample is chosen by use of a table of random numbers. As the chance of an item being chosen correlates positively with its frequency in the population, simple random sampling may generate a sample that does not include relatively rare items in the population, even though they can be of interest to researchers. One solution to this problem is *stratified random sampling*, which first divides the whole population into relatively homogeneous groups (so-called *strata*) and samples each stratum at random. In the Brown and LOB corpora, for example, the target population for each corpus was first grouped into fifteen text categories such as news reportage, academic prose and different types of fiction; samples were then drawn from each text category. Demographic sampling, which first categorizes sampling units in the population on the basis of speaker/writer age, sex and social class, is also a type of stratified sampling. Biber (1993) observes that a stratified sample is never less representative than a simple random sample.

A further decision to be made in sampling relates to sample size. For example, with written language, should we sample full texts (i.e. whole documents) or text chunks? If text chunks are to be sampled, should we sample text initial, middle or end chunks? Full text samples are certainly useful in text linguistics, yet they may potentially constitute a challenge in dealing with vexatious copyright issues (see Unit A9). Also, given its finite overall size, the coverage of a corpus including full texts may not be as balanced as a corpus including text segments of constant size, and 'the peculiarity of an individual style or topic may occasionally show through into the generalities' (Sinclair 1991a: 19). Aston and Burnard (1998: 22) argue that the notion of 'completeness' may sometimes be 'inappropriate or problematic'. As such, unless a corpus is created to study such features as textual organization, or copyright holders have granted you permission to use full texts, it is advisable to sample text segments. According to Biber (1993: 252), frequent linguistic features are quite stable in their distributions and hence short text chunks (e.g. 2,000 running words) are usually sufficient for the study of such features while rare features are more varied in their distribution and thus require larger samples. In selecting samples to be included in a corpus, however, attention must also be paid to ensure that text initial, middle and end samples are balanced.

Another sampling issue, which particularly relates to stratified sampling, is the proportion and number of samples for each text category. The numbers of samples across text categories should be proportional to their frequencies and/or weights in the target population in order for the resulting corpus to be considered as representative. Nevertheless, it has been observed that, as with defining a target population, such proportions can be difficult to determine objectively (see Hunston

2002: 28–30). Furthermore, the criteria used to classify texts into different categories or genres are often dependent on intuitions. As such, the representativeness of a corpus, as noted, should be viewed as a statement of belief rather than fact. In the Brown corpus, for example, the ratios between the fifteen text categories were determined by a panel of experts (see Table A7.1, p. 62). As for the number of samples required for each category, Biber (1993) demonstrates that ten 2,000-word samples are typically sufficient.

The above discussion suggests that in constructing a balanced, representative corpus, stratified random sampling is to be preferred over simple random sampling while different sampling methods should be used to select different types of data. For written texts, a text typology established on the basis of external criteria is highly relevant while for spoken data demographic sampling is appropriate. However, samples obtained from demographic sampling must be complemented by context-governed sampling so that some contextually governed linguistic variations can be included in the resulting corpus.

Summary

This unit introduced some important concepts in corpus linguistics – representativeness, balance and sampling. A corpus is considered representative if what we find on the basis of the corpus also holds for the language or language variety it is supposed to represent. For most corpora, representativeness is typically achieved by balancing, i.e. covering a wide variety of frequent and important text categories that are proportionally sampled from the target population. Claims of corpus representativeness and balance, however, should be interpreted in relative terms and considered as a statement of faith rather than as fact, as presently there is no objective way to balance a corpus or to measure its representativeness. Furthermore, it is only by considering the research question one has to address that one is able to determine what is an acceptable balance for the corpus one should use and whether it is suitably representative. The concepts introduced in this unit will help you to determine if a particular corpus is suitable for your intended research. They are also helpful in determining whether a research question is amenable to corpus analysis.

LOOKING AHEAD

The notions of corpus balance and representativeness will be discussed further in Units A8.3 and B1, while the potential uses of corpora in language studies will be explored in Unit A10. Units A7.9 and B2 will further develop some issues touched upon in this unit such as the monitor corpus model and the pros and cons of the corpus-based approach. In the following two units, we will introduce two further concepts in corpus linguistics, namely *mark-up* and *annotation*.

Unit A3
Corpus mark-up

A3.1 INTRODUCTION

Data collected using a sampling frame as discussed in Unit 2 form a raw corpus. Yet such data typically need to be processed before use. For example, spoken data need to be transcribed from audio recordings. Written texts may need to be rendered machine-readable, if they are not already, by keyboarding or OCR (optical character recognition) scanning. Beyond this basic processing, however, lies another form of preparatory work – corpus mark-up.

Corpus mark-up is a system of standard codes inserted into a document stored in electronic form to provide information *about* the text itself and govern formatting, printing or other processing. This is an area which often causes confusion for neophytes in corpus linguistics. This unit first explains the rationale for corpus mark-up. Following this, widely used mark-up schemes such as TEI (the Text Encoding Initiative) and CES (the Corpus Encoding Standard) are introduced. Finally we will discuss a related issue, character encoding, which may be a particularly important issue when corpora including a range of writing systems are being constructed.

A3.2 THE RATIONALE FOR CORPUS MARK-UP

Corpus mark-up is important for at least three reasons. First, as noted in Unit A2, the corpus data basically consist of samples of used language. This means that these examples of linguistic usage are taken out of the context in which they originally occurred and their contextual information is lost. Burnard (2002) compares such out-of-context examples to a laboratory specimen and argues that contextual information (i.e. metadata, or 'data about data') is needed to restore the context and to enable us to relate the specimen to its original habitat. In corpus-building, therefore, it is important to recover as much contextual information as practically possible to alleviate or compensate for such a loss (see Unit A10.8 for further discussion). Second, while it is possible to group texts and/or transcripts of similar quality together and name these files consistently (e.g. as happens with the LOB and Brown corpora, see Unit A7.4), filenames can provide only a tiny amount of extra-textual information (e.g. text types for written data and sociolinguistic variables of speakers for spoken data) and no textual information (paragraph/sentence boundaries and speech turns) at all. Yet such data are of great interest to linguists and thus should be encoded, separately from the corpus data *per se*, in a corpus (see Unit A3.3). Mark-up adds value to a corpus and allows for a broader range of research questions to be addressed as a result. Finally, pre-processing written texts, and particularly transcribing spoken data, also involves mark-up. For example in written data, when graphics/tables are removed from the original texts, placeholders must be inserted to indicate the locations and types of omissions; quotations in foreign languages should also be marked up. In spoken data, pausing and para-linguistic features such as laughter need to be marked up. Corpus mark-up is also needed to insert editorial comments, which are sometimes necessary in pre-processing written texts and transcribing spoken data. What is done in corpus mark-up has a clear parallel in existing linguistic transcription practices. Mark-up is essential in corpus-building.

A3.3 CORPUS MARK-UP SCHEMES

Having established that mark-up is important in corpus construction, we can now move on to discuss mark-up schemes. It goes without saying that extra-textual and textual information should be kept separate from the corpus data (texts or transcripts) proper. Yet there are different schemes one may use to achieve this goal. One of the earliest mark-up schemes was COCOA. COCOA references consist of a set of attribute names and values enclosed in angled brackets, as in <A WILLIAM SHAKESPEARE>, where A (author) is the *attribute name* and WILLIAM SHAKESPEARE is the *attribute value*. COCOA references, however, only encode a limited set of features such as authors, titles and dates (see McEnery and Wilson 2001: 35). Recently, a number of more ambitious metadata mark-up schemes have been proposed, including for example, the Dublin Core Metadata Initiative (DCMI; see Dekkers and Weibel 2003), the Open Language Archives Community (OLAC; see Bird and Simons 2000), the ISLE Metadata Initiative (IMDI; see Wittenburg, Peters and Broeder 2002), the Text Encoding Initiative (TEI; see Sperberg-McQueen and Burnard 2002) and the Corpus Encoding Standard (CES; see Ide and Priest-Dorman 2000). DCMI provides fifteen elements used primarily to describe authored web resources. OLAC is an extension of DCMI, which introduces refinements to narrow down the semantic scope of DCMI elements and adds an extra element to describe the language(s) covered by the resource. IMDI applies to multimedia corpora and lexical resources as well. From even this brief review it should be clear that there is currently no widely agreed standard way of representing metadata, though all of the current schemes do share many features and similarities. Possibly the most influential schemes in corpus-building are TEI and CES, hence we will discuss both of these in some detail here.

The Text Encoding Initiative (TEI) was sponsored by three major academic asso-ciations concerned with humanities computing: the Association for Computational Linguistics (ACL), the Association for Literary and Linguistic Computing (ALLC) and the Association for Computers and the Humanities (ACH). The aim of the TEI guidelines is to facilitate data exchange by standardizing the mark-up or encoding of information stored in electronic form.

In TEI, each individual text (referred to as *document*) consists of two parts: header and body (i.e. the text itself), which are in turn composed of different *elements*. In a TEI header (tagged as <teiHeader>), for example, there are four principal elements (see Burnard 2002):

- a *file description* (tagged as <fileDesc>) containing a full bibliographic description of an electronic file;
- an *encoding description* (tagged as <encodingDesc>) which describes the relationship between an electronic text and the source or sources from which it was derived;
- a *text profile* (tagged as <profileDesc>), containing a detailed description of non-bibliographic aspects of a text, specifically the languages and sub-languages used, the situation in which it was produced, the participants and their setting;
- a *revision history* (tagged as <revisionDesc>) which records the changes that have been made to a file.

Each element may contain embedded sub-elements at different levels. Of these, however, only <fileDesc> is required to be TEI-compliant; all of the others are optional. Hence, a TEI header can be very complex, or it can be very simple, depending upon the document and the degree of bibliographic control sought. Figure A3.1 shows the corpus header of the British National Corpus (World Edition) expanded to the second level. The plus symbol (+) preceding an element indicates that the element can be expanded while the minus symbol (−) means that an element has already been expanded.

In the figure, a sequence of the form <XXX> is referred to as a start tag of an element while a corresponding sequence of the form </XXX> is an end tag. It is clear that these tags appear in pairs and can be nested within other elements. For example:

<extent> Approximately 100 million words </extent>

is embedded in the <editionStmt> element, which is in turn nested in <fileDesc>. Note that the start tag of an element may also contain an *attribute-value* pair, e.g. <editionStmt n = "2.0">.

The body part of a TEI document is also conceived as being composed of elements. In this case, an element can be any unit of text, for example, chapter, paragraph, sentence or word. Formal mark-up in the body is by far rarer than in the header. It is primarily used to encode textual structures like paragraphs and sentences. Note that the TEI scheme applies to both the mark-up of metadata and the annotation of interpretative linguistic analysis (see Unit A4). For example, the article *the* can be tagged thus:

```
– <teiHeader type="corpus" creator="dominic" status="update" dat.updated="2000-10-17"
id="BNC-W">
   – <fileDesc>
   + <TITLESTMT>
   + <editionStmt n="2.0">
      <extent>Approximately 100 million words</extent>
   + <publicationStmt>
   + <sourceDesc>
   </fileDsec>
– <encodingDesc>
   + <projectDesc>
   + <samplingDecl>
   + <editorialDecl>
   + <tagsDecl>
   + <refsDecl>
   + <classDecl>
   </encodingDesc>
– <profileDesc>
      <creation>This version of the corpus contains only texts accessioned on or before
1994-11-04.</creation>
   + <langUsage>
   + <particDesc>
   </profileDesc>
– <revisionDesc>
   + <change>
   + <change>
   + <change>
   + <change n="1.0">
   </revisionDesc>
</teiHeader>
```

Figure A3.1 The corpus header of the BNC World Edition

  <w POS=AT0>the</w>

This indicates that the part of speech (POS) of *the* is an article (AT0). In the BNC, the POS tag of *the* looks like this:

  <w AT0>the

This is because end tags are omitted for the elements <s>, <w> and <c> (i.e. sentences, words and punctuation) in the BNC, the end of each being implied by the following <s>, <w> or <c>. In addition, attribute names (POS), together with the equal sign, are left out for the elements <w> and <c> to save space (see Aston and Burnard 1998: 33).

The TEI scheme can be expressed using a number of different formal languages. The first editions used the Standard Generalized Mark-up Language (SGML); the most recent edition (i.e. TEI P4, 2002) can be expressed in the Extensible Mark-up Language (XML) (Sperberg-McQueen and Burnard 2002). SGML and XML are very similar, both defining a representation scheme for texts in electronic form which is device and system independent. SGML is a very powerful mark-up language, but associated with this power is complexity. XML is a simplified subset of SGML intended to make SGML easy enough for use on the Web. Hence while all XML documents are valid SGML documents, the reverse is not true. Nevertheless, there are some important surface differences between the two mark-up languages. End tags in SGML, as noted, can optionally be left out. They cannot in XML. An attribute name (i.e. generic identifier) in SGML may or may not be case sensitive. It is always case sensitive in XML; unless it contains spaces or digits, an attribute value in SGML may be given without double (or single) quotes. Quotes are mandatory in XML.

As the TEI guidelines are expressly designed to be applicable across a broad range of applications and disciplines, treating not only textual phenomena, they are designed for maximum generality and flexibility (see Ide 1998). As such, up to 450 elements are predefined in the TEI guidelines. While these elements make TEI very powerful and suitable for the general purpose encoding of electronic texts, they also add complexity to the scheme. In contrast, the Corpus Encoding Standard (CES) is designed specifically for the encoding of language corpora. CES is described as 'simplified' TEI in that it includes only the subset of the TEI tagset relevant to corpus-based work. It also simplifies the TEI specifications. Yet CES also extends the TEI guidelines by adding new elements not covered in TEI, specifying the precise values for some attributes, marking required/recommended/optional elements, and explicating detailed semantics for elements relevant to language engineering (e.g. sentence, word, etc.) (see Ide 1998).

CES covers three principal types of mark-up: (a) document-wide mark-up, which provides a bibliographic description of the document, encoding description, etc.; (b) gross structural mark-up, which encodes structural units of text (such as volume, chapter, etc.) down to the level of paragraph (but also including footnotes, titles, headings, tables, figures, etc.) and specifies normalization to recommended character sets and entities; (c) mark-up for sub-paragraph structures, including sentences, quotations, words, abbreviations, names, dates, terms and cited words, etc. (see Ide 1998).

CES specifies a minimal encoding level that corpora must achieve to be considered standardized in terms of descriptive representation as well as general architecture. Three levels of text standardization are specified in CES: (a) the metalanguage level, (b) the syntactic level and (c) the semantic level. Standardization at the meta-language level regulates the form of the syntactic rules and the basic mechanisms of mark-up schemes. Users can use a TEI-compliant *Document Type Definition* (DTD) to define tag names as well as 'document models' which specify the relations among tags. As texts may still have different document structures and mark-ups even with the same metalanguage specifications, standardization at the syntactic level specifies precise tag names and syntactic rules for using the tags. It also provides constraints on content. However, even the same tag names can be interpreted differently by the data sender and receiver. For example, a <title> element may be intended by the data sender to indicate the name of a book while the data receiver is under no obligation to interpret it as such, because the element can also show a person's rank, honour and occupation, etc. This is why standardization at the semantic level is useful. In CES, the <h.title> element only refers to the name of a document. CES seeks to standardize at the semantic level for those elements most relevant to language-engineering applications, in particular, linguistic elements. The three levels of standardization are designed to achieve the goal of universal document interchange. Like the TEI scheme, CES not only applies to corpus mark-up, it also covers encoding conventions for the linguistic annotation of text and speech, currently including morpho-syntactic tagging (i.e. POS tagging, see Unit A4.4.1) and parallel text alignment in parallel corpora (see Unit A5.3).

CES was developed and recommended by the Expert Advisory Groups on Language Engineering Standards (EAGLES) as a TEI-compliant application of SGML that could serve as a widely accepted set of encoding standards for corpus-based work. CES is available in both SGML and XML versions. The XML version, referred to as XCES, has also developed support for additional types of annotation and resources, including discourse/dialogue, lexicons and speech (Ide, Patrice and Laurent 2000).

A3.4 CHARACTER ENCODING

Another issue related to corpus mark-up is character encoding. In the earlier SGML versions of TEI and CES, special characters in English (e.g. the pound sign, £), accented characters in European languages (e.g. those marked with an acute in French, such as: é) and other non-ASCII (American Standard Code for Information Interchange) characters were replaced by *entity references* which are delimited by & and ; (e.g. £ refers to £ and é stands for é). While declaring entity references for characters can solve the problem of representing special characters for languages which have only a small number of such characters, it is not a feasible solution for languages such as Chinese, where tens of thousands of entities would have to be declared to cover the writing system as the SGML versions of TEI and CES are primarily geared toward English and European languages.

There are many complementary standardized character codes (e.g. the ISO-8859 family of fifteen members) and competing native character sets (e.g. GB2312 and Big5 for Chinese) that corpus builders can use to avoid this problem. As noted elsewhere, (McEnery and Xiao 2005a), while these legacy encodings are efficient in handling the language(s) they are designed for, they are inadequate for the purpose of electronic data interchange in a rapidly globalizing environment. Unicode is an attempt to solve this problem. Unicode is truly multilingual in that it can display characters from a very large number of writing systems and hence it holds out the promise of providing a standard for multilingual corpus character encoding.

Unicode has also been adopted by XML as the required character set for all XML documents. With the advent of XML/Unicode, most problems previously associated with character representation in corpus-building will be greatly reduced. An XML editor enables you to input characters in most writing systems of the world directly and stores these characters in a way that is directly transferable between different computer systems, whether that be Unicode characters or as character entity references (Sperberg-McQueen and Burnard 2002). The combined use of Unicode and XML is a growing and useful trend in corpus development. As noted in the previous section, TEI and CES are both available in XML versions. XML support has made it possible for these mark-up schemes to be adopted more widely in a multilingual context.

Summary

Mark-up is an essential step in corpus-building. An understanding of corpus mark-up is also of importance to corpus users. This unit has presented the rationale for corpus mark-up. It has also reviewed a number of mark-up schemes, focusing on the TEI guidelines and CES, and reviewed briefly the issue of character encoding in corpus construction. This basic overview should provide a sound basis on which to begin corpus-building and use.

The discussions in this unit show that mark-up – especially information traditionally stored in a corpus header – often holds important information relating to context in spoken corpora and genres in written corpora. This information is crucial to the process of interpreting the data extracted from a corpus. The mark-up of the text in the body (e.g. paragraph and sentence markers) is also often very useful for linguists.

Mark-up schemes vary in complexity, as does the mark-up of individual corpora. This complexity depends on the level of detail required for particular research questions.

LOOKING AHEAD

This unit only provided a brief introduction to two major mark-up schemes, TEI and CES/XCES. Readers who wish to find further details of these schemes, or details of other schemes, should refer to their individual websites. The next unit will explore a related area of corpus construction: the annotation of interpretative linguistic analysis.

Unit A4
Corpus annotation

A4.1 INTRODUCTION

Corpus annotation is closely related to corpus mark-up. One important reason for using corpora in linguistic research is to extract linguistic information present in those corpora. But it is often the case that in order to extract such information from a corpus, a linguistic analysis must first be encoded in the corpus. The process of 'adding such interpretative, linguistic information to an electronic corpus of spoken and/or written language data' is referred to as corpus annotation (Leech 1997a: 2). Corpus annotation adds value to a corpus in that it considerably extends the range of research questions that a corpus can readily address. While corpus annotation defined in a broad sense may refer to the encoding of both textual/ contextual information and interpretative linguistic analysis, as shown by the conflation of the two often found in the literature, the term is used in a narrow sense here, referring solely to the encoding of linguistic analyses such as part-of-speech (POS) tagging and syntactic parsing in a corpus text.

Corpus annotation, as used in a narrow sense, is fundamentally distinct from corpus mark-up as discussed in Unit A3. Corpus mark-up provides relatively objectively verifiable information regarding the components of a corpus and the textual structure of each text. In contrast, corpus annotation is concerned with interpretative linguistic information. 'By calling annotation "interpretative", we signal that annotation is, at least in some degree, the product of the human mind's understanding of the text' (Leech 1997a: 2). For example, the part of speech of a word may be ambiguous and hence is more readily defined as corpus annotation than corpus mark-up. On the other hand, the sex of a speaker or writer is normally objectively verifiable and as such is a matter of mark-up, not annotation.

This unit will first discuss the advantages and disadvantages of corpus annotation. Following this is a discussion of how corpus annotation is achieved. We will then introduce the most commonly used types of corpus annotation. Finally we will briefly review standalone corpus annotation, as proposed by the Corpus Encoding Standard (CES, see Unit A3.3).

A4.2 CORPUS ANNOTATION = ADDED VALUE

Like corpus mark-up, annotation adds value to a corpus. Leech (1997a: 2) maintains that corpus annotation is 'a crucial contribution to the benefit a corpus brings, since it enriches the corpus as a source of linguistic information for future research and development'. Both Leech (*ibid.*: 4–5) and McEnery (2003: 454–455) suggest that there are at least four advantages for corpus annotation.

First, it is much easier to extract information from annotated corpora in a number of ways. Leech (*ibid.*) observes, for example, that without part-of-speech tagging (see Unit A4.4.1), it is difficult to extract *left* as an adjective from a raw corpus as its various meanings and uses cannot be identified from its orthographic form or context alone. For example, the orthographic form *left* with a meaning opposite to *right* can be an adjective, an adverb or a noun. It can also be the past or past participle form of *leave*. With appropriate part-of-speech annotations these different uses of *left* can be readily distinguished apart. Corpus annotation also enables human analysts and machines to exploit and retrieve analyses of which they are not themselves capable (McEnery 2003: 454). For example, even if you do not know Chinese, given a suitably annotated Chinese corpus, you are able to find out a great deal about Chinese using that corpus (see Case Study 6 in Section C). Speed of data extraction is another advantage of annotated corpora. Even if one is capable of undertaking the required linguistic analyses, one is quite unlikely to be able to explore a raw corpus as swiftly and reliably as one can explore an annotated corpus if one has to start by annotating the corpus oneself.

Second, an annotated corpus is a reusable resource, as annotation records linguistic analyses within the corpus that are then available for reuse. Considering that corpus annotation tends to be costly and time-consuming, reusability is a powerful argument in favour of corpus annotation (see Leech 1997a: 5).

Third, an advantage of corpus annotation, related to reusability, is multifunctionality. A corpus may have originally been annotated with one specific purpose in mind. However, corpus analyses may be reused for a variety of applications and even for purposes not originally envisaged.

Finally, corpus annotation records a linguistic analysis explicitly. As such, the corpus annotation stands as a clear and objective record of analysis that is open to scrutiny and criticism (see McEnery 2003), a laudable goal.

In addition to these advantages we can also note that corpus annotation, like a corpus *per se*, provides a standard reference resource. While a corpus may constitute a standard reference for the language variety which it is supposed to represent, corpus annotation provides a stable base of linguistic analyses, objectively recorded, so that successive studies can be compared and contrasted on a common basis.

Having outlined the advantages of corpus annotation, it is necessary to address some of the criticisms of corpus annotation. Four main criticisms of corpus annotation have been presented over the past decade.

The first criticism is that corpus annotation produces cluttered corpora. Hunston (2002: 94) argues that '[h]owever much annotation is added to a text, it is important for the researcher to be able to see the plain text, uncluttered by annotational labels'. While we agree that the plain text is important in a corpus analysis, especially in observing the patterning of words, corpus annotation does not necessarily obscure such a patterning, because most corpus exploration tools (e.g. WordSmith, MonoConc, SARA and Xaira; see Section C) do indeed allow users to suppress annotation in search results so as to allow users to view the plain text. As such this criticism is more directed at corpus browsing/retrieval tools rather than at corpus annotation *per se*.

A second criticism is that annotation imposes a linguistic analysis upon a corpus user. While it is true that corpus annotation is fundamentally interpretative in nature, there is no compulsion for corpus users to accept that analysis. They can impose their own interpretations if they will or simply ignore the annotation. The plurality of interpretations of a text is something that must be accepted from the outset when undertaking corpus annotation (see McEnery 2003: 456). Yet just leaving a corpus unannotated does not mean that there is no process of interpretation occurring when the corpus is analysed. Rather, the lack of annotation simply disguises the fact that such multiple interpretations still occur when researchers use a raw corpus. The analysis still happens, it is simply hidden from clear view. Corpus annotation should be recognized as an advantage rather than a weakness in this respect as it provides an objective record of an explicit analysis open for scrutiny – failing to annotate is not simply a failure to analyse. Failing to annotate does, however, ensure that the analysis is difficult, or indeed impossible, to recover.

A further criticism is that annotation may 'overvalue' a corpus, making it less readily accessible, updateable and expandable (see Hunston 2002: 92–93). Annotation does not necessarily makes a corpus less accessible. For example, many parsed (e.g. the Lancaster Parsed Corpus and the Susanne corpus, see Unit A7.4) and prosodically annotated corpora (e.g. the London-Lund Corpus and the Lancaster/IBM Spoken English Corpus, see Unit A7.5) are publicly available. Corpus-builders are usually happy to make their corpora available as widely as possible in spite of (or some-times because of) the huge effort that they have put into annotation. Funders are also often prepared to finance corpus construction because a valuable annotated resource will be made widely available. Public funding bodies are particularly unlikely to fund corpus-building projects which do not result in a readily accessible resource. A more common reason for not making an annotated corpus (or indeed a raw corpus) publicly available is that the copyright issues related to the corpus data prohibit it (see Unit A9). Copyright, not annotation, is the greater force in favour of restriction. The arguments relating to updating and expansion are also questionable. Unlike a monitor corpus, which is constantly updated to track rapid language change (see Unit A7.9 for further discussion), most corpora are sample corpora. A sample corpus is designed to represent a particular language variety at a particular time. For example, the LOB and Brown corpora are supposed to represent written British and American English in the early 1960s. There are indeed 'updates' for the two corpora – FLOB and Frown (see Unit A7.4). The two updated corpora respectively represent written British and American English in the early 1990s and can be used to track slower paced language change (see Unit B5.5). The need for constant expansion is only related to the dynamic monitor corpus model. It does not necessarily apply as an argument to sample corpora. Given that most corpora are sample corpora, the expandability argument is hardly important, as with a sample corpus size is typically determined when the corpus is designed. Once the corpus is created, there is generally no need for expansion.

The final criticism is related to the accuracy and consistency of corpus annotation. There are three basic methods of annotating a corpus – automatic, computer-assisted and manual (see Unit 4.3). On the one hand, as Hunston (2002: 91) argues, 'an automatic annotation program is unlikely to produce results that are 100% in accordance with what a human researcher would produce; in other words, there are likely to be errors'. Such errors also occur when humans alone analyse the texts – even the best linguist at times makes mistakes. Introducing a human factor into annotation may have another implication; as Sinclair (1992) argues, the introduction of a human element in corpus annotation, as in manual or computer-assisted annotation, results in a decline in the consistency of annotation. Taking the two points together, one might wonder why any linguist has ever carried out an analysis, as it would have been inaccurate and inconsistent! One must conclude that they have done so, and that annotators continue to do so because while inconsistency and inaccuracy in analyses are indeed observable phenomena, their impact upon an expert human analysis has been exaggerated. Also, the computer is not a sure-fire means of avoiding inaccuracy or inconsistency: the two points may also apply to machine analyses. Automatic annotation is not error free, and it may be inconsistent. If resources are altered for an annotation program – the lexicon changed, rules rewritten – then over time the output of the program will exhibit inconsistency on a scale that may well exceed that displayed by human analysts. So what should we use for corpus annotation, human analysts or the computer? Given that the value of corpus annotation is well recognized, the human analyst and the machine should complement each other, providing a balanced approach to accuracy and consistency that seeks to reduce inaccuracy and inconsistency to levels tolerable to the research question that the corpus is intended to investigate.

It is clear from the above discussion that all of the four criticisms of corpus annotation can be dismissed, with caveats, quite safely. Annotation only means undertaking and making explicit a linguistic analysis. As such, it is something that linguists have been doing for centuries.

A4.3 HOW IS CORPUS ANNOTATION ACHIEVED?

As noted earlier, corpus annotation can be achieved fully automatically, by a semi-automatic interaction between human being and the machine, or entirely manually by human analysts. To cover the three in turn, in automatic annotation, the computer works alone as an annotator by following the rules and algorithms predefined by a programmer, though rules can also be acquired by the machine via machine learning (ML), using a predefined ML algorithm. Developing an automatic annotation tool may cost time and money, but once it is completed, large quantities of data can be annotated rapidly and (assuming there are no resource changes) consistently. On occasion one may find that this work has already been undertaken elsewhere and that a program that can undertake the desired annotation is already freely available.

Some types of annotation, e.g. lemmatization and POS tagging (see Units A4.4.1 and A4.4.2) for English, French and Spanish, and segmentation and POS tagging for Chinese, can be undertaken by the machine so reliably (with a typical error rate of 3 per cent) that we may consider a wholly automated approach to their annotation. When the output from an automated process is not reliable, as is the case with most parsers (see Unit A4.4.3), or the output is reliable, but not accurate enough for a particular purpose (e.g. the training corpus used to improve an annotation tool), human correction (i.e. post-editing) is usually required. Post-editing is generally faster than undertaking annotation entirely by hand. Some annotation tools provide a human–machine interface that allows a human analyst to resolve ambiguous cases where the machine is not certain. The semi-automatic annotation process may produce more reliable results than fully automated annotation, but it is also slower and more costly. Pure manual annotation occurs where no annotation tool is available to a user, or where the accuracy of available systems is not high enough to make the time invested in manual correction less than pure manual annotation. As manual annotation is expensive and time-consuming, it is typically only feasible for small corpora. With the few exceptions mentioned above, most types of annotation presently available in large corpora were introduced either semi-automatically or manually.

A4.4 TYPES OF CORPUS ANNOTATION

Corpus annotation can be undertaken at different levels and may take various forms. For example, at the phonological level corpora can be annotated for syllable boundaries (phonetic/phonemic annotation) or prosodic features (prosodic annotation); at the morphological level corpora can be annotated in terms of prefixes, suffixes and stems (morphological annotation); at the lexical level corpora can be annotated for parts of speech (POS tagging), lemmas (lemmatization), and semantic fields (semantic annotation); at the syntactic level corpora can be annotated with syntactic analysis (parsing, treebanking or bracketing); at the discoursal level corpora can be annotated to show anaphoric relations (coreference annotation), pragmatic information like speech acts (pragmatic annotation) or stylistic features such as speech and thought presentation (stylistic annotation). Of these the most widespread type of annotation is POS tagging, which has been successfully applied to many languages; syntactic parsing is also developing rapidly while some types of annotation (e.g. discoursal and pragmatic annotations) are presently relatively undeveloped. In this unit we will introduce annotation types which are currently in general use by linguists. Readers are advised to refer to Garside, Leech and McEnery (1997: 85–90) and McEnery and Wilson (2001: 65–68) for discussions of annotation types not covered in this section.

A4.4.1 POS tagging

POS tagging (also referred to as grammatical tagging or morpho-syntactic annotation) means assigning a part-of-speech mnemonic, also known as a POS tag, to each word in a corpus. POS tagging was one of the first widely used types of corpus annotation and is today by far the most common type. It is also the most basic type of corpus annotation forming the basis of further forms of analysis such as parsing and semantic annotation. However, corpora annotated for parts of speech alone are useful for a wide scope of applications ranging from disambiguating homographs to more sophisticated uses such as computing the occurrences of word classes in a corpus (see Unit B5.5). Many linguistic analyses, e.g. the collocates of a word (see Unit A10.2 for further discussion of collocation), also depend heavily on POS tagging (see Hunston 2002: 81).

Given the advanced state of the development of POS tagging, it can be performed automatically for many languages with a precision rate good enough for most research questions. The annotation tool which automatically assigns POS tags to lexical units is called a tagger. One of the best-known and most reliable taggers for English is CLAWS (Constituent-Likelihood Automatic Word Tagging System), developed at Lancaster University (see Garside, Leech and Sampson 1987). The system employs a hybrid statistical approach enhanced by a rule-based component, idiosyncratically called the 'idiom list' (Garside and Smith 1997). This tagger is reported to have achieved an accuracy rate of 97 per cent on general written English (see Garside and Smith 1997). The system was employed to tag the British National Corpus (BNC, see Unit A7.2). POS taggers have also been developed successfully for languages such as French (Gendner 2002), Spanish (Farwell, Helmreich and Casper 1995), German (Hinrichs, Kübler, Müller and Ule 2002), Swedish (Cutting 1994) and Chinese (Chang and Chen 1993; Zhang and Liu 2002).

The POS tags used by taggers such as CLAWS can be stored in different encoding formats. For example, a POS tag can be joined with a lexical unit by the underscore as in *going_VVGK*, using TEI entity references (see Unit A3.3) as in *going&VVGK*; using SGML (*<w POS=VVGK>going</w>*, or a simplified SGML form *<w VVGK> going* as in the BNC) or in XML format (*<w POS="VVGK">going</w>*). Whatever encoding style is adopted, these formats can be translated readily between each other to meet the needs of individual corpus exploration tools. For relatively non-mark-up aware concordancers (e.g. MonoConc and WordSmith), the embedded annotation format using the underscore character may be preferred while for fully mark-up aware tools like SARA and Xaira, an SGML or XML format is preferable.

In part-of-speech annotation, the first issue that an annotator must address is how to segment the text into word tokens. The process of defining legitimate words in a running text is referred to as *word segmentation* or *tokenization*. For alphabetical languages like English, word tokens in a written text are normally delimited by a preceding and following space or new-line character. The one-to-one correspondence between orthographic and morpho-syntactic word tokens can be considered as a default with three main exceptions: multiwords (e.g. *so that* and *in spite of*), mergers (e.g. *can't* and *gonna*) and variably spelled compounds (e.g. *noticeboard, notice-board, notice board*). To give an example of how a system may treat such cases, CLAWS treats a multiword expression as a single lexical unit and assigns so-called ditto tags to the whole expression. Ditto tagging involves assigning the same POS code to each word in an idiomatic expression, marking each with a two-digit number, the first digit of which indicates the total number of words in the expression while the second indicates the number of the word in the expression. For example, the subordinating conjunction (CS) *so that* is tagged as *so_CS21 that_CS22* while the preposition (II) *in spite of* is tagged as *in_II31 spite_II32 of_II33*. In contrast, the sub-parts of mergers are considered to be separate words. For example, the contracted negated modal verb *can't* is broken apart and tagged as *ca_VM n't_XX* while the catenative *gonna* is broken apart and tagged as *gon_VVGK na_TO*. A compound is tagged as one morpho-syntactic word if it appears as one orthographic word with or without a hyphen (*noticeboard_NN1* and *notice-board _NN1*), or as two morpho-syntactic words if it appears as two orthographic words (*notice_NN1 board_NN1*).

For many other languages, word segmentation is a much more challenging task. In Chinese, for example, a written text contains a running string of characters with no delimiting spaces. Consequently, word segmentation in Chinese requires complex computer processing, which usually involves lexicon matching and the use of a statistical model. In this book we will not discuss the technical details of how segmentation is achieved by programs working on Chinese. Readers interested in this should refer to Wu and Fung (1994), Huang *et al.* (1997), Sun, Shen and Tsou (1998), Swen and Yu (1999), Feng (2001) and Zhang and Liu (2002).

A4.4.2 Lemmatization

Lemmatization is a type of annotation that reduces the inflectional variants of words to their respective lexemes (or lemmas) as they appear in dictionary entries. For example, the lemma of *do, does, did, done* and *doing* is DO while the lemma for *corpus, corpora* and *corpuses* is CORPUS. Note that in corpus linguistics, as in this book, lemmas are conventionally written in small capital letters. Lemmatization is important in vocabulary studies and lexicography, e.g. in studying the distribution pattern of lexemes and improving dictionaries and computer lexicons (see McEnery and Wilson 2001: 53; Leech 1997a: 15).

Lemmatization can automatically be performed quite reliably for many languages including, for example, English, French and Spanish (see McEnery, Wilson, Sanchez-Leon and Nieto-Serano 1997). However, the usefulness of lemmatization depends on how inflectional a language is. For highly inflectional languages like Russian and Spanish, where a lemma covers a large number of inflectional variants, lemmatization is particularly useful whereas for non-inflectional languages like Chinese, lemmatization is of limited use. As English is a language with simple inflectional morphology, which only inflects verbs for tense and nouns for plurality, lemmatization 'may be considered somewhat redundant' for English (Leech 1997a: 15). That may explain why, although quite accurate software is available for this purpose, few English corpora are lemmatized.

A4.4.3 Parsing

As noted in Unit A4.4.1, POS tagging is a basic step that often leads to further types of annotation such as parsing. Once a corpus is POS tagged, it is possible to bring these morpho-syntactic categories into higher-level syntactic relationships with one another (see McEnery and Wilson 2001: 53), in other words, to analyse the sentences in a corpus into their constituents. This procedure is referred to as *parsing*. As parsing often involves assigning phrase markers to constituents using sets of labelled brackets, parsing is sometimes referred to as *bracketing*, though strictly speaking, bracketing is specifically related to the labelling of phrase structures (PS grammar) while syntactic analysis may also cover dependency relations (constraint grammar) between words and functional labelling of elements such as subjects and objects etc. (e.g. Karlsson *et al.* 1995). As parsed corpora, especially those in a vertical indented layout (as used in the Penn Treebank, see Marcus, Santorini and Marcinkiewicz 1993), often appear similar to tree diagrams, they are sometimes known as *treebanks*. For example, *Mary visited a very nice boy* can be bracketed as follows (cited from Santorini 1991: 3):

```
(S    (NP    Mary)
      (VP    visited)
             (NP    a
                    (ADJP very nice)
                    boy)))
```

Here, *S* represents *sentence* while *NP*, *VP* and *ADJP* stand respectively for *noun*, *verb* and *adjectival phrases*.

Parsing is probably the most common type of annotation after POS tagging. It is important to most natural language processing (NLP) applications – to make sense of a natural language, an NLP system must be able to decode its syntax. Syntactically parsed treebanks are even more useful than POS tagged corpora in linguistic research, as they not only provide part-of-speech information for individual words but also indicate constituent types and membership. For example, it is much easier to study clause types using a parsed corpus. A carefully edited treebank can also be used as a grammar tutor to teach grammatical analysis to students (see McEnery, Baker and Hutchinson 1997).

While parsing can be automated, its precision rate is generally much lower than that of POS tagging (see Mitkov 2002: 194). Typically an automatically parsed corpus needs to be corrected by hand (e.g. the Penn Treebank). Some available treebanks are entirely hand crafted (e.g. the Lancaster–Leeds Treebank), though interactive computer programs (e.g. EPICS, see Garside 1993) can be used to assist in the process of manual parsing. A handcrafted or post-edited treebank can in turn be used to train an automatic parser.

Syntactic parsing, no matter whether it is automatic or manual, is typically based on some form of context-free grammar, for example, phrase-structure grammar, dependency grammar or functional grammar. Even with the same grammar, however, different annotators may use different parsing schemes, which may differ, for example, in the number of constituent types and the rules for combining each other (see McEnery and Wilson 2001: 55). For example, while the UCREL parsing scheme and the Penn Treebank scheme both employ a phrase-structure grammar and cover noun, verb, adjective, adverbial and preposition phrases, the former also distinguishes between different clause types such as adverbial clause, comparative clause, nominal clause and relative clause whereas the latter differentiates between different types of *wh*-clauses (e.g. noun, adverb and prepositional phrases).

In terms of the details encoded, parsing can be either full parsing or skeleton (shallow) parsing. While the former provides a syntactic analysis which is as detailed as possible, the latter tends to use less fine-grained constituent types. The Penn Treebank is an example of skeleton parsing. Here, for example, all noun phrases are labelled as N, whereas full parsing would distinguish between types of noun phrases (e.g. singular vs. plural). While skeleton parsing cannot provide as much information as full parsing, it allows for human analysts to parse or post-edit a corpus more speedily and consistently. Since automatic parsing is not yet sufficiently reliable (see Mooney 2003: 388; Collins 1997), human parsing or post-editing cannot be completely dispensed with in the treebanking process.

A4.4.4 Semantic annotation

Semantic annotation assigns codes indicating the semantic features or the semantic fields of the words in a text. There are actually at least two broad types of semantic annotation. The first type marks the semantic relationships between the constituents in a sentence (e.g. as happens in the Penn Treebank, see Kinsbury, Palmer and Marcus 2002) while the second type marks the semantic features of words in a text. The first type is also known as 'semantic parsing' (Mooney 2003: 389) and should, in our view, be considered as a syntactic-level annotation. We will confine ourselves to the latter type of semantic annotation in this book as this is by far the more common type at the present time. Semantic annotation is also referred to as word-sense tagging. Annotation of this type is particularly useful in content analysis. Thomas and Wilson (1996), for example, find on the basis of a semantically anno-tated corpus of doctor–patient discourse that patients are more satisfied when doctors use more interactive words (e.g. discourse particles, first- and second-person pronouns, downtoners and boosters; see Case Study 5).

Semantic annotation is a more challenging task than POS tagging and syntactic parsing, because it is principally knowledge-based (requiring ontologies and lexical resources like dictionaries and thesauri). A more statistically driven approach to the problem does seem possible, however (see Stevenson and Wilks 2003: 256–258 and Mooney 2003: 387 for a discussion of statistical and machine-learning approaches to semantic annotation).

In spite of the challenging nature of automatic sense disambiguation, work on it has met with some success. For example, Rayson and Wilson (1996) report on USAS (UCREL Semantic Analysis System), which is designed to undertake the semantic analysis of present-day English. The USAS semantic tagset is composed of twenty-one major categories which are further divided into 232 subcategories. The system first assigns a POS tag to each lexical unit (single word or idiomatic sequence) using the CLAWS tagger and then feeds the output into the semantic tagging suite called SEMTAG. Experiments with contemporary texts show that the system has a preci-sion rate of about 92 per cent (see Rayson 2001). In addition to USAS, efforts have been made elsewhere to automate semantic annotation, for example, Popov *et al.* (2003), Wilks (2003) and Guthrie (2003).

A4.4.5 Coreference annotation

Coreference annotation is a type of discourse-level annotation which has been applied to a number of corpora. The major concern of coreference annotation is coreference identification, e.g. the identification of coreferential relationships between pronouns and noun phrases. This type of annotation makes it possible to track how elements of a text are progressively interwoven so that cohesion is achieved, typically through the use of pronouns, repetition, substitution, ellipsis, and so on. A simple example of anaphoric annotation is:

> (6 the married couple 6) said that <REF=6 they were happy with <REF=6 their lot.

Here the number 6 is an index number while the less than character < indicates that a backward referential (anaphoric) link is present, i.e. *they* and *their* point backward to *the married couple* (cited from Garside, Fligelstone and Botley 1997: 68).

The annotation scheme used in the above example is the Lancaster/IBM scheme (see Fligelstone 1991, 1992), which is based on Halliday and Hasan (1976) and Quirk *et al.* (1985). This scheme aims at: (a) identifying an anaphor/cataphor and its antecedent/postcedent, or establishing whether it is identifiable; (b) identifying the direction of a referential link; (c) identifying the type of relationship (e.g. reference, substitution, ellipsis, etc.); (d) categorizing antecedents/postcedents; and (e) indicating semantic/pragmatic features (e.g. singular vs. plural, primary vs. secondary reference, exclusive vs. inclusive of addressee(s)). The Lancaster/IBM scheme was used in annotating the so-called Lancaster/IBM anaphoric treebank, which contains 100,000 words.

In addition to the Lancaster/IBM anaphoric treebank, there are a number of coreference annotated corpora, including, for example, a 65,000-word corpus resulting from the MUC (Message Understanding Conference) coreference task (Hirschman 1997), a 60,000-word corpus produced at the University of Wolverhampton (Mitkov *et al.* 2000), and 93,931 words of the Penn Treebank (Ge 1998). A much larger corpus annotated for coreference (one million words) is under construction on a project undertaken by the University of Stendhal and Xerox Research Centre Europe (Tutin *et al.* 2000).

There is so far no generally agreed upon scheme for coreference annotation (see Garside, Fligelstone and Botley 1997 for a comparison of available annotation schemes). While the Lancaster/IBM scheme proposed one approach to coreference annotation, other schemes have also been developed. For example, Botley and McEnery (2001) in work focusing solely on demonstratives propose a scheme which encodes a set of five distinctive features: recoverability of antecedent (R), direction of reference (D), phoric type (P), syntactic function (S) and antecedent type (A), with each feature constituting an unordered set consisting of values relating to different categories of demonstrative use. For example, the code DARMN represents a referential usage (R) where a nominal (N) antecedent precedes an anaphor (A) and is directly recoverable (D) while the anaphor functions syntactically as a modifier (M). A modified version of this scheme was used to analyse demonstratives in Hindi (see Baker *et al.* 2004).

Another scheme is the SGML-compliant MUC scheme, which has been used by a number of researchers to annotate coreferential links (e.g. Gaizauskas and Humphreys 1996; Mitkov *et al.* 1999). The basic MUC scheme identifies a coreferential link using a unique identity number. It also encodes the type of coreference, as shown in the following example (cited from Mitkov 2002: 134), in which *IDENT* indicates the identity relationship between anaphor and antecedent:

<COREF ID="100">The Kenya Wildlife Service</COREF> estimates

<COREF ID="101" TYPE=IDENT REF="100">it</COREF> loses $1.2 million a year in park entry fee because of fraud.

Until recently, hardly any fully automatic coreference annotation system was reported to have achieved an accuracy rate which would allow it to be used as an automated or semi-automatic system for coreference annotation (see Mitkov 2002: 169, 195). However, there is now a range of systems that facilitate coreference annotation (see Mitkov 2002 for a review). To give two examples, the first tool developed to support coreference annotation was called Xanadu, which was developed to apply the Lancaster/IBM scheme at Lancaster (see Garside 1993). A more recent tool, called CLinkA, was developed at Wolverhampton and operates by default on the MUC scheme, though the system also allows users to define their own annotation scheme (see Orasan 2000). As CLinkA supports Unicode, the tool is writing-system independent and can be used to annotate languages written in a wide range of writing systems.

A4.4.6 Pragmatic annotation

Pragmatic annotation is yet another type of annotation at the discourse level. At present the focus of pragmatic annotation appears to be on speech/dialogue acts in domain-specific dialogue such as doctor–patient discourse and telephone conversations.

A number of dialogue-based projects have been reported around the world, for example, the Edinburgh Map Task corpus (Anderson *et al.* 1991), the TRAINS corpus developed at the University of Rochester (Allen *et al.* 1996), the ATIS (Air Travel Information Service) project (Wang and Hirschberg 1992) and the German VERBMOBIL project (Alexandersson *et al.* 1997). These dialogue systems are typically domain specific and task driven. Since 1996 the Discourse Resource Initiative (DRI) has organized annual workshops in an attempt to unify previous and ongoing annotation work in dialogue coding. The DRI annotation scheme, known as DAMSL (Dialog Act Mark-up in Several Layers) specifies three layers of coding: segmentation (dividing dialogue into textual units – utterances), functional annotation (dialogue act annotation) and utterance tags (applying utterance tags that characterize the role of the utterance as a dialogue act). There are four major categories of utterance tags: (a) Communicative status (i.e. whether an utterance is intelligible and complete); (b) Information level and status (indicating the semantic content of the utterance and how it relates to the task in question); (c) Forward-looking communicative function (utterances that may constrain or affect the subsequent discourse, e.g. *assert, request, question* and *offer*); (d) Backward-looking communicative function (utterances that relate to previous parts of the discourse, e.g. *accept, backchannelling* and *answer*). Of these, only the latter two communication function types ((c) and (d)) are directly relevant to an increasingly important form of pragmatic annotation: speech act annotation. Readers are advised to refer to Leech *et al.* (2000) for further discussion of the representation and annotation of dialogue.

A good example of speech act annotation is provided by Leech and Weisser (2003). They produced an annotation scheme for their Speech Act Annotated Corpus (SPAAC) of telephone task-oriented dialogues. The SPAAC scheme consists of forty-one speech-act categories including, for example, *accept, acknowledge, answer, confirm, correct, direct, echo, exclaim* and *greet*. In addition to the assignment of these initial speech-act categories, the system also supplies supplementary syntactic, semantic and pragmatic information for each speech act in terms of form (e.g. *declarative, yes–no question, wh-question, imperative* and *fragment*), polarity (i.e. *positive* or *negative*), topic (e.g. *location, name, day, date, time* and *railcard* related to train journeys) and mode (e.g. semantic categories such as *deixis, probability* and *reason*).

Pragmatic annotation like this has not yet been fully automated. Nevertheless, human analysts can be assisted by computer programs in their annotation task. Weisser (2003), for example, has developed an efficient XML-compliant tool (SPAACy) to help human analysts to annotate speech acts semi-automatically. The MATE (Multilevel Annotation Tools Engineering) project has also produced a flexible workbench which provides support for the annotation of speech and text (see Carletta and Isard 1999).

A4.4.7 Stylistic annotation

While pragmatic annotation focuses on speech acts in dialogue, stylistic annotation is particularly associated with stylistic features in literary texts (see Leech, McEnery and Wynne 1997: 94; but see McIntyre *et al*. 2003 for an account of annotating speech and thought in spoken data). An example of annotation of this latter type is the representation of people's speech and thoughts, known as speech and thought presentation (S&TP). In stylistics, there is a long tradition of focusing on the representation of speech and thought in written fiction (e.g. Leech and Short 1981). Yet the representation of speech and thought has long been of interest not only to stylisticians, but also to researchers in applied linguistics, philosophy and psychology (see McIntyre *et al*. 2003: 513).

As far as we are aware, the only corpus which has been annotated for categories of speech and thought presentation is the Lancaster Speech, Thought and Writing Presentation Corpus (ST&WP), which is composed of a written component and a spoken component, developed from 1994 to 2003. The written section, approximately 260,000 words in size, contains three narrative genres: prose fiction, newspaper reportage and (auto)biography, which are further divided into 'serious' and 'popular' sections (see Short *et al*. 1999). The spoken section was created with the express aim of comparing S&TP in spoken and written languages systematically. It contains approximately 260,000 words, making it comparable in size to the ST&WP written section. The texts contained in the spoken corpus are drawn from two sources: sixty samples from the demographic section of the British National Corpus and sixty samples from oral history archives in the Centre for North West

Regional Studies (CNWRS) at Lancaster University (see McIntyre *et al.* 2003: 514). Both written and spoken components of the ST&WP corpus are marked up using TEI-compliant SGML (see Unit A3.3).

Given the differences between written and spoken data, the S&TP annotation schemes for the written and spoken components are slightly different. However, the main categories remain unchanged (see McIntyre *et al.* 2003: 516 for an account of modifications). The main categories include the direct category (e.g. *direct speech, direct thought* and *direct writing*), the free direct category (e.g. *free direct speech, free direct thought* and *free direct writing*), the indirect category (e.g. *indirect speech, indirect thought* and *indirect writing*), the free indirect category (*free indirect speech, free indirect thought* and *free indirect writing*), the representation of speech/thought/ writing act category, the representation of voice/internal state/writing category, and the report category (e.g. *report of speech, report of thought* and *report of writing*).

Because surface syntax cannot reliably indicate the stylistic features as outlined above, the automatic annotation of such categories is difficult. Unsurprisingly, therefore, the Lancaster ST&WP corpus was annotated entirely by human analysts.

A4.4.8 Error tagging

Error tagging is a special type of annotation which is specifically associated with learner corpora and geared toward language pedagogy (see Units A7.8, A10.8 and C1). Annotation of this kind involves assigning codes indicating the types of errors occurring in a learner corpus (see Case Study 3 in Section C). Corpora annotated for learner errors can help to reveal the relative frequency of error types produced by learners of different L1 (first language) backgrounds and proficiency levels. They are also useful when exploring features of non-native language behaviour (e.g. overuse or underuse of certain linguistic features).

At present a number of error-tagged learner corpora are available. For example, the Cambridge Learner Corpus and the Longman Learners' Corpus, which cover a variety of L1 backgrounds, are partly tagged for learner errors. In addition, a number of error-tagged learner English corpora are available which cover only one L1 background, e.g. the Chinese Learner English Corpus (CLEC), the JEFLL (Japanese EFL Learner) corpus, the SST (Standard Speaking Test) corpus of Japanese learner English and part (round 100,000 words) of the HKUST Corpus of Learner English (see Unit A7.8 for further details of these learner corpora).

Error-tagging schemes vary to some extent from one corpus to another in terms of the number and types of error codes. However, most schemes have in common error types such as *omission, addition* and *misformation*. The Cambridge scheme, for example, includes six general error types: wrong word form used (F), something missing (M), word/phrase that needs replacing (R), unnecessary word/phrase (U) and word wrongly derived (D) (see Nicholls 2003: 573–574). The CLEC scheme consists of sixty-one error types clustered in eleven categories while the SST scheme contains forty-seven learner error types.

Error tagging is a laborious and time-consuming task, as it is difficult to develop either rule-based or probabilistic programs to identify errors due in large part to a lack of information regarding error patterns and their frequencies with respect to learner groups (see Tono 2003: 804). In spite of this difficulty, a number of attempts have been made to automate part of the error-tagging process. For example, Granger and her colleagues on the ICLE project have developed a Windows-based error editor (see Dagneaux, Denness and Granger 1998); Tono *et al.* (2001) have also presented a generic error tagset and an associated error editor. In addition, some tools have also been developed for detecting specific types of errors, for example, missing articles (Mason and Uzar 2000).

A4.4.9 Problem-oriented annotation

Most types of the annotation we have considered up to now are intended to be useful for a broad range of research questions, and attempt to employ widely agreed categories or analytical schemes. Yet not all annotation schemes have that goal, and the final type of annotation explored here, problem-oriented annotation, arguably does not. Problem-oriented annotation differs in two fundamental ways from most of the annotation types discussed above. First, it is not exhaustive – only the phenomenon directly relevant to a particular research question, rather than the entire contents of a corpus, is annotated. Second, the scheme for problem-oriented annotation is developed not for its broad coverage and consensus-based theory neutrality but for its relevance to the specific research question (see McEnery and Wilson 2001: 69). Problem-oriented annotation is similar to the notion of 'local grammar', developed by Gross (1993) and Hunston and Sinclair (2000). This kind of annotation is necessary and useful for research questions that cannot be addressed using currently available annotations. Using problem-oriented anno- tation, for instance, Gross (1993) describes ways of accounting for time expressions while Meyer and Tenny (1993) study apposition in English. More recently, Hunston (1999a) uses this kind of annotation to study how people talk about sameness and difference.

Problem-oriented annotation is entirely dependent on individual research questions and the resultant annotation schemes are typically idiosyncratic to the extent that they are consequently difficult to use to explore other research questions. Nevertheless, it is a very important annotation type to keep in mind when considering a corpus-based approach to a research question. Problem-oriented annotations, as is clear from the references above, are certainly a valuable way of gaining insights into a specific research question.

A4.5 EMBEDDED VS. STANDALONE ANNOTATION

We have so far assumed that the process of annotation leads to information being mixed in the original corpus text or so-called base document when it is applied to a corpus (i.e. the annotation becomes so-called *embedded annotation*). However, the Corpus Encoding Standard (see Unit A3.3) recommends the use of *standalone annotation*, whereby the annotation information is retained in separate SGML/XML documents (with different Document Type Definitions) and linked to the original and other annotation documents in hypertext format. Standalone annotation fully addresses one of the criticisms of corpus annotation, namely the wish to be able to view a corpus in its raw form even if it is annotated, though standalone annotation is not the only solution to this problem (see Unit A4.2). In contrast to embedded annotation, standalone annotation has a number of advantages (Ide 1998) as it:

- provides control over the distribution of base documents for legal purposes;
- enables annotation to be performed on base documents that cannot easily be altered (e.g. they are read-only);
- avoids the creation of potentially unwieldy documents;
- allows multiple overlapping hierarchies;
- allows for alternative annotation schemes to be applied to the same data (e.g. different POS tagsets);
- enables new annotation levels to be added without causing problems for existing levels of annotation or search tools;
- allows annotation at one level to be changed without affecting other levels.

Standalone annotation is in principle ideal and is certainly technically feasible. It may also represent the future standard for certain types of annotation. Presently, however, there are two problems associated with standalone annotation. The first issue is related to the complexity of corpus annotation. As can be seen from the previous sections, annotation may have multiple forms in a corpus. While some of these readily allow for the separation of annotation codes from base documents (e.g. lemmatization, POS tagging and semantic annotation), others may involve much more complexity in establishing links between codes and annotated items (e.g. coreference and stylistic annotations). Even if such links can be established, they are usually prone to error. The second issue is purely practical. As far as we are aware, the currently available corpus exploration tools, including the latest versions of WordSmith (version 4, Scott 2003) and Xaira (Burnard and Todd 2003), have all been designed for use with embedded annotation. Standalone annotation, while appealing, is only useful when appropriate search tools are available for use on standalone annotated corpora.

Summary

This unit first discussed the rationale for corpus annotation in the context of addressing a number of criticisms of it, followed by a discussion of how annotation is achieved. The unit then moved on to introduce some important annotation types.

Finally, we explored the advantages, and potential problems of standalone corpus annotation.

It is clear from this discussion that the type of annotation needed in a corpus is closely associated with the research question one seeks to address using the corpus. It is also important to note that some types of annotation, e.g. POS tagging, which can be automated reliably, have a broad range of uses and form the basis of some higher-level annotations like parsing.

This unit is a basic and non-technical introduction to corpus annotation. The exploration of the annotation types presented here is also far from exhaustive.

LOOKING AHEAD

Readers interested in the in-depth discussion of corpus annotation should refer to Garside, Leech and McEnery (1997) and Mitkov (2003). In addition to some annotation types which are particularly associated with monolingual data (e.g. phonetic/phonemic and prosodic annotations), we have omitted an important type of annotation linked to multilingual corpora from our discussion: alignment.

As alignment is an important type of annotation used in building parallel corpora, alignment will be introduced in the next unit, where we will shift our focus to a discussion of multilingual corpora.

Unit A5
Multilingual corpora

A5.1 INTRODUCTION

Having covered some of the important concepts and practices in corpus linguistics, we will consider, in Units A5–A8, a range of related issues. In this unit we will consider the multilingual dimension of corpus linguistics.

While the construction and exploitation of English-language corpora still dominate corpus linguistics, corpora of other languages, particularly typologically related European languages such as French, German and Portuguese as well as Asian languages such as Chinese and Japanese, have also become available (see the website accompanying this book for a survey of well-known and influential corpora) and have added notably to the diversity of corpus-based language studies. In addition to monolingual corpora, parallel and comparable corpora have been a key focus of non-English corpus linguistics, largely because corpora of these two types are important resources for translation and contrastive studies. As Aijmer and Altenberg (1996: 12) observe, parallel and comparable corpora 'offer specific uses and possibilities' for contrastive and translation studies:

- they give new insights into the languages compared – insights that are not likely to be gained from the study of monolingual corpora;
- they can be used for a range of comparative purposes and increase our knowledge of language-specific, typological and cultural differences, as well as of universal features;
- they illuminate differences between source texts and translations, and between native and non-native texts;
- they can be used for a number of practical applications, e.g. in lexicography, language teaching and translation.

In this unit, we will address issues related to multilingual corpora. This unit consists of three sections. Unit A5.2 is concerned with terminological issues. Unit A5.3 introduces the alignment of parallel corpora.

A5.2   MULTILINGUAL CORPORA: TERMINOLOGICAL ISSUES

When we refer to a corpus involving more than one language as a multilingual corpus, the term *multilingual* is used in a broad sense. A multilingual corpus, in a narrow sense, must involve at least three languages while those involving only two languages are conventionally referred to as *bilingual* corpora. In this book, we are generally using *multilingual* to refer to corpora containing two or more languages. Given that corpora involving more than one language is a relatively new phenomenon, with most related research hailing from the early 1990s (e.g. the English–Norwegian Parallel Corpus (ENPC), see Johansson and Hofland 1994), it is unsurprising to discover that there is some confusion surrounding the termi-nology used in relation to these corpora. Generally, there are three types of corpora involving more than one language:

- Type A: Source texts plus translations, e.g. Canadian Hansard (see Brown, Lai and Mercer 1991), and Crater (see McEnery and Oakes 1995);
- Type B: Monolingual subcorpora designed using the same sampling tech-niques, e.g. the Aarhus corpus of contract law (see Faber and Lauridsen 1991);
- Type C: A combination of A and B, e.g. EMILLE (see Baker *et al.* 2004).

Different terms have been used to describe these types of corpora. For Aijmer and Altenberg (1996) and Granger (1996: 38), type A is a translation corpus whereas type B is a parallel corpus; for McEnery and Wilson (1996: 57), Baker (1993: 248, 1995, 1999) and Hunston (2002: 15), type A is a parallel corpus whereas type B is a comparable corpus; and for Johansson and Hofland (1994) and Johansson (1998: 4) the term parallel corpus applies to both types A and B. Barlow (1995, 2000: 110) assumed that a parallel corpus was type A when he developed the ParaConc corpus tool (see Case Study 6 in Section C). It is clear that some confusion centres around the term *parallel.*

In this book a *parallel* corpus is one which is composed of source texts and their translations in one or more different languages while a *comparable* corpus refers to one which is composed of L1 data collected from different languages using the same sampling techniques. When we define different types of corpora, we can use different criteria, for example, the number of languages involved, and the content or the form of the corpus. But when a criterion is decided upon, the same crite-rion must be used consistently. For example, we can say a corpus is monolingual, bilingual or multilingual if we take the number of languages involved as the criterion for definition. We can also say a corpus is a translation (L2) or a non-translation (L1) corpus if the criterion of corpus content is used. But if we choose to define corpus types by the criterion of corpus form, we must use it consistently. Then we can say a corpus is parallel if the corpus contains source texts and translations in parallel, or it is a comparable corpus if its subcorpora are comparable by applying the same sampling techniques. It is illogical, however, to refer to corpora of type A as translation corpora by the criterion of content while referring to corpora of type B as comparable corpora by the criterion of form. Consequently, in this book, we will follow McEnery and Wilson (1996) and Baker's (*ibid.*) terminology in referring to type A as parallel corpora and type B as comparable corpora. As type C is a mixture of the two, corpora of this type should be referred to as comparable corpora in a strict sense.

Parallel corpora can be bilingual or multilingual. They can be unidirectional (e.g. from English into Chinese or from Chinese into English alone), bidirectional (e.g. containing both English source texts with their Chinese translations as well as Chinese source texts with their English translations), or multidirectional (e.g. the same piece of writing with English, French and German versions). In this sense, texts which are produced simultaneously in different languages (e.g. EU and UN regulations) also belong to the category of parallel corpora (see Hunston 2002: 15). In contrast, a comparable corpus can be defined as a corpus containing components that are collected using the same sampling techniques and similar balance and representativeness (see McEnery 2003: 450), e.g. the *same proportions* of the texts of the *same genres* in the *same domains* in a range of *different languages* in the *same sampling period*. However, the subcorpora of a comparable corpus are not translations of each other. Rather, their comparability lies in their comparable sampling techniques and similar balance (see Unit A2).

By our definition, corpora containing components of varieties of the same language (e.g. the International Corpus of English, see Unit A7.6) are not comparable corpora because all corpora, as a resource for linguistic research, have 'always been pre-eminently suited for comparative studies' (Aarts 1998), either intralingual or interlingual. The Brown, LOB, Frown and FLOB corpora are typically designed for comparing language varieties synchronically and diachronically. The British National Corpus (BNC), while designed for representing modern British English, is also a useful basis for various intralingual studies (e.g. spoken vs. written, monologue vs. dialogue, and variations caused by sociolinguistic variables). Nevertheless, these corpora are generally not referred to as comparable corpora. In this book we label corpora containing components of varieties of the same language as *comparative corpora*.

While parallel and comparable corpora are supposed to be useful for different purposes (i.e. translation and contrastive studies respectively, see Unit A10.6), the two are also designed with different focuses. For a comparable corpus, the sampling frame is essential. The components representing the languages involved must match each other in terms of proportion, genre, domain and sampling period. For a parallel corpus, the sampling frame is irrelevant, because all of the corpus components are exact translations of each other. Once the source texts are selected using a certain sampling frame, it does not apply twice to translations. However, this does not mean that the construction of parallel corpora is easier. For a parallel corpus to be useful, an essential step is to *align* the source texts and their translations (see Unit A5.3), i.e. to produce a link between the two, at the sentence or word level.

Yet the automatic alignment of parallel corpora is not a trivial task for some language pairs (see Piao 2000, 2002).

Depending on the specific research question, a specialized (i.e. containing texts of a particular type, e.g. computer manuals) or general (i.e. balanced, containing as many text types as possible) corpus should be used. Parallel and comparable corpora can be of either type. For terminology extraction, specialized parallel and comparable corpora are clearly of use while for the contrast of general linguistic features such as tense and aspect, balanced corpora are supposed to be more representative of any given language in general. Existing parallel corpora appear to suggest that corpora of this type tend to be specialized (e.g. contract law and genetic engineering). This is quite natural, considering the availability of translated texts (in machine-readable form) by genre in different languages (see Johansson and Hofland 1994: 27; Mauranen 2002: 166; Aston 1999), and indeed, as will be seen in Unit A10.6, specialized parallel corpora can be especially useful in domain-specific translation research, though readers are advised to refer to Halverson (1998) for an argument for the need for representative parallel corpora. While most of the existing comparable corpora are also specialized, it is relatively easier to find comparable text types in different languages. Therefore, in relation to parallel corpora, it is more likely for comparable corpora to be designed as general balanced corpora. For instance, as the Korean National Corpus, the Chinese National Corpus (Zhou and Yu 1997) and the Polish National Corpus have adopted a sampling frame quite similar to that of the BNC (see Unit A7.2), these corpora can form a balanced comparable corpus that makes contrastive studies for these four languages possible.

Parallel and comparable corpora are used primarily for translation and contrastive studies. The two types of corpora have their own advantages and disadvantages, and thus serve different purposes. While the source and translated texts in a parallel corpus are useful for exploring 'how the same content is expressed in two languages' (Aijmer and Altenberg 1996: 13), they alone serve as a poor basis for cross-linguistic contrasts, because translations (i.e. L2 texts) cannot avoid the effect of translationese (see Hartmann 1995; Baker 1993: 243–245; Teubert 1996: 247; Gellerstam, 1996; Laviosa 1997: 315; McEnery and Wilson 2001: 71–72; McEnery and Xiao 2002). In contrast, while the components of a comparable corpus overcome translationese by populating the same sampling frame with L1 texts from different languages, they are less useful for the study of how a message is conveyed from one language to another. Also the development of application software for machine aided and machine translation, while it may be based on comparable data, has clearly benefited from having access to parallel data, for example to bootstrap example-based machine translation systems (see Unit A10.6). Nonetheless, comparable corpora are a useful resource for contrastive studies and translation studies when used in combination with parallel corpora. Note, however, that comparable corpora can be a poor basis for contrastive studies if the sampling frames for the comparable corpora are not fully comparable.

A5.3 CORPUS ALIGNMENT

We have so far assumed that parallel corpora means *aligned parallel corpora*. It is clear that simply having a corpus containing parallel texts presents problems as well as promises. Without alignment, we cannot easily determine which sentences in the target language are translations of which in the source language. An aligned parallel corpus solves this problem and makes available to researchers, language learners, etc. information regarding the translation in the parallel corpus that the users of that corpus may not be able to provide for themselves. For example, in the aligned English–Chinese CEPC–health parallel corpus which we will use in Case Study 6, you will see *What is organ donation* and *Shenme shi qiguan juanzeng* align, though it is unlikely that you are capable of identifying this translation without the aid of the annotation. As well as sentence alignment, sub-sentential-level alignment is also undertaken, notably phrase (multiword unit) or word-level alignment. In the above sentence, one might align *what* with *shenme*, *is* with *shi*, *organ* with *qiguan* and *donation* with *juanzeng*. Currently most multilingual corpus tools (e.g. ParaConc) only take pre-aligned parallel texts as input, though Multiconcord (see Woolls 2000) is able to align non-aligned parallel texts presented to the system by the user in ten European languages. In either case, alignment is an essential step in the construction and exploitation of parallel corpora.

The aim of corpus alignment is to find translation equivalents of sentences, phrases or words between the source and translated texts in a parallel corpus. Sentence alignment is generally the first step to phrase and word alignment. The source and translated texts in an aligned parallel corpus may appear in a single file, with translation equivalents aligned together. They may also appear in separate files, with the source and target text of each translation equivalent being linked together with a unique identifier or pointer (i.e. standalone annotation, as recommended by CES; see Unit A3.3). ParaConc only works on parallel corpora of the latter type.

In this unit we will present a non-technical description of sentence alignment only because this form of alignment can be achieved automatically with a relatively high degree of accuracy. Readers who are interested in the technical aspects of sentence alignment (e.g. the precise alignment algorithms) and word alignment can refer to Oakes and McEnery (2000), Piao (2000, 2002) and Simard, Foster, Hannan, Macklovitch and Plamondon (2000) for more information.

There are basically three approaches to sentence alignment: statistical (probabilistic), linguistic (knowledge-based) and hybrid. The statistical approach to sentence alignment is generally based on sentence length in terms of words (e.g. Brown, Lai and Mercer 1991) or characters (e.g. Gale and Church 1993) per sentence while the lexical approach (e.g. Haruno, Ikehara and Yamazaki 1996; Kupiek 1993) uses morpho-syntactic information to explore similarities between languages. The lexical approach may achieve more accurate alignment than the statistical approach, but it is 'necessarily slow' and not suitable for aligning large corpora (see Brown *et al.* 1991: 169). The most widely used approach to sentence alignment is the hybrid approach, which integrates linguistic knowledge into a probabilistic algorithm to achieve improved accuracy (e.g. Hofland 1996; McEnery and Oakes 1996; Simard *et al.* 2000: 49–50). As the research of alignment has focused on closely related European language pairs, sentence alignment among these language pairs has achieved a very high precision rate, e.g. 100 per cent for Polish–English alignment (McEnery and Oakes 2000: 7), 98 per cent for English–French (McEnery and Oakes 1996) and English–Norwegian alignment (Johansson and Hofland 1994). Recently, however, great success has also been achieved for typologically different languages such as English and Chinese. Piao (2000: 153), for example, reported a quite stable performance for his alignment system, with a success rate ranging from 92.93 per cent to 100 per cent on texts of various sizes and domains.

In this unit, we first clarified the confusion surrounding the terminology related to multilingual corpora. It was argued that consistent criteria should be applied in defining types of multilingual corpora. For us this means that parallel corpora refer to those that contain collections of L1 texts and their translations while comparable corpora refer to those that contain matched L1 samples from different languages. In this unit we also introduced corpus alignment, an important process applied to parallel corpora.

Summary

LOOKING AHEAD

In Unit A10.6, we will return to discuss the use of comparable and parallel corpora in contrastive and translation studies. Readers interested in exploring the further use of multilingual corpora in language studies are advised to read Aijmer, Altenberg and Johansson (1996), Johansson and Oksefjell (1998) and Botley, McEnery and Wilson (2000). In the next unit, we will discuss how to make statistical claims in corpus-based language studies.

Unit A6
Making statistical claims

A6.1 INTRODUCTION

One of the most obvious advantages of using a corpus, as compared with intuition, is that a corpus can provide reliable quantitative data (see Unit A1.5). In this unit we will consider what to do with the quantitative data that corpora provide. Our approach to this topic will be realistic: by and large most users of corpus data will not be capable of generating sophisticated statistical claims nor would they wish to do so. However, we want readers to be aware of what they should not claim on the basis of the simple descriptive statistics that they may use. Also, in this unit, we want to give guidance on how to interpret inferential statistics generated by the concordance programs used in Section C.

While statistics can be intimidating for many readers, a basic awareness of statistics is essential when adopting a corpus-based approach as 'the use of quantification in corpus linguistics typically goes well beyond simple counting' (McEnery and Wilson 2001: 81). This unit will cover the basic statistical concepts and techniques required to understand some excerpts in Section B and the case studies presented in Section C of this book while trying to avoid a complex, technical treatment of statistics. Some of these concepts and techniques, though, will be further discussed in the case studies presented in Section C of this book.

A6.2 RAW FREQUENCY AND NORMALIZED FREQUENCY

In corpus linguistics *frequency* refers to the arithmetic count of the number of linguistic elements (i.e. tokens) within a corpus that belong to each classification (i.e. type) within a particular classification scheme (e.g. the CLAWS tagset, see Unit A4.4.1). It is the most direct quantitative data a corpus can provide. Typically, frequency itself does not tell you much in terms of the validity of a hypothesis. Yet data of this type can be used in both descriptive statistics and inferential statistics (see Unit A6.3).

Note, however, that frequency data must be interpreted with caution. It is possible to use *raw frequency* (i.e. the actual count) where no comparison between corpora is necessary. However, when comparing corpora (or segments in the same corpus) of markedly different sizes, raw frequencies extracted from those corpora often need to be *normalized* to a common base (see Case Studies 2, 4, 5 and 6). For example, the swear-word *fucker(s)* occurs twenty-five times in the spoken section and fifty times in the written section of the BNC corpus (see Case Study 4). Can we say that the swear-word is twice as frequent in writing as in speech? This is clearly not true, as writing accounts for around 90 per cent of the BNC corpus whereas transcribed speech only takes up 10 per cent of the corpus (see Unit A7.2): there are nine times as much written data as spoken data. If we compare these frequencies on a common base, e.g. per million words, then we find the normalized frequency of *fucker(s)* in speech is 2.41 per million words whereas it is 0.56 in writing. Clearly this swear-word occurs much more frequently (over four times as often) in speech than in writing. Is this difference statistically significant? We will leave this question unanswered until we introduce tests for statistical significance (see Unit A6.4).

As the size of a sample may affect the level of statistical significance, the common base for normalization must be comparable to the sizes of the corpora (or corpus segments) under consideration (see Case Study 2). When we compare the spoken section (10 million words) and the written section (90 million words) of the BNC corpus, for example, it would be inappropriate to normalize frequencies to a common base of 1,000 words, as the results obtained on an irrationally enlarged or reduced common base are distorted.

A6.3 DESCRIPTIVE AND INFERENTIAL STATISTICS

Given that we have mentioned descriptive and inferential statistics above, what is the difference between the two types of statistics? Basically, descriptive statistics are used to describe a dataset, as the term suggests. Suppose a group of ten students took a test and their scores are as follows: 4, 5, 6, 6, 7, 7, 7, 9, 9 and 10. We might need to report the measure of *central tendency* of this group of test results using a single score.

There are different ways to do this. We can use the *mean*, the *mode* and the *median*. The mean is the arithmetic average, which can be calculated by adding all of the scores together and then dividing the sum by the number of scores. In our example, the mean is 7 (i.e. 70/10). The mean is the most common measure of central tendency. While the mean is a useful measure, unless one also knows how dispersed (i.e. spread out) the scores in a dataset are, the mean can be an uncertain guide. Under such circumstances other scores may help. For example, the mode is the most common score in a set of scores. In this example the mode is 7, because this score occurs more frequently than any other score. Another score one might use is the median. The median is the middle score of a set of scores ordered from lowest to the highest. For an odd number of scores the median is the central score while for an even number of scores, the median is the average of the two central scores. In the above example the median is 7 (i.e. (7+7)/2).

Introduction

There are three important ways to measure the dispersion of a dataset: the *range*, the *variance* and the *standard deviation*. The range (i.e. the difference between the highest and lowest frequencies) is a simple way to measure the dispersion of a set of data. In the above example the range is 6 (i.e. 10 – 4). However, the range is only a poor measure of dispersion because an unusually high or low score in a dataset may make the range unreasonably large, thus giving a distorted picture of the dataset. The variance measures the distance of each score in the dataset from the mean. For example, in the test results above, the variance of the score 4 is 3 (i.e. 7 – 4) while the variance of the score 9 is 2. For the whole dataset, however, the sum of these differences is always zero as some scores will be above the mean while some will be below the mean. Hence, it is meaningless to use variance to measure the dispersion of a whole dataset. Standard deviation is a useful measure in such circumstances. Standard deviation is equal to the square root of the quantity of the sum of the deviation scores squared divided by the number of scores in a dataset. It can be expressed as:

$$\sigma = \sqrt{\frac{\Sigma (F - \mu)^2}{N}}.$$

In the formula F is a score in a dataset (i.e. any of the ten scores in the above example, μ is the mean score (i.e. 7) while N is the number of scores under consideration (i.e. 10). The standard deviation in our example of test results is 1.89. When one uses standard deviation to measure the dispersion of a normally distributed dataset, i.e. where most of the items are clustered towards the centre rather than the lower or higher end of the scale, 68 per cent of the scores lie within one standard deviation of the mean, 95 per cent lie within two standard deviations of the mean, and 99.7 per cent lie within three standard deviations of the mean. In this sense, the standard deviation is a more reasonable measure of the dispersion of a dataset.

While it may be time-consuming to calculate these statistics manually, readers do not need to panic as they can be computed automatically using statistics packages such as SPSS, as shown in Case Study 5 of Section C. Note, however, that while descriptive statistics are useful in summarizing a dataset, it is inferential statistics that are typically used to formulate or test a hypothesis. Testing hypotheses in this way generally involves various statistical tests. These tests are typically used to test whether or not any differences observed are statistically significant. The sections that follow will briefly introduce the inferential statistical tests used in this book including the chi-square test, the log-likelihood (LL) test, Fisher's exact test, the MI (mutual information) test, the *t* test and the *z* test. The procedures for conducting each test are presented in the relevant case studies in Section C.

A6.4 TESTS OF STATISTICAL SIGNIFICANCE

In testing a linguistic hypothesis, it would be nice to be 100 per cent sure that the hypothesis can be accepted. Sadly, one can never be 100 per cent sure. There is always the possibility that, for example, the differences observed between two corpora have arisen by chance due to inherent variability in the data (see Oakes 1998: 1). Hence, one must state the 'level of statistical significance' at which one will accept a given hypothesis. In short, how likely is it that what you are seeing is statistically significant and what tolerance do you have for uncertainty? While we cannot be 100 per cent sure, the closer the likelihood is to 100 per cent, the more confident we can be. By convention, the general practice is that a hypothesis can be accepted only when the level of significance is less than 0.05 (i.e. $p<0.05$). In other words, one must be more than 95 per cent confident that the observed differences have not arisen by chance.

There are a number of techniques for testing statistical significance. The most commonly used statistical test in corpus linguistics is probably the chi-square test (also called the Pearson chi-square test). The chi-square test compares the difference between the observed values (e.g. the actual frequencies extracted from corpora) and the expected values (e.g. the frequencies that one would expect if no factor other than chance were affecting the frequencies; see Case Study 1 for further discussion). The greater the difference (absolute value) between the observed values and the expected values, the less likely it is that the difference is due to chance. Conversely, the closer the observed values are to the expected values, the more likely it is that the difference has arisen by chance.

Another commonly used statistical test is the log-likelihood test (also called the log-likelihood chi-square or *G*-square test). The log-likelihood (LL) test is preferred in this book, as it does not assume that data are normally distributed (see Dunning 1993; Oakes 1998). The log-likelihood statistic has a distribution similar to that of the chi-square, so the LL probability value (i.e. the p value) can be found in a statistical table for the distribution of the chi-square. To look up the *p* value, a further value is required, namely, the *degree of freedom* (or d.f.), which is computed by multiplying the number of rows less 1 with the number of columns less 1 in a frequency table (or contingency table) (see Case Study 1). For example, a contingency table with two rows and two columns has 1 degree of freedom. In both the chi-square and log-likelihood tests, the critical values with 1 d.f. are 3.83, 6.64 and 10.83 for the significance levels of 0.05, 0.01 and 0.001 respectively. A probability value p close to 0 indicates that a difference is highly significant statistically, whereas a value close to 1 indicates that a difference is almost certainly due to chance. In the BNC example in Unit A6.2, the calculated chi-square score is 42.664, and the log-likelihood score is 28.841 (1 d.f.), much greater than the critical value 10.83 for the significance level 0.001. Hence, we are more than 99.9 per cent confident that the difference in the frequencies of *fucker(s)* observed in the spoken and written sections of the BNC corpus is statistically significant.

There are many web-based chi-square or log-likelihood calculators. Readers who use a standard statistics package like SPSS can even avoid the trouble of consulting a statistical table of distribution, as the program automatically gives (Pearson) chi-square and log-likelihood scores in addition to indicating the degree of freedom and statistical significance level. It should be noted, however, that proportional data (e.g. normalized scores) cannot be used in the chi-square or log-likelihood tests. The discrepancies in corpus sizes are unimportant here, as these tests automatically compare frequencies proportionally. Note also that the chi-square or log-likelihood test may not be reliable with very low frequencies. When the expected value in a cell of a contingency table is less than 5, Fisher's exact test is more reliable. SPSS computes Fisher's exact significance level automatically if at least one of the cells of the contingency table has an expected value less than 5 when the chi-square test is selected.

A6.5 TESTS FOR SIGNIFICANT COLLOCATIONS

The term *collocation* refers to the characteristic co-occurrence patterns of words, i.e., which words typically co-occur in corpus data (see Units A10.2 and C1). Collocates can be lexical words or grammatical words. Collocations are identified using a statistical approach. Three statistical formulae are most commonly used in corpus linguistics to identify significant collocations: the MI (mutual information), *t* and *z* scores. In this section, we will briefly introduce these tests. Other statistical measures for collocation will be introduced in Case Study 1 of Section C.

MI is a statistical formula borrowed from information theory. The MI score is computed by dividing the observed frequency of the co-occurring word in the defined span for the search string (so-called *node word*), e.g. a 4:4 window, namely four words to the left and four words to the right of the node word, by the expected frequency of the co-occurring word in that span and then taking the logarithm to the base 2 of the result. The MI score is a measure of collocational strength. The higher the MI score, the stronger the link between two items. The closer to 0 the MI score gets, the more likely it is that the two items co-occur by chance. The MI score can also be negative if two items tend to shun each other. Hunston (2002: 71) proposes an MI score of 3 or higher to be taken as evidence that two items are collocates.

However, as Hunston (2002: 72) suggests, collocational strength is not always reliable in identifying meaningful collocations. We also need to know the amount of evidence available for a collocation. This means that the corpus size is also important in identifying how certain a collocation is. In this regard, the *t* test is useful as it takes corpus size into account. As such, an MI score is not as dependent upon the corpus size as a *t* score is. The *t* score can be computed by subtracting the expected frequency from the observed frequency and then dividing the result by the standard deviation (see Unit A6.3 for a discussion of standard deviation). A *t* score of 2 or higher is normally considered to be statistically significant, though the specific probability level can be looked up in a table of distribution, using the computed *t* score and the number of degrees of freedom.

While the MI test measures the strength of collocations, the *t* test measures the confidence with which we can claim that there is some association (Church and Hanks 1990). Collocations with high MI scores tend to include low-frequency words whereas those with high *t*-scores tend to show high-frequency pairs. As such, Church, Hanks and Moon (1994) suggest intersecting the two measures and looking at pairs that have high scores in both measures.

The *z* score is the number of standard deviations from the mean frequency. The *z* test compares the observed frequency with the frequency expected if only chance is affecting the distribution. In terms of the procedures of computation, the *z* score is quite similar to the *t* score whereas in terms of output, the *z* score is more akin to the MI score (see Case Study 1 in Section C). A higher *z* score indicates a greater degree of collocability of an item with the node word. The *z* test is used relatively less frequently than the MI test in corpus linguistics, but it is worth mentioning as it is used in widely used corpus tools such as TACT (Text Analytic Computer Tools) and SARA/Xaira.

Readers may wish to avoid computing the MI, *t* or *z* scores manually by taking advantage of publicly available statistics packages or corpus tools. All of the three tests for collocation introduced in this section can be undertaken using computer programs. SPSS can compute *t* and *z* scores. WordSmith (version 3) calculates the MI score, while SARA and Xaira allow users to choose from the *z* and MI scores as a measure of significant collocations. Case Study 1 in Section C of this book will show readers how to compute the *z* and MI scores using BNCWeb.

Summary

In this unit we introduced the basic concepts and techniques needed to make statistical claims on the basis of the quantitative data provided by corpora. We first noted that the frequencies extracted from corpora need to be normalized to a rational common base if corpora (or subcorpora) of different sizes are compared using descriptive statistics. The chi-square and log-likelihood scores to test statistical significance were then introduced. If the expected frequency in a cell of a contingency table has a value less than 5, Fisher's exact test is recommended. Finally, three tests for significant collocations, namely the MI, *t* and *z* scores were introduced. Further tests for collocation will be discussed in Case Study 1 in Section C.

LOOKING AHEAD

This unit serves only as a very minimal introduction to quantitative analysis in corpus linguistics. Nevertheless, some of the concepts introduced in this unit are essential in the case studies presented in Section C of this book, where we will also show readers how to carry out statistical tests using statistical packages such as SPSS.

It is our hope that this unit will raise readers' statistical awareness in taking a corpus-based approach to language studies.

Readers who wish to further explore the use of statistics in corpus linguistics can find useful discussions in Barnbrook (1996), Oakes (1998) and McEnery and Wilson (2001).

Unit A7
Using available corpora

A7.1 INTRODUCTION

Many readers will wish to use 'off the peg' corpora to carry out their work. In this unit we will introduce some of the major publicly available corpus resources and explore the pros and cons of using ready-made corpora. A corpus is always designed for a particular purpose (see Hunston 2002: 14), hence the usefulness of a ready-made corpus must be judged with regard to the purpose to which a user intends to put it. In this respect, the research question once again plays a crucial role.

There are thousands of corpora in the world, but many of them are created for specific research projects and are thus not publicly available. While abundant corpus resources for languages other than English are now available, this unit will focus upon major English corpora, which are classified in terms of their potential use: general vs. specialized corpus, written vs. spoken corpus, synchronic vs. diachronic corpus, learner corpus and monitor corpus. Note that there is some overlap in the above classification (see the summary of this unit). It is used in this unit simply to give a better account of the primary use of the relevant corpora.

A7.2 GENERAL CORPORA

A general corpus is balanced with regard to the variety of a given language. While the term balance is relative and closely related to a particular research question (see Unit A2.4), if the corpus in question claims to be general in nature, then it will typically be balanced with regard to genres and domains that typically represent the language under consideration. The corpus may contain written data, spoken data or both.

A well-known general corpus is the British National Corpus (BNC). The BNC comprises 100,106,008 words, organized in 4,124 written texts and transcripts of speech in modern British English. The corpus is designed to represent as wide a range of modern British English as possible. The written section (90 per cent) includes, among many others kinds of text, samples from regional and national newspapers, specialist periodicals and journals for all ages and interests, academic books and popular fiction, published and unpublished letters and memoranda, as well as school and university essays. The spoken section (10 per cent) includes 863 transcripts of a large amount of informal conversation, selected from respondents of different ages, from various regions and from all social classes in a demographically balanced way, together with spoken language collected in all kinds of different contexts, ranging from formal business or government meetings to radio shows and phone-ins (see Unit A2.4).

In addition to POS information, the BNC is annotated with rich metadata encoded according to the TEI guidelines, using ISO standard 8879 (SGML, see Unit A3.3). Because of its generality, as well as the use of internationally agreed standards for its encoding, the corpus is a useful resource for a very wide variety of research purposes, in fields as distinct as lexicography, artificial intelligence, speech recognition and synthesis, literary studies and, of course, linguistics. There are a number of ways one may access the BNC corpus. It can be accessed online remotely using the SARA client program (see the Appendix for the Internet address) or using the BNCWeb interface (see Case Study 1). Alternatively, if a local copy of the corpus is available, the corpus can be explored using standalone corpus exploration tools such as WordSmith Tools.

In addition to its usefulness in studying modern British English, the BNC, in combination with corpora of other languages adopting a similar sampling frame (see Unit A2.5 for a discussion of sampling frames), can provide a reliable basis for contrastive language study. A number of corpora are designed as matches for the BNC. The American National Corpus (ANC), for example, is an American match for the BNC. The ANC will contain a core corpus of at least 100 million words, comparable across genres with the BNC. Beyond this, the corpus will include an additional component of potentially several hundreds of millions of words, chosen to provide both the broadest and largest selection of texts possible. The Korean National Corpus also adopts the BNC model (see Unit A5.2), as does the Polish National Corpus (PNC) (see Lewandowska-Tomaszczyk 2003: 106).

A7.3 SPECIALIZED CORPORA

A specialized corpus is specialized relative to a general corpus. It can be domain or genre specific and is designed to represent a sub-language (see Unit A2.2). For example, the Guangzhou Petroleum English Corpus contains 411,612 words of written English from the petrochemical domain. The HKUST Computer Science Corpus is a one-million-word corpus of written English sampled from undergraduate textbooks in computer science. Both corpora are domain specific.

It is interesting to note that there has recently been much interest in the creation and exploitation of specialized corpora in academic or professional settings. For example, the Corpus of Professional Spoken American English (CPSA) has been constructed from a selection of transcripts of interactions in professional settings, containing two main subcorpora of one million words each. One subcorpus consists mainly of academic discussions such as faculty council meetings and committee meetings related to testing. The second subcorpus contains transcripts of White House press conferences, which are almost exclusively question-and-answer sessions (see Barlow 1998). The Michigan Corpus of Academic Spoken English (MICASE) is a corpus of approximately 1.7 million words (nearly 200 hours of recordings) focusing on contemporary university speech within the domain of the University of Michigan (see MICASE Manual). The entire corpus can be accessed now online at the corpus website. A much more ambitious project has been initiated by the Professional English Research Consortium (PERC), which aims to create a 100-million-word Corpus of Professional English (CPE), consisting of both spoken and written discourse used by working professionals and professionals-in-training and covering a wide range of domains such as science, engineering, technology, law, medicine, finance and other professions.

As language may vary considerably across domain (see Case Studies 4 and 6 in Section C) and genre (see Case Study 5 in Section C), specialized corpora such as those introduced above provide valuable resources for investigations in the relevant domains and genres. It is important to note that specialized corpora can also be extracted from general corpora (see the summary of this unit).

A7.4 WRITTEN CORPORA

The first modern corpus of English was a corpus of written American English, the Brown University Standard Corpus of Present-Day American English (i.e. the Brown corpus; see Kučera and Francis 1967). The corpus was compiled using 500 chunks of approximately 2,000 words of written texts. These texts were sampled from fifteen categories. All were produced in 1961. The components of the Brown corpus are given in Table A7.1.

There are a number of corpora which follow the Brown model. The Lancaster–Oslo–Bergen Corpus of British English (i.e. LOB; see Johansson, Leech and Goodluck 1978) is a British match for the Brown corpus. The corpus was created using the same sampling techniques with the exception that LOB aims to represent written British English used in 1961. The two corpora provide an ideal basis for the comparison of the two major varieties of English as used in the early 1960s. Both Brown and LOB are POS tagged. Sub-samples from both corpora have also been parsed (see Unit A4.4.3 for a discussion of parsing). The Lancaster Parsed Corpus (LPC) is a sub-sample of approximately 133,000 words taken from the LOB corpus that has been parsed. The Susanne corpus is a 128,000 word sub-sample taken from the Brown corpus that has been parsed.

Two Freiburg corpora are available to mirror the Brown/LOB relationship in the early 1990s rather than the 1960s. The Freiburg–LOB Corpus of British English (i.e. FLOB; see Hundt, Sand and Siemund 1998) and the Freiburg–Brown Corpus of American English (i.e. Frown; see Hundt, Sand and Skandera 1999) represent written British and American English as used in 1991. In addition to providing a basis for comparing the two major varieties of English in the early 1990s, the

Table A7.1 Text categories in the Brown corpus

Code	Text category	No. of samples	Proportion (%)
A	Press reportage	44	8.8
B	Press editorials	27	5.4
C	Press reviews	17	3.4
D	Religion	17	3.4
E	Skills, trades and hobbies	38	7.6
F	Popular lore	44	8.8
G	Biographies and essays	77	15.4
H	Miscellaneous (reports, official documents)	30	6.0
J	Science (academic prose)	80	16.0
K	General fiction	29	5.8
L	Mystery and detective fiction	24	4.8
M	Science fiction	6	1.2
N	Western and adventure fiction	29	5.8
P	Romantic fiction	29	5.8
R	Humour	9	1.8
Total		500	100

two Freiburg corpora also enable users to track language changes in British and American English over the intervening three decades between Brown/LOB and FLOB/Frown. The POS-tagged versions of both FLOB and Frown are available. Brown/LOB and FLOB/Frown will be used in Case Study 2 in Section C.

In addition to British and American English, a couple of corpora have been created for varieties of English using the Brown sampling model. For example, the Australian Corpus of English (i.e. ACE, also known as the Macquarie Corpus) represents written Australian English from 1986 and after; the Wellington Corpus of Written NZ English (WWC) represents written New Zealand English, covering the years between 1986 and 1990; and the Kolhapur corpus represents Indian English dating from 1978. Yet not all Brown matches focus on varieties of English. As noted in Unit A7.2, a sampling frame may cross languages as well as language varieties. An example of this using the Brown sampling frame is the Lancaster Corpus of Mandarin Chinese (i.e. LCMC; see McEnery, Xiao and Mo 2003), a Chinese match for the FLOB and Frown corpora. Such a corpus makes it possible to contrast Chinese with two major English varieties.

A7.5 SPOKEN CORPORA

In addition to the spoken part of general corpora such as the BNC and the genre-specific spoken corpora introduced in Units A7.2 and A7.3, a number of spoken English corpora are available. They include, for example, the London–Lund Corpus (LLC), the Lancaster/IBM Spoken English Corpus (SEC), the Cambridge and Nottingham Corpus of Discourse in English (CANCODE), the Santa Barbara Corpus of Spoken American English (SBCSAE) and the Wellington Corpus of Spoken New Zealand English (WSC).

The LLC is a corpus of spoken British English dating from the 1960s to the mid-1970s. The corpus consists of 100 texts, each of 5,000 words, totalling half a million running words. A distinction is made between dialogue (e.g. face-to-face conversations, telephone conversations and public discussion) and monologue (both spontaneous and prepared) in the organization of the corpus. The corpus is prosodically annotated.

The SEC corpus consists of approximately 53,000 words of spoken British English, mainly taken from radio broadcasts dating from the mid-1980s and covering a range of speech categories such as commentary, news broadcast, lecture and dialogue. The corpus is available in an orthographically transcribed form. A POS-tagged, parsed or prosodically annotated version is also available.

CANCODE is part of the Cambridge International Corpus (CIC). The corpus comprises five million words of transcribed spontaneous speech collected in Britain between 1995 and 2000, covering a wide variety of situations: casual conversation, people working together, people shopping, people finding out information, discussions and many other types of interaction. A unique feature of CANCODE is that the corpus has been coded with information pertaining to the relationship between the speakers: whether they are intimates (living together), casual acquaintances, colleagues at work or strangers. This coding allows users to look more closely at how different levels of familiarity (formality) affect the way in which people speak to each other.

The Santa Barbara Corpus of Spoken American English (SBCSAE) is part of the USA component of the International Corpus of English (i.e. ICE; see Unit A7.6). It is based on hundreds of recordings of spontaneous speech from all over the United States, representing a wide variety of people of different regional origins, ages, occupations, and ethnic and social backgrounds. It reflects the many ways that people use language in their lives: conversation, gossip, arguments, on-the-job talk, card games, city council meetings, sales pitches, classroom lectures, political speeches, bedtime stories, sermons, weddings and so on. The corpus is particularly useful for research into speech recognition as each speech file is accompanied by a transcript in which phrases are time-stamped to allow them to be linked with the audio recording from which the transcription was produced. The SBCSAE will be used in Case Study 5 in Section C.

The WSC corpus comprises one million words of spoken New Zealand English in the form of 551 extracts collected between 1988 and 1994 (99 per cent of the data from 1990–1994, the exception being eight private interviews). Formal speech/monologue accounts for 12 per cent of the data, semi-formal speech/elicited monologue 13 per cent while informal speech/dialogue accounts for 75 per cent. The unusually high proportion of private material makes the corpus a valuable resource for research into informal spoken registers.

A7.6 SYNCHRONIC CORPORA

The written English corpora introduced in Unit 7.4 are useful should one wish to compare varieties of English. The typical examples are the corpora of the Brown family: Brown and Frown for American English, LOB and FLOB for British English, ACE for Australian English, WWC for New Zealand English, and the Kolhapur corpus for Indian English (see Unit A7.4 for a description of these corpora). While these corpora are generally good for comparing national varieties of English (so-called 'world Englishes'; see Unit A10.5), the results from such a comparison must be interpreted with caution where the corpora under examination were built to represent English in different time periods (e.g. Brown vs. FLOB) or the Brown model has been modified. A more reliable basis for comparing world Englishes is the International Corpus of English (ICE), which is specifically designed for the synchronic study of world Englishes. The ICE corpus consists of a collection of twenty corpora of one million words each, each composed of written and spoken English produced after 1989 in countries or regions in which English is a first or major language (e.g. Australia, Canada, East Africa, Hong Kong as well as the UK and the USA). As the primary aim of ICE is to facilitate comparative studies of English used worldwide, each component follows a common corpus design as well as a common scheme for grammatical annotation to ensure comparability among the component corpora (see Nelson 1996). The ICE corpora are encoded at various levels, including textual mark-up, POS tagging and syntactic parsing. Readers can visit the ICE website to check the availability of the component corpora in ICE.

In contrast, there are considerably fewer corpora available for regional dialects than national varieties. This is because comparing dialects is assumed to be less meaningful than comparing varieties of a language or two distinct languages. Comparisons of dialects are even claimed by some to be 'vacuous' (Bauer 2002: 108). The spoken component of the BNC does allow users to compare dialects in Britain, but only between broadly sampled groups such as 'South', 'Midlands' and 'North' (see Aston and Burnard 1998: 31). The Longman Spoken American Corpus, which was built to match the demographically sampled component of the spoken BNC, can be used to compare regional dialects in the USA. A corpus which was built specifically for the study of English dialects is the spoken corpus of the Survey of English dialects (i.e. SED; see Beare and Scott 1999). The Survey of English Dialects was started in 1948 by Harold Orton at the University of Leeds. The initial work comprised a questionnaire-based survey of traditional dialects based on extensive interviews from 318 locations all over rural England. During the survey, a number of recordings were made as well as detailed interviews. The recordings, which were made during 1948 to 1973, consist of about sixty hours of dialogue of elderly people talking about life, work and recreation. The recordings were transcribed, with sound files linked to transcripts. The corpus is marked up in TEI-compliant SGML (see Unit A3.3) and POS tagged using CLAWS (see Unit A4.4.1).

There are presently few synchronic corpora suitable for studies of dialects and varieties for languages other than English. The LIVAC (Linguistic Variation in

Chinese Speech Communities) corpus is one of the few that exist. It contains texts from representative Chinese newspapers and the electronic media of six Chinese speech communities: Hong Kong, Taiwan, Beijing, Shanghai, Macau and Singapore. The collection of materials from these diverse communities is synchronized so that all of the components are comparable. The corpus is under construction by the City University of Hong Kong but some samples are already available.

A7.7 DIACHRONIC CORPORA

A diachronic (or historical) corpus contains texts from the same language gathered from different time periods. Typically that period is far more extensive than that covered by Brown/Frown and LOB/FLOB (see Unit A7.4) or a monitor corpus (see Unit 7.9). Corpora of this type are used to track changes in language evolution. For practical reasons, diachronic corpora typically contain only written language, though corpus builders have tried to construct corpora of speech from earlier periods, e.g., the Helsinki Dialect Corpus (see Peitsara and Vasko 2002) and the Corpus of English Dialogues 1560–1760 (see Culpeper and Kytö 2000). Perhaps the best-known diachronic corpus of English is the Helsinki Diachronic Corpus of English Texts (i.e. the Helsinki corpus), which consists of approximately 1.5 million words of English in the form of 400 text samples, dating from the eighth to eighteenth centuries. The corpus covers a wide range of genres and sociolinguistic variables and is divided into three periods (Old, Middle, and Early Modern English) and eleven subperiods (see Unit B5.4). Another diachronic English corpus of note is the ARCHER corpus (A Representative Corpus of Historical English Registers). The corpus covers both British and American English dating from 1650 to 1990, divided into fifty-year periods. Spoken data from the later periods are also included in the corpus. Yet another diachronic corpus, which is more accessible than ARCHER, is the Lampeter Corpus of Early Modern English Tracts. The Lampeter corpus contains 1.1 million words of pamphlet literature dating from 1640 and 1740. As it includes whole texts rather than smaller samples, the corpus is also useful for the study of textual organization in Early Modern English.

A7.8 LEARNER CORPORA

A type of corpus that is immediately related to the language classroom is a *learner corpus*. A learner corpus is a collection of the writing or speech of learners acquiring a second language (L2). The data collected are the L2 productions of such learners. They can be used for either cross-sectional or longitudinal analysis. The term *learner corpus* is used here as opposed to a *developmental corpus*, which consists of data produced by children acquiring their first language (L1). While L2 learner data for longitudinal analysis can also be called 'developmental' data, we use the term *developmental corpus* specifically for L1 data as opposed to *learner corpus*. Well-known developmental corpora include, for example, the Child Language Data

Exchange System (CHILDES; see MacWhinney 1992) and the Polytechnic of Wales Corpus (POW; see Souter 1993).

Probably the best-known learner corpus is the International Corpus of Learner English (ICLE; see Granger 2003a). At present the corpus contains approximately three million words of essays written by advanced learners of English (i.e. university students of English as a foreign language in their third or fourth year of study) from fourteen different mother-tongue backgrounds (French, German, Dutch, Spanish, Swedish, Finnish, Polish, Czech, Bulgarian, Russian, Italian, Hebrew, Japanese and Chinese). The error and POS-tagged version of the corpus will be available in the near future. In addition to allowing the comparison of the writing of learners from different L1 backgrounds, the corpus can be used in combination with the Louvain Corpus of Native English Essays (LOCNESS) to compare native and learner English. The ICLE corpus is available for linguistic research but cannot be used for commercial purposes.

The Longman Learners' Corpus contains ten million words of text written by students of English at a range of levels of proficiency from twenty different L1 backgrounds. The elicitation tasks used to gather the texts varied, ranging from in-class essays with or without the use of a dictionary to exam essays or assignments. Each student essay is coded by L1 background and proficiency level, among other things. The corpus is not tagged for part of speech, but part of the corpus has been error-tagged manually, although this portion is only for internal use at Longman Dictionaries. Such a corpus offers invaluable information about the mistakes students make and what they already know. The Longman Learners' Corpus is a useful resource, for example, for lexicographers and textbook materials writers who wish to produce dictionaries and coursebooks that address students' specific needs. The corpus is publicly available for commercial purposes. This corpus will be used in Case Study 3 in Section C of this book.

The Cambridge Learner Corpus (CLC) is a large collection of examples of English writing from learners of English all over the world. It contains over 20 million words and is expanding continually. The English in CLC comes from anonymized exam scripts written by students taking Cambridge ESOL English exams worldwide. The corpus currently contains 50,000 scripts from 150 countries (100 different L1 backgrounds). Each script is coded with information about the student's first language, nationality, level of English and age, etc. Over eight million words (or about 25,000 scripts) have been coded for errors. Currently, the corpus can only be used by authors and writers working for Cambridge University Press and by members of staff at Cambridge ESOL.

In addition, a number of learner English corpora are available which cover only one L1 background. For example, the HKUST Corpus of Learner English is a ten-million-word corpus composed of written essays and exam scripts of Chinese learners in Hong Kong (see Milton 1998). The Chinese Learner English Corpus (CLEC) contains one million words from writing produced by five types of Chinese learners of English ranging from middle-school students to senior English majors (Gui and Yang 2001). The SST (Standard Speaking Test) corpus contains one million words (around 300 hours of recording, or 1,200 samples transcribed from fifteen-minute oral interview tests) of error-tagged spoken English produced by Japanese learners (Izumi *et al.* 2003). The JEFLL (Japanese EFL Learner) corpus is a one-million-word corpus containing 10,000 sample essays written by Japanese learners of English from Years 7-12 in secondary schools. The JPU (Janus Pannonius University) learner corpus is a corpus of 400,000 words which contains the essays of advanced level Hungarian university students that were collected from 1992 to 1998 (Horvath 1999). The USE (Uppsala Student English) corpus contains one million words of texts written primarily by Swedish university students who are advanced learners of English with a high level of proficiency. The Polish Learner English Corpus is designed as a half-a-million-word corpus of written learner data produced by Polish learners of English from a range of learner styles at different proficiency levels, from beginning learners to post-advanced learners (see Lewandowska-Tomaszczyk 2003: 107). Readers can refer to Pravec (2002) and the Internet links given in the Appendix for a more comprehensive survey of available learner corpora.

A7.9 MONITOR CORPORA

All of the corpora (with the possible exception of CLC) introduced in the previous sections are constant in size. They are sample corpora. In contrast, a *monitor corpus* is constantly (e.g. annually, monthly or even daily) supplemented with fresh material and keeps increasing in size, though the proportion of text types included in the corpus remains constant (see Unit A2.3 for further discussion). Corpora of this type are typically much larger than sample corpora. The Bank of English (BoE) is widely acknowledged to be an example of a monitor corpus. It has increased in size progressively since its inception in the 1980s (Hunston 2002: 15) and is around 524 million words at present. The Global English Monitor Corpus, which was started in late 2001 as an electronic archive of the world's leading newspapers in English, is expected to reach billions of words within a few years. The corpus aims at monitoring language use and semantic change in English as reflected in newspapers so as to allow for research into whether the English-language discourses in Britain, the United States, Australia, Pakistan and South Africa are convergent or divergent over time. Another example of corpora of this kind is AVIATOR (Analysis of Verbal Interaction and Automated Text Retrieval), developed at the University of Birmingham, which automatically monitors language change, using a series of filters to identify and categorize new word forms, new word pairs or terms and change in meaning. However, as a monitor corpus does not have a finite size, some corpus linguists have argued that it is an 'ongoing archive' (Leech 1991: 10) rather than a true corpus.

There was an impromptu debate at a joint conference of the Association for Literary and Linguistic Computing (ALLC) and the Association for Computing in the

Humanities (ACH) at Christchurch College, Oxford in 1992 between, on the one hand, Quirk and Leech arguing in favour of the balanced sample corpus model and on the other hand Sinclair and Meijs who spoke in favour of the monitor corpus model (see Geoffrey Leech, personal communication). While the monitor corpus team won the debate in 1992, it is now clear that the sample corpus model has won the wider debate, as evidenced by it being the dominant tradition in modern corpus-building; the majority of corpora which have been built to date are balanced sample corpora, as exemplified by the pioneer English corpora Brown and LOB, and more recently by the British National Corpus. Nonetheless, the idea of the monitor corpus is still important and deserves a review here.

The monitor corpus approach was first developed in Sinclair (1991a: 24–26). Sinclair argued against static sample corpora like Brown and argued in favour of an ever growing dynamic monitor corpus. The ideas expressed in Sinclair (1991a) mirror the way people were thinking about corpora two decades ago. Unsurprisingly, Sinclair has amended his views 'as new advances come on stream' and no longer holds many of the positions held in his 1991a work (Sinclair, personal communication). However, the arguments expressed therein still have some currency, both in the writing of Sinclair (e.g. Sinclair 2004a: 187–191) and others (e.g. Tognini-Bonelli 2001, as noted in Unit A1.7). So it is worth reviewing the arguments presented by Sinclair against sample corpora. The major arguments relate to the overall corpus size (one million words) and the sample size (2,000 words). These concerns have largely been neutralized by an increase in both computer power and the availability of electronic texts (in many languages). As Aston and Burnard (1998: 22) comment, 'The continued growth in the size of corpora has generally implied an increase in sample sizes as well as the number of samples.' The overall size of the BNC, for example, is 100 million words. Accordingly, the sample size in the BNC has also increased to 40,000–50,000 words while the number of samples has increased to over 4,000. Samples of this size can no longer be said to be 'too brief', and subcategories composed of such texts can indeed 'stand as samples themselves'. Biber (1988, 1993) shows that even in corpora consisting of 2,000-word samples, frequent linguistic features are quite stable both within samples and across samples in different text categories. For relatively rare features and for vocabulary, though, Sinclair's warning is still valid.

A monitor corpus undergoes a partial self-recycling after reaching some sort of saturation, i.e. the inflow of the new data is subjected to an automatic monitoring process which will only admit new material to the corpus where that material shows some features which differ significantly from the stable part of the corpus (see Váradi 2000: 2). There are a number of difficulties with the monitor corpus model, however. First, as this approach rejects any principled attempt to balance a corpus, depending instead upon sheer size to deal with the issue (see Unit A1.7), Leech (1991: 10) refers to a monitor corpus as an 'ongoing archive', while Váradi (2000: 2) would label it as 'opportunistic'. As such, monitor corpora are a less reliable basis than balanced sample corpora for quantitative (as opposed to qualitative) analysis. Second, as this approach argues strongly in favour of whole texts, text availability becomes a difficulty in the already sensitive context of copyright. Third, it is quite confusing to indicate a specific corpus version with its word count. Under such circumstances it is only the corpus builders, not the users, who know what is contained in a specific version. Fourth, as a monitor corpus keeps growing in size, results cannot easily be compared. A monitor corpus thus loses its value as 'a standard reference' (McEnery and Wilson 2001: 32). Grönqvist (2004) suggests, rightly in our view, that '[a] system where it is possible to restore the corpus as it was at a specific time would be worth a lot' for a monitor corpus. This sugges-tion would mean that a dynamic monitor corpus should in effect consist of a series of static corpora over time. This is not current practice. One final concern of the dynamic model is that, even if the huge corpus size and required processing speed should not become a problem as the rapid development of computing technology makes this a non-issue, there is no guarantee that the same criteria will be used to filter in new data in the long term (e.g. in 200 years), meaning that even if a diachronic archive of the sort suggested is established, the comparability of the archived version of the corpus would be in doubt.

Monitor corpora are potentially useful, however. A monitor corpus is primarily designed to track changes from different periods (see Hunston 2002: 16). In this sense, a monitor corpus is similar to a diachronic corpus. However, a monitor corpus normally covers a shorter span of time but in a much more fine-grained fashion than the diachronic corpora discussed so far. It is possible, using a monitor corpus, to study relatively rapid language change, such as the development and the lifecycle of neologisms. In principle, if a monitor corpus is in existence for a very long period of time – thirty years for example – it may also be possible to study change happening at a much slower rate, e.g. grammatical change. At present, however, no monitor corpus has been in existence long enough to enable the type of research undertaken using diachronic corpora like the Helsinki corpus or sample corpora such as LOB and FLOB to be undertaken fruitfully (see Leech 2002; see also Unit B5.5).

Summary

In this unit, we introduced some of the major publicly available English corpora which are useful for a range of research purposes, including general vs. specialized corpus, written vs. spoken corpus, synchronic vs. diachronic corpus, learner corpus and monitor corpus. This discussion, however, only covers a very small proportion of the available corpus resources. Readers are advised to refer to the authors' companion website for a more comprehensive survey of well-known and influential corpora for English and other languages.

The distinctions given in this unit have been forced for the purpose of this introduction. It is not unusual to find that any given corpus will be a blend of many of the features introduced here. Consider the BNC, for example. This includes both spoken and written data. While it is a general corpus, one could extract a number of specialized corpora from it (e.g. business English). While presumably intended for use in synchronic research, the written section contains texts spanning from

1960 to 1993 (divided into two periods: 1960–1974 and 1975–1992; or for the BNC World Edition, three periods: 1960–1974, 1975–1984 and 1985–1993), so the corpus holds some data of interest to diachronic researchers. The spoken section of the BNC even contains some L2 English! So while the distinctions explored here are useful, do not think that they apply in a simple and rigid fashion to all of the corpora you may encounter.

It is also clear that while the sample and monitor corpus models have different focuses in their design criteria, corpora of both types are useful in that they serve different purposes. Specifically, a monitor corpus is better suited for identifying new words and tracking changes in usage/meaning while a representative, balanced sample corpus provides a more reliable language model. Note that the corpora used in our case studies in Section C of this book are all sample corpora.

A recurring theme throughout our discussion of corpora is that the usefulness of a given corpus depends upon the research question a user intends to investigate using that corpus. As such, while there are many corpora readily available, it is often the case that researchers and students will find that they are not able to address their research questions using ready-made corpora. In such circumstances, one must build one's own corpus.

LOOKING AHEAD

In the unit that follows, we will discuss the principal considerations involved in building the DIY corpora referred to above.

Unit A8
Going solo: DIY corpora

A8.1 INTRODUCTION

As noted in Unit A7, while there are many ready-made corpora, one may find it necessary to build one's own corpus to address a particular research question. In this unit we will discuss the principal factors one should consider when constructing such corpora. In exploring DIY ('do-it-yourself') corpora, we will revisit the key concepts introduced in Units A2–A4, and explain how they are a useful guide to the creation of DIY corpora. Additionally, we will review some of the readily available tools which may help in the process of DIY corpus-building, especially where web-based material is being used.

A8.2 CORPUS SIZE

One must be clear about one's research question (or questions) when planning to build a DIY corpus. This helps you to determine what material you will need to collect. Having developed an understanding of the type of data you need to collect, and having made sure that no ready-made corpus of such material exists, one needs to find a source of data. Assuming that the data can be found, one then has to address the question of corpus size. How large a corpus do you need? There is no easy answer to this question. The size of the corpus needed depends upon the purpose for which it is intended as well as a number of practical considerations. In the early 1960s when the processing power and storage capacity of computers were quite limited, a one-million-word corpus like Brown appeared to be as large a corpus as one could reasonably build. With the increase in computer power and the availability of machine-readable texts, however, a corpus of this size is no longer considered large and in comparison with today's giant corpora like the BNC and the Bank of English it appears somewhat small.

The availability of suitable data, especially in machine-readable form, seriously affects corpus size. In building a balanced corpus according to fixed proportions, for example, the lack of data for one text type may accordingly restrict the size of the samples of other text types taken. This is especially the case for parallel corpora, as it is common for the availability of translations to be unbalanced across text types for many languages. While it is often possible to transfer paper-based texts into electronic form using OCR software, the process costs time and money and is error prone. Hence, the availability of machine-readable data is often the main limiting factor in corpus-building.

Another factor that potentially limits the size of a DIY corpus is copyright. Unless the proposed corpus contains entirely out-of-date or copyright-free data, simply gathering available data and using them in a freely available corpus may expose the corpus-builder to legal action. When one seeks copyright clearance, one can face frustration: the construction of the corpus is your priority, not the copyright holder's. They may simply ignore you. Their silence cannot be taken as consent. Copyright clearance in building a large corpus necessitates much effort, trouble and frustration (see Unit A9 for further discussion of copyright issues relevant to corpus-building).

No matter how important legal considerations may seem, however, one should not lose sight of the paramount importance of the research question. This question controls all of your corpus-building decisions, including the decision regarding corpus size. Even if the conditions discussed above allow for a large corpus, it does not mean that a large corpus is what you want. First, the size of the corpus needed to explore a research question is dependent on the frequency and distribution of the linguistic features under consideration in that corpus (see McEnery and Wilson 2001: 80). As Leech (1991: 8–29) observes, size is not all-important. Small corpora may contain sufficient examples of frequent linguistic features. To study features like the number of present- and past-tense verbs in English, for example, a sample of 1,000 words may prove sufficient (Biber 1993). Second, small specialized corpora serve a very different yet important purpose from large multimillion-word corpora (Shimazumi and Berber-Sardinha 1996). It is understandable that corpora for lexical studies are much larger than those for grammatical studies, because when studying lexis one is interested in the frequency of the distribution of a word, which can be modelled as contrasting with all others of the same category (see Santos 1996:11). In contrast, corpora employed in quantitative studies of grammatical devices are relatively small (see Biber 1988; Givon 1995), because the syntactic freezing point is fairly low (Hakulinen *et al.* 1980: 104). Third, corpora that need extensive manual annotation (e.g. semantic annotation and pragmatic annotation; see Unit A4) are necessarily small. Fourth, many corpus tools set a ceiling on the number of concordances that can be extracted, e.g. WordSmith version 3 can extract a maximum of 16,868 concordances (version 4 does not has this limit). This makes it inconvenient for a frequent linguistic feature to be extracted from a very large corpus (see Case Studies 3 and 5 for a solution). Even if this can be done, few researchers can obtain useful information from hundreds of thousands of concordances (see Hunston 2002: 25). The data extracted defy manual analysis by a sole researcher by virtue of the sheer volume of examples discovered. Of course, we do not mean that DIY corpora must necessarily be small. A corpus small enough to produce only a dozen concordances of a linguistic feature under consideration will not be able to provide a reliable basis for quantification, though it may act as a spur to qualitative research. The point we wish to make is that the optimum size of a corpus is determined by the research question the corpus is intended to address as well as practical considerations.

A8.3 BALANCE AND REPRESENTATIVENESS

As noted in Unit A2, representativeness is a qualifying feature of a corpus. To achieve this quality, balance and sampling are important. While balance and representativeness are important considerations in corpus design, they depend on the research question and the ease with which data can be captured and thus must be interpreted in relative terms, i.e., a corpus should only be as representative as possible of the language variety under consideration. ICE is a good example of this, as each of its component subcorpora represents one national or regional variety of English; Brown and LOB represent written American and British English in 1961 respectively, while learner corpora such as ICLE represent language varieties used by learners from various L1 backgrounds or at different proficiency levels. Even a general corpus such as the BNC with 100 million words only represents modern British English in a specific time and geographical frame (see Unit A7 for a description of these corpora). It is also important to note that the lower proportion of spoken data in corpora such as the BNC does not mean that spoken language is less important or less widespread than written language. This is so simply because spoken data are more difficult and expensive to capture than written data. Corpusbuilding is of necessity a marriage of perfection and pragmatism.

Another argument supporting a loose interpretation of balance and representativeness is that these notions *per se* are open to question (see Hunston 2002: 28–30). To achieve corpus representativeness along the lines of the Brown model requires knowledge of which genre is used how often by the language community in the sampling period. Yet it is unrealistic to determine the correlation of language production and reception in various genres (see Hausser 1999: 291; Hunston 2002: 29). Readers will have an opportunity to explore the validity of the Brown model using the techniques introduced in Case Study 5 in Section C of this book. The only solution to this problem is to treat corpus-based findings with caution. It is advisable to base your claims on your corpus and avoid unreasonable generalizations (see Unit 10.15). Likewise, conclusions drawn from a particular corpus must be treated as deductions rather than facts (see also Hunston 2002: 23).

A8.4 DATA CAPTURE

For pragmatic reasons, electronic data are preferred over paper-based materials in building DIY corpora. The world-wide-web (WWW) is an important source of machine-readable data for many languages. The web pages on the Internet normally use *Hypertext Mark-up Language* (i.e. HTML) to enable browsers like Internet Explorer or Netscape to display them properly. While the tags (included in angled brackets) are typically hidden when a text is displayed in a browser, they do exist in

SECTION

A

Introduction

the source file of a web page. Hence, an important step in building DIY corpora using web pages is tidying up the downloaded data by converting web pages to plain text, or to some desired format, e.g. XML (see Unit A3.3). In this section, we will introduce some useful tools to help readers to download data from the Internet and clean up the downloaded data by removing or converting HTML tags. These tools are either freeware or commercial products available at affordable prices.

While it is possible to download data page by page, which is rather time-consuming, there are a number of tools which facilitate downloading all of the web pages on a selected website in one go (e.g. Grab-a-Site or HTTrack), or more usefully, down-loading related web pages (e.g. containing certain keywords) at one go. WordSmith version 4, for example, incorporates the WebGetter function that helps users to build DIY corpora. WebGetter downloads related web pages with the help of a search engine (Scott 2003: 87). Users can specify the minimum file length or word number (small files may contain only links to a couple of pictures and nothing much else), required language and, optionally, required words. Web pages that satisfy the requirements are downloaded simultaneously (see Scott 2003: 88–89). The WebGetter function, however, does not remove HTML mark-up or convert it to XML. The downloaded data need to be tidied up using other tools before they can be loaded into a concordancer or further annotated.

Another tool worth mentioning is the Multilingual Corpus Toolkit (MLCT; see Piao, Wilson and McEnery 2002). This toolkit is available at the website accompanying this book (see the Appendix). The MLCT runs in Java Runtime Environment (JRE) version 1.4 or above, which is freely available on the Internet. In addition to many other functions needed for multilingual-language processing (e.g. mark-up, POS tagging and concordancing), the system can be used to extract texts from the Internet. Once a web page is downloaded, it is cleaned up. One weakness of the program is that it can only download one web page at a time. Yet this weakness is compensated for by another utility that converts all of the web pages in a file folder (e.g. the web pages downloaded using the Webgetter function of WordSmith version 4) to a desired text format in one go. Another attraction of the MLCT is that it can mark up textual structure (e.g. paragraphs and sentences) automatically (see Unit A8.5).

A8.5   CORPUS MARK-UP

As noted in Unit A3, corpus mark-up is a basic step in corpus construction. Mark-up usually provides textual (e.g. paragraph and sentence) and contextual information (e.g. text type, speaker gender and bibliographic source). Textual infor-mation is useful for studying textual organization while contextual information is important in recovering the situation in which a particular corpus sample was produced, as corpora usually consist of small isolated samples extracted from larger texts. Mark-up also helps to organize corpus data in a structured way and enables explorations in language variation (see Case Study 4).

While mark-up is clearly essential for corpus construction, the degree of mark-up needed is closely related to the research question. If a corpus is constructed to compare different genres, mark-up must show text-type information; likewise, if a spoken corpus is built to explore language variation across sociolinguistic variables, then the relevant features such as speaker age, gender and social class must be marked up. Extensive metadata (see Unit A3) are encoded in general corpora such as the BNC which can serve for multiple purposes.

However, the mark-up process is usually time-consuming. Excessive mark-up may also make a corpus less readable to a casual corpus user not viewing the corpus through a mark-up-aware browsing tool which can hide such mark-up. For specialized corpora which use homogeneous data (e.g. articles downloaded from hate newsgroups on the Internet), we suggest that only basic textual information, namely paragraphs and sentences, be marked up, as this type of mark-up can be conducted relatively easily using available software. As noted, Xaira can pre-process texts in XML format. The MLCT also inserts paragraph and sentence marks automatically.

A8.6 CORPUS ANNOTATION

We noted in Unit A4 that corpus annotation is closely related to, but different from, mark-up, and can take many forms such as POS tagging, parsing, semantic annotation and so on.

The form of corpus annotation one should undertake on a corpus is primarily dependent upon one's research question. For spoken corpora designed for use in speech recognition, the annotation of prosodic features is essential whereas syntactic parsing is less important. Likewise, corpora constructed for grammatical study should be POS tagged, and preferably also parsed while those used in the study of semantics may profitably include semantic annotation. In addition to the research question, a major consideration in corpus annotation is the precision rate with which a form of annotation can be undertaken automatically. As far as the English language is concerned, automatic lemmatization and POS tagging have achieved very high success rates (typically over 97 per cent). Significant progress has also been made in parsing and semantic annotation (see Unit A4). In contrast, many other forms of annotation, such as the annotation of coreference, pragmatic features, and speech and thought representation, either cannot be conducted automatically or the output of such automatic processing requires substantial manual correction. Automatic POS tagging can also be successfully undertaken for many other languages such as French, Spanish, Chinese and Korean. Given the current status of automated corpus annotation, it is usually possible for DIY corpora intended for general language study to be annotated for parts of speech. Given that errors are inevitable in automatic annotation, corpus size should be taken into account so as to neutralize these errors. With the same precision rate of annotation, a corpus of one hundred thousand words is clearly more reliable than a corpus containing merely a few thousand words, assuming that the errors are relatively random.

A8.7 CHARACTER ENCODING

Character encoding is rarely an issue for alphabetical languages (e.g. English) which use ASCII characters. For many other languages which use different writing systems, especially for multilingual corpora which contain a wide range of writing systems, encoding is important if one wants to display the corpus properly or facilitate data interchange. For example, Chinese can be encoded using GB2312 (simplified Chinese), Big5 (traditional Chinese) or Unicode (UTF-8, UTF-7 or UTF-16). Both GB2312 and Big5 are 2-byte encoding systems that require language-specific operating systems or language support packs if the Chinese characters encoded are to be displayed properly. Language-specific encoding systems such as these make data interchange problematic. It is also quite impossible to display a document containing both simplified and traditional Chinese using these encoding systems.

Unicode solves all of these problems. Unicode is truly multilingual in that it can display the characters of a very large number of writing systems. Hence, a general trend in corpus-building is to encode corpora (especially multilingual corpora) using Unicode (e.g. the EMILLE corpora; see McEnery *et al.* 2000). Corpora encoded in Unicode can also take advantage of the latest Unicode-compliant concordancers such as Xaira (Burnard and Todd 2003) and WordSmith version 4 (Scott 2003).

Summary

This unit discussed the principal considerations involved in the creation of DIY corpora, namely, corpus size, balance and representativeness, data capture, corpus mark-up, annotation and character encoding. Throughout our discussion we have emphasized that almost every decision (with the exception of corpus encoding) is closely related to the research question one wishes to address using the corpus, though pragmatic considerations such as the availability of machine-readable data and the reliability of automatic processing tools may also affect one's decisions. We have also shown that the key concepts introduced in Units A2–A4 are a useful guide to the construction of DIY corpora.

A key theme of this unit is the usefulness of the Web in the construction of DIY corpora. The Internet is an important source of machine-readable data. It also provides many corpus-processing tools such as those that facilitate downloading web pages and mark-up conversion.

LOOKING AHEAD

Given that copyright is a sensitive issue in building DIY corpora, we will give advice in this respect in the next unit.

Unit A9
Copyright

A9.1 INTRODUCTION

We noted in Unit A8.2 that a major issue in building DIY corpora is copyright. While it is possible to use copyright-free material, such data are usually old and a corpus consisting entirely of such data is not useful if one wishes to study contemporary English, for example. Simply using copyrighted material in a corpus without the permission of the copyright holders may cause unnecessary trouble. In terms of purposes, corpora are typically of two types: for commercial purposes or for non-profit-making academic research. It is clearly unethical and illegal to use the data of other copyright holders to make money solely for oneself. Builders of commercial corpora usually reach an agreement with copyright holders as to how the profit will be shared. Publishers as copyright holders are also usually willing to contribute their data to a corpus-building project if they can benefit from the resulting corpus. However, the creation of commercial corpora is not our concern in this unit. Rather, we will focus on DIY corpora for use in non-profit-making research.

A9.2 COPING WITH COPYRIGHT: WARNING AND ADVICE

You might think that you need not worry about copyright if you are not selling your corpus to make a profit. Sadly, this is not the case. Copyright holders may still take you to court. They may, for example, suffer a loss of profit because your use of their material diminishes their ability to sell it: why buy a book when you can read it for free in a corpus (see also Amsler 2002)? Copyright issues in corpus-building are complex and unavoidable. While they have been brought up periodically for discussion by corpus linguists, there is as yet no satisfactory solution to the issue of copyright in corpus-building.

The situation is complicated further by variation in copyright law internationally. According to the copyright law of EU countries, the term of copyright for published works in which the author owns the copyright is the author's lifetime plus seventy years. Under US law, the term of copyright is the author's lifetime plus fifty years; but for works published before 1978, the copyright term is seventy-five years if the author renewed the copyright after twenty-eight years.

One is able to make some use of copyrighted text without getting clearance, however. Under the 'fair dealing' provisions of copyright law, permission need not be sought for short extracts not exceeding 400 words from prose (or a total of 800 words in a series of extracts, none exceeding 300 words); a citation from a poem should not exceed 40 lines or one quarter of the poem. So one can resort to using small samples to build perfectly legal DIY corpora on the grounds of fair usage. But the sizes of such samples are so small as to jeopardize any claim of balance or representativeness.

We maintain that the fair-use provisions as they apply to citations in published works should operate differently when they apply to corpus-building so as to allow corpus-builders to build corpora quickly and legally. Limited reproduction of copyrighted works, for instance, in chunks of 3,000 words or one-third of the whole text (whichever is shorter) should be protected under fair use for non-profit-making research and educational purposes. A position statement along these lines has been proposed by the corpus-using community articulating the point of view that distributing minimal citations of copyrighted texts and allowing the public indirect access to privately held collections of copyrighted texts for statistical purposes are a necessary part of corpus linguistics research and should be inherently protected as fair use, particularly in non-profit-making research contexts (see Cooper 2003). This aim is not a legal reality yet, however. It will undoubtedly take time for a balance between copyright and fair use for corpus-building to develop.

So, what does one do about copyright? Our general advice is: if you are in doubt, seek permission. It is usually easier to obtain permission for samples than for full texts, and easier for smaller samples than for larger ones. If you show that you are acting in good faith, and only small samples will be used in non-profit-making research, copyright holders are typically pleased to grant you permission. If some do refuse you, remember it is their right to do so; you should move on to try other copyright holders until you have enough data.

It appears easier to seek copyright clearance for web pages on the Internet than for material collected from printed publications. It has been claimed (Spoor 1996: 67) that a vast majority of the documents published on the Internet are not protected by copyright, and that many authors of texts are happy to be able to reach as many people as possible. However, readers should bear in mind that this may not be the case. For example, Cornish (1999:141) argues that probably all material available on the Web is copyrighted, and that digital publications should be treated in the same way as printed works.

Summary

Copyright law is generally formulated to prevent someone from making money from selling intellectual property belonging to other people. Unless you are making money using the intellectual property of other people, or you are somehow causing a loss of income to them, it is quite unlikely that copyright problems will arise when building a corpus. Yet copyright law is in its infancy. Different countries have different rules, and it has been argued that with reference to corpora and copyright there is very little which is obviously legal or illegal (see Kilgariff 2002). Our final word of advice is: proceed with caution.

LOOKING AHEAD

Having discussed most of the key concepts and practices in corpus linguistics in previous units, we will move on to the final unit of Section A to discuss the use of corpora in language studies.

Unit A10
Corpora and applied linguistics

A10.1 INTRODUCTION

We have so far introduced most of the important concepts and practices in corpus linguistics related either to key issues like corpus design, mark-up, annotation, and the multilingual dimension, or to ancillary issues such as making statistical claims, using ready-made and DIY corpora and copyright clearance in corpus-building. The final unit of Section A considers how corpora can be used in language studies. According to Leech (1997b: 9), corpus analysis can be illuminating 'in virtually all branches of linguistics or language learning' (see also Biber, Conrad and Reppen 1998: 11). One of the strengths of corpus data lies in their empirical nature, which pool together the intuitions of a great number of speakers and make linguistic analysis more objective (see Biber *et al.* 1998; McEnery and Wilson 2001: 103; though see Unit B2 for a discussion of this claim). In this unit we will consider the use of corpus data in a number of areas of linguistics. Units A10.2–A10.8 are concerned with the major areas of linguistics where corpora have been used while Units A10.9–A10.14 discuss other areas which have started to use corpus data. In Unit A10.15, we will also discuss the limitations of using corpora in linguistic analysis.

A10.2 LEXICOGRAPHIC AND LEXICAL STUDIES

Corpora have proved to be invaluable resources for lexicographic and lexical studies. While lexicographers, even before the advent of modern corpora, used empirical data in the form of citation slips (e.g. Samuel Johnson's *Dictionary of the English Language*), it is corpora that have revolutionized dictionary-making so that it is now nearly unheard of for new dictionaries and new editions of old dictionaries published from the 1990s onwards not to be based on corpus data. Corpora are useful in several ways for lexicographers. The greatest advantage of using corpora in lexicography lies in their machine-readable nature, which allows dictionary-makers to extract all authentic, typical examples of the usage of a lexical item from a large body of text in a few seconds. The second advantage of the corpus-based approach, which is not available when using citation slips, is the frequency information and quantification of collocation which a corpus can readily provide. Some dictionaries, e.g. *Cobuild* 1995 and *Longman* 1995, include such frequency information. Information of this sort is particularly useful for materials writers and language learners alike (see Case Study 1 in Section C for a discussion of using corpora to improve learner dictionaries). A further benefit of using corpora is related to corpus mark-up and annotation. Many available corpora (e.g. the BNC) are encoded with textual (e.g. register, genre and domain) and sociolinguistic (e.g. user gender and age) metadata which allow lexicographers to give a more accurate description of the usage of a lexical item. Corpus annotations such as part-of-speech tagging and word sense disambiguation also enable a more sensible grouping of words which are polysemous and homographs. Furthermore, a monitor corpus allows lexicographers to track subtle change in the meaning and usage of a lexical item so as to keep their dictionaries up to date. Last but not least, corpus evidence can complement or refute the intuitions of individual lexicographers, which are not always reliable (see Sinclair 1991a: 112; Atkins and Levin 1995; Meijs 1996; Murison-Bowie 1996: 184) so that dictionary entries are more accurate. The observations above are in line with Hunston (2002: 96), who summarizes the changes brought about by corpora to dictionaries and other reference books in terms of five 'emphases':

- an emphasis on frequency;
- an emphasis on collocation and phraseology;
- an emphasis on variation;
- an emphasis on lexis in grammar;
- an emphasis on authenticity.

An important area of lexicographic study is loanwords. Lexicographers have traditionally used their intuitions as criteria to decide whether to include or exclude such lexical borrowings in a dictionary. Podhakecka and Piotrowski (2003) used corpus data to evaluate the treatment of 'Russianisms' in English. Their findings, which are based on a comparison of Russian loanwords in the BNC and *Oxford English Dictionary* (OED, electronic version) as well as *Longman Dictionary of Contemporary English* (2nd edition 1987 and 3rd edition 1995), are both expected and unexpected. On the one hand, they found that half of the 360 Russian loanwords they studied occurred only once in the BNC and very few items were really frequent. This finding is hardly surprising. What is unexpected is that the items selected by the OED on the basis of etymology exhibit the same type of distribution as items selected on the basis of frequency in the BNC. This finding suggests that intuition and corpora do not always lead to different conclusions (see Unit A1.5). While Podhakecka and Piotrowski (2003) follow the traditional approach to loanword studies by analysing loanwords as singly occurring items out of context, Kurtböke and Potter (2000) demonstrated, on the basis of their study of a number of English loans in a corpus of Turkish and a number of Italian loans in a corpus of English, that collocational patterns growing around loanwords are significant and should be included in the treatment of loanwords. They also found that '[a]ssimilation criteria based on frequency counts have proved to be less reliable than previously thought, and alternative criteria such as metaphor should also be taken into account' (Kurtböke and Potter 2000: 99).

In addition to lexicography, corpora have been used extensively in lexical studies (e.g. Nattinger and DeCarrico 1992; Schmitt 2004). The focus of corpus-based lexical studies is collocation and collocational meaning, i.e. semantic prosody and semantic preference.

Collocation has been studied for at least five decades. The term *collocation* was first used by Firth (1957) when he said 'I propose to bring forward as a technical term, meaning by *collocation*, and apply the test of *collocability*' (Firth 1957: 194). According to Firth (1968: 181), 'collocations of a given word are statements of the habitual or customary places of that word'. Firth's notion of collocation is essentially quantitative (see Krishnamurthy 2000: 32). The statistical approach to collocation is accepted by many corpus linguists including, for example, Halliday (1966: 159), Greenbaum (1974: 82), Sinclair (1991a), Hoey (1991), Stubbs (1995), Partington (1998), McEnery and Wilson (2001) and Hunston (2002). All of these linguists follow Firth in that they argue that collocation refers to the characteristic co-occurrence of patterns of words. One assumes that Greenbaum's (1974: 82) definition of collocation – 'a frequent co-occurrence of two lexical items in the language' – only refers to statistically significant collocation. He reserves the terms *collocability* and *collocable* for potential co-occurrence, using *collocation* and *collocate* solely for words which frequently co-occur (*ibid.*: 80). While Greenbaum's definition does not tell us how frequent the co-occurrence of two lexical items should be to be considered as a collocation, Hoey (1991: 6–7) uses the term *collocation* only if a lexical item appears with other items 'with greater than random probability in its (textual) context'. The random probability can be measured using statistical tests such as the MI (mutual information), *t* or *z* scores (see Units A6.5 and C1).

Yet not all linguists would agree with Hoey's approach. Herbst (1996: 382), for example, argues against the statistical approach to collocation, asserting that if in Berry-Rogghe's (1972) 72,000–word corpus, 'the most frequent collocates of a word such as *house* include the determiners *the* and *this* and the verb *sell*, this is neither particularly surprising nor particularly interesting'. It is true that if we search a nominal node word such as *house*, it is to all intents and purposes inevitable that determiners like *the* and *this* will be close to the top of the frequency list of co-occurring words. The presence of determiners such as *the* and *this* tells us *house* is a noun. The collocation of a node word with a particular grammatical class of words (e.g. determiners) is normally referred to as *colligation*. The fact that grammatical words sit on the top of a frequency list does not devalue the worth of collocations derived on the basis of statistics. Rather it means that because of the high overall frequencies of such grammatical words, brought about by their frequent co-occurrence with nouns, we should be selective in our approach to any given list of collocates, being prepared, on principled grounds, to exclude such words from the list of significant collocates even though they are very frequent. WordSmith, for example, allows users to exclude such frequent items by setting an upper limit, e.g. 1 per cent of running words, from the list of collocates.

The task of determining frequency of co-occurrence manually is a daunting task, so it is no surprise that 'collocation is among the linguistic concepts which have benefited most from advances in corpus linguistics' (Krishnamurthy 2000: 33–34) in the age of the computer; the calculation of collocation statistics from electronic corpora is now a relatively trivial task given suitable software. Yet as well as being made easier to calculate, computerized corpora have freed linguists and lexicographers from an over reliance on intuition in the study of collocation. While some examples of collocation can be detected intuitively (see Deignan 1999: 23), 'particularly for obvious cases of collocation: *news* is *released, time* is *consumed,* and *computer programs run*' (Greenbaum 1974: 83), intuition is typically a poor guide to collocation. Greenbaum recognized this, and tried to address this problem by pooling the intuitions of large numbers of native speakers; he elicited data on collocation from a number of informants 'to provide access to the cumulative experience of large numbers of speakers' (*ibid.*). He had to do this because no appropriate corpus resources were available when he undertook his work in the early 1970s. In those introspection-based elicitation experiments, he found it quite unsurprising that 'people disagree on collocations' (*ibid.*). Intuition, as stated, is often a poor guide to collocation, 'because each of us has only a partial knowledge of the language, we have prejudices and preferences, our memory is weak, our imagination is powerful (so we can conceive of possible contexts for the most implausible utterances), and we tend to notice unusual words or structures but often overlook ordinary ones' (Krishnamurthy 2000: 32–33). Partington (1998: 18) also observes that 'there is no total agreement among native speakers as to which collocations are acceptable and which are not'. As Hunston (2002: 68) argues, while 'collocation can be observed informally' using intuition, 'it is more reliable to measure it statistically, and for this a corpus is essential'. This is because a corpus can reveal such probabilistic semantic patterns across many speakers' intuitions and usage, to which individual speakers have no access (Stubbs 2001a: 153).

Shifting from form to meaning, Stubbs (2002: 225) observes that 'there are always semantic relations between node and collocates, and among the collocates themselves'. The collocational meaning arising from the interaction between a given node word and its collocates might be referred to as *semantic prosody*, 'a form of meaning which is established through the proximity of a consistent series of collocates' (Louw 2000: 57). The primary function of semantic prosody is to express speaker/writer attitude or evaluation (Louw 2000: 58). Semantic prosodies are typically negative, with relatively few of them bearing an affectively positive meaning. For example, Sinclair (1987, 1991a) observes that *HAPPEN* and *SET in* habitually collocate with nouns indicating unpleasant situations. However, it is also claimed that a speaker/writer can violate a semantic prosody condition to achieve some effect in the hearer – for example irony, insincerity or humour can be diagnosed by violations of semantic prosody according to Louw (1993: 173). Semantic prosody is strongly collocational in that it operates beyond the meanings of individual words. For example, both *personal* and *price* are quite neutral, but when they co-occur, a negative prosody may result: *personal price* most frequently refers to something undesirable, as demonstrated by all such examples from the BNC (2) and the Bank of English (18).

It would appear, from the literature published on semantic prosody (including semantic preference), that it is at least as inaccessible to a speaker's conscious introspection as collocation is (cf. Louw 1993: 173; Partington 1998: 68; Hunston 2002: 142). Yet as corpora have grown in size, and tools for extracting semantic prosodies have been developed, semantic prosodies have been addressed much more frequently by linguists (see Louw 1993, 2000; Stubbs 1995; Partington 1998; Hunston 2002). The profiles of the semantic prosodies of many words and phrases have been revealed, e.g. in addition to those mentioned above, it has been suggested that CAUSE (Stubbs 1995), COMMIT (Partington 1998: 67), PEDDLE/peddler (ibid.: 70–72), dealings (ibid.: 72–74), END up verbing (Louw 2000: 54), a recipe for (Louw 2000: 63), GET oneself verbed (ibid.), FAN the flame (Stubbs 2001b: 445), signs of (ibid.: 458), ripe for (ibid.: 457), underage and teenager(s) (ibid.: 454), SIT through (Hunston 2002: 60–62), and bordering on (Schmitt and Carter 2004: 8) typically carry an unfavourable affective meaning whereas PROVIDE (Stubbs 1995) and career (Stubbs 2001b: 459) have a positive prosody.

It might be argued that the negative (or less frequently positive) prosody that belongs to an item is the result of the interplay between the item and its typical collocates. On the one hand, the item does not appear to have an affective meaning until it is in the context of its typical collocates. On the other hand, if a word has typical collocates with an affective meaning, it may take on that affective meaning even when used with atypical collocates. As the Chinese saying goes, 'he who stays near vermilion gets stained red, and he who stays near ink gets stained black' – one takes on the colour of one's company – the consequence of a word frequently keeping 'bad company' is that the use of the word alone may become enough to indicate something unfavourable (see Partington 1998: 67).

In Stubbs' (2002: 225) comment cited above, the meaning arising from the common semantic features of the collocates of a given node word can be referred to as semantic preference, which is defined 'by a lexical set of frequently occurring collocates [sharing] some semantic feature' (ibid.: 449). For example, Stubbs (2001c: 65) observes that large typically collocates with items from the same semantic set indicating 'quantities and sizes' (e.g. number(s), scale, part, quantities, amount(s)) while Partington (2004: 148) notes that 'absence/change of state' is a common feature of the collocates of maximizers such as utterly, totally, completely and entirely.

Semantic preference and semantic prosody are two distinct yet interdependent collocational meanings (see Unit B3.3). According to Sinclair (1996, 1998) and Stubbs (2001c), semantic prosody is a further level of abstraction of the relationship between lexical units: collocation (the relationship between a node and individual words), colligation (the relationship between a node and grammatical categories), semantic preference (semantic sets of collocates) and semantic prosody (affective meanings of a given node with its typical collocates). Partington (2004: 151) notes that semantic preference and semantic prosody have different operating scopes: the former relates the node item to another item from a particular semantic set whereas the latter can affect wider stretches of text. Semantic preference can be viewed as a feature of the collocates while semantic prosody is a feature of the node word. On the other hand, the two also interact. While semantic prosody 'dictates the general environment which constrains the preferential choices of the node item', semantic preference 'contributes powerfully' to building semantic prosody (Partington 2004: 151).

There are different opinions regarding whether or not semantic prosody is a type of connotative meaning. Partington (1998: 68), Stubbs (2001a: 449) and Hunston (2002: 142) appear to take it for granted that semantic prosody is connotational. However, Louw (2000: 49–50) explicitly argues that 'semantic prosodies are not merely connotational' as 'the force behind SPs [semantic prosodies] is more strongly collocational than the schematic aspects of connotation'. In our view, connotation can be collocational or non-collocational whereas semantic prosody can only be collocational.

It is important to note that lexical studies also include morphological analysis, at the sub-lexical level, of the internal structure of a word in terms of its root, prefix and suffix, where appropriate. While there is presently no morphemically annotated corpus available, University College London (UCL) is currently planning to integrate the morphological annotation into the already POS-tagged and syntactically parsed version of ICE-GB, the British component of the ICE corpus. Such morphological analysis not only greatly benefits morphologists, syntacticians and lexicographers, it is also useful for language learners. For example, Gries (2003) shows that there are some important semantic and distributional differences in adjective pairs ending with -ic and -ical, which language learners may find useful in distinguishing between the two.

A10.3 GRAMMATICAL STUDIES

Along with lexicographic and lexical studies, grammar is another area which has frequently exploited corpus data. This is because a balanced representative corpus not only provides a reliable basis for quantifying syntactic features of a language or language variety, it is also useful in testing hypotheses derived from grammatical theory. Corpora have had such a strong influence on recently published reference grammar books (at least for English) that 'even people who have never heard of a corpus are using the product of corpus-based investigation' (Hunston 2002: 96).

If *A Comprehensive Grammar of the English Language* (i.e. Quirk *et al.* 1985) is viewed as a milestone in the study of English grammar, it is fair to say that the recently published *Longman Grammar of Spoken and Written English* (i.e. LGSWE, Biber *et al.* 1999) is a new milestone. Based entirely on the 40-million-word

Longman Spoken and Written English Corpus, the new grammar gives 'a thorough description of English grammar, which is illustrated throughout with real corpus examples, and which gives equal attention to the ways speakers and writers actually use these linguistic resources' (Biber *et al.* 1999: 45).

The new corpus-based grammar is unique in many different ways, for example, by exploring the differences between written and spoken grammars and taking register variations into account. The coverage given by the grammar to spoken English is particularly important. While grammatical studies have traditionally focused on written language, the availability of spoken English corpora (see Unit A7.5) has provided unprecedented insights into spoken grammar. Recent studies have claimed that the traditional sentence-based grammar is inadequate in describing spoken language. In addition to Biber *et al.* (1999) discussed above, further work has been undertaken by Carter, Hughes and McCarthy at the University of Nottingham (the so-called Nottingham school). In a series of studies based on the CANCODE corpus (Carter and McCarthy 1995; McCarthy and Carter 1997; Hughes and McCarthy 1998; McCarthy 1998), the Nottingham school approaches spoken grammar from the perspective of discourse, as in McCarthy's (1998: 78) words, 'discourse drives grammar'. This approach has allowed the authors to discover many features of spoken grammar (e.g. initial ellipsis and topics in pre-clause slots and tails in post-clause slots) that are absent or marginalized in written grammars. For example, Carter and McCarthy (1995: 152–153) find that while indirect speech has been thoroughly covered in traditional grammars focusing on backshift in the sequencing of tenses, a frequent reporting phenomenon in spoken discourse such as reporting verbs like SAY and TELL occurring in the past progressive appears to have been overlooked. While the simple past form of a reporting verb gives more authority to the contents of the utterance, the past progressive form of a reporting verb focuses more on the event of uttering *per se*. As such, the authors suggest that the grammar of spoken language is radically different from that of written language and needs to be modelled on the basis of spoken data with no prior assumption that spoken and written grammars share the same framework. The Nottingham school's focus on the 'differentness' of spoken and written grammars is in contrast with Biber *et al.*'s (1999) position, which focuses on 'sameness' and uses the same framework to describe spoken and written language. The 'sameness' approach is taken by yet another influential English grammar, Huddleston and Pullum (2000), which comments that while '[t]here are significant and interesting differences between spoken and written language' (*ibid.*: 11), '[s]harp divergences between the syntax of speech and the syntax of writing [. . .] are rare to the point of non-existence' (*ibid.*: 13). Readers are advised to refer to Leech (2000) for a good review of corpus-based research in spoken English grammar and a comparison of the 'sameness' and 'differentness' approaches to spoken grammar.

We noted in Unit A10.2 that the corpus-based approach to grammar has led to a focus on lexis in grammatical studies. While lexical information forms, to some extent, an integral part of the grammatical description in Biber *et al.* (1999), it is the Birmingham school (e.g. Sinclair, Hunston, Francis and Manning) that focuses on lexis in their grammatical descriptions (the so-called 'pattern grammar', e.g. Hunston and Francis 2000). In fact, Sinclair *et al.* (1990) flatly reject the distinction between lexis and grammar. These authors have given prominence to the close association between pattern and meaning, as embodied in the Collins COBUILD Grammar Patterns series (e.g. Francis *et al.* 1996, 1997, 1998). Francis *et al.* (1998), for example, present over 200 patterns on the basis of their study of 10,000 nouns and adjectives in the Bank of English and relate these patterns to meaning. While pattern grammars focusing on the connection between pattern and meaning challenge the traditional distinction between lexis and grammar, they are undoubtedly useful in language learning as they provide 'a resource for vocabulary building in which the word is treated as part of a phrase rather than in isolation' (Hunston 2002: 106).

A10.4 REGISTER VARIATION AND GENRE ANALYSIS

We noted in Unit A2 that corpus design typically relies on external criteria, or situational parameters in Biber's (1993) terms (see Unit B1.2). These parameters define register in terms of the social or communicative context of their use. In Biber's works (Biber 1988: 170; Biber *et al.* 1999: 25), the terms *register* and *genre* appear to be used interchangeably. While there are other possible definitions of *register* (see Paolillo 2000: 217–218) and *genre* (as used in critical discourse analysis, where a genre is defined as 'a socially ratified way of using language in connection with a particular type of social activity (e.g. interview, narrative, exposition)', see Fairclough 1995: 14), we adopt a rather loose definition of these terms in this book so that they are less exclusive.

The corpus-based approach is well suited for the study of register variation and genre analysis because corpora, especially balanced sample corpora, typically cover a wide range of registers or genres. Oh (2000), for example, used the 2.4-million-word Switchboard corpus of informal telephone conversation and the Brown corpus (see Unit A7.4) to explore the similarities and differences between *actually* and *in fact* in written and spoken American English. He found that *actually* was 3.7 times more frequent than *in fact* in spoken discourse, and *actually* also showed a greater affinity with utterance-medial position in both written and spoken discourse.

The most powerful tool for approaching register and genre variation is perhaps the multifeature/multidimensional analytical framework (i.e. MF/MD; see Unit B4.2 for an overview and Case Study 5 in Section C for its application) established in Biber (1988), which presents a full analysis of twenty-one genres in spoken and written British English on the basis of sixty-seven functionally related linguistic features in 481 texts from the LOB and London–Lund corpora.

The MF/MD approach is based on *factor analysis*. Factor analysis is commonly used in the social and behavioural sciences to summarize the interrelationships among a large group of variables in a concise fashion (see Biber 1988: 64). Biber (1988: 63, 79) used factor analysis in concert with frequency counts of linguistic features to identify sets of features which co-occur in texts with a high frequency. He referred to these sets of features as *dimensions* or *constructs*. Biber used factor analysis to reduce sixty-seven linguistic features to seven dimensions or factors (see Unit B4.2 for further discussion). As these factors underlie linguistic features, they are conceptually clearer than the many features considered individually.

Biber (1988) used a whole chapter (chapter 5) to give a technical description of factor analysis. As we will only apply the dimensions established by Biber (see Case Study 5 in Section C), the issue of how these factors were computed will not be our concern in this book. Nevertheless, a brief, non-technical account of how factor analysis works will prove helpful to understanding Biber's MF/MD approach.

Factor analysis starts with a simple correlation matrix of all linguistic features, on the basis of which the factorial structures are established and the factor *loading* or *weight* of each linguistic feature is computed. A factor loading or weight indicates the degree to which one can generalize from a given factor to an individual linguistic feature (Biber 1988: 81). A loading can be positive or negative, indicating the direction of correlation. The greater the absolute value of a loading which a linguistic feature has on a factor, the more representative the feature is of the dimension. Biber (1988: 87) decided that only the important or salient loadings should be interpreted as part of each factor. All features having loadings with an absolute value less than 0.30 were excluded as unimportant. Due to the large number of features loading on most of the factors, Biber used a conservative cut-off point of 0.35 to decide which features were to be included in the computation of factor scores (Biber 1988: 93). When a feature has a salient loading (above 0.35) on more than one factor, it was included in the factor score of the factor on which it had the highest loading so as to ensure that each feature was included in the computation of only one factor score (Biber 1988: 93). Using the procedure above, Biber identified seven dimensions or factors:

■ Factor 1: informational versus involved production;
■ Factor 2: narrative versus non-narrative concerns;
■ Factor 3: explicit versus situation-dependent reference;
■ Factor 4: overt expression of persuasion;
■ Factor 5: abstract versus non-abstract information;
■ Factor 6: online informational elaboration;
■ Factor 7: academic hedging.

Of these, Factors 1, 3 and 5 are associated with 'oral' and 'literate' differences in English (Biber 1988: 163; Biber and Finegan 1989: 489). As the factorial structure of Factor 7 was not strong enough for a firm interpretation, it was not discussed in detail in Biber (1988).

Using the MF/MD approach, Biber (1988) was able to describe the similarities and differences of various genres in spoken and written English with reference to the different dimensions. For example, Biber (1988: 165–166) finds that along Dimensions 1 and 5, personal letters and spontaneous speech demonstrate quite similar factor scores but differ considerably along Dimensions 3 and 6. Likewise, while face-to-face conversation differs markedly from official documents along Dimensions 1, 3 and 5, they are quite similar along Dimension 4. As such, Biber (1988: 169) concludes that:

> Each dimension is associated with a different set of underlying communicative functions, and each defines a different set of similarities and differences among genres. Consideration of all dimensions is required for an adequate description of the relations among spoken and written texts.

While the MF/MD analytical framework was originally developed to compare written and spoken registers in English, this approach has been used extensively in (1) synchronic analyses of specific registers and genres (Biber 1991; Biber and Finegan 1994a; Conrad 1994; Reppen 1994; Tribble 1999) and author styles (Biber and Finegan 1994b; Connor-Linton 1988; Watson 1994); (2) diachronic studies describing the evolution of registers (Biber and Finegan 1989, 1992; Atkinson 1992, 1993) and exploring the differences between literary and non-literary genres in Early Modern English (Taavitsainen 1997); (3) register studies of non-western languages (Besnier 1988; Biber and Hared 1992, 1994; Kim and Biber 1994) and contrastive analyses (Biber 1995b). In addition, the MF/MD approach has also been applied in addressing corpus design issues (e.g. Biber 1993; see Unit B1.2) and the definitional issues of registers/genres and text types (e.g. Biber 1989). Unit B4.2 will further discuss Biber's MF/MD approach.

Lexical bundles, also called lexical chains or multiword units, are closely associated with collocations and have been an important topic in lexical studies (e.g. Stubbs 2002). More recently, Biber found that lexical bundles are also a reliable indicator of register variation (e.g. Biber and Conrad 1999; Biber 2003). Biber and Conrad (1999), for example, showed that the structural types of lexical bundles in conversation are markedly different from those in academic prose. Biber's (2003) comparative study of the distribution of fifteen major types of four-word lexical bundles (technically known as 4-grams) in the registers of conversation, classroom teaching, textbooks and academic prose indicates that lexical bundles are significantly more frequent in the two spoken registers. The distribution of lexical bundles in different registers also varies across structural types. In conversation, nearly 90 per cent of lexical bundles are declarative or interrogative clause segments. In contrast, the lexical bundles in academic prose are basically phrasal rather than clausal. Of the four registers in Biber's study, lexical bundles are considerably more frequent in classroom teaching because this register uses the types of lexical bundles associated with both conversation and academic prose.

A10.5 DIALECT DISTINCTION AND LANGUAGE VARIETY

A language variety can be broadly defined as a variant of a language that differs from another variant of the same language systematically and coherently. Varieties of a language may include, for example, the standard language (standardized for the purposes of education and public performance), dialects (geographically defined), sociolects (socially defined), idiolects (unique to individual speakers) and jargons (particular to specific domains). This book defines both *language variety* and *dialect* geographically. We refer to national variants (e.g. 'world Englishes' such as British English and American English; see Unit A7.6) as language varieties and regional variants (e.g. variants in the south and north of Britain) as dialects while other variants such as sociolects, idiolects and jargons are considered as *language variations*. So-called standard varieties of a language such as Standard English in Britain and *putonghua* ('common language') in China are simply particular dialects that have been given legal or quasi-legal status and are typically used for education (e.g. teaching the language as a foreign language) and public purposes. While a standard language is usually based on the regional dialect of a capital city, it is also marked socially. For example, while accents or dialects usually tell us where a speaker is from, RP (the notional standard form of spoken British English, which stands for 'Received Pronunciation') is a regionally neutral accent which tells us only about a speaker's social or educational but not regional background. Even though RP originated in the south-east of England, it has developed to be regionally neutral but socially marked. We do not consider standard languages as dialects as defined in this book. However, our decision is one of convenience and should not be taken to imply that we do not conceive of standard varieties as dialects. Similarly, while we will use language variety as a term that encompasses language varieties such as pidgins and creoles, we appreciate once again that we are taking something of a terminological shortcut in doing so.

Variations in dialects and language varieties are commonly found in pronunciation, spelling and word choice while grammatical differences are relatively few. Dialects typically vary quantitatively rather than qualitatively (see Bauer 2002: 108). It would appear that core grammatical structures are relatively uniform across dialects and language varieties of English (see Biber *et al.* 1999: 19–21; Huddleston and Pullum 2000: 4). For example, Biber *et al.* (1999: 398–399) observe that the *got/gotten* alternation represents an important difference between American English and British English: while the pattern *have + gotten* rarely occurs in British English, it is very frequent in American English, especially in conversations and when the combination expresses a true perfect meaning. In contrast, the use of *do* following an auxiliary (e.g. *I'm not sure that I'll go, but I **may do**)* is uncommon in American English (see Huddleston and Pullum 2000: 5). Biber (1987) also finds that nominalizations, passives and *it*-cleft structures are more frequent in American English whereas time/place adverbials, and subordinator deletion occur more frequently in British English. In Case Study 2 in Section C of this book, we will see that American English shows a strong preference for bare infinitives following *HELP* (e.g. *helped him get to his feet* and *helped finance the project*). Hundt (1998: 32), on the basis of a comparison of the frequencies and proportions of regular and irregular past-tense forms of various verbs in WWC and FLOB, finds that New Zealand English (56.4 per cent regular) and British English (68.7 per cent regular) differ significantly in this respect. She also notes that 96.7 per cent of the relevant verb forms are regular in the Brown corpus of American English, concluding that there is a difference between the three varieties of English, with New Zealand English being closer to British English. Readers must note that in Hundt's study, the difference between American English and the other two varieties might be attributed to language change (though further research is required to make it clear), as the Brown corpus sampled texts in 1961 whereas the sampling periods of WWC and FLOB are closer to each other yet much later than Brown. Tagnin and Teixeira (2003) show, on the basis of a comparable corpus of cooking recipes in four language varieties (British vs. American English, Brazilian vs. European Portuguese), that the differences between the two varieties of Portuguese at various levels (lexical, syntactic and textual) are much more marked than those between British and American English.

A10.6 CONTRASTIVE AND TRANSLATION STUDIES

This section takes linguistic comparisons one step further from dialects and varieties of the same language to different languages. This involves the use of multi-lingual corpora (see Unit A5). There are two major types of linguistic investigations based on multilingual corpora: contrastive and translation studies.

As Laviosa (1998a) observes, 'the corpus-based approach is evolving, through theoretical elaboration and empirical realisation, into a coherent, composite and rich paradigm that addresses a variety of issues pertaining to theory, description, and the practice of translation'. Corpus-based translation studies come in two broad types: theoretical and practical (Hunston 2002: 123). With reference to theory, corpora are used mainly to study the translation process by exploring how an idea in one language is conveyed in another language and by comparing the linguistic features and their frequencies in translated L2 texts and comparable L1 texts. In the practical approach, corpora provide a workbench for training translators and a basis for developing applications like machine translation (MT) and computer-assisted translation (CAT) systems. In this section, we will discuss how corpora have been used in each of these areas.

Parallel corpora are a good basis for studying how an idea in one language is conveyed in another language (see Case Study 6 in Section C). Xiao and McEnery (2002a), for example, used an English–Chinese parallel corpus containing 100,170 English words and 192,088 Chinese characters to explore how temporal and aspec-tual meanings in English were expressed in Chinese. In that study, the authors found that while both English and Chinese have a progressive aspect, the progressive has different scopes of meaning in the two languages. In English, while the progressive canonically (93.5 per cent) signals the ongoing nature of a situation (e.g. *John is singing*; Comrie 1976: 32), it has a number of other specific uses 'that do not seem to fit under the general definition of progressiveness' (Comrie 1976: 37). These 'specific uses' include its use to indicate contingent habitual or iterative situations (e.g. *I'm taking dancing lessons this winter*; Leech 1971: 27), to indicate anticipated happenings in the future (e.g. *We're visiting Aunt Rose tomorrow*; *ibid.*: 29) and some idiomatic use to add special emotive effect (e.g. *I'm continually forgetting people's names*; *ibid.*) (see Leech 1971: 27–29). In Chinese, however, the progressive marked by *zai* only corresponds to the first category above, namely, to mark the ongoing nature of dynamic situations. As such, only about 58 per cent of situations referred to by the progressive in the English source data take the progressive or the durative aspect, either marked overtly or covertly, in Chinese translations. The authors also found that the interaction between situation aspect (i.e. the inherent aspectual features of a situation, e.g. whether the situation has a natural final endpoint; see Unit A10.9) and viewpoint aspect (e.g. perfective vs. imperfective; see Unit B5.3) also influences a translator's choice of viewpoint aspect. Situations with a natural final endpoint (around 65 per cent) and situations incompatible with progressiveness (92.5 per cent of individual-level states and 75.9 per cent of achievements) are more likely to undergo viewpoint aspect shift and be presented perfectively in Chinese translations. In contrast, situations without a natural final endpoint are normally translated with the progressive marked by *zai* or the durative aspect marked by *-zhe*.

Note, however, that the direction of translation in a parallel corpus is important in studies of this kind. The corpus used in Xiao and McEnery (2002a), for example, is not suitable for studying how aspect markers in Chinese are translated into English. For that purpose, a Chinese–English parallel corpus (i.e. L1 Chinese plus L2 English) is required.

Another problem which arises with the use of a one-to-one parallel corpus (i.e. containing only one version of translation in the target language) is that the translation only represents one individual's introspection, albeit contextually and cotextually informed (see Malmkjær 1998). One possible way to overcome this problem, as suggested in Malmkjær, is to include as many versions of a translation of the same source text as possible in a parallel corpus. While this solution is certainly of benefit to translation studies, it makes the task of building parallel corpora much more difficult. It also reduces the range of data one may include in a parallel corpus, as many translated texts are only translated once. It is typically only literary works which have multiple translations of the same work available. These works tend to be non-contemporary and the different versions of the translation are usually spaced decades apart, thus making the comparison of these versions problematic.

The distinctive features of translated language can be identified by comparing translations with comparable L1 texts, thus throwing new light on the translation process and helping to identify translation norms. Laviosa (1998b), for example, in her study of L1 and L2 English narrative prose, finds that translated L2 language has four core patterns of lexical use: a relatively lower proportion of lexical words over function words, a relatively higher proportion of high-frequency words over low-frequency words, a relatively greater repetition of the most frequent words, and less variety in the words that are most frequently used. Other studies show that translated language is characterized, beyond the lexical level, by nominalization, simplification (Baker 1993, 1999), explication (i.e. increased cohesion, Øverås 1998) and sanitization (i.e. reduced connotational meanings, Kenny 1998). As we will see in Case Study 6 in Section C, the frequency of aspect markers in Chinese translations is significantly lower than that in the comparable L1 Chinese data. As these features are regular and typical of translated language, further research based upon these findings may not only uncover the translation norms or what Frawley (1984) calls the 'third code' of translation, it will also help translators and trainee translators to become aware of these problems.

The above studies demonstrate that translated language represents a version of language which we may call 'translationese'. The effect of the source language on the translations is strong enough to make the L2 data perceptibly different from the target L1 language. As such, a unidirectional parallel corpus is a poor basis for cross-linguistic contrast. This problem, however, can be alleviated by the use of a bidirectional parallel corpus (e.g. Maia 1998; Ebeling 1998), because the effect of translationese may be averaged out to some extent. In this sense, a well-matched bidirectional parallel corpus can become the bridge that brings translation and contrastive studies together. To achieve this aim, however, the same sampling frame must apply to the selection of source data in both languages. Any mismatch of proportion, genre or domain, for example, may invalidate the findings derived from such a corpus.

While we know that translated language is distinct from the target L1 language, it has been claimed that parallel corpora represent a sound basis for contrastive studies. James (1980: 178), for example, argues that 'translation equivalence is the best available basis of comparison', while Santos (1996: i) claims that 'studies based on real translations are the only sound method for contrastive analysis'. Mauranen (2002: 166) also argues, though not as strongly as James and Santos, that translated language, in spite of its special features, 'is part of natural language in use, and should be treated accordingly', because languages 'influence each other in many ways other than through translation' (*ibid.*: 165). While we agree with Mauranen that 'translations deserve to be investigated in their own right', as is done in Laviosa (1998b) and McEnery and Xiao (2002), we hold a different view of the value of parallel corpora for contrastive studies. It is true that languages in contact can influence each other, but this influence is different from the influence of a source language on translations with respect to immediacy and scope. Basically, the influence of language contact is generally gradual (or evolutionary) and less systematic than the influence of a source language on the translated language. As such, translated language is at best an unrepresentative special variant of the target language. If this special variant is confused with the target L1 language and serves alone as the basis for contrastive studies, the results are clearly misleading. This may have long-term adverse effects because contrastive studies are 'typically geared towards second language teaching and learning' (Teich 2002: 188). We would not want to misrepresent an L1 by teaching the translationese approximation of it. But parallel corpora still have a role to play in contrastive analysis. Parallel corpora can serve as a useful starting point for cross-linguistic contrasts because findings based on parallel corpora invite 'further research with monolingual corpora in both languages' (Mauranen 2002: 182). In this sense, parallel corpora are 'indispensable' to contrastive studies (*ibid.*).

With reference to practical translation studies, as corpora can be used to raise linguistic and cultural awareness in general (see Hunston 2002: 123; Bernardini 1997), they provide a useful and effective reference tool and a workbench for translators and trainees. In this respect even a monolingual corpus is helpful. Bowker (1998), for example, found that corpus-aided translations were of a higher quality with respect to subject field understanding, correct term choice and idiomatic expressions than those undertaken using conventional resources. Bernardini (1997) also suggests that traditional translation teaching should be complemented with what she calls 'LCC' (large corpora concordancing) so that trainees develop 'awareness', 'reflectiveness' and 'resourcefulness', the skills that 'distinguish a translator from those unskilled amateurs'.

In comparison to monolingual corpora, comparable corpora are more useful for translation studies. Zanettin (1998) demonstrates that small comparable corpora can be used to devise a 'translator training workshop' designed to improve students' understanding of the source texts and their ability to produce translations in the target language more fluently. In this respect, specialized comparable corpora are particularly helpful for highly domain-specific translation tasks, because when translating texts of this type, as Friedbichler and Friedbichler (1997) observe, the translator is dealing with a language which is often just as disparate from their native language as any foreign tongue. Studies show that translators with access to a comparable corpus with which to check translation problems are able to enhance their productivity and tend to make fewer mistakes when translating into their native language. When translation is from a mother tongue into a foreign language, the need for corpus tools grows exponentially and goes far beyond checking grey spots in L1 language competence against the evidence of a large corpus. For example, Gavioli and Zanettin (1998) demonstrate how a very specialized corpus of text on the subject of hepatitis helps to confirm translation hypotheses and suggest possible solutions to problems related to domain-specific translation.

While monolingual and comparable corpora are of use to translation, it is difficult to generate 'possible hypotheses as to translations' with such data (Aston 1999). Furthermore, verifying concordances is both time-consuming and error prone, which entails a loss of productivity. Parallel corpora, in contrast, provide '[g]reater certainty as to the equivalence of particular expressions', and in combination with suitable tools (e.g. ParaConc, see Case Study 6 in Section C), they enable users to 'locate all the occurrences of any expression along with the corresponding sentences in the other language' (*ibid.*). As such, parallel corpora can help translators and trainees to achieve improved precision with respect to terminology and phraseology and have been strongly recommended for these reasons (e.g. Williams 1996). A special use of a parallel corpus with one source text and many translations is that it can offer a systematic translation strategy for linguistic structures which have no direct equivalents in the target language. Buyse (1997), for example, presents a case study of the Spanish translation of the French clitics *en* and *y*, where the author illustrates how a solution is offered by a quantitative analysis of the phonetic, prosodic, morphological, semantic and discursive features of these structures in a representative parallel corpus, combined with the quantitative analysis of these structures in a comparable corpus of L1 target language. Another issue related to translator training is translation evaluation. Bowker (2001) shows that an evaluation corpus, which is composed of a parallel corpus and comparable corpora of source and target languages, can help translator trainers to evaluate student translations and provide more objective feedback.

Finally, in addition to providing assistance to human translators, parallel corpora constitute a unique resource for the development of machine translation (MT) systems. Starting in the 1990s, the established methodologies, notably, the linguistic rule-based approach to machine translation, were challenged and enriched by an approach based on parallel corpora (see Hutchins 2003: 511; Somers 2003: 513). The new approaches, such as example-based MT (EBMT) and statistical MT, were based on parallel corpora. To take an example, EBMT works by matching any sentence to be translated against a database of aligned texts previously translated to extract suitable examples which are then combined to generate the correct translation of the input sentence (see Somers: *ibid.*). As well as automatic MT systems, parallel corpora have also been used to develop computer-assisted translation (CAT) tools for human translators, such as translation memories (TM), bilingual concordancers and translator-oriented word processors (see Somer 2003; Wu 2002).

The main concern of this section is the potential value of parallel and comparable corpora to translation and contrastive studies. Parallel corpora are undoubtedly a useful starting point for contrastive research, which may lead to further research in contrastive studies based upon comparable corpora. In contrast, comparable corpora used alone are less useful for translation studies. Nonetheless, they certainly serve as a reliable basis for contrastive studies. It appears then that a carefully matched bidirectional parallel corpus provides a sound basis for both translation and contrastive studies. Yet the ideal bidirectional parallel corpus will often not be easy, or even possible, to build because of the heterogeneous pattern of translation between languages and genres. So we must accept that, for practical reasons alone, we will often be working with corpora that, while they are useful, are not ideal for either translation or contrastive studies. We will return to the exploitation of the use of parallel and comparable corpora in Units B5.2–B5.3 and Case Study 6 in Section C of this book.

A10.7 DIACHRONIC STUDY AND LANGUAGE CHANGE

This section shifts our focus from the synchronic studies discussed in the previous sections to diachronic studies and language change. The nature of diachronic study determines its reliance on empirical historical data. Diachronic study is perhaps one of the few areas which can only be investigated using corpus data. This is because the intuitions of modern speakers have little to offer regarding the language used hundreds or even tens of years before.

We noted in Unit A7.7 that while a number of corpora (e.g. LOB vs. FLOB, and Brown vs. Frown) are suitable for the diachronic study of English, the most famous corpus of this kind is the Helsinki corpus, produced by the English Department of the University of Helsinki. Following the creation of the corpus, the analysis of the corpus was carried out on their subsequent project 'English in transition: change through variation', which produced three volumes of studies: *Early English in the Computer Age: Exploration through the Helsinki Corpus* (Rissanen, Kytö and Palander-Collin 1993), *English in Transition: Corpus-based Studies in Linguistic Variation and Genre Styles* (Rissanen, Kytö and Heikkonen 1997a), and *Grammaticalization at Work: Studies of Long-term Developments in English* (Rissanen, Kytö and Heikkonen 1997b). The Helsinki corpus not only sampled different periods covering one millennium, it also encoded genre and sociolinguistic information (e.g. author rank, sex and age; see Rissanen *et al.* 1997a: 3). This allowed the authors of these volumes to go beyond simply dating and reporting change by combining diachronic, sociolinguistic and genre studies.

Peitsara (1993), for example, in her study of prepositional phrases introducing agency in passive constructions in the Early Modern and Modern English (*c.*1350–1640) components in the Helsinki corpus, finds that while at the beginning of the period *by* and *of* were equally frequent, by the end of the period, *by* had gained prominence to the extent that it was three times more frequent than *of* by the fifteenth century. This trend accelerated over time, so that by the sixteenth century it was eight times more frequent than *of.* Furthermore, she notes that such a contrast was particularly marked in the genre of official documents and correspondences. Likewise, based on the Corpus of Early English Correspondence (developed at the University of Helsinki), Nevalainen (2000) observes that in Early Modern English, female authors led the move in replacing the verbal suffix *-th* with *-s* and using *you* in subject position whereas male authors took the lead in replacing double negation with single negation.

Such findings can only have been made via the use of properly composed diachronic corpora. This research, and much more beside (see Units B5.4 and B5.5), has been enabled by the production of diachronic corpora.

A10.8 LANGUAGE LEARNING AND TEACHING

The early 1990s saw an increasing interest in applying the findings of corpus-based research to language pedagogy. This is apparent when one looks at the published literature. In addition to a large number of journal articles, at least nine single-authored or edited volumes have recently been produced on the topic of teaching and language corpora: Wichmann *et al.* (1997), Kettemann and Marko (2000), Burnard and McEnery (2000), Aston (2001), Hunston (2002), Granger *et al.* (2002), Tan (2002), Aston *et al.* (2004) and Sinclair (2004b). These works cover a wide range of issues related to using corpora in language pedagogy, e.g. corpus-based language description, corpus analysis in classroom and learner corpora (see Keck 2004).

In the opening chapter of *Teaching and Language Corpora* (Wichmann *et al.* 1997), Leech noted that a convergence between teaching and language corpora was apparent. That convergence has three focuses, as noted by Leech (1997b): the direct use of corpora in teaching (teaching about, teaching to exploit and exploiting to teach), the indirect use of corpora in teaching (reference publishing, materials development and language testing) and further teaching-oriented corpus development (LSP corpora, L1 developmental corpora and L2 learner corpora). These three focuses of convergence are worthy of note.

Of these focuses, perhaps the most relevant for this book are 'teaching about' and 'teaching to exploit'. 'Teaching about' means teaching corpus linguistics as an academic subject like other sub-disciplines of linguistics such as sociolinguistics or discourse analysis. Corpus linguistics has now found its way into the curricula for linguistics and language-related degree programmes at both postgraduate and undergraduate levels. 'Teaching to exploit' means providing students with 'hands-on' know-how, as emphasized in this book, so that they can exploit corpora for their own purposes. Once the student has acquired the necessary knowledge and techniques of corpus-based language study, learning activity may become student centred. If 'teaching about' is viewed as being associated typically with students of linguistics and languages, 'teaching to exploit' relates to students of all subjects which involve language study/learning. 'Exploiting to teach' means using a corpus-based approach to teaching language and linguistics courses, which would otherwise be taught using non-corpus-based methods. As for the indirect use of corpora in language teaching, we have already noted in Units A10.2 and A10.3 that corpora have revolutionized reference publishing in a manner such that people who have never heard of a corpus are using the products of corpus research. As we will see later in this section, corpora also have a lot to offer in terms of syllabus design, materials development and language testing. Finally, teaching-oriented corpora are particularly useful in teaching languages for specific purposes (LSP corpora) and in research on L1 (developmental corpora) and L2 (learner corpora) language acquisition. In the remainder of this section, we will introduce the uses of corpora in a number of areas in language pedagogy, including syllabus design and materials development, using corpora in classroom, teaching domain-specific language and professional communication, teacher training, language testing, as well as learner corpus research.

While corpora have been used extensively to provide more accurate descriptions of language use (see Units A10.2–A10.5), a number of scholars have also used corpus data directly to look critically at existing TEFL (Teaching English as a Foreign Language) syllabuses and teaching materials. Mindt (1996), for example, finds that the use of grammatical structures in textbooks for teaching English differs considerably from the use of these structures in L1 English. He observes that one common failure of English textbooks is that they teach 'a kind of school English which does not seem to exist outside the foreign language classroom' (1996: 232). As such, learners often find it difficult to communicate successfully with native speakers. A simple yet important role of corpora in language education is to provide more realistic examples of language usage. In addition, however, corpora may provide data, especially frequency data, which may further alter what is taught. For example, on the basis of a comparison of the frequencies of modal verbs, future time expressions and conditional clauses in corpora and their grading in textbooks used widely in Germany, Mindt (*ibid.*) concludes that one problem with non-corpus-based syllabuses is that the order in which those items are taught in syllabuses 'very often does not correspond to what one might reasonably expect from corpus data of spoken and written English', arguing that teaching syllabuses should be based on empirical evidence rather than tradition and intuition with frequency of usage as a guide to priority for teaching (1996: 245–246; see discussion below).

Hunston (2002: 189) echoes Mindt suggesting that 'the experience of using corpora should lead to rather different views of syllabus design'. The type of syllabus she discusses extensively is a 'lexical syllabus', originally proposed by Sinclair and Renouf (1988) and outlined fully by Willis (1990). According to Sinclair and Renouf (1988: 148), a lexical syllabus would focus on '(a) the commonest word forms in a language; (b) the central patterns of usage; (c) the combinations which they usually form'. While the term may occasionally be misinterpreted to indicate a syllabus consisting solely of vocabulary items, a lexical syllabus actually covers 'all aspects of language, differing from a conventional syllabus only in that the central concept of organization is lexis' (Hunston 2002: 189). Sinclair (2000: 191) would say that the grammar covered in a lexical syllabus is 'lexical grammar', not 'lexico-grammar', which attempts to 'build a grammar and lexis on an equal basis'. Indeed, as Murison-Bowie (1996: 185) observes, 'in using corpora in a teaching context, it is frequently difficult to distinguish what is a lexical investigation and what is a syntactic one. One leads to the other, and this can be used to advantage in a teaching/learning context.' Sinclair and his colleagues' proposal for a lexical syllabus is echoed by Lewis (1993, 1997a, 1997b, 2000), who provides strong support for the lexical approach to language teaching.

While syllabus design and materials development are closely associated with what to teach, corpora have also provided valuable insights into how to teach. The issue of how to use corpora in the language classroom has been discussed extensively in the literature. With the corpus-based approach to language pedagogy, the traditional 'three Ps' (presentation–practice–production) approach to teaching may not be entirely suitable. Instead, the more exploratory approach of 'three Is' (illustration–interaction–induction) may be more appropriate, where 'illustration' means looking at real data, 'interaction' means discussing and sharing opinions and observations, and 'induction' means making one's own rule for a particular feature, which 'will be refined and honed as more and more data is encountered' (see Carter and McCarthy 1995: 155). This progressive induction approach is what Murison-Bowie (1996: 191) and Aston (1997) would call the interlanguage approach: partial and incomplete generalizations are drawn from limited data as a stage on the way towards a fully satisfactory rule. While the 'three Is' approach was originally proposed by Carter and McCarthy (1995) to teach spoken grammar, it may also apply to language education as a whole, in our view.

It is certainly clear that the teaching approach focusing on 'three Is' is in line with Johns' (1991) concept of 'data-driven learning (DDL)'. Johns was perhaps among the first to realize the potential of corpora for language learners (e.g. Higgins and Johns 1984). In his opinion, 'research is too serious to be left to the researchers' (1991: 2). As such, he argues that the language learner should be encouraged to become 'a research worker whose learning needs to be driven by access to linguistic data' (*ibid.*). Indeed, as Kennedy (2003) observes, language learning is a process of learning 'explicit knowledge' with awareness, which requires a great deal of exposure to language data. Data-driven learning can be either teacher directed or learner led (i.e. discovery learning) to suit the needs of learners at different levels, but it is basically learner centred. This autonomous learning process 'gives the student the realistic expectation of breaking new ground as a "researcher", doing something which is a unique and individual contribution' (Leech 1997b: 10).

Johns (1991) identifies three stages of inductive reasoning with corpora in the DDL approach: observation (of concordanced evidence), classification (of salient features) and generalization (of rules). The three stages roughly correspond to Carter and McCarthy's 'three Is'. The DDL approach is basically different from the 'three Ps' approach in that the former is bottom-up induction whereas the latter is top-down deduction. The direct use of corpora and concordancing in the language classroom has been discussed extensively in the literature (e.g. Tribble 1991, 1997, 2000, 2003; Tribble and Jones 1990, 1997; Flowerdew 1993; Karpati 1995; Kettemann 1995, 1996; Wichmann 1995; Woolls 1998; Aston 2001; Osborne 2001), covering a wide range of issues including, for example, underlying theories, methods and techniques, and problems and solutions.

In addition to teaching English as a second or foreign language in general, a great deal of attention has been paid to domain-specific language use and professional communication (e.g. English for specific purposes and English for academic purposes). For example, Thurstun and Candlin (1997, 1998) explore the use of concordancing in teaching writing and vocabulary in academic English; Hyland

(1999) studies the metadiscourse in introductory coursebooks (see Unit B4.3); Thompson and Tribble (2001) examine citation practices in academic text; Koester (2002) argues, on the basis of an analysis of the performance of speech acts in workshop conversations, for a discourse approach to teaching communicative functions in spoken English; Yang and Allison (2003) study the organizational structure in research articles in applied linguistics; Carter and McCarthy (2004) explore, on the basis of the CANCODE corpus, a range of social contexts in which creative uses of language are manifested; Hinkel (2004) compares the use of tense, aspect and the passive in L1 and L2 academic texts.

There are two other areas of language education in which corpora have recently been used: language teacher training and language testing. For learners to benefit from the use of corpora, language teachers must first of all be equipped with a sound knowledge of the corpus-based approach. It is unsurprising to discover then that corpora have been used in training language teachers (e.g. Conrad 1999; Allan 1999, 2002; Seidlhofer 2000, 2002; O'Keeffe and Farr 2003). Another emerging area of language pedagogy which has started to use the corpus-based approach is language testing. Alderson (1996) envisaged the possible uses of corpora in this area: test construction, compilation and selection; test presentation; response capture; test scoring, and calculation and delivery of results. He concludes that '[t]he potential advantages of basing our tests on real language data, of making data-based judgments about candidates' abilities, knowledge and performance are clear enough. A crucial question is whether the possible advantages are born out in practice' (Alderson 1996: 258–259). The concern raised in Alderson's conclusion appears to have been addressed satisfactorily. Choi, Kim and Boo (2003) find that computer-based tests are comparable to paper-based tests. A number of corpus-based studies of language testing have been reported. For example, Coniam (1997) demonstrated how to use word frequency data extracted from corpora to generate cloze tests automatically. Kaszubski and Wojnowska (2003) presented a corpus-based program for building sentence-based ELT exercises – TestBuilder. The program can process raw and POS-tagged corpora, tagged on the fly by a built-in POS tagger, and uses this as input for test material selection. Indeed, corpora have recently been used by major providers of test services for a number of purposes: (a) as an archive of examination scripts; (b) to develop test materials; (c) to optimize test procedures; (d) to improve the quality of test marking; (e) to validate tests; and (f) to standardize tests (see Ball 2001; Hunston 2002: 205). For example, the University of Cambridge Local Examinations Syndicate (UCLES) is active in both corpus development (e.g. Cambridge Learner Corpus, Cambridge Corpus of Spoken English, Business English Text Corpus and Corpus YLE Speaking Tests) and the analysis of native-English corpora and learner corpora. At UCLES, native-English corpora such as the BNC are used 'to investigate collocations, authentic stems and appropriate distractors which enable item writers to base their examination tasks on real texts' (Ball 2001: 7); the corpus-based approach is used to explore 'the distinguishing features in the writing performance of EFL/ESL learners or users taking the Cambridge English examinations' and how to incorporate these into 'a single scale of bands, that is, a common scale, describing different levels of

L2 writing proficiency' (Hawkey 2001: 9); corpora are also used for the purpose of speaking assessment (Ball and Wilson 2002; Taylor 2003) and to develop domain-specific (e.g. business English) wordlists for use in test materials (Ball 2002; Horner and Strutt 2004).

One of the most exciting recent developments in corpus-based language studies has been the creation and use of learner corpora in language pedagogy and inter-language studies. At the pre-conference workshop on learner corpora affiliated to the International Symposium of Corpus Linguistics 2003 held at the University of Lancaster, the workshop organizers, Tono and Meunier, observed that learner corpora are no longer in their infancy but are going through their nominal teenage years: they are full of promise but not yet fully developed. In language pedagogy, the implications of learner corpora have been explored for curriculum design, materials development and teaching methodology (see Keck 2004: 99). The inter-face between L1 and L2 materials has been explored. Meunier (2002), for example, argues that frequency information obtained from native-speaker corpora alone is not sufficient to inform curriculum and materials design. Rather, 'it is important to strike a balance between frequency, difficulty and pedagogical relevance. That is exactly where learner corpus research comes into play to help weigh the importance of each of these' (Meunier 2002: 123). Meunier also advocates the use of learner data in the classroom, suggesting that exercises such as comparing learner and native-speaker data and analysing errors in learner language will help students to notice gaps between their interlanguage and the language they are learning. Interlanguage studies based on learner corpora which have been undertaken so far focus on what Granger (2002) calls 'Contrastive Interlanguage Analysis (CIA)', which compares learner data and native-speaker data, or language produced by learners from different L1 backgrounds. The first type of comparison typically aims to identify under or overuse of particular linguistic features in learner lan-guage while the second type aims to uncover L1 interference or transfer. In addition to CIA, learner corpora have also been used to investigate the order of acqui-sition of particular morphemes (see Case Study 3 in Section C). Readers can refer to Granger *et al.* (2002) for recent work in the use of learner corpora, and read Granger (2003b) for a more general discussion of the applications of learner corpora.

Before we close the discussion in this section, it is appropriate to address some objections to the use of corpora in language learning and teaching. While frequency and authenticity are often considered two of the most important advantages of using corpora, they are also the motivation for criticism of the corpus-based approach from language pedagogy researchers. For example, Cook (1998: 61) argues that corpus data impoverishes language learning by giving undue promi-nence to what is simply frequent at the expense of rarer but more effective or salient expressions. Widdowson (1990, 2000) argues that corpus data is authentic only in a very limited sense in that it is decontextualized (i.e. traces of texts rather than discourse) and must be recontextualized in language teaching. Nevertheless, it can also be argued reasonably that:

on the contrary, using corpus data not only increases the chances of learners being confronted with relatively infrequent instances of language use, but also of their being able to see in what way such uses are atypical, in what contexts they do appear, and how they fit in with the pattern of more prototypical uses.

(Osborne 2001: 486)

This view is echoed by Goethals (2003: 424), who argues that 'frequency ranking will be a parameter for sequencing and grading learning materials' because '[f]requency is a measure of *probability* of usefulness' and '[h]igh-frequency words constitute a core vocabulary that is useful above the incidental choice of text of one teacher or textbook author'. Hunston (2002: 194–195) observes that '[i]tems which are important though infrequent seem to be those that echo texts which have a high cultural value', though in many cases 'cultural salience is not clearly at odds with frequency'. While frequency information is readily available from corpora, no corpus linguist has ever argued that the most frequent is most important. On the contrary, Kennedy (1998: 290) argues that frequency 'should be only one of the criteria used to influence instruction' and that '[t]he facts about language and language use which emerge from corpus analyses should never be allowed to become a burden for pedagogy'. As such, raw frequency data is often adjusted for use in a syllabus, as reported in Renouf (1987: 168). It would be inappropriate, therefore, for language teachers, syllabus designers and materials writers to ignore 'compelling frequency evidence already available', as pointed out by Leech (1997b: 16), who argues that:

> Whatever the imperfections of the simple equation 'most frequent' = 'most important to learn', it is difficult to deny that frequency information becoming available from corpora has an important empirical input to language learning materials.

If we leave objections to the use of frequency data to one side, Widdowson (1990, 2000) also questions the use of authentic texts in language teaching. In his opinion, authenticity of language in the classroom is 'an illusion' (1990: 44) because even though corpus data may be authentic in one sense, its authenticity of purpose is destroyed by its use with an unintended audience of language learners (see Murison-Bowie 1996: 189; see Units B2.2 and B6.2 for further discussion). The implication of Widdowson's argument is that only language produced for imaginary situations in the classroom is 'authentic'. However, as argued by Fox (1987), invented examples often do not reflect nuances of usage. That is perhaps why, as Mindt (1996: 232) observes, students who have been taught 'school English' cannot readily cope with English used by native speakers in real conversation. As such, Wichmann (1997: xvi) argues that in language teaching, 'the preference for "authentic" texts requires both learners and teachers to cope with language which the textbooks do not predict'.

In conclusion, it is our view that corpora will not only revolutionize the teaching of subjects such as grammar in the twenty-first century (see Conrad 2000), they will also fundamentally change the ways we approach language pedagogy, including both what is taught and how it is taught.

We have so far reviewed the applications of corpora in major areas of language studies. The sections that follow will discuss other areas which have started to use corpus data.

A10.9 SEMANTICS

We have already touched upon semantics at the lexical level when we discussed semantic prosody/preference and pattern meanings in Unit A10.2. But corpora are also more generally important in semantics in that they provide objective criteria for assigning meanings to linguistic items and establish more firmly the notions of fuzzy categories and gradience (see McEnery and Wilson 2001: 112–113), as demonstrated by Mindt (1991). This section considers semantics in more general terms, with reference to the two functions of corpus data as identified above by McEnery and Wilson (*ibid.*).

Corpora have been used to detect subtle semantic distinctions in near synonyms. Tognini-Bonelli (2001: 35–39), for example, finds that *largely* can be used to introduce cause and reason and co-occurs with morphological and semantic negatives, but *broadly* cannot; yet while *broadly* can be used as a discourse disjunct for argumentation and to express similarity or agreement, *largely* cannot. Gilquin (2003) seeks to combine the corpus-based approach with the cognitive theory of frame semantics in her study of the causative verbs GET and HAVE. The study shows that the two verbs have a number of features in common but also exhibit important differences. For example, both verbs are used predominantly with an animate causer. Yet while with GET the causee is most often animate, the frequencies of animate and inanimate causees are very similar with HAVE. Nevertheless, when causees are expressed as an object (i.e. not demoted), the proportion of animates and inanimates is reversed, with a majority of animates with GET and a predominance of inanimates with HAVE. While Tognini-Bonelli (2001) and Gilquin (2003) can be considered as examples of assigning meanings to linguistic items, Kaltenböck (2003) further exemplifies the role of corpus data in providing evidence for fuzzy categories and gradience in his study of the syntactic and semantic status of anticipatory *it*. Kaltenböck finds that both the approach which takes anticipatory *it* to have an inherent cataphoric function (i.e. referring *it*), and the view that it is a meaningless, semantically empty dummy element (i.e. prop *it*), as have been proposed previously, are problematic as they fail to take into account the actual use of anticipatory *it* in context. The analysis of instances actually occurring in ICE-GB showed very clearly that delimiting the class of *it*-extraposition (and hence anticipatory *it*) is by no means a matter of 'either–or' but has to allow for fuzzy boundaries (Kaltenböck 2003: 236): 'anticipatory *it* takes an intermediate position between prop *it* and referring *it*, all of which are linked by a scale of gradience specifying their scope of reference (wide vs. narrow)' (Kaltenböck 2003: 235). The functionalist approach taken by Kaltenböck (2003) is in sharp contrast to the purely formalist approach which, relying exclusively on conceptual evidence, identifies anticipatory *it* as meaningless. Kaltenböck argues that:

> the two approaches operate with different concepts of meaning: a formalist will be interested in the meaning of a particular form as represented in the speaker's competence, while for the view expressed here 'meaning' not only resides in isolated items but is also the result of their interaction with contextual factors.
>
> (Kaltenböck 2003: 253)

Let us now turn to a core area of semantics: aspect. According to Smith (1997: 1), 'aspect is the semantic domain of the temporal structure of situations and their presentation'. Aspect has traditionally been approached without recourse to corpus data. More recently, however, corpus data have been exploited to inform aspect theory. Xiao and McEnery (2004a), for example, have developed a corpus-based two-level model of situation aspect, in which situation aspect is modelled as verb classes at the lexical level and as situation types at the sentential level. Situation types are the composite result of the rule-based interaction between verb classes and complements, arguments, peripheral adjuncts and viewpoint aspect at the nucleus, core and clause levels. With a framework consisting of a lexicon, a layered clause structure and a set of rules mapping verb classes onto situation types, the model was developed and tested using an English corpus and a Chinese corpus. The model has not only provided a more refined aspectual classification and given a more systematic account of the compositional nature of situation aspect than previous models, but it has also shown that intuitions are not always reliable (e.g. the incorrect postulation of the effect of external arguments). We will return to discuss aspect in Unit B5.3 and Case Study 6 of Section C of this book.

The examples cited above demonstrate that corpora do have a role to play in the study of meaning, not only at the lexical level but in other core areas of semantics as well. Corpus-based semantic studies are often labour-intensive and time-consuming because many semantic features cannot be annotated automatically (consider e.g. causer vs. causee and animate vs. inanimate in Gilquin's (2003) study of causative *GET/HAVE*). Yet the interesting findings from such studies certainly make the time and effort worthwhile. In the next section we will review the use of corpora in pragmatics.

A10.10 PRAGMATICS

As noted in Unit A4.4.6, pragmatics is strongly – though not exclusively – associated with spoken discourse. This is hardly surprising considering that written registers tend to be referentially explicit whereas spoken registers typically 'permit extensive reference to the physical and temporal situation of discourse' (Biber 1988: 144). In Kennedy's (1998: 174) words, 'What we say and how we say it is influenced by who we are talking to and where the interaction is taking place.' Until the mid-1990s corpus-based pragmatic studies were severely constrained because there was only one reasonably large, publicly available corpus which was sufficiently marked up for prosodic and discourse features, the London–Lund Corpus (i.e. LLC; see Unit A7.5, and see Kennedy 1998: 174). It is, therefore, unsurprising that earlier corpus-based work on pragmatics was based fairly exclusively on the LLC. For example, Svartvik (1980), on the basis of a sample of 45,000 words from the LLC, found that the discourse marker *well* is an important device which allows the speaker time to think online while keeping a turn in conversation. The pragmatic functions of *well* include polite disagreement, qualified refusal, reinforcement, modification, indirect and partial answers, and delaying tactics. Aijmer's (1987) study of *oh* and *ah* in a 170,000-word sample from the LLC provides a full account of the major pragmatic functions of the two 'disjunct markers' (Jefferson 1978: 221). Tottie (1991), on the basis of a comparison of the LLC and the Santa Barbara Corpus of Spoken American English (i.e. SBCSAE; see Unit A7.5), finds that American speakers use backchannel agreement markers (e.g. *yeah, sure* and *right*) three times as frequently as British speakers.

Aijmer (1987: 63) notes that one of the pragmatic functions of *oh* and *ah* is to signal 'a shift or development to something not foreseen by the speaker', thus construing what comes afterwards as 'topically not coherent' (Jefferson 1978: 221). Discourse markers such as *anyway, however* and *still* help to establish coherence in spoken discourse (see Lenk 1995, 1998a, 1998b). Lenk (1998b), for example, uses the LLC and SBCSAE corpora to investigate how *however* and *still* are involved in the process of achieving conversational coherence. It was found that 'the function of both of these discourse markers is to connect parts of the discourse that are not immediately adjacent, or that are not topically related' (Lenk 1998b: 256). Nevertheless, while '*however* closes digressions that are relevant to the development of the main topic, or that bear interactional significance', '*still* closes off subjective comments within a quasi-objective narration or presentation of facts' (Lenk 1998b: 256). It is also interesting to note that *however* is used as a discourse marker only in British English (Lenk 1998b: 251).

Spoken language, and face-to-face conversation in particular, takes place on the basis of a shared context, avoids elaboration or specification of reference, and reflects the needs for real-time processing (Leech 2000). It is, therefore, hardly surprising that conversation is more vague than most written genres. Vagueness is pervasive in conversation where it plays an important role. The most obvious reason for using vague expressions is uncertainty at the time of speaking. In this case, vagueness allows speakers to maintain fluency even though they lack information about a given quantity, quality or identity, or, when such information is potentially available, they cannot access or process it in time. However, speakers may still choose to be vague even when they could in principle be more precise. This is because vague language can serve a number of pragmatic functions. Jucker, Smith and Lüdge (2003), for example, analyse the vague additives (i.e. approximators, downtoners, vague category identifiers and shields) and instances of lexical vagueness (i.e. vague quantifying expressions, vague adverbs of frequency, vague adverbs of likelihood and placeholder words) in a corpus of semi-controlled spoken interactions between students in California. They find that vagueness is an interactional strategy which plays an important role in managing conversational implicature. First, vague expressions may serve as focusing devices, directing the hearer's attention to the most relevant information. Second, vague expressions of quantities provide information about the significance of the quantity and may provide a reference point in terms of a scale. Third, vague expressions may also convey several aspects of propositional attitude (e.g. conveying different levels of certainty regarding the propositional content, conveying the newsworthiness or expectedness of a statement, and conveying evaluative meaning). Finally, vague expressions may serve various social functions (serving as politeness strategies, softening implicit complaints and criticisms, and providing a way of establishing a social bond). As such, vague language helps to 'guide the hearer towards the best interpretation of the speaker's intention' (Jucker, Smith and Lüdge 2003: 1766).

Similarly, Drave (2002) studies vague language (VL) in intercultural conversations. The corpus he used was the Hong Kong Corpus of Conversational English (HKCCE), a corpus consisting of 98,310 words of native-speaker English (NSE) and 84,208 words of English produced by native speakers of Cantonese (NSC). Drave (2002: 27) finds that vague language can be used in naturally occurring conversations strategically for promoting politeness and intersubjectivity and for managing asymmetries of knowledge, particularly in intercultural interaction. It was found that while quantitatively NSE seems to be 'vaguer' than NSC, the two groups do not differ qualitatively, 'with very few VL items being used exclusively by one group or the other and the rank orders of VL items of the most frequent items virtually identical' (Drave 2002: 29).

McEnery, Baker and Cheepen (2002) explored the relationship between directness and lexical markers of politeness with reference to operator requests to 'hold the line', using a corpus of telephone-based transactional dialogues. They found that of the various types of request strategies (bare imperative, deletion, conditional *if*, prediction and question), only the bare imperatives were unambiguously direct while all of the other types were to some extent indirect imperatives. It is also interesting to note that while bare imperatives are the most common request strategy, they are typically softened by mitigators such as *please* and *just* (McEnery, Baker and Cheepen 2002: 64–65).

While politeness strategies are particularly important in transactional dialogues as explored by McEnery, Baker and Cheepen (2002), conversation is not always polite. Complaining is unavoidable. Laforest (2002) presents an interesting study which characterizes 'the complaint/complaint-response sequence in everyday conversations between people who are on intimate terms' (Laforest 2002: 1596), in this case, peer family members (i.e. husbands/wives and brothers/sisters). The complaints exchanged between people who are not peers (i.e. parents vs. children) were excluded in order to neutralize the variation introduced by a difference in hierarchical position between interactants. The data used in this study were taken from a corpus of about fifty hours of family conversations recorded in Montreal. The complaints analysed in this study illustrated the numerous ways in which speakers expressed dissatisfaction with the behaviour of people close to them. They had preferential realization patterns that could be linked in part to the intimacy of the relationship between the interactants: in many ways, they were uttered without the special precautions generally associated with face-threatening acts (FTAs) outside the private sphere (Laforest 2002: 1617–1618). Laforest found that while the complainees most often reject the blame levelled at them, well-characterized arguments are virtually absent from the corpus; the entry into the argument is negotiated in the speech turns that follow the complaint–response sequence, and the argument only breaks out if the complainer questions the value of the complainee's response. The study also shows that both complainer and complainee use various strategies for avoiding an argument and, more often than not, succeed in doing so (Laforest 2002: 1596).

Nowadays, pragmatic studies are more varied than before. One area of increasing interest is historical pragmatics which, like general diachronic studies, depends heavily upon corpus data. For example, Arnovick (2000) examines the speech event of parting, focusing on the development of *Goodbye*, which was originally an explicit blessing *God be with you*. She finds that the formal development from *God be with you* to *Goodbye* is linked to functional shifts. In the English Drama section of the Chadwyck-Healey corpus, the original form, which appeared in closing sections of dialogue in Early Modern English, was used as a blessing as well as a greeting at parting while the contracted form became stronger in the force of the polite closing greeting. Arnovick's study shows that the end of the seventeenth century and the beginning of the eighteenth century marked a crucial period during which the blessing declined and the closing form *Goodbye* increased in frequency. Jucker and Taavitsainen (2000) undertake a diachronic analysis of one particular speech act, i.e. insults, through the history of English on the basis of a corpus composed of both literary and non-literary data. Their analysis of written materials of the past periods indicates an evident bias towards conventionalized insults. Most early examples are found in literary texts, which reflect generic conventions of the time and the culture that gave rise to these literary forms. Jacobsson (2002) used a pilot version of the Corpus of English Dialogues (CED; see Unit A7.7) to study gratitude expressions such as *Thank you* and *Thanks* in Early Modern English. The author found that while these expressions themselves were probably the same in the Early Modern period as they are today, they 'had not developed the discourse-marking features of today's British English; nor is it possible to see the complex patterns of thanking in different turn-positions in the CED material' (Jacobsson 2002: 78). Biber (2004) explores, on the basis of the ARCHER corpus (see Unit A7.7), the patterns of historical change in the preferred devices used to mark stance across the past three centuries. He finds that of the grammatical categories marking stance, modal verbs have undergone a decrease in use whereas other devices such as semi-modals, stance adverbials and stance complement clause constructions have all increased in use across the historical periods in his study (Biber 2004: 129).

Pragmatics is an area in which more and more corpus data are being used. However, meanings dependent upon pragmatics cannot easily be detected automatically. As in semantics, the automatic extraction is not likely unless the corpora used for such studies have been annotated manually with the required analyses.

A10.11 SOCIOLINGUISTICS

While sociolinguistics has traditionally been based upon empirical data, the use of standard corpora in this field has been limited. The expansion of corpus work in sociolinguistics appears to have been hampered by three problems: the operationalization of sociolinguistic theory into measurable categories suitable for corpus research, the lack of sociolinguistic metadata encoded in currently available corpora and the lack of sociolinguistically rigorous sampling in corpus construction (see McEnery and Wilson 2001: 116).

Corpus-based sociolinguistic studies have so far largely been restricted to the area of gender studies at the lexical level. For example, Kjellmer (1986) compared the frequencies of masculine and feminine pronouns and lexical items *man/men* and *woman/women* in the Brown and LOB corpora. It was found that female items are considerably less frequent than male items in both corpora, though female items were more frequent in British English. It is also interesting to note that female items were more frequent in imaginative (especially romantic fiction) than informative genres. Sigley (1997) found some significant differences in the distribution patterns of relative clauses used by male and female speakers/writers at different educational levels in New Zealand English. Caldas-Coulthard and Moon (1999) found on the basis of a newspaper corpus that women were frequently modified by adjectives indicating physical appearance (e.g. *beautiful, pretty* and *lovely*) whereas men were frequently modified by adjectives indicating importance (e.g. *key, big, great* and *main*). Similarly, Hunston (1999b) noted that while *right* is used to modify both men and women, the typical meaning of *right* co-occurring with men is work-related ('the right man for the job') whereas the typical meaning of *right* co-occurring with women is man-related ('the right woman for this man'). Hunston (2002: 121) provided two alternative explanations for this: that women are perceived to be 'less significant in the world of paid work', or that 'men are construed as less emotionally competent because they more frequently need "the right woman" to make their lives complete'. In either case, women are not treated identically (at least in linguistic terms) in society. Holmes (1993a, 1993b, 1993c, 1997) has published widely on sexism in English, e.g. the epicene terms such as -*man* and *he*, gender-neutral terms like *chairperson*, and sexist suffixes like -*ess* and -*ette*. Holmes and Sigley (2002), for example, used Brown/LOB and Frown/FLOB/WWC to track social change in patterns of gender marking between 1961 and 1991. They found that

> while women continue to be the linguistically marked gender, there is some
> evidence to support a positive interpretation of many of the patterns

identified in the most recent corpora, since the relevant marked contexts reflect inroads made by women into occupational domains previously considered as exclusively male.

(Holmes and Sigley 2002: 261)

While Holmes and Sigley (2002) approached gender marking from a diachronic perspective, Baranowski (2002) approached the issue in a contrastive context. Baranowski investigated the epicene pronominal usage of *he, he or she* and singular *they* in two corpora of written English (one for British English and the other for American English), and found that the traditional form *he* is no longer pre-dominant while singular *they* is most likely to be used. The form *he or she* is shown to be used rather rarely. The study also reveals that American writers are more conservative in their choice of a singular epicene pronoun. In gender studies like these, however, it is important to evaluate and classify usages in context (see Holmes 1994), which can be time-consuming and hard to decide sometimes.

In addition to sexism, femininity and sexual identity are two other important areas of gender studies which have started to use corpus data. For example, Coates (1999) used a corpus of women's (and girls') 'backstage talk' to explore their self-presentation in contexts where they seem most relaxed and most off-record, focusing on 'those aspects of women's backstage performance of self which do not fit prevailing norms of femininity' (Coates 1999: 65). Coates argued that the backstage talk 'provides women with an arena where norms can be subverted and challenged and alternative selves explored' while acknowledging 'such talk helps to maintain the heteropatriarchal order, by providing an outlet for the frustrations of frontstage performance'. Thorne and Coupland (1998: 234) studied, on the basis of a corpus of 200 lesbian and gay male dating advertisement texts, a range of discursive devices and conventions used in formulating sexual/self-gendered iden-tities. They also discussed these discourse practices in relation to a social critique of contemporary gay attitudes, belief and lifestyles in the UK. Baker (2004) undertook a corpus-based keyword analysis of the debates over a Bill to equalize the age of sexual consent for gay men with the age of consent for heterosexual sex at 16 years in the House of Lords in the UK between 1998 and 2000 (see Unit C5.5 for further discussion of keywords). Baker's analysis uncovered the main lexical differences between oppositional stances and helped to shed new light on the ways in which discourses of homosexuality were constructed by the Lords. For example, it was found that *homosexual* was associated with acts whereas *gay* was associated with identities. While those who argued for the reform focused on equality and tolerance, those who argued against it linked homosexuality to danger, ill health, crime and unnatural behaviour.

While corpus-based sociolinguistic research has focused on language and gender, corpora have also started to play a role in a wide range of more general issues in sociolinguistics. For example, Banjo (1996) discussed the role that ICE-Nigeria is expected to play in language planning in Nigeria; Florey (1998: 207) drew upon a corpus of incantations 'in order to address the issue of the extent to which specialised sociocultural and associated linguistic knowledge persists in a context of language shift'; Puchta and Potter (1999) analysed question formats in a corpus of German market research focus groups (i.e. 'a carefully planned discussion designed to obtain perceptions on a defined area of interest in a permissive, non-threatening environment', see Krueger 1994: 6) in an attempt 'to show how elaborate questions [i.e. 'questions which include a range of reformulations and rewordings' (Puchta and Potter 1999: 314)] in focus groups are organized in ways which provide the kinds of answers that the focus group moderators require' (Puchta and Potter 1999: 332); de Beaugrande (1998: 134) drew data from the Bank of English to show that terms like *stability* and *instability* are not 'self-consciously neutral', but rather they are socially charged to serve social interests. Dailey-O'Cain (2000) explored the sociolinguistic distribution (sex and age) of focuser *like* (as in *And there were* like *people blocking, you know?*) and quotative *like* (as in *Maya's* **like**, *'Kim come over here and be with me and Brett'*) as well as attitudes towards these markers.

In a more general context of addressing the debate over ideal vs. real language, de Beaugrande (1998: 131) argues that sociolinguistics may have been affected, during its formative stages, as a result of the long-term tradition of idealizing language and disconnecting it from speech and society. Unsurprisingly, sociolinguistics has traditionally focused on phonological and grammatical variations in terms of 'features and rules' (de Beaugrande 1998: 133). He observes that the use of corpus data can bring sociolinguistics 'some interesting prospects' (de Beaugrande 1998: 137) in that '[r]eal data also indicate that much of the socially relevant variation within a language does not concern the phonological and syntactic variations' (de Beaugrande 1998: 133). In this sense, the

> corpus can help sociolinguistics engage with issues and variations in usage that are less tidy and abstract than phonetics, phonology, and grammar, and more proximate to the socially vital issues of the day . . . Corpus data can help us monitor the ongoing collocational approximation and contestation of terms that refer to the social conditions themselves and discursively position these in respect to the interests of various social groups.
>
> (de Beaugrande 1998: 135)

With the increasing availability of corpora which encode rich sociolinguistic metadata (e.g. the BNC), the corpus-based approach is expected to play a more important role in sociolinguistics. To give an example of this new role, readers will have an opportunity to explore, in Case Study 4 in Section C, the patterns of swearing in modern British English along with such dimensions as sex, age, social class of speakers and writers encoded in the BNC.

A10.12 DISCOURSE ANALYSIS

Closely allied with sociolinguistics is discourse analysis (DA), especially critical discourse analysis (CDA), which is mainly concerned with the studies of ideology, power and culture (see Fairclough 1995). While both corpus linguistics and DA rely heavily on real language, Leech (2000: 678–680) observes that there is 'a cultural divide' between the two: while DA emphasizes the integrity of text, corpus linguistics tends to use representative samples; while DA is primarily qualitative, corpus linguistics is essentially quantitative; while DA focuses on the contents expressed by language, corpus linguistics is interested in language *per se*; while the collector, transcriber and analyst are often the same person in DA, this is rarely the case in corpus linguistics; while the data used in DA are rarely widely available, corpora are typically made widely available. It is also important to note that some terms used in DA are defined differently from corpus linguistics. Apart from *genre* as noted previously, for example, *keywords* in DA refers to words that have a particular significance in a given discourse. The cultural divide, however, is now diminishing. McEnery and Wilson (2001: 114) note that there are some important 'points of contact' between DA and corpus linguistics: the common computer-aided analytic techniques, and the great potential of standard corpora in DA as control data. Because the corpus-based approach tends to obscure 'the character of each text as a text' and 'the role of the text producer and the society of which they are a part' (Hunston 2002: 110), some DA authors have avoided using corpus data. For example, Martin (1999: 52) argues that analysing a lot of text from a corpus simultaneously would force the analyst to lose 'contact with text'. Yet Stubbs (1997) and de Beaugrande (1999, 2001), among many others, have insisted that corpora are indeed useful for studies of this kind.

Specialized corpora are particularly useful in discourse analysis and most of the recently published studies of ideology and culture are based on specialized corpora. Political discourse is perhaps the most important and most widely used data in discourse analysis. This is perhaps because politics is '[o]ne area of social life in which the increasing salience of discourse has been especially apparent' (Johnson, Culpeper and Suhr 2003: 41). For example, Sotillo and Starace-Nastasi (1999) undertook a critical discourse analysis on the basis of a corpus of 123 Letters to the Editors (LEs) of two weekly newspapers written by candidates for political office, their supporters and opponents in an American working-class town. They found that gender and class markers were salient in the discourse of LEs. With regard to class, there is an antagonistic dialogue between residents of the third ward (working class) and those of the second and first wards (middle class): middle-class residents of the first and second wards remain unsympathetic to the concerns of third-ward residents, especially to their claims of a deteriorating quality of life. With respect to the saliency of gender in LEs, qualitative differences were found between males and females in writing style, lexical and syntactic choices, and tone of communication. For example, men used more qualifiers and intensifiers than women, and women writers of LEs were often less confrontational and more conciliatory than their male counterparts in their criticism of those in power.

Teubert (2000) studied the language of Euroscepticism in Britain on the basis of a corpus of texts downloaded from websites which take an antagonistic attitude towards the European Union. Corpus analysis techniques like collocation and phraseology enabled Teubert to make explicit what was implied but not stated by Eurosceptics: only Britain in the whole of Europe is a true democracy with a truly accountable government (Teubert 2000: 76–77). Similarly, Fairclough's (2000) comparative analysis of keywords (in the sense as used in corpus linguistics) in a corpus of the British Prime Minister Blair's speeches and other documents from New Labour and a corpus of documents from Old Labour Party showed that the party has changed its ideology, as reflected by its language.

Johnson, Culpeper and Suhr (2003) explored discourses of political correctness (PC) in a corpus of articles gathered from three broadsheet newspapers in the UK between 1994 and 1999. Their frequency and (statistically defined) keyword analyses showed that while the overall frequency of so-called PC-related terms ('political correctness', 'politically correct', etc.) generally declined in the five-year period, there was an interesting link between the frequency of such terms and the ways in which they have been drawn upon as a means of framing debates over Blair and the Labour Party throughout the period in question.

Saraceni (2003) analysed two corpora of interviews and speeches related to the war in Iraq in an attempt 'to understand the extent to which, at least in linguistic terms, the ideas of Blair and Bush may not be as alike as one might be tempted to believe'. His analysis revealed some important differences in the ways in which Blair and Bush use language and in what they actually say. While Bush's rhetoric is typically right wing, Blair's discourse is more enigmatic, lacking many of the characteristics of right-wing rhetoric but not typical of left-wing rhetoric either (Saraceni 2003: 12). The marked contrast between words and actions in this case is a good example of a complex issue which the corpus-based approach alone cannot resolve.

Partington (2003) provides a full, corpus-based account of the discourse of White House press briefing, in an attempt 'to show how it is possible to use concordance technology and the detailed linguistic evidence available in corpora to enhance the study of the discourse features of a particular genre of the language' (Partington 2003: 3). The major corpus resource used by him is a corpus consisting of forty-eight briefings, amounting to approximately 250,000 words. The work presented in Partington (*ibid.*) represents an unusual contribution to corpus-based discourse analysis because a large part of the book is devoted to devising 'a suitable method-ology to study features of interaction in large bodies of texts, in corpora' (Partington 2003: 5). Such methodologies are particularly important in the context of most studies in discourse analysis undertaken so far having been based on corpora of a number of single texts (e.g. Pardo 2001).

In addition to political discourse, corpora have been used in analysing a number of other types of discourse, for example, academic discourse (e.g. Piper 2000), business discourse (e.g. Koller 2004), everyday demotic discourse (Carter and McCarthy

2004), legal discourse (e.g. Graham 2001), media discourse (e.g. Downs 2002; Moore 2002; Pan 2002; Page 2003), medical discourse (e.g. Salager-Meyer, Ariza and Zambrano 2003), and workshop discourse (e.g. Holmes and Marra 2002).

The works reviewed so far are all based mainly on specialized corpora, though some of them (e.g. Piper 2000; Johnson, Culpeper and Suhr 2003; Partington 2003) have used general corpora such as the BNC for comparative purposes. In contrast, there has been far less work in discourse analysis that is based directly on general corpora. There are a number of reasons for this. First, most discourse analysts prefer to study whole texts – general corpora are typically composed of samples. Second, with a few exceptions (e.g. the BNC), most general corpora have not encoded variables required for discourse analysis (e.g. metadata relating to the language producer). Third, most general corpora have not included spoken data for spoken discourse analysis yet, as Partington (2003: 262) observes, some linguists only consider spoken language as discourse. Finally, the field of discourse analysis has historically been accustomed to analysing a small number of single texts whereas general corpora provide a much larger number of texts. There are, however, a number of studies which are based on general corpora. For example, Stubbs (1996) gives numerous examples of what he calls 'cultural keywords' in the Bank of English; de Beaugrande (1999) compared the ideologies as reflected by 'liberal' and its derivatives (e.g. 'liberalism', 'liberalization') in the UK and the US-based corpus resources as well as in the Corpus of South African English (i.e. CSAE, which was originally developed as part of the ICE corpus).

In conclusion, while the corpus-based approach to discourse analysis is still in its infancy, corpora (either specialized or general) do present a real opportunity for discourse analysis, because the automatic analysis of a large number of texts at one time 'can throw into relief the non-obvious in a single text' (Partington 2003: 7). As de Beaugrande (1999) comments:

> Obviously, the methods for doing a 'critical discourse analysis' of corpus data are far from established yet. Even when we have examined a fairly large set of attestations, we cannot be certain whether our own interpretations of key items and collocations are genuinely representative of the large populations who produced the data. But we can be fairly confident of accessing a range of interpretative issues that is both wider and more precise than we could access by relying on our own personal usages and intuitions. Moreover, when we observe our own ideological position in contest with others, we are less likely to overlook it or take it for granted.
>
> (de Beaugrande 1999: 287)

A10.13 STYLISTICS AND LITERARY STUDIES

Style is closely allied to registers/genres and dialects/language varieties (see Unit B4), because stylistic shifts in usage may be observed with reference to features associated with either particular situations of use or particular groups of speakers (see Schilling-Estes 2002: 375). In this section, we will consider only what Carter (1999: 195) calls 'literary language'. Literariness is typically present in, but not restricted to, literary texts. However, given that most work in stylistics focuses upon literary texts, the accent of this section will fall upon literary studies.

Stylisticians are typically interested in individual works by individual authors rather than language or language variety as such. Hence while they may be interested in computer-aided text analysis, the use of corpora in stylistics and literary studies appears to be limited (see McEnery and Wilson 2001: 117). Nevertheless, as we will see shortly, corpora and corpus analysis techniques are useful in a number of ways: the study of prose style, the study of individual authorial styles and authorship attribution, literary appreciation and criticism, teaching stylistics and the study of literariness in discourses other than literary texts have all been the focus of corpus-based study.

As noted in Unit A4.4.7, one of the focuses in the study of prose stylistics is the representation of people's speech and thoughts. Leech and Short (1981) developed an influential model of speech and thought presentation, which has been used by many scholars for literary and non-literary analysis (e.g. McKenzie 1987; Roeh and Nir 1990; Simpson 1993). The model was tested and further refined in Short, Semino and Culpeper (1996), and Semino, Short and Culpeper (1997). Readers can refer to Unit A4.4.7 for a description of the speech and thought categories in the model. Using this model, Semino, Short and Wynne (1999) studied hypothetical words and thoughts in contemporary British narratives; Short, Semino and Wynne (2002) explored the notion of faithfulness in discourse presentation; Semino and Short (2004) provide a comprehensive account of speech, thought and writing presentation in fictional and non-fictional narratives.

The corpus-based approach has also been used to study the authorial styles of individual authors. Corpora used in such studies are basically specialized. For example, if the focus is on the stylistic shift of a single author, the corpus consists of their early and later works, or works of theirs that belong to different genres (e.g. plays and essays); if the focus is on the comparison of different authorial styles, the corpus then consists of works by the authors under consideration. However, as Hunston (2002: 128) argues, using a large, general corpus can provide 'a means of establishing a norm for comparison when discussing features of literary style'. The methodology used in studying authorial styles often goes beyond simple counting; rather it typically relies heavily upon sophisticated statistical approaches such as MF/MD (see Unit A10.4; e.g. Watson 1994), Principal Component Analysis (e.g. Binongo and Smith 1999a) and multivariate analysis (or more specifically, cluster analysis, e.g. Watson 1999; Hoover 2003b). The combination of stylistics and computation and statistics has given birth to a new interdisciplinary area referred to as 'stylometry' (Holmes 1998; Binongo and Smith 1999b), 'stylometrics' (Hunston 2002: 128), 'computational stylistics' (Merriam 2003) or 'statistical stylistics' (Hoover 2001, 2002).

Watson (1994) applied Biber's (1988) MF/MD stylistic model in his critical analysis of the complete prose works of the Australian Aboriginal author Mudrooroo Nyoongah to explore a perceived diachronic stylistic shift. He found that Nyoongah has shifted in style towards a more oral and abstract form of expression throughout his career and suggested that this shift 'may be indicative of Nyoongah's steadily progressive identification with his Aboriginality' (Watson 1994: 280). In another study of Nyoongah's early prose fiction (five novels), Watson (1999) used cluster analysis to explore the notion of involvement, more specifically *eventuality* (certainty vs. doubt) and *affect* (positive vs. negative). The analysis grouped *Wildcat*, *Sand* and *Doin* into one cluster and grouped *Doctor* and *Ghost* into another cluster, which represent two very distinct styles. The first cluster is more affective and representative of informal, unplanned language, using more certainty adverbs, certainty verbs and expressions of affect; in contrast, the second cluster is more typical of more structured, integrated discourse, highlighted by a greater use of adjectives, in particular doubt adjectives and negative affect adjectives, and a very low expression of affect.

Binongo and Smith (1999a, 1999b) applied Principal Component Analysis in their studies of authorial styles. In Binongo and Smith (1999b), for example, the authors studied the distribution of twenty-five prepositions in Oscar Wilde's plays and essays. They found that when the plays and essays are brought into a single analysis, the difference in genre predominates over other factors, though the distinction is not clear-cut, with a gradual change from plays to essays (Binongo and Smith 1999b: 785–786).

In addition to stylistic variation, authorship attribution is another focus of literary stylistics. In a series of papers published in *Literary and Linguistic Computing*, Hoover (2001, 2002, 2003a, 2003b) tested and modified cluster analysis techniques which have traditionally been used in studies of stylistic variation and authorship attribution. Hoover (2001) noted that cluster analyses of frequent words typically achieved an accuracy rate of less than 90 per cent for contemporary novels. Hoover (2002) found that when frequent word sequences were used instead of frequent words, or in addition to them, in cluster analyses, the accuracy often improved, sometimes drastically. In Hoover (2003a), the author compared the accuracies when using frequent words, frequent sequences and frequent collocations, and found that cluster analysis based on frequent collocations provided a more accurate and robust method for authorship attribution. Hoover (2003b) proposed yet another modification to traditional authorship attribution techniques to measure stylistic variation. The new approach takes into consideration locally frequent words, a modification which is justified when one considers that authorship attribution focuses on similarities persisting across differences whereas the study of style variation focuses on variations of authorial style. Lexical choice is certainly part of authorial style. The modified approach has achieved improved results on some frequently studied texts, including Orwell's *1984* and Golding's *The Inheritors*. Readers can refer to Haenlein (1999) for a full account of the corpus-based approach to authorship attribution.

Authorship is only one of the factors which affect stylistic variation. Merriam (2003) demonstrated, on the basis of fourteen texts by three authors, that three other factors, proposed originally by Labbé and Labbé (2001), namely the vocabulary of the period, treatment of theme and genre, also contributed to intertextual stylistic variation.

Louw (1997: 240) observed that '[t]he opportunity for corpora to play a role in literary criticism has increased greatly over the last decade'. He reported on a number of examples from his students' projects which showed that 'corpus data can provide powerful support for a reader's intuition' on the one hand while at the same time providing 'insights into aspects of "literariness", in this case the importance of collocational meaning, which has hitherto not been thought of by critics' (Louw 1997: 247). Likewise, Jackson (1997) provided a detailed account of how corpora and corpus analysis techniques can be used in teaching students about style.

While we have so far been concerned with literary texts, literariness is not restricted to literature, as noted at the beginning of this section. Carter (1999) explored, using the CANCODE corpus, the extent to which typically non-literary discourses like everyday conversation can display literary properties. He concluded that:

> The opposition of literary to non-literary language is an unhelpful one and the notion of literary language as a yes/no category should be replaced by one which sees literary language as a continuum, a cline of literariness in language use with some uses of language being marked as more literary than others.
>
> (Carter 1999: 207)

A10.14 FORENSIC LINGUISTICS

The final example of the use of corpora and corpus analysis techniques which we will consider in this section is forensic linguistics, the study of language related to court trials and linguistic evidence. This is perhaps the most applied and exciting area where corpus linguistics has started to play a role because court verdicts can very clearly affect people's lives. Corpora have been used in forensic linguistics in a number of ways, e.g. in general studies of legal language (e.g. Langford 1999; Philip 1999) and courtroom discourses (e.g. Stubbs 1996; Heffer 1999; Szakos and Wang 1999; Cotterill 2001), and in the attribution of authorship of linguistic evidence. For example, such texts as confession/witness statements (e.g. Coulthard 1993) and blackmail/ransom/suicide notes related to specific cases (e.g. Baldauf 1999) have been studied. Corpora have also been used in detecting plagiarism (e.g. Johnson 1997; Woolls and Coulthard 1998).

Legal language has a number of words which either say things about doing and happening (e.g. *intention* and *negligence*) or refer to doing things with words (e.g. AGREE and PROMISE). Such keywords are central to an understanding of the law but are often defined obscurely in statutes and judgements. Langford (1999) used corpus evidence to demonstrate how the meanings of words such as *intention*, *recklessness* and *negligence* can be stated simply and clearly in words that anyone can understand. When L2 data are involved, defining legal terms becomes a more challenging task. Dictionaries are sometimes unhelpful in this regard. Philip (1999) showed how parallel corpora, in this case, a corpus of European Community directives and judgements, could be used to identify actual translation equivalents in Italian and English.

Courtroom discourses are connected to the 'fact-finding' procedure, which attempts to reconstruct reality through language, e.g. prosecutor's presentation, the eye-witness's narratives, the defendant's defence and the judge's summing-up. As people may choose to interpret language in different ways according to their own conventions, experiences or purposes, the same word may not mean the same thing to different people. Unsurprisingly, the prosecutor and the defendant produce conflicting accounts of the same event. While the judge's summing-up and the eyewitness's testimonies are supposed to be impartial, studies show that they can also be evaluative.

Stubbs (1996) gave an example based on his own experience in analysing a judge's summing-up in a real court case, which involved a man being accused of hitting another man. The judge's summing-up used a number of words that had a semantic preference for anger, e.g. *aggravated, annoyed, irritation, mad* and *temper*. The judge also quoted the witness who claimed to have been hit, using the word *reeled* four times. The word *reeled* was used with reference to the person being hit falling backwards after he had allegedly been assaulted. If we look at how the word REEL is used in the BNC, we can see that it is often used to connote violence or confusion due to some sort of outside force. The word carries an implication that the man was struck or pushed quite violently and was therefore likely to be remembered by the jury because of the number of times it was repeated by the judge (who, being the most important person in the courtroom, holds a lot of power and may be assumed to be able to influence people), and because it paints quite a dramatic picture. Another unusual aspect of the judge's speech was his use of modal verbs, which are used typically to indicate possibility or give permission. The judge used two modal verbs in particular, *may* and *might*, a total of thirty-one times in his speech and the majority of these occurred in phrases such as *you may think that, you may feel, you may find* and *you may say to yourselves* . . . Stubbs found that only three of these could truly be said to indicate possibility. In the other cases it was used to signal what the judge actually thought about something. Given the importance of the judge in the courtroom, the implication of phrases such as *you may think* can become 'it would be reasonable or natural for you to think that . . .' or even 'I am instructing you to think that . . .'. Supported by corpus evidence, Stubbs claimed that in a number of ways, the judge was using linguistic strategies in order to influence the jury.

While the court imposes severe constraints on the witness's right to evaluate in their narratives, the overall evaluative point of the narration is perhaps most clear in this context. Heffer (1999) explored, on the basis of a small corpus of eyewitness accounts in the trial of Timothy McVeigh, the 'Oklahoma Bomber', some of the linguistic means by which lawyer and witness cooperate in direct examination to circumvent the law of evidence and convey evaluation. He found that while witnesses seldom evaluate explicitly, a combination of a careful examination strategy and emotional involvement can result in highly effective narratives replete with evaluative elements.

Cotterill (2001) explored the semantic prosodies in the prosecution and the defence presented by both parties in the O. J. Simpson criminal trial, drawing upon data from the Bank of English. The prosecution repeatedly exploited the negative semantic prosodies of such terms as ENCOUNTER, CONTROL and *cycle of* in order to deconstruct the professional image of Simpson as a football icon and moviestar, wishing to 'expose' the other side of Simpson. Cotterill found that in the Bank of English, ENCOUNTER typically refers to an inanimate entity and collocates with such words as *prejudice, obstacles, problems, a glass ceiling* (used metaphorically to refer to a barrier in one's career), *hazards, resistance, opposition*, and *risks*, all of which are negative. The modifiers of *resistance* (*stiff*) and *opposition* (*fierce*) also indicate violence. An analysis of the agents and objects of CONTROL in the corpus was also revealing. Corpus evidence shows that the typical agents of CONTROL are authority figures or representatives from government or official bodies (e.g. police), while the objects of CONTROL often refer to something bad or dangerous (e.g. chemical weapons, terrorist activities). It appears then, in this context, that CONTROL is legitimate only when the controller has some degree of authority and when what is controlled is bad or dangerous. Cotterill (2001: 299) suggested that the prosecutor was constructing Simpson as a man who was entirely unjustified and unreasonable, and excessively obsessed with discipline and authority. Another group of collocates of CONTROL in the corpus refers to various emotional states or conditions. But in this context, it appears that women tend to control their emotions while men tend to control their temper. In this way, Simpson was portrayed as a violent and abusive husband who finally lost his temper and murdered his emotionally vulnerable wife. The corpus shows that *cycle of* collocates strongly with negative events and situations (e.g. *violence* and *revenge killings*), and cycles tend to increase in severity over a long period of time. These two characteristics were just what the prosecutor believed the Simpson case displayed (Cotterill 2001: 301). The defence attorney, on the other hand, attempted to minimize and neutralize the negative prosodies evoked by the prosecution through a series of carefully selected lexical choices and the manipulation of semantic prosodies in his response. For example, he repeatedly conceptualized Simpson's assaults as 'incidents' (a relatively more neutral term), and used a series of verbal process nominalizations (i.e. *dispute, discussion* and *conversation*) in his defence statement. *Incidents* only occur at random rather than systematically. The Bank of English shows that at the top of the collocate list of *incident* (MI, 4:4 window) is *unrelated*. The defence attorney used the term *incident* to de-emphasize the systematic nature of Simpson's attacks and imply that Simpson only lost control and beat his wife occasionally and that these events were unrelated. Nominalization not only de-emphasized Simpson's role by removing agency from a number of references to the attacks, it also turned a violent actional event into a non-violent verbal event.

In the fact-finding procedure of court trials, the coherence of the defendant's account is an important criterion which may be used to measure its reliability. Szakos and Wang (1999) presented a corpus-based study of coherence phenomena in the investigative dialogues between judges and criminals. Their study was based on the Taiwanese Courtroom Spoken Corpus, which includes thirty criminal cases with seventeen different types of crimes. The authors demonstrated that word frequency patterns and concordancing of corpus data could assist judges in finding out the truth and arriving at fair judgments.

Another important issue in legal cases is to establish the authorship of a particular text, e.g. a confession statement, a blackmail note, a ransom note, or a suicide note. We have already discussed authorship attribution of literary texts (see Unit A10.13). The techniques used in those contexts, such as Principal Component Analysis and cluster analysis, however, are rarely useful in forensic linguistics, because the texts in legal cases are typically very short, sometimes only a few hundred words. The techniques used in forensic linguistics are quite different from those for authorship attribution of literary texts. Forensic linguists often rely on comparing an anonymous incriminated text with a suspect's writings and/or data from general corpora.

Baldauf (1999), for example, reported on the work undertaken at the 'linguistic text analysis' section of the Bundeskriminalamt (BKA) in Wiesbaden, Germany, which has been dealing with the linguistic analysis of written texts, mainly in serious cases of blackmail, for more than ten years. During this time a method has been established that consists partly of computer-assisted research on a steadily growing corpus of more than 1,500 authentic incriminated texts and partly of *ad-hoc*, case-specific linguistic analysis.

Perhaps the most famous example of authorship attribution in forensic linguistics is the case of Derek Bentley, who was hanged in the UK in 1953 for allegedly encouraging his young companion Chris Craig to shoot a policeman. The evidence that weighed against him was a confession statement which he signed in police custody but later claimed at the trial that the police had 'helped' him produce. Coulthard (see 1993, 1994) found that in Bentley's confession, the word *then* was unusually frequent: it occurred ten times in his 582-word confession statement, ranking as the eighth most frequent word in the statement. In contrast, the word ranked fifty-eighth in a corpus of spoken English and eighty-third in the Bank of English (on average once every 500 words). Coulthard also examined six other statements, three made by other witnesses and three by police officers, including two involved in the Bentley case. The word *then* occurred just once in the witnesses' 930-word statements whereas it occurred twenty-nine times – once in every seventy-eight words in the police statements. Another anomaly Coulthard noticed was the position of *then*. The sequence subject + *then* (e.g. *I then*, *Chris then*) was unusually frequent in Bentley's confession. For example, *I then* occurred three times (once every 190 words) in his statement. In contrast, in a 1.5-million-word corpus of spoken English, the sequence occurred just nine times (once every 165,000 words). No instance of *I then* was found in ordinary witness statements, but nine occurrences were found in the police statement. The spoken data in the Bank of English showed *then I* was ten times as frequent as *I then*. It appeared that the sequence subject + *then* was characteristic of the police statement. Although the police denied Bentley's claim and said that the statement was a verbatim record of what Bentley had actually said, the unusual frequency of *then* and its abnormal position could be taken to be indicative of some intrusion of the policemen's register in the statement. The case was reopened in 1993, forty years after Derek was hanged. Malcolm Coulthard, a forensic linguist, was commissioned to examine the confession as part of an appeal to get a posthumous pardon for Derek Bentley by his family. The appeal was initially rejected by the Home Secretary; but in 1998, another court of appeal overthrew the original conviction and found Derek Bentley innocent. In 1999 the Home Secretary awarded compensation to the Bentley family.

An issue related to authorship attribution in forensic linguistics is plagiarism, which is sometimes subject to civil or criminal legal action, and in the context of education, subject to disciplinary action. Corpus analysis techniques have also been used in detecting plagiarism. For example, Johnson (1997) carried out a corpus-based study in which she compared lexical vocabulary and hapaxes (i.e. words that occur only once) in student essays suspected of plagiarism in order to determine whether those essays had been copied. Woolls and Coulthard (1998) demonstrated how a series of corpus-based computer programs could be used to analyse texts of doubtful or disputed authorship.

Readers can refer to Coulthard (1994), Heffer (1999) and Kredens (2000) for further discussion of the use of corpora in forensic linguistics. While forensic linguistics is a potentially promising area in which corpora can play a role, it may take some time to persuade members of the legal profession to accept forensic linguistic evidence. Yet in real-life cases, Coulthard's testimony helped to bring a happy ending to the Bentley case. Other cases have been less successful, however. Stubbs's evidence against the judge's biased summing-up was not accepted by the Lord Chief Justice who looked at the appeal. But whatever initial outcomes, forensic linguistics needs to demonstrate that it can indeed arrive at correct answers so that the discipline can gain more credibility. For this, more experimental tests need to be carried out where linguists are given problems to solve where the answer is already known by an independent judge.

A10.15 WHAT CORPORA CANNOT TELL US

We have so far reviewed the use of corpora and corpus analysis techniques in a wide range of areas of language studies. This review might give the misleading impression that corpora are all-powerful and capable of solving all sorts of language problems. But in fact, they are not. This section will briefly discuss a number of limitations of the corpus-based approach to language studies. We will return to discuss the pros and cons of using corpora in Unit B2. For the moment, let us review the problems with using corpora that we have noted so far.

First, corpora do not provide negative evidence. This means that they cannot tell us what is possible or not possible. Everything included in a corpus is what language users have actually produced. A corpus, however large or balanced, cannot be exhaustive except in a very limited range of cases. Nevertheless, a representative corpus can show what is central and typical in language.

Second, corpora can yield findings but rarely provide explanations for what is observed. These explanations must be developed using other methodologies, including intuition.

Third, the use of corpora as a methodology also defines the boundaries of any given study. As we have emphasized throughout the book, the usefulness of corpora in language studies depends upon the research question being investigated. As Hunston (2002: 20) argues, 'They are invaluable for doing what they do, and what they do not do must be done in another way.' It is also important, as will be seen in Units B3–B6 as well as in Section C of this book, that readers learn how to formulate research questions amenable to corpus-based investigation.

Finally, it is important to keep in mind that the findings based on a particular corpus only tell us what is true in that corpus, though a representative corpus allows us to make reasonable generalizations about the population from which the corpus was sampled. Nevertheless, unwarranted generalizations can be misleading.

The development of the corpus-based approach as a tool in language studies has been compared to the invention of telescopes in astronomy (Stubbs 1996: 231). If it is ridiculous to criticize a telescope for not being a microscope, it is equally pointless to criticize the corpus-based approach for not doing what it is not intended to do (Stubbs 1999).

This final unit of Section A reviewed the corpus-based approach to language studies, drawing examples from a wide range of studies. The first part of this unit (Units A10.2–A10.8) explored the major areas in linguistics which have used corpus data. They include lexicographic and lexical studies (Unit A10.2), grammatical studies (Unit A10.3), register variation and genre analysis (Unit A10.4), dialect studies and language varieties (Unit A10.5), contrastive and translation studies (Unit A10.6), diachronic studies and language change (Unit A10.7), and language learning and teaching (Unit A10.8). These areas will be further discussed in Section B and explored in Section C of this book. The second part of this unit (Units A10.9–A10.14) introduced other areas of linguistics in which the corpus-based

Summary

approach has started to play a role. They include semantics (Unit A10.9), pragmatics (Unit A10.10), sociolinguistics (Unit A10.11), discourse analysis (Unit A10.12), stylistics and literary studies (Unit A10.13), and forensic linguistics (Unit A10.14). In Unit A10.15, we also discussed a number of limitations of the corpus-based approach to language studies, which readers should keep in mind when reading the excerpts in Section B and exploring specific research questions in Section C of this book. These warnings are also useful when readers pursue their own corpus-based language studies.

LOOKING AHEAD

Having introduced the key concepts in corpus linguistics and having considered the applications of corpora in language studies, we are now ready to move on to Section B of the book, which will further discuss, on the basis of excerpts from published works, major issues in corpus linguistics and the use of corpora in linguistics.

SECTION B
Extension

Section A introduced some important concepts in corpus linguistics. We also briefly considered the use of corpora in a range of areas of language studies. In this section, readers will get an opportunity to read excerpts from published material which will go into a number of research areas in more depth. The excerpts presented in this section have been selected carefully using a number of criteria. The primary criterion is the originality, importance and influence of the published work in the area of study. The second criterion is its current relevance. Given the second criterion, it is unsurprising that, with a few exceptions, the majority of the works in this section were published in or after 1998. The final criterion is a pragmatic one – some materials, while interesting, simply did not fit well with the overall design of the book. We are fully aware that a book of this size cannot possibly include all of the publications which meet the stated criteria. Also, the recentness of data included here can be viewed as an advantage or a disadvantage, depending upon one's viewpoint. Those who view it as a disadvantage might argue that the book is wanting in historical background. Nevertheless, it can also be argued reasonably that the focus on current research is as important as historical depth. Readers interested in the historical dimension of corpus linguistics should look to Biber, Conrad and Reppen (1998), Kennedy (1998), and McEnery and Wilson (2001), which have already covered much of the history of corpus analysis. Furthermore, readers can refer to McCarthy and Sampson (2004) for an anthology of important publications on corpus linguistics including papers from its early years.

The excerpts selected using the stated criteria are designed to help readers understand a number of key concepts in corpus linguistics and bring them up to date with the latest developments in corpus-based language studies. They are also selected to get readers familiarized with a particular area of study so that they will be ready to explore the case studies in Section C. Note that in order to save space in this book, the excerpts are presented without notes or references. Readers are advised to refer to the original publications for these. We would also like to remind readers that the terminology used in each excerpt may differ slightly from that adopted in this book. At no point, however, does this slight imprecision interfere with the general argument presented.

This section consists of two parts. Part 1 'Important and controversial issues' (Units B1–B2) discusses further some important or controversial issues in corpus linguistics introduced in Section A, namely corpus representativeness and balance (Unit B1), and the pros and cons of the corpus-based approach (Unit B2). Part 2 'Corpus linguistics in action' (Units B3–B6) presents corpus-based studies in some of the areas we considered in Section A including, for example, lexical and grammatical studies (Unit B3), language variation (Unit B4), contrastive and diachronic studies (Unit B5), and finally language teaching and learning (Unit B6).

Unit B1
Corpus representativeness and balance

B1.1 INTRODUCTION

We learned from Units A1 and A2 that one of the commonly accepted defining features of a corpus is representativeness. Representativeness is typically achieved by balancing the corpus through sampling a wide range of text categories which are defined primarily in terms of external criteria. It was also noted that it could be difficult both to define a target population and to determine the proportions across text categories. In this unit, we discuss corpus representativeness and balance, using two excerpts from published work. This discussion will provide a more thorough grounding in these ideas than has been achieved so far in the book.

B1.2 BIBER (1993)

Biber has published widely on the issue of corpus design. In this section we present an extract from his article 'Representativeness in corpus design', originally published in *Literary and Linguistic Computing* in 1993. In this article, Biber addresses a number of issues related to how to achieve corpus representativeness, including the meaning of representativeness, defining a target population, stratified vs. proportional sampling, sampling within texts and issues relating to sample size. Biber's ideas of corpus representativeness are generally accepted and certainly widely reported (e.g. McEnery and Wilson 2001; Tognini-Bonelli 2001; Hunston 2002). The extract below is from the first section of the article.

Biber, D. 1993. 'Representativeness in corpus design'. *Literary and Linguistic Computing* **8/4: 243–57.**

Text B1.2
D. Biber

Some of the first considerations in constructing a corpus concern the overall design: for example, the kinds of texts included, the number of texts, the selection of particular texts, the selection of text samples from within texts, and the length of text samples. Each of these involves a sampling decision, either conscious or not.

The use of computer-based corpora provides a solid empirical foundation for general purpose language tools and descriptions, and enables analyses of a scope not otherwise possible. However, a corpus must be 'representative' in order to be appropriately used as the basis for generalizations concerning a language as a whole; for

D. Biber

example, corpus-based dictionaries, grammars, and general part-of-speech taggers are applications requiring a representative basis (cf. Biber, 1993b).

Typically researchers focus on sample size as the most important consideration in achieving representativeness: how many texts must be included in the corpus, and how many words per text sample. Books on sampling theory, however, emphasize that sample size is not the most important consideration in selecting a representative sample; rather, a thorough definition of the target population and decisions concerning the method of sampling are prior considerations. Representativeness refers to the extent to which a sample includes the full range of variability in a population. In corpus design, variability can be considered from situational and from linguistic perspectives, and both of these are important in determining representativeness. Thus a corpus design can be evaluated for the extent to which it includes: (1) the range of text types in a language, and (2) the range of linguistic distributions in a language.

Any selection of texts is a sample. Whether or not a sample is 'representative', however, depends first of all on the extent to which it is selected from the range of text types in the target population; an assessment of this representativeness thus depends on a prior full definition of the 'population' that the sample is intended to represent, and the techniques used to select the sample from that population. Definition of the target population has at least two aspects: (1) the boundaries of the population – what texts are included and excluded from the population; (2) hierarchical organization within the population – what text categories are included in the population, and what are their definitions. In designing text corpora, these concerns are often not given sufficient attention, and samples are collected without a prior definition of the target population. As a result, there is no possible way to evaluate the adequacy or representativeness of such a corpus (because there is no well-defined conception of what the sample is intended to represent).

In addition, the representativeness of a corpus depends on the extent to which it includes the range of linguistic distributions in the population; i.e. different linguistic features are differently distributed (within texts, across texts, across text types), and a representative corpus must enable analysis of these various distributions. This condition of linguistic representativeness depends on the first condition; i.e. if a corpus does not represent the range of text types in a population, it will not represent the range of linguistic distributions. In addition, linguistic representativeness depends on issues such as the number of words per text sample, the number of samples per 'text', and the number of texts per text type. [. . .]

However, the issue of population definition is the first concern in corpus design. To illustrate, consider the population definitions underlying the Brown corpus (Francis and Kucera 1964/79) and the LOB corpus (Johansson et al., 1978). These target populations were defined both with respect to their boundaries (all published English texts printed in 1961, in the United States and United Kingdom respectively), and their hierarchical organizations (fifteen major text categories and numerous subgenre distinctions within these categories). In constructing these corpora, the compilers also had good 'sampling frames', enabling probabilistic, random sampling of the population. A sampling frame is an operational definition of the population, an itemized listing of population members from which a representative sample can be chosen. The LOB corpus manual (Johansson et al., 1978) is fairly explicit about the sampling frame used: for books, the target population was operationalized as all 1961 publications listed in *The British National Bibliography Cumulated Subject Index, 1960–1964* (which is based on the subject divisions of the Dewey Decimal Classification system), and for periodicals and newspapers, the target population was operationalized as all 1961 publications listed in *Willing's Press Guide* (1961). In the case of the Brown corpus, the sampling frame was the collection of books and periodicals in the Brown University Library and the Providence Athenaeum; this sampling frame is less representative of the total texts in print in 1961 than the frames used for construction of the Lancaster–Oslo/Bergen (LOB) corpus, but it provided well-defined boundaries and an itemized listing of members. In choosing and evaluating a sampling frame, considerations of efficiency and cost effectiveness must be balanced against higher degrees of representativeness.

Given an adequate sampling frame, it is possible to select a probabilistic sample. There are several kinds of probabilistic samples, but they all rely on random selection. In a simple random sampling, all texts in the population have an equal chance of being selected. For example, if all entries in the *British National Bibliography* were numbered sequentially, then a table of random numbers could be used to select a random sample of books. Another method of probabilistic sampling, which was apparently used in the construction of the Brown and LOB corpora, is 'stratified sampling'. In this method, subgroups are identified within the target population (in this case, the genres), and then each of those 'strata' are sampled using random techniques. This approach has the advantage of guaranteeing that all strata are adequately represented while at the same time selecting a non-biased sample within each stratum (i.e. in the case of the Brown and LOB corpora, there was 100 per cent representation at the level of genre categories and an unbiased selection of texts within each genre).

Note that, for two reasons, a careful definition and analysis of the non-linguistic characteristics of the target population is a crucial prerequisite to sampling decisions. First, it is not possible to identify an adequate sampling frame or to evaluate the extent to which a particular sample represents a population until the population itself has been carefully defined. A good illustration is a corpus intended to represent the spoken texts in a language. As there are no catalogues or bibliographies of spoken texts, and since we are all constantly expanding the universe of spoken texts in our everyday conversations, identifying an adequate sampling frame in this case is difficult: but without a prior definition of the boundaries and parameters of speech within a language, evaluation of a given sample is not possible.

The second motivation for a prior definition of the population is that stratified samples are almost always more representative than non-stratified samples (and they are nevertheless representative). This is because identified strata can be fully represented (100% sampling) in the proportions desired, rather than depending on random selection techniques. In statistical terms, the between-group variance is typically larger than within-group variance and thus a sample that forces representation across identifiable groups will be more representative overall. Returning to the Brown and LOB corpora, a prior identification of the genre categories (e.g. press reportage, academic prose, and mystery fiction) and subgenre categories (e.g. medicine, mathematics, and humanities within the genre of academic prose) guaranteed 100% representation at those two levels; i.e. the corpus builders attempted to compile an exhaustive listing of the major text categories of published English prose, and all of these categories were included in the corpus design. Therefore, random sampling techniques were required only to obtain a representative selection of texts from within each subgenre. The alternative, a random selection from the universe of all published texts, would depend on a large sample and the probabilities associated with random selection to assure representation of the range of variation at all levels (across genres, subgenres, and texts within subgenres), a more difficult task.

B1.3 ATKINS, CLEAR AND OSTLER (1992)

The excerpt included in this section is extracted from Atkins *et al.*'s paper 'Corpus design criteria', originally published in *Literary and Linguistic Computing* in 1992. This excerpt (section 4 of the paper) addresses the major difficulties in defining a target population, contrasting the sets of texts received vs. those produced by a target group, and the internal (linguistic) vs. external (social) means of defining such groups.

Atkins, S., Clear, J. and Ostler, N. 1992. 'Corpus design criteria'. *Literary and Linguistic Computing* 7/1: 1–16.

Text B1.3
S. Atkins,
J. Clear and
N. Ostler

4 Population and sampling

In building a natural language corpus one would like ideally to adhere to the theoretical principles of statistic sampling and inference. Unfortunately, the standard approaches to statistical sampling are hardly applicable to building a language corpus. First, it is very difficult (often impossible) to delimit the total population in any rigorous way. Textbooks on statistical methods almost always focus on clearly defined populations. Secondly, even if the population could be delimited, because of the sheer size of the population and given current and foreseeable resources, it will always be possible to demonstrate that some feature of the population is not adequately represented in the sample. Thirdly, there is no obvious unit of language (words? sentences? texts?) which is to be sampled and which can be used to define the population. We may sample words or sentences or 'texts' among other things. Despite these difficulties, some practical basis for progress can be established. An approach suggested by Woods, Fletcher, and Hughes is to accept the results of each study as though any sampling had been carried out in the theoretically 'correct' way, to attempt to foresee possible objections. In corpus linguistics such a pragmatic approach seems the only course of action. Moreover, there is a tendency to overstate the possibility and effects of experimental error: indeed, good scientific estimation of the possibility and scale of experimental error in statistics of natural language corpora is seldom carried out at all.

All samples are *biased* in some way. Indeed the sampling problem is precisely that a corpus is inevitably biased in some respects. The corpus users must continually evaluate the results drawn from their studies and should be encouraged to report them [. . .].

The difficulty of drawing firm conclusions when the number of observed instances is few underlines the methodological point made by Woods, Fletcher, and Hughes: that researchers should question how the sample was obtained and assess whether this is likely to have a bearing on the validity of the conclusions reached.

4.1 *Defining the Population*

When a corpus is being set up as a sample with the intention that observation of the sample will allow us to make generalizations about language, then the relationship between the sample and the target population is very important. The more highly

S. Atkins,
J. Clear and
N. Ostler

specialized the language to be sampled in the corpus, the fewer will be the problems in defining the texts to be sampled. For a general-language corpus, however, there is a primary decision to be made about whether to sample the language that people hear and read (their *reception*) or the language that they speak and write (their *production*).

Defining the population in terms of language reception assigns tremendous weight to a tiny proportion of the writers and speakers whose language output is received by a very wide audience through the media. However, most linguists would reject the suggestion that the language of the daily tabloid newspapers (though they may have a very wide reception) can be taken to represent the language production of any individual member of the speech community.

The corpus builder has to remain aware of the reception and production aspects, and though texts which have a wide reception are by definition easier to come by, if the corpus is to be a true reflection of native speaker usage, then every effort must be made to include as much production material as possible. For a large proportion of the language community, writing (certainly any extended composition) is a rare language activity. Judged on either of these scales, private conversation merits inclusion as a significant component of a representative general language corpus. Judged in terms of production, personal and business correspondence and other informal written communications form a valuable contribution to the corpus.

To summarize, we can define the language to be sampled in terms of language production (many producers each with few receivers) and language reception (few producers but each with many receivers). Production is likely to be greatly influenced by reception, but technically only production defines the language variety under investigation. However, collection of a representative sample of total language production is not feasible. The compiler of a general language corpus will have to evaluate text samples on the basis of *both* reception and production.

4.2 *Describing the Population*

A distinction between external and internal criteria is of particular importance for constructing a corpus for linguistic analysis. The internal criteria are those which are essentially *linguistic*: for example, to classify a text as formal/informal is to classify it according to its linguistic characteristics (lexis/diction and syntax). External criteria are those which are essentially *non-linguistic*. Section 6 contains a list of attributes which we consider relevant to the description of the language population from which corpus texts are to be sampled. These attributes, however, are all founded upon extra-linguistic features of texts (external evidence). Of course, the internal criteria are not independent of the external ones and the interrelation between them is one of the areas of study for which a corpus is of primary value. In general, external criteria can be determined without reading the text in question, thereby ensuring that no linguistic judgements are being made. The initial selection of texts for inclusion in a corpus will inevitably be based on external evidence primarily. Once the text is captured and subject to analysis there will be a range of linguistic features of the text which will contribute to its characterization in terms of internal evidence. A corpus selected entirely on internal criteria would yield no information about the relation between language and its context of situation. A corpus selected entirely on external criteria would be liable to miss significant variation among texts since its categories are not motivated by textual (but by contextual) factors.

Summary

This unit discussed in more detail the key concepts of corpus representativeness and balance as introduced in Unit A2. It is clear that in order to achieve corpus balance and representativeness, it is essential to define the target population and apply appropriate sampling techniques. There is also a consensus that external (or situational, social or extra-linguistic) rather than internal (or linguistic) criteria should be used in initial corpus design. It is important to note that corpus representativeness and balance are also closely associated with the sample vs. monitor corpus models. Readers are advised to refer to Units A2.3 and A7.9 for a discussion of this debate.

LOOKING AHEAD

In the next unit, we will discuss the pros and cons of the corpus-based approach.

Unit B2
Objections to corpora: an ongoing debate

B2.1 INTRODUCTION

A more controversial issue than the issue of representativeness/balance is the question of whether corpus data should be used at all in linguistic analysis, language teaching and language learning. From the 1950s onwards, the corpus-based approach to linguistics was severely criticized, notably by Noam Chomsky (see Unit A1.2; see also Aarts 2001; McEnery and Wilson 2001: 5–12). Chomsky's criticism represented an extreme argument against using corpus data. Such a hostile attitude towards corpora has lost credibility in recent years to the extent that the value of corpora is no longer questioned seriously (see Nelson 2000). However, among those who support the use of corpora there are divergent views on their usefulness for certain purposes. As Murison-Bowie (1996: 182) observes, '[t]he strong case suggests that without a corpus (or corpora) there is no meaningful work to be done. The weak case is that there are additional descriptive pedagogic perspectives facilitated by corpus-based work which improve our knowledge of the language and our ability to use it.' The scholars holding the 'strong' view of corpus use include John Sinclair and Michael Stubbs, while those who hold the so-called 'weak' view of corpus use include, for example, Henry Widdowson. In this unit we will include three excerpts from published material to give readers an opportunity to understand the different viewpoints and to form their own views. The first excerpt is from an article by Widdowson, published in *Applied Linguistics* in 2000, where he outlines some reservations he has about the use of corpus data. The second excerpt is a response to Widdowson from Michael Stubbs, published in *Applied Linguistics* in 2001. The final excerpt is cited from de Beaugrande's article which summarizes the debate between Widdowson and Sinclair over the role of corpora, particularly in language teaching.

B2.2 WIDDOWSON (2000)

Widdowson has been mischaracterized as being anti-corpus linguistics. According to Widdowson (personal communication), however, this is not true: 'What I am critical about are the claims that have been made for it, and that's a very different thing, of course.' Widdowson (2000) criticizes some of the claims that have been made in corpus linguistics and CDA (see Unit A10.12). The issues about corpus linguistic claims raised in this article are developed further in Widdowson (2003) while those relating to discourse analysis (especially CDA) are taken up in Widdowson (2004). The excerpt below, cited from Widdowson (2000), focuses on his criticisms of corpus linguistics.

Text B2.2
H. Widdowson

Widdowson, H. 2000. 'The limitations of linguistics applied'. *Applied Linguistics* 21/1: 3–25.

I would argue, then, that linguistics applied is, in effect, misapplied linguistics. And I want now to give some substance to this argument by giving detailed (and critical) consideration to two developments in E-language description that have become extremely influential in our field over the 20 years since this journal was founded. One of these is corpus linguistics: the quantitative analysis of text *en masse*. The other is critical linguistics: the qualitative analysis of particular texts. Each claims to have something quite radical to reveal about language use: corpus analysis about the language that people actually produce, and critical analysis about what they really mean by it. And each also makes claims for the relevance of their analyses to the formulation of problems as experienced in the real world which I believe to be questionable. In this respect, both are, to my mind, examples of linguistics applied. They warrant close attention because an examination of their analyses and the significance claimed for them seem to me to bring out the issues I have raised in clear relief. Furthermore, the identification of shortcomings (as I see them) at the same time, more positively, points out where applied linguistics might come in.

Corpus linguistics first. There is no doubt that this is an immensely important development in descriptive linguistics. That is not the issue here. The quantitative analysis of text by computer reveals facts about actual language behaviour which are not, or at least not immediately, accessible to intuition. There are frequencies of occurrence of words, and regular patterns of collocational co-occurrence, which users are unaware of, though they must be part of their competence in a procedural sense since they would not otherwise be attested. They are third person observed data ('When do they use the word X?') which are different from the first person data of introspection ('When do I use the word X?'), and the second person data of elicitation ('When do you use the word X?'). Corpus analysis reveals textual facts, fascinating profiles of produced language, and its concordances are always springing surprises. They do indeed reveal a reality about language usage which was hitherto not evident to its users.

But this achievement of corpus analysis at the same time necessarily defines its limitations. For one thing, since what is revealed is contrary to intuition, then it cannot represent the reality of first person awareness. We get third person facts of what people do, but not the facts of what people know, nor what they think they do: they come from the perspective of the observer looking on, not the introspective of the insider. In ethnomethodical terms, we do not get member categories of description. Furthermore, it can only be one aspect of what they do that is captured by such quantitative analysis. For, obviously enough, the computer can only cope with the material products of what people do when they use language. It can only analyse the textual traces of the processes whereby meaning is achieved: it cannot account for the complex interplay of linguistic and contextual factors whereby discourse is enacted. It cannot produce ethnographic descriptions of language use. In reference to Hymes's components of communicative competence (Hymes 1972), we can say that corpus analysis deals with the textually attested, but not with the encoded possible, nor the contextually appropriate.

To point out these rather obvious limitations is not to undervalue corpus analysis but to define more clearly where its value lies. What it can do is reveal the properties of text, and that is impressive enough. But it is necessarily only a partial account of real language. For there are certain aspects of linguistic reality that it cannot reveal at all. In this respect, the linguistics of the attested is just as partial as the linguistics of the possible.

Problems arise when this partial description is directly applied to determine language prescription for pedagogic use, when claims are made that this provides the only language worth teaching. Now that we know what real language looks like, the argument runs, we expose learners to it and rid our classrooms of contrivance. This follows the common tradition of dependency whereby the language subject is designed in reference to, indeed in deference to, developments in the linguistics discipline. So it was that previously structuralist linguistics defined language content in terms of the formal units of the possible. So it is now that corpus linguistics defines language content in terms of the authentic patterns of the attested. Linguistics applied in both cases. For in both cases, what is not taken into account is the pedagogic perspective, the contextual conditions that have to be met in the classroom for language to be a reality for the learners. Whether you are dealing with the possible or the attested, you still have to make them appropriate for learning. And it is just such conditions that applied linguistics has somehow to take cognizance of.

There are two points (at least) to be made about the direct application of linguistic description of the kind that corpora provide, and both are fairly obvious. The first is that the textual product that is subjected to quantitative analysis is itself a static abstraction. The texts which are collected in a corpus have a reflected reality: they are only real because of the presupposed reality of the discourses of which they are a trace. This is decontexualized language, which is why it is only partially real. If the language is to be realized as use, it has to be recontextualized. The textual findings of frequencies and co-occurrences have to be contextually reconstituted in the classroom for their reality to be realized, and this reconstitution must obviously be based on very different contextual conditions than those which activated the texts in the first place. The contextual authenticity from which textual features originally derived cannot be ratified by language learners precisely *because* they are learners and do not know (yet) how to do it. It is sometimes assumed to be self-evident that real language is bound to be motivating, but this must depend on whether learners can make it real.

The first point, then, is that however the language is to be contextually abstracted, as units of the possible or the attested, they have to be recontextualized in the classroom so as to make them real for learners. And effective for learning. This is the second point. All language is realized as use in respect to some purpose or other. The purpose of language use in the classroom is to induce learning, and it is appropriate to the extent that it fulfils that purpose. There is a widespread assumption that the classroom is of its nature an unreal place and that this has to be countered by having it replicate the world outside as closely as possible. In the foreign language classroom, this world is taken to mean that of the native speakers of the language concerned. But there seems no good reason why the classroom cannot be a place of created context, like a theatre, where the community of learners live and move and have their being in imagined worlds, purposeful and real for them. To conceive of the classroom in this way is to acknowledge that what is being taught and learned is something designed as a *subject*, not the language as experienced by its native speaker users but something that native speakers cannot experience at all, namely a foreign language. And its foreignness has to be locally accounted for by the devising of appropriate contexts in the classroom which have to activate the process of learning.

This design of the subject is the concern of applied linguistics, whereby descriptive findings are pedagogically treated to make them appropriate as prescription. And the findings of corpus descriptions are potentially highly serviceable to this purpose. It would be a grave mistake to disregard the attested, as it would be to disregard the possible. After all, for many learners at least, the language as realized by its users is the goal to which they aspire and to which they will seek to approximate by the process of gradual authentication. But it would be equally mistaken to suppose that what is textually attested uniquely represents real language and that this reality should define the foreign language subject. A number of people concerned with foreign language pedagogy have expressed reservations along similar lines about the assumption that the findings of corpus linguistics should determine the content of the language subject (Cook 1998; Owen 1993; Widdowson 1991).

It is important to stress that the expression of such reservations does not amount to a denial of the pedagogic potential of corpus description, particularly, perhaps, in the *process* of analysis, in the use of concordancing to develop discovery procedures for learners (see Tribble and Jones 1998; Wichmann *et al.* 1997). Nor do these reservations betoken a conservative allegiance to outmoded ideas or a stubborn refusal to countenance change, as has sometimes been suggested. Rather it is an effort to refer these descriptive developments to applied linguistic principles by subjecting them to critical appraisal, so as to establish criteria of relevance. It is, of course, important that we should take new modes of description, and their findings, into account in the design of language instruction, but that is very different from accepting them on trust and without question.

To make the point more clearly, let me refer to a particular example. It has been John Sinclair's innovative vision more than anything else that has been the impetus behind developments in the corpus description of English, and he speaks with unique authority as a linguist. He has recently offered a number of precepts for language teachers, the first of which is: *Present real examples only*. These precepts are, as he himself acknowledges, based entirely on descriptive data: 'They are not concerned with psychological or pedagogical approaches to language teaching' (Sinclair 1997: 30). But it seems obvious that if they do not take pedagogic considerations into account, they cannot reasonably be taken as pedagogical precepts. As proposals informed, and so limited, by a linguistic perspective, they may well be worth thinking about, but that is another thing. And to be critically cautious in this way is not at all to confirm teachers in the belief that they know everything they need to know about the language they teach. But Sinclair thinks it is:

> A few leading figures in applied linguistics (e.g. Widdowson 1992) effectively endorse this complacency by casting doubt on the relevance of corpus findings to the process of teaching and learning languages.
>
> (Sinclair 1997: 30)

But to cast doubt is to express uncertainty about a claim, not to reject it out of hand. It can only be construed as negative if you assume the self-evident validity of linguistics applied. But from an applied linguistic point of view, casting doubt on the relevance of linguistic description for pedagogic prescription is, I would argue, precisely what we should be about. And this is particularly so in this case. Since, on Sinclair's own admission, the claim for relevance is not informed by pedagogic considerations, it seems only reasonable to entertain some doubt. Indeed, I would argue that the value of such proposed precepts is precisely *because* they provoke a critical response. The alternative is to accept the relevance unilaterally as a self-evident fact, and this means to fashion pedagogic reality to fit the descriptive findings: a clear case of linguistics applied (see also Aston 1995).

I have argued that corpus linguistics provides us with the description of text, not discourse. Although textual findings may well alert us to possible discourse signifi-cance and send us back to their contextual source, such significance cannot be read off from the data. The factual data constitute evidence of the textual product: what evidence they might provide of the discourse process is a matter for further enquiry. The same is true, I think, of the other area of description I want to consider. In spite of its name, critical discourse analysis is, I would maintain, also an exercise in text description. And it, too, has a way of assigning discourse significance to textual facts. The supposed area of relevant application is here, however, much broader and of much greater moment. Whereas corpus descriptions have been brought to bear on matters of language pedagogy, critical discourse analysis is concerned with education in a more general sense: it is directed at making people more sociopolitically aware of the way language is used to manipulate them. The purpose is to be applauded. It is hard to think of one which is of greater social significance or more squarely within the scope of applied linguistics. But the question needs to be raised again as to what kind of enquiry this is, and whether here, too, we should take the relevance of its findings on trust, or cast a doubt or two.

B2.3 STUBBS (2001b)

As Widdowson's criticisms focus largely on corpus linguistics, Stubbs's response mainly focuses upon the nature of data and methods in corpus linguistics while also addressing the criticism of critical discourse analysis in passing. Stubbs totally bypasses the criticism of the use of corpus data in language teaching. However, readers will have an opportunity to consider this latter criticism in the next section. In the excerpt presented below Stubbs argues that Widdowson's criticism 'is flawed by its misinterpretation of the data, methods and central concepts of corpus linguistics'. Reader can refer to de Beaugrande (2001) for a detailed critical analysis of Widdowson (2000).

Stubbs, M. 2001b. 'Texts, corpora, and problems of interpretation: a response to Widdowson'. *Applied Linguistics* **22/2: 149–172.**

Text B2.3
M. Stubbs

The background arguments: description and applications

There are two background arguments in Widdowson. The first is a long-running debate, to which Widdowson himself contributed so influentially, namely: can concepts from theoretical linguistics be applied directly to real world problems (the 'linguistics applied' position), or must applied linguistics develop its own theories, which mediate and interpret findings both from linguistics and also from other disciplines (the 'applied linguistics' position)? Nowadays, partly thanks to Widdowson, the second position may seem self-evident, though whether we need a separate layer of mediation is doubtful. In line with the second position, Widdowson questions whether descriptions of language use, especially those based on corpora, can be applied to textual interpretation.

The second argument is that, since the 1980s, linguistics has undergone a profound shift from a primary interest in internalized I-language to externalized E-language (Chomsky 1988), that is from introspective to attested data. Two developments have led to this increased interest in 'real' language: the technology which now allows corpus linguists to describe very large quantities of text; and the attempt by critical discourse analysts to reveal the ideological assumptions of texts. Widdowson argues that neither perspective, on I-language or E-language, provides the whole truth. Presumably, therefore, they should be combined, though Widdowson makes no proposal as to how this might be done.

Widdowson accepts that corpus linguistics is 'an immensely important development in descriptive linguistics', which has revealed a previously unsuspected 'reality about language usage' (p. 6), but he emphasizes that this provides 'only a partial account of real language' (p. 7). The partiality is evident, he argues, in the lack of correspondence between corpus findings and native speaker intuitions: since they are contrary to intuition, they cannot be the full story.

So, the problems concern the relations between linguistic descriptions, the unsuspected reality which they reveal, and interpretations of these descriptions. And this involves very different things: interpretations are subjective, but they must nevertheless be related to findings which are objective, insofar as they have been discovered by replicable methods in publicly accessible data. In the context of critical discourse analysis, this leads us into deep Whorfian waters, when patterns of language use are related to ideologies held by individuals or social groups (Stubbs 1997b). We must try to disentangle public data and private interpretations, cause and correlation, and also weak and strong forms of Whorfian arguments. For example, it might be that systematic differences in language use correlate with, but do not cause, identifiable ideologies. Everything therefore depends on whether we can provide a clear statement of the logic of the positions.

The data and methods of corpus linguistics

First therefore, we require an accurate statement of the data and methods of corpus linguistics.

Possible, attested, and probable

Widdowson (2000: 7) follows Hymes (1972) in distinguishing between what is formally possible, contextually appropriate, and actually attested, and claims (p. 7) that corpus linguistics deals only with the textually attested. He then repeatedly opposes 'the attested' and 'the possible' (pp. 7–8, 23, but also pp. 10, 19). The misleading nature of this opposition becomes most apparent perhaps in this statement (p. 8): 'it would be . . . mistaken to suppose that what is textually attested uniquely represents real language'.

But who supposes this? Not, as far as I am aware, any corpus linguists. Corpus linguistics is not concerned with what happens to occur (at least once): indeed its methods are generally designed to exclude unique instances, which can have no statistical significance. It is concerned with a much deeper notion: what frequently and typically occurs. What frequently occurs in texts is only a small proportion of what seems to be possible in the system (Pawley and Syder 1983), and the more relevant opposition is between what is possible and what is probable (Kennedy 1992).

In any case, instances can be interpreted only against a background of what is typical. Corpus linguistics therefore investigates relations between frequency and typicality, and instance and norm. It aims at a theory of the typical, on the grounds that this has to be the basis of interpreting what is attested but unusual. Priority is given to describing the commonest uses of the commonest words. (Sinclair *et al.* (1998) illustrate software which gives an operational definition of typicality.)

Widdowson's repeated use of the term 'attested' subtly colours his whole argument. It is important to be clear whether any given data fragment has actually occurred, or whether it has been invented by the linguist as an illustration. But any single occurrence is, in itself, of little interest for the description of the language as a whole.

Observational data, introspective data, and mental models

Widdowson distinguishes (p. 6) three complementary types of data: third-person observations, second-person elicitations, and first-person intuitions. What do *they* actually say? What would *you* say? And what do I think I say? (See also Widdowson 1996b: 72–3.) This is a valuable and elegant suggestion, but Widdowson does not discuss how these three levels of reality relate to each other, or how such relations could be empirically investigated.

Long before corpus linguistics, we knew that people do not talk as they believe they do, and corpus linguists now often point out how radically intuition and use may diverge. Certainly, these relations between behavioural and psycholinguistic data are under-investigated, but a start has been made. Fillmore (1992) provides a detailed argument for combining corpus-based and introspective data; Moon (1998) uses corpus data to propose lexical schemas and prototypes; and Sinclair (1991a: 113) proposes a specific hypothesis about the systematic relation between intuition and use. In order to answer questions such as 'what is the meaning of a given linguistic form?', we have to study quantitative data on its uses, admit the variability of the examples, and formulate a prototype.

Partiality, point of view, and reality

Widdowson argues that 'the linguistics of the attested is just as partial as the linguistics of the possible' (p. 7, also pp. 3, 5, 24), but admits that 'all enquiry is partial' (p. 23). He is also sceptical of attempts to study language in the 'real' world (pp. 3, 5), yet he concedes that corpus analysis reveals 'a reality about language usage which was hitherto not evident to users' (p. 6). Burrows elegantly formulates the paradoxical nature of this reality:

> Computer-based concordances, supported by statistical analysis, now make it possible to enter hitherto inaccessible regions of the language |which| defy the most accurate memory and the finest powers of discrimination.
>
> (Burrows 1987: 2–3)

137

M. Stubbs

So, what is it that we can see from this new point of view? A set of concordance lines is a sample of a node word together with a sample of its linguistic environments, often defined as a span of words to left and right. In Saussurean (1916: 171) terms, a syntagmatic relation holds between items *in praesentia*, which co-occur in a linear string. A concordance line is a fragment of *parole*, where a single instance of syntagmatic relations can be observed. We are interested in more, however, than what happens to have occurred once in such a fragment. A paradigmatic relation is a potential relation between items *in absentia*, which have a psychological reality ('des termes *in absentia* dans une série mnémonique virtuelle', *ibid.*: 171). If paradigmatic relations are seen as a virtual mental phenomenon, then they are unobservable.

In an individual text, neither repeated syntagmatic relations, nor any paradigmatic relations at all, are observable. However, a concordance makes it possible to observe repeated events: it makes visible, at the same time, what frequently co-occurs syntagmatically, and how much constraint there is on the paradigmatic choices. The co-occurrences are visible on the horizontal (syntagmatic) axis of the individual concordance lines. The repeated paradigmatic choices – what frequently recurs – are equally visible on the vertical axis: especially if concordance lines are re-ordered alphabetically to left or right (Tognini-Bonelli 1996).

Since concordances make repetitions visible, this can lead to an emphasis on the repetitive and routine nature of language use, possibly at the cost of striking individual occurrences (the difficult relation between frequency and salience again). Frequency is not necessarily the same as interpretative significance: an occurrence might be significant in a text precisely because it is rare in a corpus. But unexpectedness is recognizable only against the norm.

These repetitions can now be studied. A major part of the patterning revealed by concordances is the extent of phraseology, which is not obvious to speakers, and has indeed been ignored by many linguists. The patterns have been discovered, but not created, by the computer. The test of this claim, and a major strength of computer-assisted corpus analysis, is that findings can be replicated on publicly accessible data: there is always an implicit prediction that you will find the same patterns in independent corpora. These probabilistic semantic patterns (collocations, colligations, etc.) revealed across many speakers' usage in corpora are not within the control of individual speakers, and are not reducible to anything else (Carter and Sealey 2000). Where I agree with Widdowson is in his insistence that their cognitive influence has yet to be stated clearly.

Interpretation and convention

Widdowson emphasizes the different possible interpretations of lexical and grammatical features.

However, one of the deepest problems – which Widdowson does not raise – is the relation between interpretation and convention. It is currently fashionable to emphasize the interpretative aspects of text analysis, and to play down the pervasive patterning in data, and many theorists are sceptical of the view that meanings are explicit in text. This scepticism is evident both in linguistic theories of pragmatics, such as relevance theory (Sperber and Wilson 1995), and also in a broad tradition of interpretative sociology (to which Widdowson, p. 6, alludes), in work by Garfinkel and Cicourel onwards.

Batstone (1995), also with reference to critical discourse analysis, tries to distinguish between stable semantic (notional) aspects of textual meaning and unstable context-dependent pragmatic (attitudinal) meaning. However, Levinson (1983: 11) points out that some pragmatic meanings are conventionally encoded. And a major finding of corpus linguistics is that pragmatic meanings, including evaluative connotations, are more frequently conventionally encoded than is often realized (Kay 1995; Moon 1998; Channell 2000). Both convention and interpretation are involved, but it is an empirical question to decide how much meaning is expressed by conventional form-meaning relations, and how much has to be inferred.

Concepts of convention and norm raise problems in the not infrequent cases when interpretations diverge. I have no space here for detailed examples, but readers might check the divergent connotations given for *cronies* in different corpus-based dictionaries. Is it a neutral word for '(male?) friends'? Or a pejorative word connoting 'disreputable friends'? Or does it even imply 'criminal activities'? These divergences are themselves open to empirical corpus study.

Process and product

Widdowson repeatedly argues that corpus linguistics provides us with a description of text as product, not discourse as process (pp. 6, 9, 10). Since a text is a 'static semantic patchwork' (pp. 7, 17, 22), which has been taken out of its social context of inference and interpretation, we can study only 'textual traces' (pp. 7, 11, 21, 22) of discourse process.

This is perfectly true, though the problem is very widespread in empirical disciplines. Recognizing the problem obviously does not solve it, but it shows that corpus linguistics is trying to develop observational, empirical methods of studying meaning, which are open to the same tests as are applied in other disciplines. For example, consider the parallels between corpus linguistics and geology, which both assume a relation between process and product. By and large, the processes are invisible, and must be inferred from the products.

Geologists are interested in processes which are not directly observable, because they take place across vast periods of time. What is observable is individual rocks and geographical formations: these products are the observable traces of processes which have often taken place a long time in the past. They are highly variable, because any specific instance is due to the local environment. Nevertheless, these variable products are due to highly general processes of destruction (such as erosion) and construction (such as sedimentation) (Love 1991).

Corpus linguists are interested in processes which are not directly observable because they are instantiated across the language use of many different speakers and writers. What is directly observable is the individual products, such as utterances and word combinations. (In addition, repetitions of such patterns, across time, can be made observable if different occurrences are displayed by concordancers and other software: see above.) These individual word combinations are the observable traces of general patterns of collocation and colligation. They are highly variable due to local socio-linguistic contexts. Nevertheless, these variable products are due to highly general processes of probability and speaker expectation.

Summary

Widdowson's account of corpus linguistics, and hence of associated problems of interpretation, lacks a discussion of

- the empirical, observational methods used in corpus semantics;
- the ontological status of the patterns which are revealed;
- the balance in language use of convention and interpretation;
- the relation between individual instances and general patterns.

B2.4   WIDDOWSON (1991) vs. SINCLAIR (1991b): A SUMMARY

Stubbs (2001b) does not consider Widdowson's (2000) criticism of the application of corpus data in language teaching simply because he believes that the criticism is 'over a non-issue' and it is 'much ado about nothing' (*ibid.*: 170). Yet Widdowson's criticism was not a new one and has been condoned by others (see Seidlhofer 2003: 77–123 for a discussion of the controversy). Indeed the opinions expressed on the usefulness of corpora in language teaching were at least ten years old when Widdowson (2000) was published. As early as 1991, at the Georgetown University Round Table on Languages and Linguistics, there was a heated debate between Widdowson and Sinclair over the use of corpus data in language learning. The paper by de Beaugrande provides a critical review of this debate. The following is an excerpt from his paper.

Text B2.4
R. de
Beaugrande

de Beaugrande, R. [date unknown]. 'Large corpora and applied linguistics: H. G. Widdowson versus J. McH. Sinclair'. Accessed 16 April 2004 (at http://beaugrande.bizland.com/WiddowSincS.htm).

In 1991, a controversy arose at the Georgetown University Round Table on Languages and Linguistics during an interchange between Henry Widdowson and John Sinclair. After carefully analysing the two published papers and separately discussing the issues with each of the two linguists, I have concluded that their respective positions are closer together than the controversy might suggest. Widdowson seems to have argued from some positions which are not actually his, and attributed to his opponent some positions which are definitely not Sinclair's.

   A predictable crux of the controversy was how corpus evidence might relate to the 'competence' of native speakers on the one hand and to the needs of learners of English as a Foreign Language (hereafter EFL) on the other. As a noted spokesperson for applied linguistics in EFL, Widdowson (1991: 14) felt provoked by Sinclair's typical criticisms, and cited this one: 'we are teaching English in ignorance of a vast amount of basic fact' (Sinclair 1985: 282). To be sure, Sinclair has not blamed the teachers, but the sources they are offered, such as dictionaries, viz:

> Teachers and learners have become used to a diet of manufactured, doctored, lop-sided, unnatural, peculiar, and even bizarre examples through which, in

the absence of anything better, traditional dictionaries present the language.
It is perhaps the main barrier to real fluency.

(1988: 6f)

Nonetheless, Widdowson seemed indignant that 'linguists' who have debarred 'discrimination against languages' should practice 'discrimination against ideas about language'; and that 'linguists have no hesitation in saying that certain ideas held by the uninformed commoner or language teacher are ill-conceived, inadequate, or hopelessly wrong', and in 'rubbishing the theories of colleagues with relish in prescribing their own' (1991: 11). By these tactics, each linguist's 'point of view is sustained by eliminating all others, so that the diversity of experience is reduced in the interests of intellectual security' (1991: 11).

My own detailed studies of the discourse of theoretical linguists in considerable detail (e.g. Beaugrande 1991) confirm Widdowson's remarks. But we should make due allowance for the fact that theoretical linguistics has been largely an enterprise for replacing real language with ideal language existing nowhere except in some 'linguistic theory' (cf. Beaugrande 1997a, 1997b, 1998a, 1998b). In consequence, the major resources for rationally adjudicating theories or models become unavailable, and debaters merely contest that 'my idealisation is better than yours!' At that stage, 'rubbishing the theories of colleagues' and 'eliminating' other 'points of view' become prominent tactics.

The same mode of linguistics would naturally shower 'haughty disapproval, not to say disdain' upon the attempts of 'applied linguists' to 'appropriate' its 'ideas', as Widdowson (1997: 146) has more recently complained (see Beaugrande 1998b for a riposte posted on this website). This posture is not just the ordinary casual 'disdain' of authentic experts for ordinary people. It is the calculated defence of a *sham expertise* that could be severely imperiled by applications, e.g., ones that would quickly debunk Chomsky's (1965: 33) straight-faced denial that 'information regarding situational context' 'plays any role in how language is acquired, once the mechanism' – the 'language acquisition device' – 'is put to work' 'by the child'.

So those earlier polemic tactics ensued from replacing real language with ideal language, whereas the arguments Widdowson was castigating here were being marshalled *against* this very replacement by Sinclair, as they have also been by Pike, Chafe, Firth, Halliday, Hasan, Schegloff, Roy Harris, and many others. Unfortunately, the reinstatement of real language at the rightful centre of modern linguistics cannot be achieved without strenuous 'discrimination against ideas about language' which *really are* 'ill-conceived, inadequate, or hopelessly wrong' but which have been enthroned by linguists whose 'theories' must be sustained by 'rubbishing' the others. And, our own objective is *just the opposite* of 'reducing' the 'diversity of experience' 'in the interests of intellectual security'; we are resolve to *disrupt* the *unearned* 'intellectual security' of linguists, theoretical or applied, who have indeed 'reduced the diversity of experience' of language and discourse and left us with a 'trivial picture' (Halliday 1997: 25).

Widdowson's paper proposed a contrast between the two positions. Whereas the one claims 'objectivity' and 'correctness' in 'descriptions of language', the other adopts 'the relativist or pluralist position on the nature of knowledge':

The principles or equality and objectivity are comfortable illusions. Descriptions of language are not more or less correct but more or less influential, and therefore prescriptive in effect. They tell us less about truth

141

than about power, about the privilege and prestige accorded to acknowledged authority . . . We cannot any longer be sure of our facts. It is not a very
comfortable position to be in.

(1991: 11f)

Despite the first person pronouns ('us', 'we'), Widdowson avoided committing
himself to this 'pluralist position', but he did imply that Sinclair opposes it by invoking
'basic fact' 'about which teachers were previously ignorant' (Widdowson 1991: 12).

Widdowson then posed the rhetorical question 'what kind of fact is it that comes
out of computer analysis of a corpus of text?' (1991: 12). Characteristically, he did not
answer it here or anywhere else in the paper by quoting a single 'corpus fact'; at one
point, he speculated on the 'relative frequency' of specific words without 'having any
evidence immediately to hand' (1991: 17). Instead, he evoked the 'distinction' drawn
between 'externalised language' versus 'internalised language' (1991: 12) by none
other than Chomsky, the linguist who has memorably taken the most 'relish' in
'rubbishing the theories of colleagues' while 'prescribing his own'. Moreover, Chomsky
(1991: 89) has 'doubted very much that linguistics has anything to contribute' to
'teaching' (Chomsky 1991: 89), as Widdowson (1990: 9f) has elsewhere acknowledged
even whilst rating 'Chomsky's position as consistent with the position I expressed'
(but see below). The genuine opposition is still between real language versus ideal
language, which, I have asserted, can seriously mislead the language teaching profession.

Widdowson (1991: 12–15) also invoked a further series of oppositions or
dichotomies we might do well to deconstruct. These included 'competence' versus
'performance' (of course); 'the possible' versus 'the performed' (after Hymes 1972);
'knowledge' in 'the mind' versus 'behaviour' (Chomsky again); and 'first person' versus
'third person perspective' (Widdowson's own theme, e.g. 1997: 158f), which should
not be misconstrued as referring to the morphology of English verbs. Sinclair was
reproached for conveying the 'clear implication' that the corpus is identical with the
language, and for excluding the first pole of each opposition while allowing only for
the second:

> You do not represent language beyond the corpus: the language is repre-
> sented by the corpus. What is not attested in the data is not English; not real
> English at any rate . . . what is not part of the corpus is not part of compe-
> tence . . . What is not performed is just not possible.
>
> (Widdowson 1991: 14)

Against this supposed position of 'the work of Sinclair and his colleagues',
Widdowson quoted Greenbaum (1988: 83) that 'the major function of the corpus is'
'to supply examples that represent language beyond the corpus'. But this position is
just as much Sinclair's, e.g.: 'language users treat the regular patterns as jumping off
points, and create endless variations to suit particular purposes' (Sinclair 1991: 492).
His real position should concur with the notion the collocability and colligability of
the lexicogrammar of English are partly realised by the collocations and grammatical
colligations of discourse and partially innovated against (Beaugrande 2000).

Sinclair was astounded to be stuck in the straw-man realist position of 'what is not
attested in the data is not real English' and 'what is not performed is just not possible'.
If he held those positions, he would stop expanding the corpus straightaway because
nothing more is 'possible' and because any differing data would be 'not real English',

R. de
Beaugrande

whereas he has in fact insisted, at times to the dismay of agitated project sponsors, that the corpus must be hugely expanded. He would also have to assume that the sources of his corpus are the linguistic equivalent of the sum total all 'possible' sources, whereas he candidly asserts that a much wider selection of spoken data would have already been included but for severe problems of labour and expense.

The evolution of modern linguistics proffers an ironic context for another one of Widdowson's (1991: 13) polarities: 'Chomsky's view is that you go for the possible, Sinclair's view is that you go for the performed'. By any realistic measure, Chomsky's programme has always gone for the *impossible*, advocating, with tireless self-confidence, one project after another that never materialise and never could – a 'grammar' that is 'autonomous and independent of meaning'; a solution to 'the general problem of analysing the process of "understanding" ' by 'explaining how kernel sentences are understood'; an account of how human 'children' 'acquire language' by 'inventing a generative grammar that defines well-formedness and assigns interpretations to sentences even though linguistic data' are 'deficient' (1957: 17, 92; 1965: 201); and more others than I have room to list here (for a thorough analysis of Chomskyan discourse, see now Beaugrande 1998b).

Here we can look to Hjelmslev (1969 [1943]: 17) for the most striking formulation, this one concerning the 'possible': 'the linguistic theoretician must' 'foresee all conceivable possibilities', including 'texts and languages that have not appeared in practice' and 'some of which will probably never be realised'. Easy enough to say once you decide (as we saw Hjelmslev do) that 'linguistic theory cannot be verified (confirmed or invalidated) by reference to any existing texts and languages'.

Chomsky (1965: 25, 27) fulfilled Hjelmslev's vision in the most facile manner when he simply installed, by fiat, just such a 'theory' in the 'language acquisition device' of the human child: 'as a precondition for language learning' the child 'must possess a linguistic theory that specifies the form of the grammar of a possible human language' plus 'a strategy for selecting a grammar' by 'determining which of the humanly possible languages is that of the community'. This is definitely not the position of Widdowson, who has firmly rejected the concept of 'internalisation' by means of a 'universal Chomskyan language acquisition device' (1990: 19).

The conception of the 'possible' is too abstract to be very useful for language pedagogy anyway. Learners of English as a non-native language produce many utterances which may not seem possible to the teacher's intuition, but, as I have noted, we are currently finding new motives for doubting the reliability of intuition. Far more relevant is what is or is not both 'possible' and 'performed' at the learners' *current stage of skills and knowledge*, since that is all we can realistically hope to build upon. There, we can productively orient our approach toward large corpora of *learners' English*, such as have been collected by Sylviane Granger at the University of Louvain (cf. Granger 1996) and by John Milton at the Hong Kong University of Science and Technology (cf. Milton and Freeman 1996). Such data can also systematically alert teachers and learners to typical problems such as language interference.

Another of Widdowson's polarities we might deconstruct is the one between 'knowledge' in 'the mind' versus 'behaviour', the latter term perhaps reminding language teachers of behaviourist pedagogy and Skinnerean behaviourism. But linking a large corpus with behaviour and behaviourist methods would be flawed for at least two reasons. The more obvious reason is that the behaviourist 'audio-lingual' method with its pattern drills and prefabricated dialogues was based on mechanical language patterns more than on authentic data; it equated language with behaviour in order to reduce language, whose relative complexity it could not grasp, to behaviour, whose

143

relative simplicity seemed ideal for 'conditioning', 'reinforcement' and so on; and the method was backed up by heavy behaviourist commitments in general pedagogy and by the prestige and authority of American military language institutes, where 'drills' are literally the 'order of the day'. Nor does Sinclair advocate a teaching method whereby learners parrot back corpus data; on the contrary, he has expressly counselled against 'heaping raw texts into the classroom, which is becoming quite fashionable', and in favour of having 'the patterns of language to be taught undergo pedagogic processing' (1996).

The more subtle reason is that corpus data are not equivalent to 'behaviour' in the 'externalised' sense which Widdowson's polarities imply and which is often encountered in discussions of pedagogy, e.g., when a 'syllabus' 'identifies' 'behavioural skills' (Sinclair 1988: 175). Instead, they are *discourse*, and the distinction is crucial. External behaviour consists of observable corporeal enactments, of which the classic examples in behaviourist research were running mazes, pulling levers, and pressing keys. Discourse is behaviour in that externalised sense only as an array of articulatory and acoustic operations, or, for written language, of inscriptions and visual recognitions; and no one has for a long time – certainly not Sinclair – proposed to describe language in those terms, nor does a corpus represent language that way. When discourse realises lexical collocability and grammatical colligability by means of collocations and colligations, the 'performed' continually re-specifies and adjusts the contours of the 'possible'. In parallel, 'knowledge' in 'the mind' decides the *significance* of the 'behaviour'. Sinclair's true position is that these operations are far more delicate and specific than we can determine without extensive corpus data. Moreover, analysing corpus data is less equivalent to *observing behaviour* than to *participating in discourse*.

Summary

This unit presented three excerpts from published material in order to explore the pros and cons of the corpus-based approach. These characterize well the so-called strong and weak cases for the use of corpus data. Between these two poles are many milder (positive or negative) reactions to corpus data (see Nelson 2000, section 5.3.3 for an overview of these reactions). Nevertheless, the discussion in this unit clearly shows that while some reservations remain about the use of corpus data, corpora have generally been accepted as valuable linguistic resources. Readers are reminded that the corpus-based approach and the intuition-based approach are not conflicting but complementary (see Unit A1.5). We have already noted that the corpus-based approach is not all-powerful (see Unit A10.15). The usefulness of a corpus is typically dependent on the research question researchers intend to address using the corpus. Also, corpora do not necessarily provide explanations for what we see. This remains the task of the human analyst, drawing upon a wide range of resources and methodologies. Nevertheless, corpora are undoubtedly valuable resources in linguistic analysis and language teaching, as has been shown in Unit A10 and will be demonstrated in the second part (Units B3–B6) of this Section.

Unit B3
Lexical and grammatical studies

B3.1 INTRODUCTION

We noted in Units A10.2 and A10.3 that lexical and grammatical studies are probably the areas that have benefited most from corpus data. This unit presents four excerpts which discuss the use of corpora in these areas. The first excerpt, Krishnamurthy (2000) demonstrates the use of corpora in collocation analysis, which is followed by an excerpt from Partington (2004), which studies semantic preference. For grammatical studies, Carter and McCarthy (1999) explore the English GET-passive in spoken discourse while Kreyer (2003) compares genitive and *of*-construction in written English.

B3.2 KRISHNAMURTHY (2000)

In this excerpt, Krishnamurthy briefly reviews the British tradition of text analysis, from Firth to Sinclair, which is closely tied to collocation. On the basis of this review, Krishnamurthy discusses the relevance of corpus linguistics to collocation analysis. This excerpt provides background knowledge for Case Study 1 in Section C, where we will explore collocations in the BNC and discuss the implications of our findings for pedagogical lexicography.

Krishnamurthy, R. 2000. 'Collocation: from *silly ass* to lexical sets' in Heffer C., Sauntson H. and Fox G. (eds) *Words in Context: A Tribute to John Sinclair on his Retirement*. Birmingham: University of Birmingham.

Text B3.2
R. Krishnamurthy

2 Collocation theory

We are generally indebted to Firth for channeling the attention of linguists towards lexis (Halliday 1966: 14) and specifically for originating the concept of collocation. Writing from the perspective of stylistics, and viewing meaning as dispersed in a range of techniques working at a series of levels, Firth said: 'I propose to bring forward as a technical term, meaning by *collocation*, and to apply the test of *collocability*' (1957: 194).

Firth established the distinction between cognitive and semantic approaches to word-meaning on the one hand, and the linguistic feature of collocation on the other (196): 'Meaning by collocation is an abstraction at the syntagmatic level and is not directly concerned with the conceptual or idea approach to the meaning of words. One

R. Krishnamurthy

of the meanings of *night* is its collocability with *dark*, and of *dark*, of course, collocation with *night*'. He then proceeded to develop the notion of collocation with reference to examples from specific registers, genres, authors, and texts.

His first example concerned the meaning by collocation of *ass* in the colloquial English of his day, in sentences like 'You silly ass!'. He suggested that the set of potential adjectives with *ass* was limited (e.g. *silly, obstinate, stupid, awful*; and *young* rather than *old*) and that the plural form *asses* was not very common in this meaning.

In the next example, he discussed collocation in the language of Edward Lear's limericks and noted that '*man* is generally preceded by *old*, never by *young* . . . One of the "meanings" of *man* in this language is to be immediately preceded by *old* in collocations of the type, *There was an Old Man of* . . . The collocability of *lady* is most frequently with *young*, but *person* with either *old* or *young*. In this amusing language, there is no *boy* or *young man* or *woman*, neither are there any plurals for *man, person,* or *lady*.'

Throughout his discussion of collocation, Firth implied a quantitative basis for the notion, stating actual numbers of occurrences for words in Lear's limericks as well as using expressions like *habitual, commonest, frequently, not very common, general, usual* and *more restricted*.

Halliday identified the need to measure the distance between two collocating items in a text: 'some measure of significant proximity, either a scale or at least a cut-off point' (1966: 152). Importantly, he brought in the concept of probability, thereby validating the need for data, quantitative analyses, and the use of statistics: 'The occurrence of an item in a collocational environment can only be discussed in terms of probability' (159). He also first suggested the idea of using collocation to identify lexical sets, which will be explored further at the end of this paper: 'It is the similarity of their collocational restriction which enables us to consider grouping lexical items into lexical sets' (156).

Sinclair had already started to collect data and perform quantitative analyses using computers in the 1960s. He devised computational methods of looking at collocation in a corpus, and introduced the parameter of position (Sinclair *et al.* 1970: 8): 'Collocations of very frequent words are positionally restricted . . . Collocation which is positionally free . . . will commonly be an indication of lexical patterning' [Sinclair *et al.* 1970 is now reprinted as Krishnamurthy (ed.) 2004]. The very frequent words are of course mainly grammatical words, and Firth had already suggested the separate term *colligation* for collocations involving these. It is the positionally free i.e. lexical, co-occurrences which are now usually termed *collocations*.

In later work, Sinclair presented the 'open choice principle' and the 'idiom principle' as two simultaneously available speaker strategies, with collocation as an important aspect of the latter (1987b: 325): 'Collocation . . . illustrates the idiom principle. On some occasions, words appear to be chosen in pairs or groups and these are not necessarily adjacent'. He used the corpus frequency of node and collocate to distinguish between *downward* collocation, involving a more frequent node A with a less frequent collocate B, and *upward* collocation: 'Upward collocation of course is the weaker pattern in statistical terms, and the words tend to be elements of grammatical frames, or superordinates. Downward collocation by contrast gives us a semantic analysis of a word' (326).

3 Corpus linguistics

R. Krishnamurthy

'In the past, linguists and lexicographers relied mostly on native-speaker intuitions. These were often incorrect, or at least inexact, because each of us has only a partial knowledge of the language, we have prejudices and preferences, our memory is weak, our imagination is powerful (so we can conceive of possible contexts for the most implausible utterances), and we tend to notice unusual words or structures but often overlook ordinary ones' (Butterfield and Krishnamurthy forthcoming) [later published as Butterfield and Krishnamurthy (2000)]. To this one can add that intuition-based made-up examples in dictionaries have been shown to be poor, especially as regards collocation (Krishnamurthy 1996: 145–6; 1997: 45–6, 54–5).

Technological advances in computers, the assembling of large language corpora, and the development of computational techniques for corpus analysis have made possible performance-oriented descriptions of language based on data, in contrast to the previous competence-oriented, intuition-based ones. Indeed, as English becomes a global language, no individual or group can keep up with language change on a worldwide scale; and with the arrival of the Internet in particular, these changes are taking place too fast for our intuitions to assimilate them (Butterfield and Krishnamurthy forthcoming).

Hunston and Francis (2000: 14) equate Sinclair's work with corpus linguistics and argue that it 'prioritises a method, or group of methods, and a kind of data rather than a theory'. The central position occupied by 'a method, or group of methods' in corpus linguistics suggests that advances in methodology will represent progress in this field.

The first step in the established methodology is pattern recognition, to identify the objects of study. For example, the corpus linguistics definition of a word is usually 'a sequence of characters bounded by spaces'. Though this definition may be unsatisfactory, it allows us to proceed in a reasonably objective manner. Other classificatory tasks have been carried out successfully, such as the morphological grouping of word-forms into lemmas (lemmatization) and the syntactic grouping of word-forms into word-classes (part-of-speech tagging), and semantic and pragmatic annotations of corpora are currently being attempted, but the fundamental weakness of these operations is that they crucially depend on pre-existing ideas about language.

The second step in the methodology is the generation of frequency lists, which enable us to place the objects of study in a hierarchy. If we accept that the rank of a word-form in a corpus frequency list has some relationship to the importance of that word-form in the linguistic system, frequency lists enable us to decide, on a more objective basis, which word-forms to analyse.

Concordances represent the third stage in the methodology. Concordances allow us to observe the behaviour of a particular word-form in detail. The close inspection of numerous examples of a word-form, together with some context from the original source text, will probably always remain the ultimate process of verification for attributing any linguistic feature to that word-form. As regards collocation, the ability of the computer to sort the examples alphabetically by the words occurring to the left or right of the target word (keyword or node) enable us to notice more easily patterns involving adjacent words, but collocates at a greater distance can still be difficult to spot. And it is impossible for the human brain to distinguish 'statistically significant' collocations merely from the patterns observed in the concordances.

Collocational tools offer the fourth objective methodological element in corpus analysis. Collocation is among the linguistic concepts which have benefited most from the advances in corpus linguistics. Only with large-scale computer corpora can we raise the status of collocation beyond the simple definition 'the co-occurrence of two lexical items in a text within a certain proximity', which privileges every vagary of performance-error, idiolect or creativity equally, and establish collocation as a powerful organisational principle of language.

With large corpora, we can discuss 'statistically significant' collocations, both those which operate across all language types, as well as those which are restricted in their distribution to particular linguistic modes, genres, varieties, and so on. Computer-generated lists of collocates for a word-form, whether based on raw frequency or more sophisticated statistical measures, focus our attention on prominent candidates for significant collocation, and collocation profiles including positional information make more detailed analysis of syntagmatic or phraseological units possible.

Using the ideas expressed in the academic literature described in Section 2, we might state the primary requirements of collocational software as follows: a) co-occurrences should be identifiable; b) the span or window of collocation (i.e. the distance between collocating items) should be specifiable and adjustable; c) the frequency of co-occurrence should be calculable; d) statistical measures that enhance the notion of 'significance' should be available; e) positional information i.e. where the collocate occurs with respect to the node, should be available; f) if one wants to distinguish between colligation and collocation, it should be possible to distinguish between grammar words and lexical words among the collocates; g) it should be possible to check the distribution of a collocate across source texts to see whether it is restricted to a particular author, mode, vintage, genre, variety, domain etc.

B3.3 PARTINGTON (2004)

Semantic prosody and semantic preference are two important concepts related to collocation (see Unit A10.2). Semantic prosody refers to the collocational meaning hidden between words, or in Louw's (2000: 57) terms, 'a form of meaning which is established through the proximity of a consistent series of collocates'. For example, *HAPPEN* typically refers to some unpleasant situation. Semantic preference, on the other hand, refers to the frequent co-occurrence of a lexical item with a group of semantically related words, or so-called 'lexical set' (Hoey 1997: 3). In this excerpt Partington explores semantic preference in English.

Text B3.3
A. Partington

Partington, A. 2004. '"Utterly content in each other's company": semantic prosody and semantic preference'. *International Journal of Corpus Linguistics* 9/1: 131–156.

2 Semantic preference

2.1 *Introduction and definition*

Stubbs (2001) following Sinclair (1996, 1998) lists four separate kinds of relation between lexical units, in ascending order of abstraction:

(i)   collocation: the relationship between lexical item and other lexical items;
(ii) colligation: the relationship between lexical item and a grammatical category: 'For example, the word-form *cases* frequently co-occurs with the grammatical category of quantifier, in phrases such as *in some cases, in many cases*' (Stubbs 2001:65);
(iii) semantic preference;
(iv) semantic (Stubbs prefers the term *discourse*) prosody.

The third of these, *semantic preference*, is defined by Stubbs as 'the relation, not between individual words, but between a lemma or word-form and a set of semantically related words' (2001:65). He cites the item *large* which often co-occurs with words for 'quantities and sizes', such as *number(s), scale, part, amounts, quantities*. Elsewhere he explains that an item shows semantic preference when it co-occurs with 'a class of words which share some semantic feature (such as words to do with "medicine" or "change")' (2001:88).

Partington (1998: 34–39) examines the intricate semantic preferences of the item *sheer*, an intensifying adjective. This study also illustrates how the typical syntactic realisations of the phrases involving this item are interdependent on those meaning preferences. A concordance of the item was prepared from the newspaper and academic corpora combined [. . .]. Further analysis showed how it collocated with a number of items from specific semantic sets. These included (i) 'magnitude', 'weight' or 'volume', e.g. *the sheer volume of reliable information, and sheer size of the stadium*, (ii) items expressing 'force', 'strength' or 'energy', e.g. *the sheer force of his presence*. A typical phraseology here was found to be '*the sheer* (magnitude or force word) *of* (noun phrase)'.

A third group consisted of words expressing (iii) 'persistence', e.g. '*sometimes through sheer insistence*'. But here the typical structure is not '*the sheer* (noun phrase) *of* (noun phrase)'. Instead we find *sheer* frequently preceded by words expressing means or manner, e.g. *through, out of, by, because of, by virtue of*.

In yet another group, *sheer* collocates with nouns expressing (iv) 'strong emotion', e.g. *sheer joy in life, in moments of sheer exhilaration* and (v) physical quality e.g. *he didn't have . . . the sheer glamour of evil*. This use is often found as part of a list of qualities or emotions, e.g. *nothing can replace the skill, wit, or sheer expertise . . .*

Partington (1998: 39–47) then goes on to compare this behaviour with other items sometimes considered synonymous with *sheer*, such as *complete, pure* and *absolute*, and discovers that none of them share these semantic preferences and are involved in different typical syntactic structures.

2.2 *Group preference*

In the previous section we explored the syntactic–semantic conduct of a single item. In another, earlier study using the then 10 million-word *Cobuild* corpus of general English, Partington (1991) examines the collocational behaviour of the group of items called *maximizers* by Quirk *et al.* (1985), a subset of *amplifying intensifiers*. They include *absolutely, perfectly, entirely, completely, thoroughly, totally* and *utterly*. The first of these, *absolutely*, displays a distinct semantic preference in collocating with items which have a strong or superlative sense: among its significant collocates (i.e. those which co-occur with the keyword three times or more) in the *Cobuild* corpus were: *delighted, enchanting, splendid, preposterous, appalling, intolerable*. There appears to be an even balance between favourable and unfavourable items. This preference is well documented in

149

A. Partington

modern corpus-based dictionaries: '*Absolutely* can be used to add force to a strong adjective' (*Cambridge International Dictionary of English* 1995: 5).

Perfectly, on the other hand, exhibits a distinct tendency to co-occur with 'good things', including:

> *capable, correct, fit, good, happy, harmless, healthy, lovely, marvellous, natural*

but the fact that we also find *ridiculous* and *odd* demonstrates that language users are able to swim against the current – can 'switch off' primings – when they seek particular creative effects. Semantic prosody and preference do not ordain that counter examples *cannot* happen, just that they *seldom* happen. And the value and status of such counter instances could not be more momentous. As Hoey (forthcoming) [later published as Hoey (2004)] tells us 'fluency comes from conformity to them' whereas 'creativity comes from the switching off of primings'.

Of particular interest to the present study, however, is the behaviour of a subgroup within the maximizers which consists of *completely, entirely, totally* and *utterly*. These four have a great deal in common, in particular, they share a large number of collocates (i.e. there is a high degree of *collocational overlap* amongst them). In contrast there is very little collocational overlap between these items and *absolutely* or *perfectly* or, indeed, any of the other items listed in Quirk *et al.* as amplifiers.

A closer investigation of their individual significant collocates was most intriguing. If we examine *utterly*, which is, as it were, the 'purest specimen' of the group, we discover that the modified items almost invariably express either the general sense of 'absence of a quality' or some kind of 'change of state'. Those collocates which fall into the first category are: *helpless, useless, unable, forgotten*; those in the second category are: *changed, different*; whereas *failed, ruined, destroyed* seem to fall into both categories. Only two collocates could be interpreted as having a semantic element of 'favourable' – *pleasant* and *clear*. This data coincides with Greenbaum's (1970: 73) and Louw's (1993: 160–161) observation that *utterly* tends to have unfavourable implications. This said, the existence of *utterly pleasant* demonstrates again how tendencies are not inviolable and can be exploited by speakers for particular effects, e.g. (from the *Cobuild* written corpus):

> (58) Their relationship in fact was so complete that they were *utterly content in each other's company.*

However, the semantic preference of *utterly* for 'absence' and 'change' is more fundamental still. Of course, these preferences and the bad prosody may well be connected. In universal terms, in human psychology the presence of something is preferable to its absence (to have is better than to have not). In equally universal terms, change causes anxiety to the human psyche (see Hunston (forthcoming) [later published as Hunston (2004)] on the value of *change*).

Turning to *totally* we find again a large number of 'absence' or 'lack of' collocates:

> *bald, exempt, incapable, irrelevant, lost, oblivious, uneducated, unemployed, unexpected, unknown, unpredictable, unsuited, ignored, excluded, unfamiliar, blind, ignorant, meaningless, unaware, unable, vanished, naked, without*

and also a set of 'change of state', 'transformation' words:

destroyed, different, transformed, absorbed, failed

Completely co-occurs with the following 'absence' words:

devoid, disappeared, empty, forgotten, hopeless, ignored, lost, oblivious, vanished, gone, lacking, unexpected, bald, naked, unaware, innocent, blank, unknown, finished (and, perhaps, *dry, alone*)

and these expressing 'change':

altered, changed, destroyed, different.

For *entirely* we find, in the first category:

different, forgotten, unrelated, without, abandoned, unfamiliar, lost, ignorant, lacking, unnecessary, unknown (and, perhaps, *alone, isolated*)

for 'change' we have *different*.

The collocates of *entirely*, however, also seem to encompass a slightly wider range of senses than those of the others. They include a number of words which express an opposition between dependence–independence or relatedness–unrelatedness:

dependent, due, self-sufficient, unrelated, without, isolated.

One last maximizer to deserve a mention is *thoroughly*. This was found in the company of words relating to emotions and states of mind: *annoyed, approved, enjoyed, confused, happy, sure, disgruntled*. It also, strikingly, often co-occurred with words which have something to do with water and washing: *wet, dry, absorbed, cleaned, filtered, muddied* as well as the verbs *wash* and *rinse*. This amplifier evidently retains traces of its ancient sense of *thorough-like*, of penetration, and both water and emotions penetrate 'through and through'.

We might summarize these observations as follows:

Maximizer	Preference for	Prosody
absolutely	hyperbole, superlatives	
perfectly		favourable
utterly	absence/change of state	unfavourable
totally	absence/change of state	
completely	absence/change of state	
entirely	absence/change of state, (in)dependency	
thoroughly	emotions/liquid penetration	

So far, then, we have found evidence of the existence of the following major types of semantic preference: 'factual'–'non-factual', 'absence', 'change', 'emotions' and perhaps 'dependence'–'independence'. This suggests that there may well be closer links than is generally assumed between grammar and lexico-semantic features, in the sense that the two areas may share a number of similar categories and dichotomies. 'Absence', as a marked lexico-semantic feature contrasting with the unmarked feature 'presence', would seem reminiscent of negativity, marked in relation to the unmarked positive, in the grammatical system of *polarity*. In addition, the averral of factuality or non-factuality is also accomplished grammatically through choices in the system of verbal epistemic *modality* (with the major difference, however, that the latter is scalar rather than polar or antithetical). Finally, dependence and independence are the two basic relations between clauses. We may tentatively surmise that more particular clausal relations such as causality, contrast and hypotheticality also have their expression at the level of semantic preference.

We hypothesize, then, that a number of the major grammatical functions are reflected at the lexical level in the phenomenon of preference. This should come as no surprise if we accept that linguistic categories are largely modelled by functional communicative needs. Clearly, the same communicative pressures are active on language at both 'higher' grammatical and 'lower' lexical levels. One of the great challenges currently facing modern linguistics is to describe the precise relationship between these two levels, and semantic preference may well prove a fruitful area of research.

B3.4 CARTER AND McCARTHY (1999)

Carter and McCarthy (1999) discuss the interpersonal meaning of the GET-passive in a 1.5-million-word sample from the CANCODE spoken English corpus and outline some implications for an interpersonal grammar. This excerpt is taken from the discussion and conclusion sections of their paper.

Text B3.4
R. Carter and
M. McCarthy

Carter, R. and McCarthy, M. 1999. 'The English *get*-passive in spoken discourse: description and implication for an interpersonal grammar'. *English Language and Literature* 3/1: 41–58.

5 Discussion

The key to understanding the *get*-passive is that it highlights the stance of the speaker in context towards the event and the grammatical subject. It is a clear case where examining sentences and jettisoning the people who produce them and their contexts of production is inadequate. The *get*-passive might indeed be a linguistic puzzle, but it is considerably demystified the moment we look upon it as something the speaker overlays onto events to mark his/her stance towards those events and their subjects. Some linguists have recognized this, most notably Lakoff (1971), Stein (1979), and Hübler (1991), but the benefit of examining real spoken data is that intuitions on that score can be supported by figures showing actual usage. Our conclusion is that the *get*-passive coincides mostly with adverse or problematic circumstances, but these are adverse/problematic as judged by the speaker. Get also coincides overwhelmingly with the absence of an explicit agent, suggesting that emphasis is on the event/process and the person or thing experiencing the process encoded in the verb phrase, rather than its cause or agent. We have also made tentative statements, supported by (albeit limited) statistics, about the frequency of particular verbs, the collocational tendencies these suggest, and the relative absence of adverbials. But in all cases, such statements are no more than probabilities.

R. Carter and
M. McCarthy

At this point we may usefully distinguish between deterministic grammar and probabilistic grammar. Deterministic grammar deals with matters of structural prescription (e.g. that *be-* and *get-*passives are always formed with the past participle of verbs, rather than the base-form or *ing-*form). Such determinism enables grammars of languages to be codified in a relatively straightforward way, and has served linguists well for centuries. Probabilistic grammar is concerned with statements of what forms are most likely to occur in particular contexts of use, and the probabilities may be stronger or weaker. Itkonen's (1980: 338) contrast between 'correct sentences' and 'factually uttered sentences' is apt here. Probabilistic grammars need real corpus data to substantiate their claims, but statistical data alone are insufficient; evaluation and interpretation are still necessary to gauge the form-function relationships in individual contexts, from which probabilistic statements can then be derived. Probabilistic grammar proposals are not new: Halliday (1961: 259) talked of the fundamental nature of language as probabilistic and not as 'always this and never that'. More recently, Halliday has returned to this theme with considerable quantitative evidence from the study of corpora. He is primarily concerned with how frequently the terms in binary grammatical systems (e.g. *present* versus *nonpresent*) actually occur in relation to each other, and argues that the statistical facts of occurrence are 'an essential property of the system – as essential as the terms of the opposition itself' (1991: 31). Halliday recognizes that a probabilistic statement such as 'agentless *get-*passives are nine times more frequent than *get-*passives with agents' has little predictive power, but argues that it is important for interpretation of the choice of form. Halliday (1992) stresses further that the different probabilities of occurrence in different registers is also important, since it is unlikely that terms in opposition will be equiprobable in a corpus reflecting any given register. This is true of a general language corpus as well, and the one must be measured against the other. Several of Halliday's followers within systemic-functional linguistics have also further pursued the matter of unequal probabilities of occurrence of particular forms: Nesbitt and Plum (1988) take a predominantly quantitative line in their study of the distribution of clause complexes in real data, and are interested in what is more likely and less likely to occur, rather than what is possible. Here, though, we go beyond the statistics of occurrence and are interested in the relationship between the probabilism of forms and their relationships to contexts. In the case of our type (a) *get-*passives, the probabilities are that *get* will occur in informal contexts when speakers are marking attitude. Most probably that attitude denotes concern, problematicness in some way, or, at the very least, noteworthiness of the event beyond its simple fact of occurring. Indeed, no deterministic statement about when speakers will choose *get* instead of *be* can be made; judgements about adversativeness, problematicness, noteworthiness, etc. are socioculturally founded and are emergent in the interaction rather than immanent in the semantics of verb choice, or of selection of voice or aspect. Over and above these concerns are the broader questions of probability of occurrence within particular generic types of spoken text: most of our *get-*passives occur in narrating and reporting contexts. It may be possible to show that probabilities of form–functional correlations are an integral characteristic of genres and one of the means whereby they can be adequately described by linguists. Genre derives from patterned social activity, and those patterns of activity emerge from the accumulated interactions of participants; their linguistic traces are the probabilities upon which grammars can be constructed. Since genres reflect complex activities, the plotting of probabilities should not be mono-dimensional but should investigate the likelihood of different features from different grammatical ranks and categories clustering in any specified context, rather in the way that Biber (1995) demonstrates.

R. Carter and
M. McCarthy

Any grammar which attempts to explicate interpersonal meaning cannot but be probabilistic (i.e. interpretive rather than predictive, to utilize Halliday's terms), since interpersonal meanings are emergent in interaction. This brings us squarely back to our other types of pseudo-passives [. . .]. The passive gradient itself cannot be prescribed deterministically or predicted absolutely. Possible choices of precise structural configuration [. . .] depend on how the speaker cares to position the subject, event and (possible) agents and circumstances relative to judgements about perceived responsibility and involvement of the participants, the inclusion of essential information, and affective factors such as distaste, humour, amazement, etc. reflecting the speaker's reaction to the events. Within particular genres (e.g. gossip, anecdotes), such affective positioning may be more regularly socioculturally conditioned, and manifested in a greater frequency of occurrence of particular forms.

We can now return to some of our other types of structures and see how they occur in ways that highlight their interpersonal meanings just as we did in the case of the type (a) *get*-passives. (28) shows three different choices of perspective on the verb *frame*, concluding with a type (g) structure:

(28) [Speakers are discussing some photographs]
S1 I'm afraid I can't afford to frame them, but erm . . .
S2 But do you want them framed?
S1 I'd love to have them framed.
S2 Well if that's the case then the next time we come [S1 Yeah] we'll take them with us [S1 Mm] and then we'll have them framed. [90113001]

In S1's first turn, the simple active is chosen, and agency is ambiguous, though likely to mean 'I cannot afford to pay someone else to frame them', which would be a challenge to S1's positive face (self-esteem) in Brown and Levinson's (1987) terms. S2's response equally avoids explicit mention of agency, thus preserving face (consider the possible alternatives: *Do you want to have them framed? Do you want them to be framed?*, both of which do or could carry greater implications of outside agency), and focuses on the subject and her needs. S1 then openly admits a desire to have an outside agency perform the task, and S2 agrees. Interpersonal equilibrium is maintained, face is preserved, by strategic choices of perspective upon patient and agent.

(29) includes structures of types (b) and (c):

(29) S1 Do you think school had an impact on you?
S2 Massive, massive, erm but I left it all to the last minute. I, you know, I kept telling myself well I'll work in the end, and in the end I did, but it was in the end, very much in the last two, in the last, like in the last couple of days, project work and whatnot. I'd stay up forty eight hours to **get it done** and stuff like that, which er . . . and I realized, you know, then that, you know, if you put, if I put my mind to what I could do you know . . . but I realized also that it's much easier if you work all the way through, and I had to **get myself organized** then. There was no point you know just leaving it. I had to do it you know. [90175001]

The speaker is centring himself as the topic, and his actions and their consequences for him. Simple active-voice choices on the two highlighted verb-phrases would have been possible, but would not carry the same affective focus on self-discipline, organization and achievement of the speaker's goals; *get*, with its focus on the subject-as-recipient, expresses these aspects of the speaker's narrative evaluation much more powerfully than simple, canonical active-voice alternatives could have done.

6 Conclusion

An interpersonal grammar, if such is needed (and we would argue that our corpus evidence shows that conventional types of description are inadequate to the task of explicating the difference between the various alternatives on the passive gradient), must necessarily be stated in probabilistic/interpretive terms. This does not weaken such a grammar; on the contrary, it lends strength to the enterprise of examining grammar in context, which many grammarians, especially those working within the field of discourse grammar, are currently engaged in, and offers the possibility of harnessing the power of computerized corpora in the service of qualitative research that reaches beyond the bare statistics of occurrence.

   Get-passives and related structures are not the only grammatical features to display strong interpersonal meanings that are best explicated in probabilistic and interpretive terms. McCarthy and Carter (1997) account for right-dislocated elements in this way, using spoken corpus evidence, and McCarthy (1998) investigates a number of grammatical features including speech reporting, tense and aspect, and idiom selection from a similar perspective. We are encouraged in our claims for the *get*-passive by the fact that linguists who have previously investigated the phenomenon have instinctively homed in on features connected with the affective and interactive domains, finding it generally impossible to explain the choice of *get* solely by conventional semantic or syntactic criteria. The present paper has attempted to put the weight of corpus evidence behind other linguists' sound intuitions and to state more precisely the contextual conditions in which the *get*-passive and related forms are likely to occur. Our investigation has, we hope, sharpened the description of the structures and taken a step forward in the understanding of how an interpersonal grammar of English might be formulated.

B3.5 KREYER (2003)

Kreyer (2003) explores the use of genitive and *of*-construction on the basis of 519 instances of the *of*-construction and 179 instances of the genitive in a 45,000-word subcorpus taken from the written section of the BNC. It is argued that the variation of the genitive and *of*-construction can be explained with regard to two major underlying factors, namely 'processability' and the 'degree of human involvement'. This excerpt is from the discussion section of the paper.

Text B3.5
R. Kreyer

Kreyer, R. 2003. 'Genitive and *of*-construction in modern written English: processability and human involvement'. *International Journal of Corpus Linguistics* **8/2: 169–207.**

5 Discussion: processability and human involvement

In this study the variation of genitive and *of*-construction has been analysed with regard to three underlying factors, namely the lexical class of the modifier, the semantic relationship expressed by the constructions, and weight and syntactic complexity. It was an important objective to develop a descriptive framework for each of these factors which, while being sufficient from the view-point of linguistic description, would at the same time allow an efficient statistical analysis. With regard to the first conditioning factor a modified version of Quirk *et al.*'s gender scale, the personality scale, seemed most suitable. To capture the variety of semantic relationships expressed by the two constructions, a paraphrasation system based on traditional categories was applied. The influence of weight and syntactic complexity was analysed separately for instances of premodification and postmodification. The former could conveniently be described in terms of the number of premodifying items of head and modifier. With the latter, the most common types of postmodification (finite clause, non-finite clause and prepositional phrase) were distinguished from apposition and coordination.

The statistical analysis of the conditioning factors has shown that all of them influence the choice of construction. With regard to the lexical class of the modifier, the analysis essentially supported the ranking of the modifiers as depicted on the personality scale. However, the surprising results for collective modifiers indicated that these, as far as the choice between genitive and *of*-construction is concerned, tend to be regarded as a non-personal collectivity. The influence of the semantic relationship was demonstrated by the fact that six out of nine categories had a decisive influence on the choice of construction. With many of these categories a preference for certain classes of modifiers was observed, which contributed to the immediate effect of the semantic relationship. The impact of premodification was shown to be most decisive with extremely modifier- and head-heavy constructions, which led to a favouring of the *of*-construction ('mod+3..', 'mod+2') or the genitive ('head+3..'), respectively. With regard to postmodification the data showed that a *proximity-principle* is at work, i.e. those constructions are usually favoured which guarantee that related constituents are in the vicinity of one another.

So far the conditioning factors have, for the most part, been analysed in isolation from each other. Some concluding remarks on the relative power of the different factors and the way they interact might therefore be helpful to draw a more comprehensive picture of the variation of genitive and *of*-construction in modern written English. In Table 9, factor levels with decisive influence on the choice of construction have been ranked according to the preference of *of*-constructions. The line in the middle of the table divides those factor levels which lead to a significant deviance from the corpus norm (genitive vs. *of*-construction: 25.6%/74.4%) in favour of the *of*-construction (upper half) or the genitive (lower half).

The ranking of the factors gives a first impression of their power. Those factors which are at the extreme ends of the hierarchy have the strongest influence on the choice of construction. The pervasive importance of syntactic factors is most obvious with regard to postmodified modifiers, which impose extremely heavy constraints

Table 9 Hierarchy of decisive factors

Factor level	of *(rel. freq.)*
postmodified modifier (N_1)	100.0%
non-personal (lexical)	98.5%
'objective' relationship (semantic)	98.3%
$N_1 + 3..$ (weight of premodification)	96.8%
'attributive' relationship (semantic)	88.1%
$N_1 + 2$ (weight of premodification)	84.5%
'partitive' relationship (semantic)	81.3%
personified (lexical)	57.1%
personal common noun (lexical)	49.5%
'origin' relationship (semantic)	40.7%
preposition N_2 (right-branching)	40.5%
'kinship' relationship (semantic)	33.3%
$N_2 + 3..$ (weight of premodification)	33.3%
'disposal' relationship (semantic)	30.8%
'possessive' relationship (semantic)	23.9%
personal proper name (lexical)	14.9%

on the choice of construction. These constraints even overrule powerful lexical constraints as can be seen in examples (63) and (64), here repeated as (100) and (101):

(100) The aggressive ardour of the professional golfer who might try to cut the slight dogleg and set himself up for an easier shot into the two-tier green (CS4)
(101) The coming of our friends from the west (ABC)

In these cases, the underlying factor seems to be the requirement of structural and referential clarity, which above has been referred to as the 'proximity principle'. Only if this requirement is met can other factors exert their influence. The lexical class of the modifier shows a decisive influence towards the personal and non-personal poles of the personality scale. With regard to proper names, this factor is only overruled by considerations of weight and syntactic complexity, as the examples above show. Similarly, we find that the occurrence of genitives with non-personal modifiers is restricted to cases of heavy or complex heads, as in example (34), here repeated as (102):

(102) that term's list of the morning lectures for the first-year undergraduates (AOF)

The influence of weight and syntactic complexity is also strongly felt when semantic relationships that favour the genitive, such as 'kinship' or 'possession', show instances of *of*-construction (examples (103) and (104) ((49), (50)).

(103) the son of the Royal Bucks secretary (CS4)
(104) the realms of more important kings (CB6)

Again, if considerations of weight and complexity are not relevant the usual choice with these kinds of relationships is the genitive.

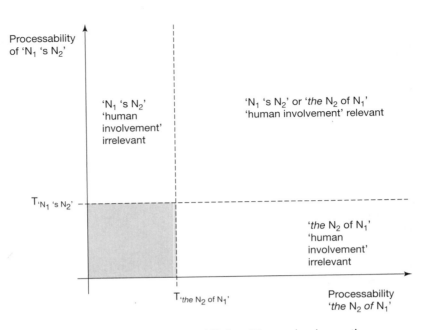

Figure 3 The interaction of 'processability' and 'human involvement'

If we look at the results of this study from a more remote perspective, it seems as if the variation of genitive and *of*-construction can to a large extent be described by two more fundamental principles. The discussion in the previous paragraph has shown that considerations of weight and complexity are decisive with a number of instances and may overrule powerful lexical and semantic factors. This influence can be described by the more general term 'processability'. The second factor, i.e. the semantic and lexical aspect, can largely be described in terms of 'human involvement'. This is obvious with the lexical class of the modifier but also holds true for semantic relationship: mostly we think about 'possession', 'disposal' and 'kinship' in terms of our own species whereas, with partitive or objective relationships, which show a preference for the *of*-construction, the notion of associated human beings is usually very faint. In conclusion, therefore, it might be suggested that a possible descriptive framework for the variation of genitive and *of*-construction could be based on the aspects of 'processability' and 'degree of human involvement'.

As to the relative powers of these two factors the data reveal that considerations of 'processability' are more important than the influence of 'degree of human involvement': if, for example, the choice of the genitive led to extreme difficulties of processing, an *of*-construction would be used, regardless of lexical or semantic factors that might indicate genitive. However, instances of heavy modification of head or modifier occur in only 36 per cent of all cases. Although, then, 'human involvement' may not counteract 'processability' in extreme cases, it can exert its influence in almost two thirds of all phenomena, i.e. in those cases where 'processability' is guaranteed by both kinds of constructions ('N_1's N_2' and '*the* N_2 of N_1'). This situation is depicted in Figure 3. The vertical and the horizontal axes show the processability of genitive ('N_1's N_2') and *of*-construction ('*the* N_2 of N_1'), respectively. For both constructions, there exist threshold levels, $T_{'N1's N2'}$ and $T_{'the N2 of N1'}$, below which the respective constructions will be extremely difficult to process. In cases where the processability for one construction is below the threshold the alternative construction will be used, regardless of considerations of 'human involvement'; in such cases, this factor is irrelevant. 'Human involvement', however, is relevant in those cases where the choice of construction does not influence processability.

To sum up: in this article, I have attempted to develop a more general description of the variation of genitive and *of*-construction. Starting off from the study of four isolated factors, two basic underlying principles, 'processability' and 'human involvement' have been identified which, to a large extent, account for the variation of genitive and *of*-construction. However, this description can still be further refined since secondary factors, such as information status, might be integrated into the above framework. These factors will most probably show their influence in those cases where 'processability' is guaranteed by both constructions and where 'human involvement' is not decisive. Instances which would be left unaccounted for by the two major factors might then be explained and an even more detailed description of the variation of genitive *of*-construction could be arrived at.

This unit used four excerpts to illustrate the applications of language corpora in lexical and grammatical studies. In lexical studies collocation and semantic prosody/preference can only be quantified reliably on the basis of corpus data. We will return to lexical studies in Case Study 1 in Section C, where readers will explore pedagogically oriented corpus-based lexicography. In grammatical studies a corpus-based approach is useful in formulating and testing syntactic theories. It often provides unexpected insights into language use.

Summary

LOOKING AHEAD

Readers will have an opportunity to explore, in Case Study 2 in Section C, the syntactic conditions which may influence a language user's choice between a *to*-infinitive and a bare infinitive following *HELP*. But before that, the next unit discusses the use of corpora in the study of language variation.

Unit B4
Language variation studies

B4.1 INTRODUCTION

When people use language in different social and communicative contexts, their language often differs in terms of both grammatical and lexical choice. Biber *et al.* (1999: 24) indicate that different registers or genres demonstrate consistent patterning. The authors find that many descriptions of general English, based on an averaging of patterns across registers, often obscure such register variation and are thus inaccurate and misleading. People who use the same language in different regions and countries may also talk differently. This unit presents four excerpts from published research in the area of language variation. The first extract, from Biber (1995a), provides an overview of Biber's framework of multifeature/ multidimensional (MF/MD) analysis (see also Unit A10.4 and Case Study 5 in Section C). In the second excerpt, Hyland (1999) undertakes a genre analysis on the basis of corpora of textbooks and research articles. The last two excerpts, Lehmann (2002) and Kachru (2003), are concerned with the regional variation of English.

B4.2 BIBER (1995a)

Biber and his colleagues have explored register and genre variation from three different perspectives: synchronic (e.g. Biber 1985, 1987, 1988), diachronic (e.g. Biber and Finegan 1989) and contrastive (e.g. Biber 1995b). Biber's MF/MD analysis framework has been well received as it establishes a link between form and function. This excerpt outlines the MF/MD approach and provides a background for Case Study 5 in Section C, which will compare conversation and speech in American English using Biber's approach and WordSmith Tools.

Text B4.2
D. Biber

Biber, D. 1995a. 'On the role of computational, statistical, and interpretive techniques in multi-dimensional analysis of register variation'. *Text* 15/3: 314–370.

2 Overview of the multi-dimensional approach to register variation

The multi-dimensional approach to register variation was originally developed for comparative analyses of spoken and written registers in English (e.g., Biber, 1986,

1988). Methodologically, the approach uses computer-based text corpora, computational tools to identify linguistic features in texts, and multivariate statistical techniques to analyse the co-occurrence relations among linguistic features, thereby identifying underlying dimensions of variation in a language.

The primary research goal of the multidimensional approach is to provide comprehensive descriptions of the patterns of register variation, including (1) identification of the underlying linguistic parameters, or dimensions, of variation, and (2) specification of the linguistic similarities and differences among registers with respect to those dimensions. Two primary motivations for the multi-dimensional approach are the assumptions that: (1) generalizations concerning register variation in a language must be based on analysis of the full range of spoken and written registers; and (2) no single linguistic parameter is adequate in itself to capture the range of similarities and differences among spoken and written registers. The approach thus requires analysis of numerous spoken and written registers with respect to numerous linguistic features.

Some of the general characteristics of the multi-dimensional approach are:

1. It is corpus-based, depending on analysis of a large collection of naturally-occurring texts.
2. It uses automated computational techniques to analyse linguistic features in texts. This characteristic enables distributional analysis of many linguistic features across many texts and text varieties.
3. It uses interactive computational techniques to check the analysis of ambiguous linguistic features, ensuring accuracy in the final feature counts.
4. The research goal of the approach is the linguistic analysis of texts, registers, and text types, rather than analysis of individual linguistic constructions.
5. The approach is explicitly multi-dimensional. That is, it is assumed that multiple parameters of variation will be operative in any discourse domain.
6. The approach is quantitative. Analyses are based on frequency counts of linguistic features, describing the relative distributions of features across texts. Multivariate statistical techniques are used to identify co-occurrence patterns among linguistic features and to analyse the relations among texts.
7. The approach synthesizes quantitative and functional methodological techniques. That is, the quantitative statistical analyses are interpreted in functional terms, to determine the underlying communicative functions associated with each empirically determined set of co-occurring linguistic features. The approach is based on the assumption that statistical co-occurrence patterns reflect underlying shared communicative functions.

Dimensions represent distinct groupings of linguistic features that have been empirically determined to co-occur with significant frequencies in texts. It is important to note that the co-occurrence patterns underlying dimensions are identified quantitatively (by a statistical factor analysis) and not on any a priori basis. Dimensions are subsequently interpreted in terms of the communicative functions shared by the co-occurring features. Interpretive labels are posited for each dimension, such as 'Involved versus Informational Production' and 'Narrative versus Non-narrative Concerns'.

In earlier synchronic multi-dimensional analyses of English (e.g., Biber 1986, 1988), approximately 500 texts from 23 registers were analysed, including face-to-face conversations, interviews, public speeches, broadcasts, letters, press reportage, official documents, academic prose, and fiction. Subsequent analyses have used this

Extension

approach to analyse texts from a number of more specialized registers, such as elementary school textbooks and student writing, job interviews, and the writings of individual authors. Linguistic features analysed in these studies include both lexical and grammatical characteristics of texts (see section 2.3 below).

Individual texts, or groups of texts called registers, can be compared along each dimension. Two registers are similar along a dimension to the extent that they use the co-occurring features of the dimension in similar ways. Multi-dimensional analyses show that a pair of registers are often similar along one dimension (i.e., with respect to one set of co-occurring linguistic features) but quite different along another dimension (i.e., with respect to another set of features).

2.1 The use of automated and interactive computational techniques in multi-dimensional analyses

The use of automated and semi-automated (i.e., interactive) computational techniques is a practical rather than necessary aspect of multi-dimensional analyses. Such analyses by hand would be extremely time-consuming, and they are often considerably less reliable and accurate than analyses by computer.

Before the use of computers, empirical discourse analyses were typically based on a few thousand words of text; an analysis of 10,000 words was regarded as a major undertaking that required a long research period. Similarly it was possible to consider only a relatively restricted range of linguistic characteristics; analyses considering 10 different linguistic characteristics were regarded as major projects. In contrast, early multi-dimensional analyses employing computational techniques were based on a much more adequate and representative database: a text corpus over 100 times as large as in most previous analyses (nearly 1 million words of text), and inclusion of a very wide range of linguistic characteristics (67 different features in Biber [1988]).

Needless to say, some linguistic analyses must be checked interactively, because current automated techniques are not sufficiently accurate. For example, the distinction between some past tense verbs and past participial verbs functioning as post-nominal modifiers is notoriously hard for automated computer analyses. All automated grammatical taggers have difficulties dealing with distinctions such as this, and as a result, it is necessary to include interactive post-editing to insure accuracy [. . .].

2.2 Methodological overview of the multi-dimensional approach

The multi-dimensional approach involves the following methodological steps:

1. Texts are collected, transcribed (in the case of spoken texts), and input into the computer. The situational characteristics of each spoken and written register are noted during data collection.
2. The published literature is reviewed, and if necessary supplemented by original grammatical research, to determine the range of linguistic features to be included in the analysis, together with functional associations of individual features (see, for example, Aijmer, 1984; Altenberg, 1984; Beaman, 1984; Chafe, 1982; Coates, 1983; Schiffrin, 1981, 1987; Tannen, 1982; Thompson, 1983; Tottie, 1986).

3. Computer programs are developed for automated grammatical analysis, to 'tag' all relevant linguistic features in texts.
4. The entire corpus of texts is tagged automatically by computer.
5. All texts are post-edited interactively to insure that the linguistic features are accurately identified.
6. Additional computer programs are developed and run to compute frequency counts of each linguistic feature in each text of the corpus.
7. The co-occurrence patterns among linguistic features (across all texts in the corpus) are analysed, using a factor analysis of the frequency counts.
8. The co-occurrence patterns identified by the factor analysis are interpreted functionally as underlying dimensions of variation.
9. Dimension scores for each text are computed by summing the major linguistic features empirically grouped on each dimension; the mean dimension scores for each register are then compared to analyse the salient linguistic similarities and differences among spoken and written registers.
10. The functional interpretation of each dimension is revised based on the distribution of spoken and written registers along the dimension.

2.3 *Choice of linguistic features included in multidimensional analyses*

Although the co-occurrence patterns underlying dimensions are determined empirically, those patterns depend on the prior choice of linguistic features to be used in the analysis. Most multi-dimensional analyses to date have focused on lexical, grammatical, and syntactic features, with the goal of being as inclusive as possible. That is, any linguistic characteristic that can be interpreted as having functional associations is a candidate for inclusion in multi-dimensional analyses. Previous analyses have included:

– lexical features, such as type-token ratio and word length;
– semantic features relating to lexical classes, such as hedges, emphatics, speech act verbs, mental verbs;
– grammatical feature classes, such as nouns, prepositional phrases, attributive and predicative adjectives, past tense verbs, perfect aspect verbs, personal pronouns; and
– syntactic features, such as relative clauses, adverbial clauses, *that* complement clauses, passive postnominal participial clauses.

One characteristic of multi-dimensional analyses is that they can be extended by investigating the role of additional features in relation to previously determined dimensions. For example, Biber (1992b) analyses the distribution and function of linguistic features marking reference and cohesion within texts, showing how these features relate to the previously identified multi-dimensional structure of English. While some cohesion features function as part of previously identified dimensions, other cohesion features co-occur in new patterns to define additional dimensions associated with the marking of reference in discourse.

Future multi-dimensional analyses could be extended to include linguistic features from additional domains, such as the frequency of various rhetorical devices or the frequency of different organizational patterns. Any text characteristic that is encoded in language and can be reliably identified and counted is a potential candidate for

D. Biber

Table 1 Summary of functions, linguistic features, and characteristic registers for the five major English dimensions identified in Biber (1988)

Functions	Linguistic features	Characteristic registers
Dimension 1 'Involved versus informational production'		
Involved (Inter)personal focus Interactive Personal stance On-line production	1st and 2nd person pronouns, questions, reductions, stance verbs, hedges, emphatics, adverbial subordination	Conversations, personal letters, public conversations
Informational Careful production Faceless	nouns, adjectives, prepositional phrases, long words	informational exposition, e.g., official documents, academic prose
Dimension 2 'Narrative versus non-narrative concerns'		
Narrative	past tense, perfect aspect, 3rd person pronouns, speech act (public) verbs	fiction
Non-narrative	present tense, attributive adjectives	exposition, broadcasts, professional letters, telephone conversations
Dimension 3 'Elaborated versus situation-dependent reference'		
Elaborated Situation-independent reference	WH relative clauses, pied-piping constructions, phrasal coordination	official documents, professional letters, written exposition
Situation-dependent reference	time and place adverbials	broadcasts, conversations, fiction, personal letters
On-line production		
Dimension 4 'Overt expression of persuasion'		
Overt argumentation and persuasion	modals (prediction, necessity, possibility), suasive verbs, conditional subordination	professional letters, editorials
Not overtly argumentative	–	broadcasts, press reviews
Dimension 5 'Abstract versus non-abstract style'		
Abstract style	agentless passives, by passives, passive dependent clauses	technical prose, other academic prose, official documents
Non-abstract	–	conversations, fiction, personal letters, public speeches, public conversations, broadcasts

inclusion. Multi-dimensional analyses to date have focused primarily on a wide range of lexical and grammatical characteristics, but these analyses could be usefully extended to include consideration of language characteristics from other linguistic levels.

2.4 *Summary of the* 1988 *multi-dimensional analysis of register variation in English*

As noted in the introduction, it is important to distinguish between the multi-dimensional approach to register variation and multi-dimensional studies of particular discourse domains in particular languages. Watson focuses on the multi-dimensional analysis of English register variation presented in Biber (1988); this study provides the fullest account of multi-dimensional methodology and a synchronic analysis of the relations among adult spoken and written registers.

Five major dimensions are identified and interpreted in Biber (1988: especially chapters 6–7). Each comprises a set of co-occurring linguistic features; each defines a different configuration of similarities and differences among spoken and written registers; and each has distinct functional underpinnings. The five dimensions are interpretively labeled as follows:

1. Involved versus Informational Production
2. Narrative versus Non-narrative Concerns
3. Elaborated versus Situation-Dependent Reference
4. Overt Expression of Persuasion
5. Abstract versus Non-abstract Style

The primary communicative functions, major co-occurring features, and characteristic registers associated with each dimension are summarized in Table 1. Registers differ systematically along each of these dimensions, relating to functional considerations such as interactiveness, involvement, purpose, and production circumstances; and these functions are in turn realized by systematic co-occurrence patterns among linguistic features. [. . .]

Two major conclusions come out of the 1988 multi-dimensional analysis of register variation in English: (1) no single dimension of variation is adequate in itself to account for the range of similarities and differences among registers – rather, multi-dimensional analyses are required; and (2) there is no absolute difference between spoken and written language rather, particular types of speech and writing are more or less similar with respect to different dimensions.

B4.3 HYLAND (1999)

Hyland (1999) compares the features of the specific genres of metadiscourse in introductory coursebooks and research articles on the basis of a corpus consisting of extracts from twenty-one university textbooks for different disciplines and a similar corpus of research articles. This excerpt presents the methodology and findings of the paper.

Text B4.3
K. Hyland

Hyland, K. 1999. 'Talking to students: metadiscourse in introductory coursebooks'. *English for Specific Purposes* **18/1: 3–26.**

Corpus and procedure

The corpus consists of extracts from 21 introductory coursebooks in three academic disciplines: microbiology, marketing and applied linguistics, comprising almost 124 000 words [. . .]. The average length of the extracts was 5 900 words (range 3 305–10 678) consisting of complete chapters (16) or substantial sections of chapters beginning with the introductory matter and comprising entire contiguous sub-sections (5). The textbooks were selected from reading lists for introductory undergraduate courses and all extracts were among those recommended by teachers as containing 'core' reading matter. A parallel corpus of 21 research articles (121 000 words/average length 5 771 words) was compiled for comparison from the current issues of prestigious journals recommended by expert informants in the same three disciplines. The corpora were analysed independently by myself and two research assistants by coding all items of metadiscourse according to the schema outlined above. An inter-rater reliability of 0.83 (Kappa) was obtained, indicating a high degree of agreement.

Findings

Overall, the quantitative analysis revealed the importance of metadiscourse in these textbooks with an average of 405 examples per text; about one every 15 words. It should be noted here that the expression of devices according to a word count is not intended to represent the *proportion* of text formed by metadiscourse. Clearly, metadiscourse typically has clause-level (or higher) scope and I have standardised the raw figures to a common basis merely to compare the *occurrence*, rather than the length, of metadiscourse in corpora of unequal sizes. Table 2 shows that writers used far more textual than interpersonal forms in this corpus, and that connectives and code glosses were the most frequent devices in each discipline. The numerical preponderance of textual devices emphasises the common interpretation of metatext as guiding the reading process by indicating discourse organisation and clarifying propositional meanings.

The tables show some obvious disciplinary variations in metadiscourse use. The applied linguistics texts comprise considerably more evidentials and relational markers, the biology authors favoured hedges, and marketing textbooks had fewer evidentials and endophorics. Perhaps more interesting however are the cross-discipline similarities, with all three fields containing comparable total use and a near identical proportion of textual and interpersonal forms. In particular, all disciplines showed a high use of logical connectives and code glosses which together comprised about half of all cases, demonstrating that the principal concern of textbook authors is to present information clearly and explicitly.

A comparison with the research articles revealed strikingly similar total frequencies of metadiscourse in the two corpora, but a considerable difference in the proportion of the two main categories (Table 3). The increase in interpersonal metadiscourse from about a third of all cases in the textbooks to nearly half in the RAs shows the critical importance of these forms in persuasive prose.

As can be seen, devices used to assist comprehension of propositional information, such as connectives, code glosses and endophoric markers, were less frequent in the

Table 2 Metadiscourse in academic textbooks per 1,000 words (% of total)

Category	Biology		Applied linguistics		Marketing	
Logical connectives	32.3	(43.2)	17.8	(30.6)	34.4	(48.8)
Code glosses	9.4	(12.6)	9.6	(15.6)	9.7	(13.8)
Endophoric markers	6.4	(8.6)	4.5	(7.3)	2.5	(3.5)
Frame markers	2.5	(3.3)	4.6	(7.4)	4.2	(6.0)
Evidentials	3.2	(4.2)	5.3	(8.6)	1.0	(1.5)
Textual	**53.8**	**(71.9)**	**42.8**	**(69.4)**	**51.9**	**(73.7)**
Hedges	8.9	(12.0)	4.7	(7.7)	5.9	(8.4)
Emphatics	5.0	(6.7)	2.4	(3.9)	3.3	(4.7)
Attitude markers	4.1	(5.5)	3.5	(5.6)	5.5	(7.9)
Relational markers	2.2	(3.0)	6.1	(9.8)	2.5	(3.5)
Person markers	0.7	(0.9)	2.2	(3.6)	2.2	(3.6)
Interpersonal	**21.0**	**(28.1)**	**18.9**	**(30.6)**	**18.9**	**(30.6)**
Totals	**74.8**	**(100)**	**61.7**	**(100)**	**70.4**	**(100)**

Table 3 Ranked metadiscourse categories (combined disciplines)

	Textbooks Items per 1,000 words	% of total	Research articles Items per 1,000 words	% of total
Textual	**49.1**	**71.7**	**34.8**	**52.6**
Interpersonal	**19.4**	**28.3**	**31.4**	**47.4**
Subcategory				
Logical connectives	28.1	40.9	12.3	18.5
Code glosses	9.6	14.0	7.6	11.5
Hedges	6.4	9.4	16.7	25.3
Endophoric markers	4.4	6.5	3.2	4.9
Attitude markers	4.3	6.3	4.5	6.8
Frame markers	3.8	5.5	5.6	8.5
Relational markers	3.7	5.4	2.5	3.8
Emphatics	3.5	5.1	4.2	6.3
Evidentials	3.3	4.8	6.1	9.3
Person markers	1.4	2.1	3.5	5.2
Grand Totals	**68.5**	**100%**	**66.2**	**100%**

articles while those typically used to assist persuasion, such as hedges, emphatics, evidentials and person markers, were more frequent. Hedges were almost three times more common in the RAs and represented the most frequent metadiscourse feature, demonstrating the importance of distinguishing established from new claims in research writing and the need for authors to evaluate their assertions in ways that their peers are likely to find persuasive.

When separating the texts by both discipline and genre we find that the tables above mask a number of variations in metadiscourse use. Table 4 shows that the over-all density levels differed markedly in biology, with almost 25% more metadiscourse in the textbooks than the RAs, due mainly to a heavier use of textual forms. Biology was also the only discipline where there was little change in the proportions of interpersonal and textual features between the two genres, while the interpersonal frequencies increased dramatically in the applied linguistics and marketing RAs.

Extension

Table 4 Metadiscourse in textbooks and RAs per 1,000 words

	Biology Textbook	RA	Applied linguistics Textbook	RA	Marketing Textbook	RA
Textual	53.8	40.1	42.8	30.1	51.9	36.6
	71.9%	66.8%	69.4%	49.2%	73.7%	49.7%
Interpersonal	21.0	19.9	18.9	31.0	18.5	37.0
	28.1%	33.2%	30.6%	50.8%	26.3%	50.3%
Totals	74.8	59.9	61.7	60.1	70.4	73.6

Table 5 Proportions of metadiscourse in RAs and textbooks

Category	Biology TB	RA	Applied linguistics TB	RA	Marketing TB	RA
Logical connectives:	43.2	18.8	30.6	18.1	48.8	18.7
Frame markers	3.3	8.6	7.4	7.6	6.0	9.0
Endophoric markers	8.6	7.7	7.3	4.1	3.5	4.4
Evidentials	4.2	16.2	8.6	7.3	1.5	8.0
Code glosses	12.6	15.4	15.6	12.1	13.8	9.6
Textual	**71.9**	**66.8**	**69.4**	**49.2**	**73.7**	**49.7**
Hedges	12.0	20.0	7.7	25.6	8.4	27.0
Emphatics	6.7	5.8	3.9	7.4	4.7	5.7
Attitude markers	5.5	2.2	5.6	8.8	7.9	7.0
Relational markers	3.0	1.2	9.8	4.1	3.5	4.5
Person markers	0.9	4.0	3.6	4.8	1.8	6.0
Interpersonal	**28.1**	**33.2**	**30.6**	**50.8**	**26.3**	**50.3**
Total %	100	100	100	100	100	100

Table 5 shows that the use of logical connectives was highest in textbooks in all disciplines and that the RAs contained a higher proportion of hedges, person and frame markers. Biologists showed the greatest variation, both across genres and disciplines, with substantial genre differences in most categories. While the marketing and applied linguistics texts were more uniform between genres, both contained large differences in hedges and connectives. Substantial genre variations were also apparent in the use of evidentials and person markers in marketing and endophoric and relation markers in applied linguistics. In general, metadiscourse variations were more pronounced between genres than disciplines, particularly for high frequency items, and the textbooks tended to exhibit greater disciplinary diversity than the RAs.

Discussion

Textbooks, as a specific form of language use and social interaction, both represent particular processes of production and interpretation, and link to the social practices of the institutions within which they are created. We might expect, then, that metadiscourse variations will reflect the different roles that textbooks and research papers play in the social structures of disciplinary activity and anticipate that their use will contain clues about how these texts were produced and the purposes they serve. Metadiscourse is grounded in the rhetorical purposes of writers and sensitive to their perceptions of audience, both of which differ markedly between the two genres. One audience consists of an established community of disciplinary peers familiar with the conceptual frameworks and specialised literacies of their discipline. The other is relatively undifferentiated in terms of its experience of academic discourse, often possessing little more than a general purpose EAP competence in the early under-graduate years (e.g. Leki and Carson 1994). As a result of such contextual differences, what can be said, and what needs to be said, differs considerably. It is therefore interesting to speculate on the patterns observed and I will consider textual and interpersonal variations in turn.

B4.4 LEHMANN (2002)

Lehmann (2002) presents a large-scale study of zero-subject relative constructions (ZSRs) on the basis of the demographically sampled spoken BNC and the five-million-word Longman Spoken American Corpus (LSAC). This study shows that there is a sharp difference between American English which has 2.5 per cent subject relatives with a zero relativizer and British English which has 13 per cent.

Lehmann, H. 2002. 'Zero subject relative constructions in American and British English'. *New Frontiers in Corpus Research*, **pp. 163–177. Amsterdam: Rodopi.**

Text B4.4
H. Lehmann

6 Results

The analysis left me with 94 instances of ZSRs in 5 million words in LSAC and 205 instances in 4.2 million words in the spoken demographic sample of the BNC. This certainly is a strong indication that ZSRs are about two and a half times more frequent in British English than in American English. However, as a consequence of the principle of accountability there are problems with accounting frequency per million running words. After all it could be the case that subject relative constructions allowing for a possible realization by zero are less frequent in American English overall. For this reason it is important to account for the frequency of ZSRs taking into account the overall frequency of possible occurrences including surface relativizers. The results of such an analysis are shown in Table 1.

Table 1 shows that taking into account occurrences and non-occurrences of ZSRs does not reduce the difference found above. In fact, taking into account possible occurrences results in an even greater difference between American and British English, with ZSRs being over five times more frequent in British English than in American English. Thus the results in Table 1 firmly establish a pronounced difference in the use of ZSRs between these two major varieties of English.

Table 1 also shows a striking difference in the frequency of subject relative constructions observed by the retrieval patterns. Subject relative constructions conforming to the retrieval patterns are twice as frequent in American English as in British English.

Another interesting aspect for analysis is the different matrix clauses in which ZSR complexes occur. Here I will follow Shnukal (1981), who defines four major types exemplified by (22)–(25).

Extension

Table 1 Realization forms of subject relatives in American and British English

American English				British English			
surface		zero		surface		zero	
N	%	n	%	n	%	n	%
3647	97.5%	94	2.5%	1376	87%	205	13%

Table 2 Types of ZSRs in American and British English

Types	American English		British English	
	n	%	n	%
existential *there*	27	29%	126	61%
Cleft	24	26%	25	12%
Be	14	15%	8	4%
Have	9	10%	15	7%
Others	20	21%	31	15%

(22) there's this woman Ø went out to like some Caribbean or something to have a vacation and then she met this guy (LSAC: 118901:?)

(23) It was Joanne Ø said you'd go down there, so you said alright. (BNC:KDG: 1795:PS000)

(24) this dog I got friendly with, they were people Ø got in there for the summer, got and just abandon it so there's all these dogs running around the coast. (LSAC:165301#dr2791)

(25) well I mean we had one girl Ø didn't know what she was going about, . . . (BNC:KDW:6217:PS1C1)

The first type represented by (22) is characterized by existential *there* in the matrix clause. The second type features an *it*-cleft construction, as in (23). The third type has the verb *be* as a main verb, as in (24). The fourth type of matrix clause is characterized by the verb *have* as a main verb, as in (25). These are the most frequent matrix clause types discussed by Shnukal (1981). There are other less frequent verbs used in the matrix clauses in my material as in (26)–(31).

(26) . . . and erm thought knock on the doors and see, ask people Ø had seen it and (BNC:KD5:9674:PS0JX)

(27) knife at the back of the saw, they, it is a bit dangerous, erm where's the guard Ø goes at the top. (BNC:KDM:07067:PS0RD)

(28) And I can handle any bastard Ø gets in here. (BNC:KDY:0658:PSI42)

(29) and it was talking in there <u>about one woman Ø asked the waiter to go to bed with him when she was ordering something</u>. (LSAC:151103:2173)

(30) It's like people who eat marmalade Ø has no peel in it. (BNC:KPU: 2690:PS584)

(31) either you kill each other until finally you get to one Ø gives in so one becomes the master and one becomes the slave. (LSAC:165001:2757)

(26)–(31) show that the construction is not limited to the matrix clause types exemplified in (22)–(25). Table 2 shows the distribution of the four main types and other matrix clause choices.

Table 2 shows that the ranking of matrix clause types in American and British English is fairly similar. The only exceptions are constructions with the verb *be* and the verb *have* which are reversed in the order of their ranking. The most striking difference is found with existential *there* constructions, which cover 61% of all ZSR constructions in British English and only 29% in American English.

In the following I will try to analyse the distribution of the ZSR construction with the help of the annotation provided by the BNC and the LSAC. Both corpora are annotated with social variables for individual speakers. However, not all speakers are annotated, as it was impossible to obtain the relevant data from all interlocutors who happened to be recorded. The use of speaker annotation divides the corpora into parts of unequal size. To cope with this problem I prepared databases containing annotation and word-counts for the individual speakers. This information was then used for normalization and thus made direct comparison possible.

LSAC contains information about the ethnicity of speakers. Given the presence of ZSRs in AAVE [African American Vernacular English] documented in Tottie and Harvie (1999) and Harvie (1998), it is interesting to see if African Americans use ZSRs with a higher frequency than other Americans. Table 3 highlights the problem of correlating social variables with a low frequency phenomenon like ZSRs. The slightly higher frequency of ZSRs produced by African Americans is undermined by the fact that it is based on only four instances. The conclusion that can be drawn from Table 3, nevertheless, is that the majority of the occurrences are produced by European Americans and African Americans. The presence of ZSRs in spoken American English can thus not be attributed to the language use of one single ethnic group like AAVE. The absence of ZSRs from all other ethnic groups is certainly noteworthy. The high frequency of ZSRs for which speaker ethnicity is not indicated certainly raises the question of the observer's paradox. Speakers for which there is no annotation available are likely to be passers by. They may therefore be less conscious of being recorded.

Table 3 Distribution of ZSRs over ethnic groups in spoken American English

Ethnicity	No. of words	ZSR (n)	ZSRs per 1 million words
White	2,493,493	55	22
Not indicated	800,820	34	42
Black/African-American	145,989	4	27
Other	84,474	1	12
Multiple/Mixed ethnicity	67,520	–	–
Chicano/Mexican-American	59,884	–	–
American Indian/Native American	56,280	–	–
Latino/Other Hispanic	54,893	–	–
Filipino/Filipino-American	22,967	–	–
Polynesian/Pacific Islander	13,424	–	–
Chinese/Chinese-American	11,397	–	–
Korean/Korean-American	10,874	–	–
Japanese/Japanese-American	8,319	–	–
Puerto Rican	1,446	–	–
Arab/Arab-American	404	–	–
Viet/Thai/Other Asian	347	–	–

Table 4 Distribution of ZSRs in the LSAC according to age of speaker

Age of speaker	n	No. of words	Freq. per 1m words
0–14	1	46246	21.6
15–24	11	852081	12.9
25–34	18	803259	22.4
35–44	7	694733	10.0
45–59	19	889398	21.4
60+	10	295592	33.8

Another interesting variable is the age of speakers presented in Table 4.

Here again no clear picture emerges. The highest frequency for the group 60+ might suggest that ZSRs are used more frequently by older speakers. However, the data for the other age groups doesn't support such a trend. The gender of speakers using ZSRs is remarkably even: female speakers with 19 instances per million words, and male speakers with 18 instances per million words. Nor is there any support for the hypothesis that speakers using ZSRs belong to a lower social class. In terms of occupation we find professors, graduate students, lawyers, bankers as well as a cashier and a seamstress who produce instances of ZSRs.

The analysis of social variables for the British data was more successful. This is to be expected given the higher number of instances available for a breakdown according to the individual social variables, firstly on speaker age. Table 5 shows the frequency of ZSRs according to age of speakers.

Table 5 and its graphical representation in Figure 1 show a clear increase of the use of ZSRs with increasing age of speaker. However, such a result might be attributed to a difference in frequency of all the subject relatives under observation and not only to zero realizations. Table 6 shows the proportion of SSR [surface subject relative] and ZSR constructions according to age of speaker.

Table 6 shows that the trend observed in Table 5 and Figure 1 can't be attributed to subject relatives in general. Zero as a relativizer choice is still twice as frequent in the age group 60+ than in the age group 0–14. Figure 2 shows a graphical representation of the frequency information in Tables 4 and 5. It helps us to visualize both the distribution of subject relatives in general and the distribution of surface and zero variants.

While the younger speakers certainly use fewer subject relatives, this cannot explain away the trend found in the distribution of ZSRs. This is documented by the proportion of realizations by zero, which increases with the age of speaker. Shnukal (1981: 322) comes to a similar conclusion for a dialect of Australian English.

Table 5 Distribution of ZSRs in the BNC according to age of speaker

Age of speaker	n	frequency per 1m. words
0–14	8	19.2
15–24	9	21.5
25–34	25	36.3
35–44	36	51.3
45–59	51	72.3
60+	49	74.2
not available	27	42.9

Table 6 Proportion of SSRs and ZSRs according to age of speaker in the BNC

Age of speaker	Surface		Zero	
	n	%	n	%
0–14	95	92.2	8	7.8
15–24	114	92.7	9	7.3
25–34	223	89.9	25	10.1
35–44	248	87.3	36	12.7
45–59	246	82.8	51	17.2
60+	273	84.7	49	15.3

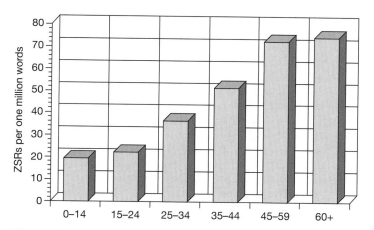

Figure 1 Distribution of ZSRs in the BNC according to age of speakers

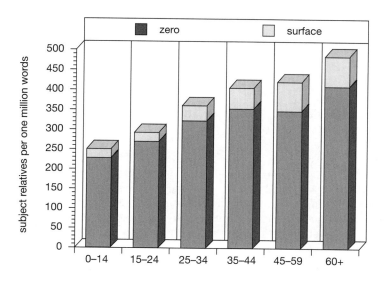

Figure 2 ZSRs and SSRs per million words in the BNC

The most important findings presented above are the difference between American English and British English and the fact that younger speakers use fewer ZSRs than older speakers. Given that, synchronically, language change is only observable as variation, a variation phenomenon like the realization form of subject relatives lends itself to speculation about an ongoing language change. On the assumption that language acquisition is completed at a certain age between 16 and 25, we may conclude that we are indeed observing an ongoing language change in British English, with an observable decrease of the use of ZSRs from the older to the younger generation. This is particularly important because variation and change do not mutually imply each other. While it is sound to extrapolate from ongoing language change to the presence of variation, the reverse does not hold. From observation of variation we may not extrapolate to the presence of language change. Variation phenomena can represent differences in registers, which may remain stable over time. Thus speaker age presents the only means of observing language change in synchronic corpora.

However, using speaker age for documenting language change is certainly not uncontroversial. Only under the assumption that language use remains stable after the phase of language acquisition can speaker age be used for documenting ongoing language change. Even if language acquisition is completed at the age of about 18, this does not necessarily mean that the frequency of use of the acquired repertoire remains stable over the course of an adult's life.

The finding that ZSRs are over five times more frequent in British English than in American English could mean that the same language change – loss of ZSRs – has progressed further in American English. This may have been caused by the large number of immigrants speaking Western European languages like German, French, Italian and Spanish, which only have overt relativizers.

B4.5 KACHRU (2003)

Kachru (2003) uses a small corpus to explore the uses of definite reference across four regional varieties of English: Indian, Nigerian, Singaporean and American. The study indicates that the use of definite descriptions is likely to differ in 'Englishes' used in different parts of the world.

Text B4.5
Y. Kachru

Kachru, Y. 2003. 'On definite reference in world Englishes'. *World Englishes* 22/4: 497–510.

The corpus collected for the study consisted of a number of letters to the editor from several newspapers in India, Nigeria, Singapore and the USA. The letters were published between March 5 and April 6, 2000. The total corpus was just over 15,000 words which yielded 945 noun phrases with the definite article *the*. The rationale for choice of data source was that newspapers correspond to a more casual style of writing and within newspapers the letters to the editor represented the least edited and most typical of individual style.

The classification of definite NPs in Quirk *et al.*, cited in Table 1, though useful in the classroom devoted to pedagogical grammar of English at a university setting, was too sketchy to serve the purposes of an analysis of definite reference in a larger corpus with the focus I have already mentioned. Although Quirk *et al.* (1985) also discuss several other categories of nouns with definite and indefinite articles, the classification suggested in Poesio and Vieira (1998) seemed more suitable for my purposes since it was developed for large-scale corpus analysis. Poesio and Vieira ran two experiments to determine how 'good' (i.e., how much they agree among themselves about analysing definite descriptions) naive subjects are at doing the form of linguistic analysis presupposed by current schemes for classifying definite descriptions. Their subjects were asked to classify definite descriptions found in a corpus of natural language texts according to classification schemes developed starting from the taxonomies proposed in Hawkins (1978) and Prince (1981, 1992). The experiments were also designed to assess the feasibility of a system to process definite descriptions on unrestricted text and to collect data that could be used for their implementation.

I coded the noun phrases in my corpus according to the classification of noun phrases with the definite article *the* given in 1–6 in A below. This still left some definite NPs encountered in the corpus unaccounted for. I therefore had to add the classes 7–9 to the list of categories. There are still problems with the classification, which I will mention toward the end.

A. Classification of definite NPs
1. Anaphoric (definite NPs that cospecify with a discourse entity already introduced in the discourse).
   John bought a car. **The car/vehicle** *turned out to be a lemon.*
2. Immediate situation (definite **NP** used to refer to an object in the situation of utterance; it may be visible or inferred).
   At the dining table: *Please pass* **the salt!**
   Sign at the zoo: *Don't feed* **the bears!**
3. Larger situation (in which the speaker appeals to the hearer's knowledge of entities that exist in the non-immediate or larger situation of utterance knowledge that speakers and hearers share by being members of the same community).
   On a specific campus, talking about lunch: *Shall we meet in* **the ballroom?**
4. Associative anaphoric (speaker and hearer may have (shared) knowledge of the relations between certain objects (the triggers) and their components and attributes (the associates); associative anaphoric use exploits such knowledge).
   There was an accident at the intersection. **The car** *was smashed, but* **the passengers** *and* **the driver** *escaped without serious injury.*
5. Unfamiliar (definite NPs that are not anaphoric, do not rely on information about the situation of utterance, and are not associates of some triggers in the previous discourse).

   (a) NP complements
       the fact/suggestion *that . . .* , **the place** *where . . .*
   (b) Nominal modifiers
       the color *maroon,* **the number** *three*
   (c) Referential relative
       The book *that you were reading . . .*
   (d) Associative clause (definite NPs that specify both the trigger and the associate)
       The OP ED page *of the* NY Times *. . .*
   (e) Unexplanatory modifiers
       The last person *to leave the party was an old woman.*

6. Institutional ('sporadic reference' in Quirk *et al.*, 1985)
   The USA, The UN
7. Fixed collocations ('the logical use of the' in Quirk *et al.*, 1985)
   the first flight to Denver, . . . catch **the last bus** . . .
8. Generic
   the musk ox, the tiger . . .
9. Idioms
   a shot in **the arm**

All the noun phrases with the definite article *the* in the corpus were coded in terms of the categories listed in 1–9 in A above. [. . .] I am not giving all the data on each piece of text and even each variety, mainly in view of space considerations.

The distribution of forms according to the classification in A is in Table 4. Although there are more occurrences of definite NPs of classes 1, 3, 4, and 5d, all anaphoric in some sense, the numbers still do not represent the anaphoric use as the most frequent use of definite NPs. This is clear from the percentages involved (Table 5).

The direct anaphoric referential NPs constitute under four tenths of the total use of definite NPs. Even if we combine the direct and indirect anaphoric referential use (i.e., classes 1 and 4), the percentage is still just about half of the total. Classes 3 and 5c are referential, but not anaphoric, and class 5d performs a deictic rather than a referential function. The other classes have a purely grammatical function. The occurrences in other categories are so small that it is hard to even speculate about their significance.

Discussion and interpretation

What is interesting about Tables 4 and 5 is that they do not point to a great deal of difference across varieties. This strengthens the claims that institutionalized varieties of English are not the same as learner varieties referred to by the term interlanguage. They are not 'interference varieties', as Quirk *et al.* (1985) characterize them.

The results, however, raise a question about my third observation that in view of the descriptions of Asian and African varieties of English, it is reasonable to assume that world Englishes will exhibit differences in their use of definite NPs. Do the results presented here render this assumption invalid? I would submit that it is difficult to come to any conclusion on the basis of the small corpus I have analysed so far. We need to have a much larger corpus with many more different types of texts to determine if inter-variety differences exist.

There is, however, another possibility. The data documented in earlier descriptions have not paid much attention to the cline of bilingualism in English (B. Kachru, 1965: 393–6). If we take the acrolectal varieties of English, there may be very little difference across them. As the users of the institutionalized varieties of English gain proficiency in the language and become users of the acrolectal variety, their cognitive abilities obviously make it possible for them to perceive and conceptualize grammatical structures which do not operate in their substratum languages. This is true of an entire range of grammatical phenomena. There is no reason why this should not be true also of the deictic and anaphoric relations and their exponents, which would explain their use of definite NPs similar to the Inner Circle users. The non-Inner Circle users' internalizing of the system of definite NPs in English is not precluded by their other language experience. This is an empirical question and needs to be investigated.

Table 4 Distribution of definite NPs across varieties

| | Classes | | | | | | | | | | | | |
	1	3	4	5a	5b	5c	5d	5e	6	7	8	9	Total NPs
USA E	75	20	27	7	6	12	34	1	11	2	5	2	202
IndE	101	55	26	8	1	7	66		6	11	5	5	291
S'Pore E	84	26	28	14	5	8	37	1	5	7	2	2	219
Niger E	84	13	39	7	1	10	43		13	15		2	227

Table 5 Percentages of NPs in classes across varieties

	USA E	Ind E	S'pore E	Niger E
1	37	35	38	37
3	10	19	12	6
4	13	9	13	17
5d	17	22	17	19
1 + 4	50	43	50	54

Summary

This unit was concerned with language variation. It first introduced Biber's MF/MD approach to register and genre analysis. The other three excerpts in this unit explored variation in specific genres and language varieties.

LOOKING AHEAD

In Case Study 5 in Section C of this book, we will compare Biber's analytic framework with an approach that uses WordSmith, which is less technically demanding and can approximate a Biber-style analysis. We will also, in Case Study 2 in Section C, consider the differences between British and American English, the two major varieties of English. While the excerpts presented in this unit are synchronic studies of a single language, we will explore language variation from contrastive and diachronic perspectives in the next unit.

Unit B5
Contrastive and diachronic studies

B5.1 INTRODUCTION

As noted in Units A10.4–A10.7, corpora are well suited to comparative and diachronic studies. Of the various types of corpora introduced in Unit A7, comparable and parallel corpora are particularly useful in contrastive and translation studies (see Unit A5). Likewise, diachronic studies have always, in a sense, been corpus-based (see also Bauer 2002: 109). This unit presents four excerpts from published material to demonstrate the use of corpora in these two types of language studies. The first two excerpts are concerned with contrastive analysis while the latter two explore language change.

B5.2 ALTENBERG AND GRANGER (2002)

This excerpt discusses the use of comparable and parallel corpora (or 'translation corpora' in the authors' term) in contrastive linguistics (CL), focusing on lexis. Readers are reminded that their proposal to base cross-linguistic contrast on parallel corpora is potentially problematic, as noted in Unit A10.6.

> **Text B5.2**
> **B. Altenberg**
> **and S. Granger**

Altenberg, B. and Granger, S. 2002. 'Recent trends in cross-linguistic lexical studies' in B. Altenberg and S. Granger (eds) *Lexis in Contrast*, pp. 3–48. Amsterdam: John Benjamins.

3 Theoretical and methodological issues

3.1 *Some contrastive approaches*

Traditionally, CL has been described as involving three methodological steps: description, juxtaposition and comparison (see e.g. Krzeszowski 1990: 35). The description includes selection of the items to be compared and a preliminary characterisation of these in terms of some language-independent theoretical model. The juxtaposition involves a search for, and identification of, cross-linguistic equivalents. In the comparison proper the degree and type of correspondence between the compared items are specified.

Modern lexical CL often follows this procedure, but a characteristic feature of recent corpus-based contrastive work is the great variety of approaches employed. This is

B. Altenberg
and S. Granger

largely due to the expansion of the field and the new research possibilities that multilingual corpora and search tools offer. The methodology chosen and the delicacy of the analysis depend to a large extent on the purpose of the analysis, e.g. whether it is primarily 'theoretical' (focusing on a contrastive description of the languages involved) or 'practical' (intended to serve the needs of a particular application). This in turn may determine the role that the corpus is allowed to play in the analysis. One distinction that is sometimes made in corpus linguistics, and which is also applicable to CL, is that between 'corpus-based' and 'corpus-driven' approaches (see e.g. Francis 1993 and Tognini Bonelli 2001 and in this volume). The former may involve any work – theory-driven or data-driven – that makes use of a corpus for language description, but it is also used in a restricted sense to refer to studies which start from a model postulating a cross-linguistic difference or similarity on theoretical grounds and use a multilingual corpus to confirm, refute or enrich the theory. The latter approach, on the other hand, may start from an implicit or loosely formulated assumption but uses the corpus primarily to discover types and degrees of cross-linguistic correspondence and to arrive at theoretical statements. In practice, however, the distinction may be slight. The difference lies rather in the importance attached to the initial assumptions and the role that the data play in the analysis. Here we shall use the term 'corpus-based' as an umbrella term covering both types of corpus-informed studies.

In the following sections we shall briefly examine some of the theoretical and methodological issues involved and how these have been approached in some recent corpus-based contrastive studies of lexis.

3.2 *Tertium comparationis and translation equivalence*

Any cross-linguistic comparison presupposes that the compared items are in some sense similar or comparable. That is, to be able to say that certain categories in two languages are similar or different it is necessary that they have some common ground, or *tertium comparationis*. For lexis it is obvious that the compared items should express 'the same thing', i.e. have the same (or at least similar) meaning and pragmatic function' (see James 1980: 90f.). However, what exactly this 'thing' is is not always obvious, and the problem of identifying *a tertium comparationis* in CL has been discussed a great deal in the past (see e.g. James 1980:169ff., Krzeszowski 1990, and Chesterman 1998: 27ff.).

Krzeszowski (1990:23f) has distinguished seven types of equivalence: statistical equivalence, translation equivalence, system equivalence, semanticosyntactic equivalence, rule equivalence, substantive equivalence and pragmatic equivalence. However, although there is something to say for this taxonomic approach, it seems that the only way we can be sure that we are comparing like with like is to rely on translation equivalence (see James 1980: 178). Chesterman (1998: 37ff.) develops this in the following way. Any notion of equivalence is a matter of judgement. Similarly, cross-linguistic equivalence is not absolute, but a matter of judgement or, more precisely, translation competence. 'On this view, estimations of any kind of equivalence that involves meaning must be based on translation competence, precisely because such estimations require the ability to move *between* utterances in different languages. Translation competence, after all, involves the ability to *relate* two things' (*ibid.*: 39).

The fact that equivalence is a relative concept also has another consequence. It is not realistic to proceed from a *tertium comparationis* that is based on 'identity of meaning'. For one thing, this would be putting the cart before the horse and we would run the risk of methodological circularity: the result of the contrastive analysis would be no more than the initial assumption (cf. Krzeszowski 1990: 20). For another, the area we want to explore is often fuzzy and impossible to define satisfactorily (e.g. epistemic modality or pragmatic particles). In such cases we cannot start from a *tertium comparationis* that is founded on equivalence in a strict sense (identity of meaning). Instead, what we have to do – and what we generally do – is to start from a perceived or assumed similarity between cross-linguistic items (cf. James 1980: 168f.). Viewed in this way, CL becomes a way of refining initial assumptions of similarity. Chesterman (1998: 58) expresses this as follows:

> In this methodology, the *tertium comparationis* is thus what we aim to arrive at, after a rigorous analysis; it crystallizes whatever is (to some extent) common to X and Y. It is thus an explicit specification of the initial comparability criterion, but it is not identical with it – hence there is no circularity here. Using an economic metaphor, we could say that the *tertium comparationis* thus arrived at adds value to the initial perception of comparability, in that the analysis has added explicitness, precision, perhaps formalization; it may also have provided added information, added insights, added perception.

The crucial role that translation equivalence plays in CL has important methodological consequences. We have already described the differences between comparable corpora and translation corpora [. . .]. When items are compared across comparable corpora, it is difficult to know if we are comparing like with like. Any judgement about cross-linguistic equivalence (or similarity) must be based on the researcher's translation competence: This is true at both ends of the analysis: initially, when items are selected for comparison, and finally, when the results of the comparison are evaluated. When we use translation corpora the situation is different. Although we normally start with an initial assumption about cross-linguistic similarity – the very basis for comparing anything at all – we can place more reliance on the translations found in the corpus. The corpus can be said to lend an element of empirical inter-subjectivity to the concept of equivalence, especially if the corpus represents a variety of translators.

However, despite the usefulness of translation corpora, to what extent can we trust the translations we find in them? Can we treat all the translations that turn up as cross-linguistic equivalents? There does not seem to be a simple answer to this question. In one sense, every translation is worth considering as a potential translation equivalent as it reflects the translator's 'competence': However, translations are rarely literal renderings of the original. Translators transfer texts from one language (and culture) to another and the translation therefore tends to deviate in various ways from the original. We have already mentioned possible translation effects – traces of the source language or universal translation strategies – and they may involve additions, omissions and various kinds of 'free' renderings that are either uncalled for or motivated by cultural and communicative considerations.

How, then, can we determine which translations should be regarded as 'equivalents' in a stricter sense? One solution has been to resort to the procedure of 'back-translation' (see Ivir 1983, 1987), i.e. to restrict the comparison to forms in L2 that can be translated back into the original forms in L1. This is likely to eliminate irrelevant differences that are due to the translator's idiosyncrasies or motivated by particular communicative or textual strategies.

Another solution is to rely on recurrent translation patterns, i.e. to resort to a quantitative notion of translation equivalence (cf. Kzreszowski 1990: 27). If several translators have used the same translation, this obviously increases its relevance. However, this too implies a risk: by restricting the comparison to recurrent translations we may throw away valuable evidence and miss the cross-linguistic insights that 'unexpected' translations often provide.

A variant of this approach which combines Ivir's idea of back-translation and a quantitative notion of equivalence is to calculate what has been called the 'mutual correspondence' (or translatability) of two items in a bidirectional translation corpus (see Altenberg 1999). If an item x in language A is always translated by y in language B and, conversely, item y in language B is always translated by x in language A, they will have a mutual correspondence of 100%. If they are never translated by each other their mutual correspondence will be 0%. In other words, the higher the mutual correspondence value is, the greater the equivalence between the compared items is likely to be. Although the mutual correspondence of categories in different languages seldom reaches 100% in a translation corpus (even 80% seems to be a comparatively high value), a statistical measure of translation equivalence can be a valuable diagnostic of the degree of correspondence between items or categories in different languages (see e.g. Altenberg 1999 and Ebeling 1999: 257ff.). However, it does not tell us where to draw the line between equivalence and non-equivalence. Ultimately, the notion of equivalence is a matter of judgement, reflecting either the researcher's or the translator's bilingual competence. Both involve a judgement of translation equivalence.

B5.3 McENERY, XIAO AND MO (2003)

McEnery, Xiao and Mo (2003) explore aspect marking in English and Chinese, using the FLOB/Frown corpora and a comparable Chinese corpus, the Lancaster Corpus of Mandarin Chinese (LCMC) (see Unit A7.4 for a description of the three corpora). The study demonstrates some important similarities and differences in the distribution of aspect markers in Chinese, British English and American English. This excerpt provides background knowledge for Case Study 6 in Section C and demonstrates how comparable corpora may be used to explore a specific feature cross-linguistically.

McEnery, A., Xiao, Z. and Mo, L. 2003. 'Aspect marking in English and Chinese'. *Literary and Linguistic Computing* 18/4: 361–378.

Text B5.3
A. McEnery,
Z. Xiao and
L. Mo

Having built LCMC, we decided to use the corpus to test a claim made by McEnery and Xiao (2002: 224–5); McEnery and Xiao, based on a study of public health documents in Chinese and English, claimed that aspect markers occur significantly more frequently in narrative texts than in expository texts. However, McEnery and Xiao only studied one genre. Does this claim hold across a wider range of genres? Also, they only contrasted British English and Chinese. Is the claim true when American English and Chinese are contrasted, or American English and British English? We decided to explore these questions by examining the distribution of aspect markers

A. McEnery,
Z. Xiao and
L. Mo

in the fifteen text categories of the LCMC and FLOB/Frown corpora. In so doing, we were also able to compare the distribution patterns of aspect markers in Chinese and British/American English.

However, before proceeding to the analysis, a brief description of the aspect system of Chinese is needed as Chinese has a very complicated aspect marker system. In Chinese the perfective aspect is marked by *-le*, *-guo*, verb reduplication and resultative verb complements (RVCs) while the imperfective aspect is marked by *zai*, *-zhe*, *-qilai*, and *-xiaqu* (cf. Xiao and McEnery, forthcoming) [later published as Xiao and McEnery (2004b)]. In addition, covert aspect marking is also an important strategy used to express aspectual meanings in Chinese discourse (cf. McEnery and Xiao, 2002: 212). However, as the tagger we used only annotated *-le*, *-guo*, *zai* and *-zhe*, we decided to explore these four aspect markers in LCMC in this study. The frequencies of these aspect markers in LCMC are as shown in Table 4.

English is a less aspectual language with regard to grammatical aspect marking than Chinese. English only differentiates between the simplex viewpoints of the progressive, the perfect and the simple aspect in addition to the complex viewpoint of the perfect progressive (c.f. Biber, Johansson, Leech, Conrad and Finegan, 1999: 461; Svalberg and Chuchu, 1998). In English, perfective meaning is most commonly expressed by the simple past (cf. Brinton, 1988: 52), though the perfect can also mark perfectivity (Dahl, 1999: 34). Imperfective meaning is typically signalled by the progressive, and less often by the perfect progressive. For the purpose of contrasting English aspect marking with Chinese we counted the distribution of the four aspects of English. The frequencies of aspect markers in FLOB and Frown are given in Tables 5–6.

Tables 4–6 show that in both LCMC and FLOB/Frown, the text categories where the frequency of aspect markers is above average (categories L, M, N, P, R, and K) or near to the average (categories A and G) are the five fiction categories plus humour, biography, and press reportage. The text types where aspect markers occur least frequently include reports/official documents, academic prose, skills/trades/

Table 4 Distribution of aspect markers in LCMC

Average	Text type	Words (10k)	Frequency	Frequency per 10k words	Per cent
Above the average	K	5.8	1674	289	12.00%
	M	1.2	322	268	11.13%
	P	5.8	1384	238	9.88%
	R	1.8	387	215	8.92%
	L	4.8	1024	214	8.88%
	G	15.4	3140	204	8.47%
	N	5.8	1107	191	7.93%
	A	8.8	1539	175	7.26%
Average	Average of frequency per 10k words: 161 (6.68%)				
Below the average	F	8.8	1057	120	4.98%
	C	3.4	365	108	4.48%
	D	3.4	363	106	4.40%
	B	5.4	561	104	4.32%
	J	16.0	1355	84	3.49%
	E	7.6	412	54	2.24%
	H	6.0	231	39	1.62%

A. McEnery,
Z. Xiao and
L. Mo

Table 5 Distribution of aspect markers in FLOB

Average	Text type	Words (10k)	Frequency	Frequency per 10k words	Per cent
Above (or	P	5.8	5673	978	11.17%
near to) the	L	4.8	4624	963	11.00%
average	N	5.8	5255	906	10.34%
	K	5.8	5169	891	10.17%
	M	1.2	997	831	9.49%
	R	1.8	1313	729	8.32%
	A	8.8	5166	587	6.70%
	G	15.4	8257	536	6.12%
Average	Average of frequency per 10k words: 584 (6.67%)				
Below the	D	3.4	1317	388	4.43%
average	F	8.8	3353	381	4.35%
	E	7.6	2724	358	4.09%
	B	5.4	1886	349	3.98%
	H	6.0	1740	290	3.31%
	C	3.4	978	288	3.29%
	J	16.0	4524	283	3.23%

Table 6 Distribution of aspect markers in Frown

Average	Text type	Words (10k)	Frequency	Frequency per 10k words	Per cent
Above (or	L	4.8	4546	947	10.95%
near to) the	M	1.2	1119	933	10.78%
average	N	5.8	5349	922	10.66%
	P	5.8	5238	903	10.44%
	R	1.8	1534	852	9.85%
	K	5.8	4815	830	9.59%
	A	8.8	4816	547	6.32%
	G	15.4	7799	506	5.58%
Average	Average of frequency per 10k words: 577 (6.67%)				
Below the	F	8.8	3397	386	4.46%
average	B	5.4	1893	351	4.06%
	E	7.6	2617	344	3.98%
	C	3.4	1155	340	3.93%
	D	3.4	1053	310	3.58%
	J	16.0	4024	252	2.91%
	H	6.0	1368	228	2.64%

hobbies, press reviews, press editorials, religion, and popular lore. In both Ch
and the two major varieties of English considered here, there is a great dif'
in usage between the first and second groups of texts, which indicates that
are basically different. Text types like fiction, humour, and biography are '
whereas reports/official documents, academic prose, and skills/trades/ho'
expository. Press reportage is a transitory category which is more akin to
texts.

A. McEnery,
Z. Xiao and
L. Mo

Table 7 Distribution of aspect markers in narrative and expository texts

Corpus	Discourse type	Categories	Words	Markers	LL score	Sig. level
LCMC	Narrative	K–R, A, G	494000	10577	2796.53	<0.001
	Expository	B–F, H, J	506000	4344		
FLOB	Narrative	K–R, A, G	494000	36454	7771.37	<0.001
	Expository	B–F, H, J	506000	16522		
Frown	Narrative	K–R, A, G	494000	35216	7950.98	<0.001
	Expository	B–F, H, J	506000	15507		

Log-likelihood (LL) tests indicate that in both Chinese and the two varieties of English, the differences between the distribution of aspect markers in narrative and expository texts are statistically significant (see Table 7). In all of the three corpora, aspect markers occur in narrative texts twice as frequently as in expository texts (2.43 times in LCMC, 2.21 times in FLOB, and 2.27 times in Frown), which means that the higher frequency of aspect markers in narrative texts over expository texts is a common feature of Chinese and the two major varieties of English.

These findings confirm those of McEnery and Xiao (2002) and allow us to generalize this claim from the domain studied by McEnery and Xiao, public health, to English/Chinese in general. As can be seen from Figure 1, while the two languages differ typologically, they show a strikingly similar distribution pattern of aspect markers. It is also interesting to note that while British English and American English have developed variations in spelling (e.g. *behaviour* vs. *behavior*), word choice (e.g. *petrol* vs. *gasoline*), and grammar (e.g. American English has two participle forms for the verb *get*, namely *got* and *gotten* whereas British English only uses the form *got*) (cf. Biber *et al.*, 1999: 19), their use of aspect is strikingly similar – the curves for the distribution of aspect markers for FLOB and Frown are almost identical to each other (see Figure 1).

Chinese and English, however, do show some differences in the distribution of aspect markers, as shown in Figure 2. The figure shows the frequencies of aspect markers, as percentages, in the fifteen text categories in the three corpora. As can be seen, by comparison to the two major varieties of English, aspect markers in Chinese

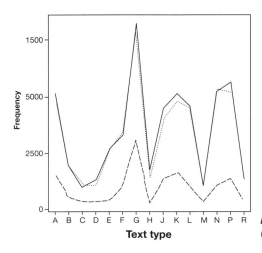

Figure 1 Distribution of aspect markers (frequency)

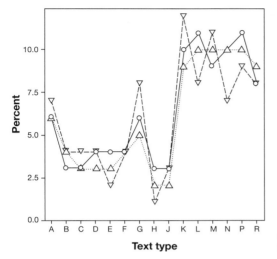

Figure 2 Distribution of aspect markers (percentage)

occur more frequently in categories G and K but less frequently in N, L, H, and E. The relatively low frequency of aspect markers in category N (martial arts fiction) in relation to other fiction types [. . .] is shown even more markedly in the contrast of the N category between LCMC and FLOB/Frown. British English and American English also differ in that the latter variety does not show such a marked fluctuation in aspect marking in narrative texts, notably in biography and the five types of fiction.

B5.4   KILPIÖ (1997)

Kilpiö (1997) examines, on the basis of the Helsinki corpus (see Unit A7.7), two distinct areas connected to verb *BE*: developments in its morphology and developments in its functional load from Old English (OE) to Early Modern English (EModE). This excerpt discusses the developments in the functions of *BE*. The data cover four sub-periods OE1-4 (OE1: –850 A. D., OE2: 850–950 A. D., OE3: 950–1050 A. D., OE4: 1050–1150 A. D.), ME1 (1150–1250 A. D.), ME3 (1350–1420 A. D.) and EModE1 (1500–1570 A. D.).

Kilpiö, M. 1997. 'On the forms and functions of the verb *be* from Old to Modern English'. In M. Rissanen, M. Kytö and K. Heikkonen (eds) *English in Transition: Corpus-based Studies in Linguistic Variation and Genre Styles*, pp. 101–120. Berlin: Mouton de Gruyter.

Text B5.4
M. Kilpiö

3.3 Developments in the functions of *be*

In his discussion of the use of *be* as a tense auxiliary, Mustanoja makes the following remark: "It is perhaps not without significance that while *be* is becoming an auxiliary *par excellence* of the passive voice, it is losing ground as an auxiliary of the perfect and pluperfect tenses" (Mustanoja 1960: 501). There is indeed good reason to assume that developments in different parts of the verbal system are not separate and autonomous but interdependent.

3.3.1 Chronological trends in the relative share of the main functions of be: a survey of present tense form from OE to EModE1

Table 6 presents an overview of the relative share of the three main uses of the verb *be* from Old to Early Modern English in the present tense, indicative and subjunctive.

The overall impression gained from the statistics in Table 6 is one of great stability in the relative share of the different functions of *be* throughout the periods studied. For a discussion of the implications of this, see section 3.3.

Table 7 gives the breakdown of the auxiliary uses of *be* in the periods studied, throughout which the use of *be* as a passive auxiliary is the most important. With rare constructions like the progressive the method of sampling adopted here clearly involves a random factor. As the corresponding eight OE examples have been classified as copular constructions, only ME3 contains examples of the progressive (see, however, Table 9 below for EModE1 instances of the progressive).

As can be seen, neither the *be to* construction, illustrated above by (10), nor the *be about to* construction are common in any of our periods. The rather high OE percentage is evidently due to the commonness in OE of the (particularly deontic) construction of the type seen in (19):

> (19) Nu ge habbað gehyred anrædlice hwæt eow *to donne is* and hwæt eow *to forgane is*. (Ælfric, *Letter to Wulfsige* 34)
> 'Now you have heard definitely what you are to do and what you are to abstain from.'

The rise of *be to* in EModE1 after being rather dormant in the two ME periods is in accordance with Mustanoja (1960: 524), who says that the "construction is comparatively infrequent in OE and early ME, but becomes more common in later ME and early Mod.E".

3.3.2 The relative share of the main functions in ME3 and EModE1 in finite past tense forms and in non-finite forms

As stated above [. . .] in connection with the statistics presented in Table 6, the overall impression gained from a survey of the relative share of the three main functions of *be* is one of great stability. Particularly with regard to the transition from Middle English to Early Modern English this runs counter to the expectations that the relative share of auxiliary uses at the expense of the remaining two uses would rise. It is for this reason that I here supplement the information provided by Table 6 by considering the main functions of *be* in past tense forms and in non-finite forms of *be* for the last two subperiods, ME3 and EModE1.

There are immediately obvious features of the relative shares of the main functions of *be* in the light of Tables 6 and 9. The first is that with past tense forms, auxiliary uses are relatively more common and copular uses correspondingly less common than with

M. Kilpiö

Table 6 Relative share of the three main functions of *be* in OE, ME1, ME3 and EModE1 in the select corpus (every 10th instance): present indicative and subjunctive

	OE		ME1		ME3		EModE1	
	N	%	N	%	N	%	N	%
Copular uses	527	65%	176	68%	276	64%	235	64%
Auxiliary uses	231	28%	59	23%	119	28%	103	28%
Main verb, non-copular	56	7%	22	9%	34	8%	31	8%
Total instances	814		257		429		369	

Table 7 Types of auxiliary uses

	OE		ME1		ME3		EModE1	
	N	%	N	%	N	%	N	%
Passive auxiliary	202	88%	52	88%	95	80%	93	90%
Pass. or tense auxiliary	19	8%	1	2%	7	6%	4	4%
Tense auxiliary	10	4%	6	10%	12	10%	6	6%
Progressive (ME-)	–	–	0	0%	5	4%	0	0%
Totals	231		59		119		103	

Table 8 Quasi-auxiliary uses of *be* included in the copular instances

	OE	ME1	ME3	EModE1
Be to	19	3	3	7
Be about to	–	–	–	1

Percentage of *be to* constructions of all copular constructions:
OE 3.6%, ME1 1.8%, ME3 1.1%, EModE1 3%

the present tense forms in subperiods ME3 and EModE1. The difference is of the same magnitude in both subperiods studied as appears from the following juxtaposition of percentages. The figures before the slash (/) give the percentage met in the present, the one after the slash the percentage met in the past tense:

ME3: copular 64%/54%; auxiliary 28%/37%; main verb, noncopular 8%/9%.
EModE1: copular 64%/54%; auxiliary 28%/39%; main verb, noncopular 8%/7%.

There is no obvious explanation for the difference between the present and past tense of *be* with regard to the relative frequency of the main uses of the verb.

Table 9 Relative share of the three main functions of *be* in a select corpus (every 8th instance)[a] of past tense forms of *be* in ME3 and EModE1 and the breakdown of the auxiliary uses between different types of auxiliaries

Function of be	ME3		EModE1	
	N	%	N	%
Copular	120	54%	126	54%
Auxiliary	82	37%	91	39%
Main verb, non-copular	19	9%	16	7%
Totals	221	100%	233	100%
Auxiliary uses				
– Passive auxiliary	71		81	
– Passive or tense auxiliary	4		3	
– Tense auxiliary	4		4	
– Progressive auxiliary	3		3	
Total auxiliaries	82		91	

[a] Every 8th, not every 10th instance was analysed here. The solution adopted was purely practical since the structure of the WordCruncher program makes the selection of every 8th example speedier and more mechanical than 10th.

The second noticeable thing that emerges from Table 9 is that when we move from ME3 to EModE1 there are no big changes in the relative proportions of the main uses; thus the addition of the past tense to the survey does not change the picture of relative stability gained from a study of the present tense forms.

Table 9 also shows the distribution of past tense forms of *be* between different auxiliary uses. The figures can be compared with those in Table 7; they show a similar kind of breakdown where the use of *be* as a passive auxiliary is preponderant (87% of the ME3 and 89% of the EModE1 auxiliary instances of *was*, *were*, etc. represent the passive auxiliary).

The data in Table 10 consists of those non-finite forms of *be*, infinitives, past participles and *-ing* forms in ME3 and EModE1 which are used in verb phrases so as to represent one of the three main functions of the verb *be*. Thus, to give a couple of examples, in (20) the infinitive has the function of a non-copular main verb, in (21) the past participle has the function of a passive auxiliary and in (22) the *-ing* form, a present participle, functions as a copula:

(20) Lat *be* soche falsheed; (*The Cloud of Unknowing* 23)
'Let such falsehood be'

(21) But [in] this thing hath *ben* discoveryd to the [that] thow seydest that thow wistest not a litel herbyforn (Chaucer, *Boethius' De Consolatione Philosophiae* 436.C2)
'But in this thing has been revealed to you what you said that you did not know a little before this time'

(22) yᵉ mylner *beyng* wᵗyn asked who was ther (*A Hundred Mery Talys* 36)
'the miller, being within, asked who was there'

Compared with the division of finite forms of *be* between the different functions of the verb set out in Tables 6 and 9 above, the breakdown of non-finite forms seen in

M. Kilpiö

Table 10 Relative share of the main functions of *be* in a select corpus (every 10th instance) of nonfinite forms of *be*

	ME3		EModE1	
	N	%	N	%
Infinitive				
Copular	43	40%	42	37%
Auxiliary	57	52%	66	58%
Main verb, non-copular	9	8%	6	5%
	109	100%	114	100%
Past participle				
Copular	7	54%	12	60%
Auxiliary	5	38%	7	35%
Main verb, non-copular	1	8%	1	5%
	13	100%	20	100%
-ing form				
Copular	2	100%	13	68%
Auxiliary	0	0%	6	32%
Main verb, non-copular	0	0%	0	0%
	2	100%	19	100%
All non-finite forms				
Copular	52	42%	67	44%
Auxiliary	62	50%	79	52%
Main verb, non-copular	10	8%	7	4%
Total forms analysed	124	100%	153	100%

Table 10 again presents a different kind of picture. As only infinitives are represented by a large enough number of instances to enable us to make reliable statistical comparisons between the two periods examined, the main focus will be on this non-finite form. It is worth noticing that with infinitives, both in ME3 and in EModE1, the auxiliary uses are the most common function of the infinitive (52% of the infinitive instances in ME3, 58% in EModE1). In the infinitive there is also a rise in the percentage of auxiliary uses when we move from ME3 to EModE1. By the same token, the relative shares of copular and non-copular main verb uses decrease in EModE1 compared to ME3.

It is interesting to note that the finiteness or non-finiteness of the form of *be* affects its distribution between the copular and auxiliary uses. This is understandable in view of the general tendency to increase three-verb groups in 16th century English and the natural avoidance of non-finite copulas of the type illustrated by example (22).

Of the auxiliary instances, the majority represent the passive auxiliary both in ME3 and EModE. Thus of the 57 infinitives used as auxiliaries in ME3 56 are passive auxiliaries and one is a tense auxiliary; all five past participles with auxiliary function represent the passive auxiliary. In subperiod EModE1, all the non-finite forms with auxiliary function represent the passive auxiliary. This confirms the picture gained from finite forms of *be* functioning as an auxiliary.

One feature in Table 10 that points the way to future developments is the great increase in the number of occurrences of *being* used either as a gerund or as a present participle when we move from subperiod ME3 to EModE3. This expansion naturally paves the way to the enrichment of the morphology of the progressive.

B5.5 MAIR, HUNDT, LEECH AND SMITH (2002)

While Kilpiö (1997) traces language in transition over several centuries, Mair, Hundt, Leech and Smith (2002) explore language change occurring over a shorter span of time. This paper compares part-of-speech tag frequencies in two matching one-million-word reference corpora of standard British English, LOB and FLOB (see Unit A7.4). The study shows a significant rise in the frequency of nouns, which is not paralleled by a corresponding decrease in verbs. This excerpt examines frequency changes among subcategories and combinations of nouns and provides an explanation from both a diachronic and a synchronic perspective.

Mair, C., Hundt, M., Leech, G. and Smith, N. 2002. 'Short-term diachronic shifts in part-of-speech frequencies'. *International Journal of Corpus Linguistics* 7/2: 245–264.

Text B5.5
C. Mair,
M. Hundt,
G. Leech and
N. Smith

3 Frequency changes among subcategories and combinations of nouns

Leaving aside discussion of other word classes, we may at this stage look more closely at the noun category from yet a further viewpoint: let us consider the frequency of different subcategories of nouns, to find out if the noun increase between LOB and F-LOB is concentrated in one subcategory rather than another.

The striking feature of Table 3 [. . .] is the consistency of the increase in the use of nouns across different categories and subcategories. However, although all three of these important subclasses of nouns show the same increase, they do so to markedly different degrees. The most significant increase of all is that of proper nouns, which amounts to 11%. Why the texts of F-LOB contain so many more proper nouns than the texts of LOB is not one of the questions to be answered in this article, but one suggestion which may contribute to the answer is that F-LOB reflects a greater prevalence of acronyms in the 1990s, as shown in Table 4.

Most proper nouns which are printed entirely in capitals are acronyms: words such as UNO, UNICEF, RSPCA, etc. Although these do not make up a large proportion of all proper nouns, it is worth noting a remarkable difference between their incidence in the two corpora: acronyms appear to be nearly twice as frequent in F-LOB as in LOB.

We now illustrate another way of attacking the issue of the higher frequency of nouns in F-LOB. This is to obtain counts of noun + noun sequences, to see what change if any has taken place between LOB and F-LOB. There is more than a suspicion that the favoured Germanic way of forming complex lexical expressions – the combining of nouns – is making a comeback in the later 20th century, and it may be further suspected that this change is more salient in newswriting (Press) than in other categories: witness the well-known multiple-noun headlines such as:

> BT *strike threat over plans to chop* 1,000 (F-LOB text A06)
> *Flagship hospital boss out* (F-LOB text A07)

To investigate this, our first tactic was to count all tags N* N*: that is, any noun (including proper nouns) followed by other noun. The results showed a vastly significant increase in the use of noun + noun sequences in F-LOB, as shown in Table 5.

C. Mair,
M. Hundt,
G. Leech and
N. Smith

Table 3 Frequency of selected noun subcategories in the LOB and F-LOB corpora

Subcorpus	LOB corpus		F-LOB corpus		Difference	
	Raw freq.	per million	raw freq.	per million	% of LOB	log likelihood
Singular common nouns						
Press	28047	157754	28772	161386	+2.3%	7.4
Gen. Prose	65631	158274	67996	164335	+3.8%	47.2
Learned	27254	169473	27592	172093	+1.5%	3.2
Fiction	32764	127726	34278	133450	+4.5%	32.2
Total	153696	152206	158638	157186	+3.3%	80.9
Plural common nouns						
Press	9214	51825	9835	55166	+6.4%	18.6
Gen. Prose	23844	57501	26117	63119	+9.8%	108.4
Learned	9806	60977	10783	67256	+10.3%	49.4
Fiction	8037	31331	9213	35868	+14.5%	78.7
Total	50901	50407	55948	55436	+10.0%	241.3
Proper nouns						
Press	12246	68879	12413	69626	+1.1%	0.7
Gen. Prose	14432	34804	17579	42486	+22.1%	316.9
Learned	3765	23412	4551	28383	+21.2%	76.7
Fiction	9229	35978	9474	36885	+2.5%	2.9
Total	39672	39287	44017	43614	+11.0%	228.1

Table 4 Proper nouns consisting entirely of capital letters: comparison of frequency in LOB and F-LOB

Subcorpus	LOB corpus		F-LOB corpus		Difference	
	Raw freq.	per million	raw freq.	per million	% of LOB	log likelihood
Press	775	4372	857	4811	+10.0%	3.7
Gen. Prose	391	946	1196	2895	+205.9%	428.1
Learned	98	617	615	3852	+524.1%	414.7
Fiction	166	648	188	731	+12.8%	1.3
Total	1430	1422	2856	2833	+99.2%	479.7

Strikingly, the most dramatic increases of noun + noun sequences are not found in Press (A–C), where it could be expected, but rather in other categories, particularly General Prose. It was decided to try other variants, but surprisingly, it was not combinations ending with a proper name, but combinations ending with a common noun that showed the steepest increase of occurrence. In Table 6, we compare LOB and F-LOB in terms of sequences of noun + common noun.

The table shows a very marked difference – an increase of 27.5% in F-LOB above the frequency in LOB. Note that the Noun + Common noun rise is a feature of every text category A–R, not just the four block groupings used in this paper; whereas Noun + Proper Noun sequences rise in only 6 of the 15 text categories.

C. Mair,
M. Hundt,
G. Leech and
N. Smith

Table 5 Noun + noun sequences: comparison of frequency in the LOB and F-LOB corpora

Subcorpus	LOB corpus		F-LOB corpus		Difference	
	Raw freq.	per million	raw freq.	per million	% of LOB	log likelihood
Press	9876	55714	10874	61045	+9.6%	43.3
Gen. Prose	12938	31306	16229	39277	+25.5%	372.8
Learned	5260	33127	5961	37336	+12.7%	40.0
Fiction	4127	16121	4952	19261	+19.5%	71.6
Total	32201	32030	38016	37711	+17.7%	466.3

Table 6 Sequences of Noun + Common noun: comparison of the LOB and F-LOB corpora (excluding tags NNB, NNL*, and NNA, which are invariably associated with naming expressions)

Subcorpus	LOB corpus		F-LOB corpus		Difference	
	Raw freq.	per million	raw freq.	per million	% of LOB	log likelihood
Press	5098	28760	6376	35794	+24.5%	136.5
Gen. Prose	8756	21187	11562	27982	+32.1%	389.4
Learned	4459	28083	5235	32788	+16.8%	58.0
Fiction	2448	9562	3366	13092	+36.9%	141.7
Total	20761	20651	26539	26326	+27.5%	691.9

4 Shifts in part-of-speech frequencies: diachronic and synchronic factors

To cast further light on tag frequency in a diachronic perspective, it is instructive to relate the observed changes to the synchronic variation manifest in a given corpus at any one time. In their exhaustive analysis of the tagged LOB corpus, Johansson and Hofland, for example, have shown tag frequencies to vary quite drastically from genre to genre (1989/I:7–39, in particular 15). Our figures, which are based on the C8 re-tagging of LOB and therefore differ from theirs in minor ways, are in Table 7.

In the wake of Johansson and Hofland's pioneering effort there have been a number of further corpus-based studies of part-of-speech distribution – most recently Biber *et al.*'s (1999) *Longman Grammar of Spoken and Written English*. None of them – including Hudson's (1994) facetiously titled 'About 37% of Word-Tokens are Nouns' – casts doubt on the strong tie between genre/text-type and the frequency of nouns and verbs.

Stated in the most simple terms, the major result of all such research is the following: information orientation appears to promote the use of nouns, whereas narration is characterised by a higher incidence of verbs. LOB does not contain any spoken language, so that it is impossible to ascertain without further data analysis to what extent the results from the Fiction (K–R) sections, through the incorporation of fictional dialogue, represent the situation in speech. However, Leech *et al.* (2001: 294–295) gives comparative percentages for the frequency of nouns and verbs as in Table 8, demonstrating that the high verb-to-noun ratio shown for fiction in Table 7 is even higher in general spoken corpus material.

What does all this mean in terms of the diachronic analysis attempted in the present paper? First and foremost, the extent of the synchronic variation observed makes clear that smallish shifts in part-of-speech ratios over time must be interpreted

C. Mair,
M. Hundt,
G. Leech and
N. Smith

Table 7 Noun and verb frequencies in LOB (given as percentages)

	Nouns	Verbs
Fiction	20.0	21.9
Nonfiction (all)	26.9	16.4
Nonfiction/press (A–C)	29.6	16.6
Nonfiction/science (J)	26.2	15.5
Total	25.1	17.8

Table 8 Noun and verb frequencies in the BNC sampler (given as percentages)

	Nouns	Verbs
Written texts	28.4	17.3
Spoken transcriptions	14.6	23.1

with extreme caution. After all, what is the significance of a 5.3% increase in nouns in the corpus overall, when at any given time there is a much greater scope for variation based on genre?

Changes in tag frequencies thus do not reflect grammatical change directly. Rather, they may hold a clue to the puzzle of how grammatical innovations spread in actual usage, namely at differential speeds through different genres. To illustrate this general assumption, consider a concrete case at hand, namely the rise in verbs of 7.3 per cent observed in our reportage samples (sections A in LOB and F-LOB). This is not a direct sign of a grammatical change, but shows a style change. Reportage over the past thirty years has moved a little closer towards other genres rich in verbs – represented by fiction and conversation in our corpora. Such colloquialisation and informalisation of news writing is a sociocultural rather than a linguistic phenomenon – and has been plausibly accounted for by critical discourse analysts, sociologists and historians (cf., e.g., Fairclough 1992). But in due course, it will no doubt have consequences for the linguistic system, because the new stylistic climate will speed up the demise of many lexical and grammatical archaisms and prevent the establishment of new lexical and grammatical markers of more formal or literary diction.

Standard English is primarily defined through its lexicon, and through its grammar. On a textual level, however, standard English is also usage, style and choice. This is, after all, the level on which we immediately recognise the standard British English of the beginning of the 20th century and distinguish it from 1960s and 1990s English, or tell British standard English apart from American standard English – long before we confirm such first intuitions through laborious counts of grammatical or lexicogrammatical variables such as the proportion of analytical and synthetic comparatives/ superlatives or the prevalence of regularised *spoiled* and *burned* against their irregular counter-parts *spoilt* and *burnt*. At this level of language change – for lack of a better term one might speak of changes in grammar-in-text – the comparison of tag frequencies will usefully complement the quantitative study of lexical frequencies and the qualitative analysis of individual examples. In addition, the study of changing stylistic fashions and genre conventions is an interdisciplinary undertaking, linking linguistics, sociology and cultural history. The investigation of corpora may thus yield insights which are useful far beyond the field of linguistics itself, and this is a prospect we need not be unhappy about at all.

Summary

This unit demonstrated the use of corpora in contrastive and diachronic studies, with particular reference to multilingual corpora and diachronic corpora. Readers are reminded that while parallel corpora are useful in translation studies, they are typically complemented by comparable corpora when used in contrastive studies (see Unit A10.6).

LOOKING AHEAD

As we will see in Case Study 6 in Section C, translated language is distinct from L1 language. We noted earlier that diachronic studies would not really have been possible without corpus data. Diachronic corpora are useful in tracking developments in the syntactic, semantic and functional distributions of linguistic features in both the long and short terms. In Case Study 2 readers will have an opportunity to explore how language change over three decades (from the early 1960s to the early 1990s) has influenced speakers' choice between a *to*-infinitive and a bare infinitive following *HELP*. In the next unit, the final unit in Section B, we will demonstrate the use of corpora in an important area of linguistics – language teaching and learning.

Unit B6
Language teaching and learning

B6.1 INTRODUCTION

While the usefulness of corpora in language pedagogy is an area of ongoing debate (see Unit B2.4), we noted in Unit A10.8 that there has been an increase in interest in recent years in the corpus-based approach to language teaching and learning. This unit uses three excerpts from published papers to discuss the theoretical and practical issues related to using corpora in language education, focusing on English as a second or foreign language.

B6.2 GAVIOLI AND ASTON (2001)

We noted in Unit B2.4 that the use of corpora in language pedagogy is a topic causing ongoing debate. Among those who support using corpus data in language teaching there has been considerable discussion of how far teaching syllabuses and materials should be 'corpus-driven'. Gavioli and Aston (2001) summarize this debate and argue that corpora should not only be viewed as resources which help teachers to decide what to teach, they should also be viewed as resources from which learners may learn directly. This excerpt cites the first four sections from their paper.

Gavioli, L. and Aston, G. 2001. 'Enriching reality: language corpora in language pedagogy'. *ELT* Journal 55/3: 238–246.

Text B6.2
L. Gavioli and
G. Aston

Introduction

Ever since the *Cobuild* project started producing corpus-based dictionaries, grammars, and materials for ELT, applied linguists have been divided between those who have seen the findings and methods of corpus linguistics as providing new ways forward in language teaching, and those who have warned against over-enthusiasm. In a debate in ELT *Journal* 52/1 (1998), Ron Carter and Guy Cook focused on two of the main terms of this argument. First, they asked how far the analysis of corpora provides descriptions of the workings of 'real English'; second, they asked whether such English is what foreign learners need. In this paper, we begin by summarizing our own position on these issues, and then go on to argue that the terms of this debate should be redefined in relation to learners' needs to experience language as 'real' for themselves.

L. Gavioli and
G. Aston

Can corpora capture reality?

The largest corpora of English are still smaller than the average adult user's experience of the language, and very different in their composition (most notably in the ratio of speech to writing). Nonetheless, they provide evidence about linguistic performance which can undoubtedly be helpful in deciding what we should teach.

First, they can be used to test claims based purely on intuition. For instance, Carter (1998: 43) proposes that the word 'real' 'invariably carries positive associations', as in 'Real ale', 'Get real!', 'Real English', 'that real country taste', etc. But if we look up 'real' in the 100-million word British National Corpus (BNC), the picture is rather different. We find that the most frequent lexical items to collocate with 'real' are 'world(s)', 'life/ lives', 'term(s)', and 'problem(s)'. Can we really say that 'the real world', 'real life', 'in real terms', or, most strikingly, 'a real problem', have positive associations? The corpus evidence makes it clear that the linguistic 'fact' Carter proposes is over-generalized, and suggests that we might want to reformulate it somewhat for teaching purposes. Second, corpora can help clarify our motives for teaching particular features. Carter discusses a number of spoken formulae which carry 'cultural' content, including expressions referring to other nations: 'Dutch courage', 'to go Dutch', 'double-Dutch', 'Dutch cap', 'Dutch auction', 'then I'm a Dutchman', etc. He goes on to claim:

> Here we learn several useful and widely used phrases, but we can also learn something about British insularity, and that distrust of foreigners to the point where the British can be interpreted as believing almost all of them to be either unintelligible, untrustworthy, or 'unreal'.
>
> (Carter 1998: 49)

Judging from publicly-available corpora of speech, however, these expressions are far from 'widely used'. In the spoken component of the BNC (10 million words), 'go Dutch' and 'double-Dutch' each occur twice, 'I'm a Dutchman' once, while 'Dutch cap', 'Dutch courage', and 'Dutch auction' are not found at all. A similarly-sized British speech component of the Bank of English presents an even more desolate picture: there are four instances of 'double-Dutch', and that is all. Given these very low frequencies, these items would only seem worth teaching if we have other good reasons for doing so. In the passage cited, Carter actually suggests two such reasons: 'double-Dutch, 'go Dutch', and indeed, 'Dutch cap', could all be useful expressions for a learner wishing to avoid social embarrassment in Britain; and the study of British insularity, as revealed through linguistic references to foreign nationals and nations, could constitute a stimulating activity which could increase learners' awareness of cultural issues.

The inclusion in syllabuses of language which is very rare in large corpora thus calls for justification, and the same is equally true for the exclusion of language which is common. As we saw with 'real', corpora can remind us of frequent uses which might otherwise tend to be ignored. Thus McCarthy and Carter (1995) notice the frequency in speech of the semi-modal 'tend to' (it occurs almost as often as 'ought' in the BNC spoken component). Although this verb has traditionally received little attention in teaching, it arguably provides learners with a valid alternative to frequency adverbs such as 'usually' and 'often'. A more problematic case noted by the same authors is that of structures with 'tails' (as in 'That's enough, *don't you think*?'), which are rarely found among the prototypical patterns presented by textbooks. While their frequency

L. Gavioli and
G. Aston

in conversation suggests they should be included in syllabuses, other considerations may argue against this, at any rate from the perspective of spoken production. Their use being highly context-dependent, they seem difficult to teach and harder to master than other markers of affect with similar functions. The point is that while corpora do not tell us what we should teach, they can help us make better-informed decisions, and oblige us to motivate those decisions more carefully.

Can corpora provide valid models for learners?

Most existing corpora are collections of spoken and/or written texts produced by native speakers. Both Cook (1998) and Carter (1998) ask whether learners in fact need to imitate native-speaker behaviour, and whether, in consequence, corpus data are relevant to them as models – a doubt, incidentally, which relates not only to corpora, but to 'authentic' materials in general. There is, however, no reason to assume that the materials we present to learners should constitute models for imitation (were this the case, it would be difficult to imagine a role for literature, advertising, or other 'creative' genres in the language classroom), and it would be wrong to expect corpus data to do so either. When linguists abstract generalized patterns from corpora, and interpret the data as exemplifying them, these patterns are rarely immediately apparent. Sinclair, who attempted to include only actual corpus instances as examples in the *Cobuild* dictionary (Sinclair 1995), reports how difficult it was to find instances which reflected 'typical' usage in every respect (Sinclair and Kirby 1990: 114–15). The *Cobuild* team was, moreover, only looking for single sentences exemplifying a limited range of features. The chances of finding a complete corpus text which consistently shows typical usage is minimal, so if we want to propose a model of conversation at the hairdresser's, we will almost certainly do better to use an invented dialogue than a corpus extract – though we may want to compare it with corpus extracts before proposing it to students.

It is precisely because they do not simply offer models to imitate, however, that corpus data seems valuable for learners. As Leech and Candlin (1986: xiv–xvi) observed well over a decade ago, data from corpora has to be interpreted subjectively. Their reality, from this point of view, is a characteristic not just of the data, but above all of the interpretative process. For learners, the reality of corpus data would seem principally to lie in the extent to which they can interpret them to create models of their own.

From real texts to real discourse

In one of his most widely-quoted distinctions, Widdowson (1978) contrasts *genuineness* (a quality of texts) and *authenticity* (a quality of discourse interpretation). Viewed in these terms, corpora of naturally-occurring texts provide samples of genuine language, since they are produced by speakers and writers with real communicative goals. The reproduction of such samples in pedagogic contexts does not, however, guarantee them authenticity as discourse, which depends on their context of reception. In their discussion, both Carter (1998) and Cook (1998) seem to treat reality as an inherent characteristic of materials, i.e. as a matter of genuineness of the text. But if – as communicative language teaching has traditionally held – learning is primarily a product of discourse authenticity, the question is not whether corpora represent reality, but rather whether their use can create conditions that will enable learners to engage in real discourse, authenticating it on their terms – and whether this engagement can lead to language learning.

Widdowson (1998) claims that learners will often be unable to authenticate real texts, since they do not belong to the community for which those texts are designed, and are therefore unqualified to participate in the discourse process. This, however, overlooks the fact that there is an alternative way of authenticating discourse, by adopting the role of an observer (Aston 1988). While the participant interacts with the text as an intended recipient, the observer views this interaction from the outside, adopting a critical, analytic perspective. Observer as well as participant roles can allow learning: observation allows strategies of interaction to be noticed, while participation allows such strategies to be tested.

Corpora clearly allow many opportunities to authenticate discourse through observation. As already noted, unlike the examples provided by textbooks and dictionaries, the samples of language provided by corpus data do not immediately illustrate particular linguistic patterns. A concordance does not make sense in itself: sense has to be attributed to it by the reader, who must infer patterns which will as far as possible account for the data. In other words, a concordance can be viewed as a text that provokes 'a pragmatic reaction' in the observer (Widdowson 1998: 713). As we shall see in the following examples, this pragmatic reaction can also constitute a focus for discourse participation, thereby allowing learners to alternate and integrate these two roles.

B6.3   THURSTUN AND CANDLIN (1998)

Thurstun and Candlin (1998) explore ways of using concordancing in teaching the vocabulary of academic English. In this excerpt, the authors discuss the rationale for their decision to focus in detail on a restricted set of vocabulary items.

Text B6.3
J. Thurstun and
C. Candlin

Thurstun, J. and Candlin, C. 1998. 'Concordancing and the teaching of the vocabulary of academic English'. *English for Specific Purposes* 17: 267–280.

Introduction

Since concordancing programs have become available to teachers and students, their possibilities have been seen as offering new and exciting directions for developing teaching materials, enabling students themselves to make direct discoveries about language (Johns 1991a; Tribble & Jones 1990) and as an aid to course design (Flowerdew 1993). This particular project has used the concordancing program, *Microconcord*, and the *Microconcord Corpus of Academic Texts* (1993) to develop teaching materials for independent study of the vocabulary of academic English.

It was decided to develop corpus-based learning materials that would be of assistance to students from any discipline, focusing on lexical items shared across various disciplines. Li & Pemberton (1994: 184) point out that tertiary students do not necessarily find discipline-specific technical vocabulary difficult:

J. Thurstun and
C. Candlin

Rather, it is the vocabulary with a middle frequency of occurrence across texts of various disciplines that students find most problematic.

Nation (1990) refers to this range of vocabulary items as "academic vocabulary".

Rationale

The features of this project which require preliminary explanation are firstly, the decision to focus in detail on a restricted set of vocabulary items, and secondly the use of concordancing techniques to provide the student with intensive exposure to the use of these items.

In choosing the vocabulary items to be dealt with in this project, we began with the extensive University Word List cited in Nation (1990). Using this list, we developed categories of vocabulary items according to the various rhetorical purposes they can serve in academic writing. We then selected items according to frequency of use cited by Nation and our own perception (based on having marked many hundreds of student essays and in consultation with teachers of English for Academic Purposes) of the extent to which their investigation would be helpful to students. In this way, we created a list of about 150 examples [. . .] attempting to group them according to purpose. We will refer to these purposes as rhetorical functions. Further selection was based on frequency counts provided by *Microconcord*, using the *Microconcord Corpus of Academic Texts*. The main rhetorical functions we identified, and the keywords for each function on which the project finally focused were:

- Stating the topic of your writing
  - factor
  - issue
  - concept
- Referring to the research literature
  - evidence
  - research
  - source
- Reporting the research of others
  - according to
  - suggest
  - claim
- Expressing opinions tentatively
  - may
  - possible
  - unlikely
  - probably
- Explaining procedures undertaken in a study
  - identification
  - analysis
  - criteria
- Drawing conclusions
  - conclude
  - summarize
  - it is clear
  - thus

J. Thurstun and
C. Candlin

Such a focus on particular rhetorical functions provides a purposeful basis for learning and potentially some structuring for the teaching of academic writing skills. The intensive focus on a limited number of vocabulary items is characteristic of concordance-based materials and is supported by the experience of Tim Johns (University of Birmingham, UK, personal communication). As with Li & Pemberton (1994), students, in his view, do not necessarily need to master a wide range of academic terms in order to write acceptable academic essays. They do, however, need to be competent users of a restricted set of "semi technical" vocabulary items. Pickard (1994: 218) suggested that, when preparing concordance-based material, there is

> a potential tension between the aims of wanting to expose students to a variety of vocabulary as a means of encouraging variety in their writing, and using a concordancer to search for a keyword. Through selection of key, frequent words how does one encourage variety?

Variety, however, is not necessarily an end to be pursued for its own sake in the teaching of academic writing, and Pickard goes on to point out that, by drawing students' attention to collocates of the keyword, concordance-based study has considerable potential for expanding student vocabulary while dealing in detail with selected items.

Academics from four Australian universities responded in a recent study (Bush *et al.* 1996) to questions about their expectations of student writing. Results indicated that accurate and appropriate use of academic vocabulary is considered to be extremely important, but there is much more concern that students convey their ideas clearly than that they attempt to rely on jargon.

These comments and studies supported our view that the most useful approach to helping students unfamiliar with the vocabulary required in academic writing would be to focus on intensive work on a few of the most useful lexical items selected as typically realising each of the rhetorical functions listed.

These three or four selected words for each rhetorical function are all frequently used, most appearing more than once every 6000 words in the corpus. Words such as *unlikely* and forms associated with *summary* are not used quite so frequently in the corpus of professional, published work, (appearing with a frequency of 1/12600 and 1/13254 respectively) but were nonetheless included given their usefulness for student writers, particularly for dealing with modality and the creation of final statements. A range of grammatical forms of each word in question was included where appropriate.

Concordance-based materials offer the learner a rich experience of language (in this case, the language of academic English). Concordancing has been used in this project to present students with the opportunity to condense and intensify the process of learning through exposure to multiple examples of the same vocabulary item in context, and to promote awareness of collocational relationships. According to Nattinger (1988: 63),

> guessing vocabulary in context is the most frequent way we discover the meaning of new words.

Johns (1991b) has argued that the central justification for using concordance-based materials is that they can help to develop this ability to guess the meaning and use of unknown words from context. In our materials, exposure to concordances for the purpose of discovering meaning focuses learner attention on the central importance of collocational relationships in connection with the keywords. The broad objective of the materials is to develop the writing competence of students by promoting discovery of meaning and by making students aware of representative patterns of language use and of selected grammatical structures. This awareness is accompanied by guided opportunities for research, practice and improvisation.

At various stages in the preparation of this material, as with Flowerdew (1993: 240) who found "areas where concordancing has revealed a discrepancy between published materials and the specialist corpus", we also encountered language use which questioned the standard patterns usually recommended to EAP students by teachers and grammar books. For example, it was found that the plural form, *researches*, occurred in the corpus on ten occasions, indicating that it is, in fact, accepted practice in published texts though usually not accepted by markers of student essays. Although we did not draw student attention to this specifically, we decided to modify questions about the use of this form so that students were not obliged to understand that it is never used in its plural form. Likewise, the standard advice to students to use the past tense of the reporting verb for author-prominent statements (see Weissberg & Buker 1990: 45, who advise students that "in these citations the *simple past tense* is used in the verb of report") was not supported by the corpus, these reporting verbs being shown to be used more frequently in the present tense.

B6.4 CONRAD (1999)

Conrad (1999) presents a corpus-based study of linking adverbials (e.g. *therefore* and *in other words*), on the basis of which she suggests that it is important that a language teacher do more than use classroom concordancing and lexical or lexico-grammatical analyses if language teaching is to take full advantage of the corpus-based approach. This excerpt is taken from section 1 of her paper.

Conrad, S. 1999. 'The importance of corpus-based research for language teachers'. *System* 27: 1–18.

Text B6.4
S. Conrad

Interest in the use of language corpora and computer analysis tools for language education has grown tremendously in the past decade. Understandably, articles written for language teachers have emphasized the use of corpora and computers in the classroom. The greatest attention has been paid to the use of concordancers – software programs whose primary purpose is to display words or simple grammatical items with their surrounding context. Writers emphasize the usefulness of concordancing for vocabulary and grammar development because it facilitates the use of authentic language, makes students more active and independent analysers of language, and provides empirical evidence about language use (Johns, 1986, 1994; Taylor, 1991; Hanson-Smith, 1993; Aston, 1995; Stevens, 1995; Qiao and Sussex, 1996; Cobb, 1997). In addition, articles about corpora and computer-assisted analyses have also addressed the development of cloze tests (Coniam, 1997) and of test construction in general (Alderson, 1996). Textbooks also are beginning to integrate the use of corpora; e.g. a recent textbook for spoken English (Carter and McCarthy, 1997) is designed around extracts from a spoken language corpus.

S. Conrad

There is no denying that these publications provide important information for language teachers. However, teachers may get the impression that these articles represent the only ways that language corpora can be useful to them. On the contrary, the growing field of corpus linguistics offers much more for teachers who want to understand language use and design effective materials for their students. In fact, even if teachers do not have computer expertise or computer facilities in their schools, corpus-based studies can be valuable resources for them.

The previous corpus-based work addressed to teachers has commonly been constrained in two ways. First, most of the articles for teachers stick to small-scale analyses. Usually, a small collection of texts – often compiled by convenience rather than following a principled design – is used, and analyses typically consist of looking at all the occurrences of a certain word or reading a transcript from the corpus. These analyses do provide interesting information, but many of the most useful aspects of corpus-based research are lost. For example, studies with larger, more diverse corpora can make comparisons in the characteristics across varieties of language (e.g. spoken conversation vs academic articles, or research articles in one discipline vs other disciplines), and thus better meet the needs of students or teachers in special purpose situations. Studies that include statistical analyses or even frequency data can identify strong patterns in language use that we do not recognize intuitively – patterns that may be very helpful to discuss with our students.

In addition, previous studies aimed at teachers rarely go beyond lexical or lexicogrammatical analyses; i.e. they concentrate on studies of words alone or words in connection with a grammatical feature (e.g. verbs occurring before *that* complement clauses) and do not undertake more complex grammatical analyses. Even one of the best-known publications covering analysis of a large corpus (Sinclair, 1991) focuses on lexical and lexico-grammatical analyses. In general, therefore, the fact that corpus-based studies can also provide insight into complex grammatical and discourse features remains unknown to many teachers. Even less well known is that corpus-based studies can address the interactions of many aspects of a grammatical feature: e.g. the frequency, syntactic forms of the feature, typical lexical items realizing the feature, and differences in use across language varieties can all be analysed together – and can all be tied to the communicative functions fulfilled by the feature.

In sum, the limited types of studies that have been addressed to teachers have run the risk of restricting teachers' appreciation of corpus linguistics. However, corpus linguistics is a means of studying and describing language use which offers a great deal beyond classroom concordancing and lexical/lexico-grammatical analyses. Practising teachers and teachers-in-training can learn a great deal from corpus-based studies and, in fact, owe it to their students to share the insights into language use that corpus linguistics provides.

Summary

In this final unit of Section B, we discussed the theoretical and practical issues of the corpus-based approach to language teaching and learning, using three excerpts from published material. The discussion not only showed that corpora are a valuable resource for language education, it also warned readers of potential problems of using corpora in language pedagogy.

LOOKING AHEAD

In Section C, we will return to the learning issue in Case Study 3 where readers will be engaged in an interlanguage analysis on the basis of the Longman Learners' Corpus.

Section C, the final Section of this book, will explore some of the areas in language studies which we have introduced in Section A and further discussed in this Section B.

SECTION C
Exploration

Having introduced the key concepts in corpus linguistics and presented excerpts from published material, we now want to engage readers in a series of case studies. These case studies investigate research questions in some of the areas of linguistic analysis introduced in Section A and further discussed in Section B. Each case study starts with an overview of the background knowledge needed for the study and a brief description of the corpus data used. Then it explores, together with the reader, a particular research question using specific tools (a corpus exploration tool and/or a statistics package). This is where the reader learns how to 'do' corpus linguistics, as the process of investigating the data using the package(s) concerned will be spelled out step by step, using text and screenshots. Thus by the end of each case study, a corpus has been introduced, the reader has learned how to use a retrieval package and some research questions have been explored. Readers are then encouraged to explore a related research question using the same corpus data, tools and techniques. Readers can visit the authors' companion website given in the Appendix for details of the availability of corpora and tools used in these case studies.

This section consists of six case studies. Case Study 1 explores the area of pedagog-ical lexicography on the basis of the BNC corpus (Word Edition), using BNCWeb. The focus of this study is on collocation analysis and the study seeks to describe collocation patterns of *sweet* from the BNC and integrate that information into a description of a dictionary entry. Case Study 2 uses four corpora of the Brown family to explore the potential factors that may influence a language user's choice of a full or bare infinitive after *HELP*, which include language variety (British English vs. American English), language change (English in the early 1960s and the early 1990s) and a range of syntactic conditions (e.g. an intervening nominal phrase, a preceding infinitive marker and the passive). This case study also introduces MonoConc Pro and SPSS. Case Study 3 uses WordSmith version 4 and the Japanese component of the Longman Learners' Corpus to study second-language acquisition of English grammatical morphemes. Case Study 4 uses the metadata encoded in the BNC (version 2) pertaining to demographic features such as user age, gender and social class, and textual features such as register, publication medium and domain to explore such dimensions of variation to discover a general pattern of swearing (more specifically the use of the word *FUCK*) in modern British English. This case study demonstrates how to use BNCWeb to make complex queries and provides readers with an opportunity to practice using SPSS. Case Study 5 compares two approaches to genre analysis – Biber's (1988) multifeature/multidimensional analysis and Tribble's (1999) use of the keyword function of WordSmith – through a comparison of speech and conversation in American English. This study introduces some advanced functions of WordSmith version 3. The final case study uses parallel and comparable corpora of English and Chinese to examine the effect of domain, text type and translation upon aspect marking in Chinese. This study also introduces parallel concordancing.

We would remind the readers that for each case study alternate versions of the study are available on our companion website covering most concordance packages. Note also that if any of the results gained by the readers do not match those given here they should check the website for an update.

Most of the case studies in this Section are based upon articles published elsewhere by the authors, as indicated in individual units. Readers interested in particular research questions can refer to our full papers for further discussion.

Unit C1
Collocation and pedagogical lexicography

CASE STUDY 1

C1.1 INTRODUCTION

We introduced collocation statistics in Unit A6.5 and discussed the use of corpora in lexicographic and collocation studies in Units A10.2 and B3.2. These units should have provided you with a solid grounding on which to undertake the case study in this unit, which will explore how to use BNCWeb to augment the collocation information available in learner dictionaries.

Most EFL (English as a Foreign Language) learner dictionaries published in the UK at present claim to be based on corpus data. Yet corpus-based learner dictionaries have a quite short history: it was only in 1987 that the *Collins COBUILD English Dictionary* was published as the first 'fully corpus-based' dictionary. Yet the impact of this corpus-based dictionary was such that most other publishers in the ELT market followed Collins' lead. By 1995, the new editions of major learner dictionaries such as the *Longman Dictionary of Contemporary English* (LDOCE, third edition), the *Oxford Advanced Learner's Dictionary* (OALD, fifth edition) and a newcomer, the *Cambridge International Dictionary of English* (CIDE, first edition) all claimed to be based on corpus evidence in one way or another.

Yet what is a corpus-based learner dictionary? The most common use of corpora in dictionary-making is for the selection of entries based on frequency information (see Unit A10.2). This is not a new approach. Scholars such as Thorndike and Barnhart used frequency information to select the entries for elementary school dictionaries in the 1930s (Thorndike 1935). It is rather surprising, therefore, that it was not until 1995 that such word frequency marking was introduced into EFL learner dictionaries by UK publishers. This is even more unusual when one considers that in countries like Japan this sort of frequency information had already been introduced in learner dictionaries in the early 1960s in such a way that each entry was marked with special symbols (e.g. an asterisk, a dagger, etc.) to indicate its relative frequency. Vagaries of history aside, it is clear that corpus-based learner dictionaries now exhibit one important feature – they include quantitative data extracted from a corpus.

Another important feature of corpus-based learner dictionaries, related to frequency information again, is that such dictionaries typically select the vocabulary used from a controlled set when defining the entry for a word. Producing definitions in an L2 that language learners can understand is a problem; language learners may not have a very well-developed L2 vocabulary. This makes it necessary and desirable for dictionary-makers to limit the vocabulary they use when defining words in a dictionary. This notion, encapsulated in the term 'defining vocabulary', is not new – it was discussed by the vocabulary control movement in the 1930s in the United States (see Ogden 1930). However, it was not until the publication of LDOCE (first edition, 1978) that the words used for defining dictionary entries were actually limited to a set of 2,000 words. Nowadays, most learner dictionary-makers prepare a list of defining words, usually ranging from 2,000 to 2,500 words, based on the frequency information extracted from corpora as well as on the lexicographers' experience of defining words.

Another important use of corpus data for lexicography is in the area of example selection. This is true of learner dictionaries also. Traditionally, for unabridged dictionaries such as the *Oxford English Dictionary* and the *Webster's International Dictionary of American English*, examples were often selected from a large collection of citations held on cards. Nowadays most dictionaries of English use corpora as the source of their examples (see Unit A10.2). Hence one might be tempted to say that when learner dictionaries do so they are following a trend that is common to all dictionaries. Yet this is not quite true. In the case of learner dictionaries, there was a tradition of using examples invented by lexicographers, rather than authentic materials, in dictionary production. This decision was influenced very strongly by the work of lexicographers working on learner dictionaries such as Harold E. Palmer and his successor A. S. Hornby, who worked together to produce the *Idiomatic and Syntactic English Dictionary* (ISED) in 1942, which was later published in the UK as the first edition of the *Oxford Advanced Learner's Dictionary* (OALD). Their reason for resisting authentic examples was simple: they believed that foreign language learners have difficulty understanding authentic materials and therefore have to be presented with simple, rewritten examples in which the use of a given word is highlighted to show its syntactic and semantic properties. It was corpus-based learner dictionary work which challenged this received wisdom: the COBUILD project broke with tradition and used authentic data extracted from corpora to produce illustrative examples for a learner dictionary. While there was disagreement among lexicographers concerning the value of authentic examples from corpora (see Unit A10.8), the second edition of COBUILD (1995) continued this policy and shifted to only using corpus examples. COBUILD represents an extreme case. Other dictionaries, such as LDOCE or OALD, have adopted some examples from corpora, but they do not strictly follow the policy of 'authentic examples only' and use rewritten examples from corpora whenever they view it as necessary. Nonetheless, the use of authentic examples in learner dictionaries is an area where corpus-based learner dictionaries have innovated.

Though the discussion so far outlines some ways in which corpora have changed learner dictionaries the discussion is illustrative rather than exhaustive. Yet even this short review shows that corpora have had a major impact upon the form and content of learner dictionaries. As well as providing information which can embellish existing lexicographic practice corpora may also make available new data over and above simple frequency data. A good example of this is data related to collocations, which represent, arguably, the greatest contribution that corpora have made to learner-focused lexicography. For the last two decades, increasing attention has been paid to information about lexical combinability (see Benson *et al.* 1986) or phraseology (see Cowie 1998). Although there have been some publications in this area, including dictionaries such as the *BBI Combinatory Dictionary of English* (1986) and *Kenkyusha's New Dictionary of English Collocations* (edited by S. Katsumata 1939, 1958, 1995), it was only quite recently that a more serious attempt was made to incorporate collocation information from corpora into a dictionary. Hence in this case study, we will look at the derivation and use of collocation information for learner dictionaries. In doing so we will first show how to extract collocation information from corpora, in this case the BNC using BNCWeb. We will also show that different kinds of collocation statistics are used for different purposes. Following from this we will choose one entry from an EFL learner's dictionary, LDOCE, and examine how corpus data have helped to improve the description of collocation information in its fourth edition in comparison with its first edition. Finally, we will explore the possibility of further improving collocation information in learner dictionaries by examining collocation data. While this study focuses on EFL dictionary-making, it should be apparent that the techniques and findings of this case study are also applicable to second language lexicography for other languages.

C1.2 COLLOCATION INFORMATION

Let us first explore how to extract collocation information from the BNC. We assume that you will be able to access the BNC (World Edition) via BNCWeb. In this study we will look at what collocates with *sweet*, specifically looking at what nouns co-occur with *sweet* to see whether there is a pattern in the distribution of *sweet* relative to these nouns. At this point you may want to check your own intuitions before proceeding – which noun is typically premodified by *sweet*? Jot your answers down before proceeding should you wish to do so, then consider your responses after looking at the corpus.

C1.2.1 Collocation analysis using BNCWeb

Let us first examine the collocation statistics provided by BNCWeb. We will take *sweet* as an example. To find out the collocation patterns of *sweet* in the BNC using BNCWeb, follow the steps described below:

1. Activate BNCWeb. You will see the default query window of BNCWeb (Figure C1.1).

2. Type in the search word *sweet* in the search window and click the 'Start Query' button (Figure C1.2).

3. The results window will appear with some raw data listed (e.g. the number of matches, range, normalized frequencies) (Figure C1.3).

4. If you click the 'KWIC View' button, you will see the KWIC concordance (Figure C1.4). You can browse the concordance lines if you want.

5. Now select 'Collocations' from the drop-down menu next to the 'KWIC/ Sentence View' button and press the 'Go!' button (Figure C1.5).

6. A new window will appear which allows you to adjust the 'Collocation Settings'. Here you can simply press 'Submit' to continue (Figure C1.6).

7. The collocation database will open (Figure C1.7). This table will display various collocation statistics according to the parameters you set in the upper-half of the window.

8. Since we are interested in the collocation patterns of *sweet* followed by a noun, we will define the window span as '+1 to +3' and choose 'any noun' in the 'Filter result by tag' box. Choose 'Rank by frequency' in the 'Statistics' box and press 'Go'. This will enable you to get a list of nouns collocating with *sweet*, ordered by raw frequency, shown in Figure C1.8.

At this stage, we need to examine the list carefully to check whether the words listed are truly collocates of the node word *sweet*. Also, from a lexicographer's viewpoint, it is important to judge whether the combination of the words (e.g. *sweet smell*) should be dealt with under the main entry *sweet* or under a separate entry (e.g. *sweet tooth*), or simply ignored (e.g. *Sweet Maxwell*, in which case *Sweet* is a person's name).

9. Now we can extract more detailed collocation information. Clicking on the word in the second column ('Word') will display different kinds of statistical measures (e.g. mutual information, log-likelihood, log-log, observed/expected, z score and MI3), showing the distribution of the collocate across the individual positions of the chosen window span. Figure C1.9 shows the details of the collocates of *smell*.

C1.2.2 Collocation statistics

Having obtained the various collocation statistics using BNCWeb, it is now appropriate to discuss their characteristics. These statistical measures are commonly used in corpus linguistics (see Unit A6.5).

The most basic statistic used for the calculation of collocations is raw frequency. As shown in Figure C1.8, the word *smell* ranks first in the column 'As collocate'. The raw frequency is 71, which means that the word *sweet* co-occurs with the word *smell* 71 times (with *sweet* as a pre-modifier) in the whole BNC. The word ranked second is *shop*, which is pre-modified by *sweet* 50 times. For learner dictionaries, the list is quite useful because we can choose the collocates which tend to occur

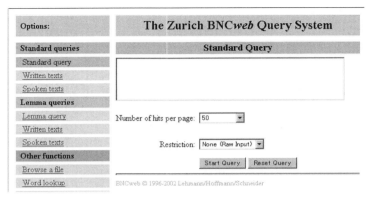

Figure C1.1 BNCWeb interface

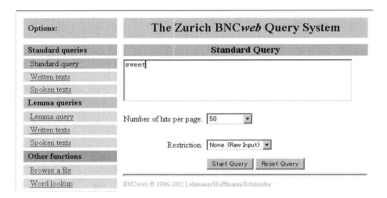

Figure C1.2 Start query

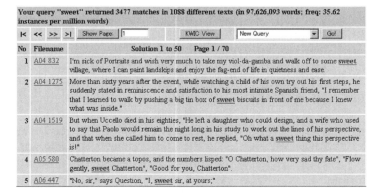

Figure C1.3 Result window

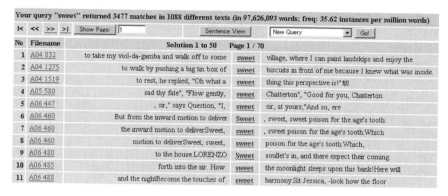

Figure C1.4 KWIC view

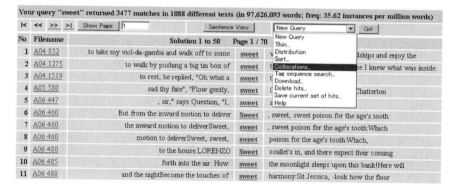

Figure C1.5 Menu: collocation

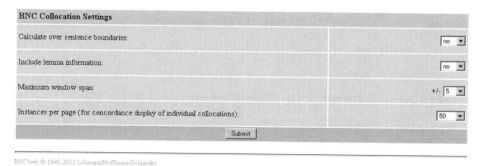

Figure C1.6 Collocation setting

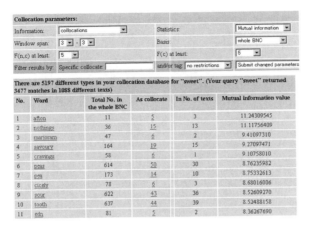

No.	Word	Total No. in the whole BNC	As collocate	In No. of texts	Mutual information value
1	afton	11	5	3	11.24309545
2	nothings	36	15	13	11.11756409
3	marjoram	47	6	2	9.41097310
4	savoury	164	19	15	9.27097471
5	cravings	58	6	1	9.10758010
6	peas	614	50	30	8.76235982
7	pea	173	14	10	8.75332613
8	cicely	78	6	3	8.68016006
9	sour	622	43	36	8.52609270
10	tooth	637	44	39	8.52488158
11	edn	81	5	2	8.36267690

Figure C1.7 Collocation database

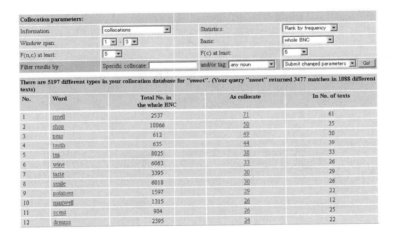

No.	Word	Total No. in the whole BNC	As collocate	In No. of texts
1	smell	2537	71	61
2	shop	10066	50	35
3	peas	612	49	30
4	tooth	635	44	39
5	tea	8025	38	33
6	wine	6063	33	26
7	taste	3395	30	29
8	smile	6018	30	26
9	potatoes	1597	29	22
10	maxwell	1315	26	12
11	scent	904	26	25
12	dreams	2395	24	22

Figure C1.8 Adjusting parameters

Collocation information for the node "sweet" and "smell" with tag restriction *any noun* (2537 occurrences in whole BNC)

Type of Statistics	Value (for window span 1 to 3)
Mutual information	8.22143845
Log-likelihood	826.830177
Log-log	50.55976742
Observed/expected	295.8333
Z-score	145.07967490
MI3	20.52093269

Within the window 1 to 3, *smell* with tag restriction *any noun* occurs 71 times in 61 different files.

Distance	No. of Occurrences	In No. of Files	Percent
1	55	45	77.46%
2	7	7	9.86%
3	9	9	12.68%
Total	71		100%

Figure C1.9 Collocation information

quite frequently and look familiar even to learners of English. Yet as you can see, when sorted by raw frequency of co-occurrence, frequent words crowd into the top of the collocate list. This holds out the possibility that they may not be collocates as such, rather they may simply be high-frequency words. Raw frequency is a poor guide to collocation. Look, for instance, at the third column 'Total No. in the whole BNC' for the words *smell* and *shop*. You can see immediately the difference in total frequency between the two words (2,537 times for *smell* and 10,066 times for *shop*). The raw frequency is not a reliable measure as the total number of occurrences of the word *shop* in the whole BNC is almost four times greater than that of *smell*. In the case of *smell* and *shop*, while the raw frequency also shows that *sweet smell* is a stronger collocation than *sweet shop*, we have to doubt the reliability of the raw frequency as a measure for collocations as it indicates that the combination *sweet shop* (ranks second) is stronger than *sweet peas* (ranks third) (see Figure C1.8). In the case of *sweet peas*, *peas* collocates with *sweet* 49 times while its total frequency in the whole BNC is only 612. This indicates that *peas* shows a very strong preference to collocate with *sweet*, certainly stronger than *shop*, which occurs in the BNC 10,066 times but collocates with *sweet* only 50 times (see Figure C1.8). In order to measure the strength of association we need to move away from the raw frequency and use other collocation statistics instead which can capture this relative strength of word combination.

One measure which takes into account the total frequencies of a node word and a collocate in relation to the size of the entire corpus is the 'observed/expected' score. This measure basically shows how far the results differ from what one would expect by chance alone. To derive a list of collocates sorted by the 'observed/expected' score using BNCWeb, select 'Observed/expected' from the pull-down menu for 'statistics' and press 'Go' in Figure C1.8. The results should look like those given in Figure C1.10. The list in the figure indicates that *smell* ranks eleventh, with an observed/expected score of 298.4599 while *shop* ranks forty-second, with an observed/expected score of 52.7938. This rank order is hardly surprising because, as noted, the raw frequency can also give this result. However, if we consider *peas* and *shop* again, we can see immediately the advantage of the observed/expected measure over the raw frequency. The observed/expected score for *pea* is 868.0599 (ranks fifth; *peas* ranks sixth, with an observed/expected score of 853.8720) whereas the score for *shop* is 52.9738 (ranks forty-second). This shows clearly that the association between *sweet* and *peas* is much stronger than that between *sweet* and *shop*.

A more sophisticated statistical measure than the observed/expected score provided by BNCWeb is the z-score. The z-score is a measure which adjusts for the general frequencies of the words involved in a potential collocation and shows how much more frequent the collocation of a word with the node word is than one would expect from their general frequencies (see Unit A6.5). To get a list of collocates sorted by the z-score using BNCWeb, select 'Z-score' from the pull-down menu for 'statistics' and press 'Go' in Figure C1.8. The results are given in Figure C1.11. The z-score measure is widely used and built into corpus tools such as SARA and its new XML-aware variant Xaira. However, as Dunning (1993) observes, this measure

There are 5197 different types in your collocation database for "sweet". (Your query "sweet" returned 3477 matches in 1088 different texts)

No.	Word	Total No. in the whole BNC	As collocate	In No. of texts	Observed / expected value
1	afton	11	5	3	4847.5851
2	nothings	36	15	13	4443.6197
3	marjoram	47	5	2	1134.5412
4	smelling	53	5	5	1006.1026
5	pea	172	14	10	868.0559
6	peas	612	49	30	853.8720
7	savoury	69	5	5	772.8034
8	tooth	635	44	39	738.9705
9	peppers	204	8	6	418.2230
10	scent	904	26	25	306.7277
11	smell	2537	71	61	298.4599
12	dessert	302	8	7	282.5083
13	fragrance	324	8	8	263.3256
14	chestnut	433	10	10	246.2976
15	perfume	522	12	12	245.1652
16	chariot	225	5	5	236.9931
17	sherry	568	12	11	225.3103
18	aroma	337	7	6	221.5217
19	potato	859	17	11	211.0590
20	maxwell	1315	26	12	210.8607

Figure C1.10 Observed/expected values

There are 5197 different types in your collocation database for "sweet". (Your query "sweet" returned 3477 matches in 1088 different texts)

No.	Word	Total No. in the whole BNC	As collocate	In No. of texts	Z-score value
1	nothings	36	15	13	258.17555938
2	peas	612	49	30	204.29802298
3	tooth	635	44	39	180.07311116
4	afton	11	5	3	155.68563956
5	smell	2537	71	61	145.07967490
6	pea	172	14	10	110.08220731
7	scent	904	26	25	89.02810980
8	marjoram	47	5	2	75.31708493
9	potatoes	1597	29	22	74.55396829
10	maxwell	1315	26	12	73.70174714
11	smelling	53	5	5	70.92600999
12	savoury	69	5	5	62.03689890
13	potato	859	17	11	59.61818989
14	peppers	204	8	6	57.69814759
15	perfume	522	12	12	54.01422902
16	taste	3395	30	29	52.60471316
17	sherry	568	12	11	51.78091689
18	shop	10066	50	35	50.50016367
19	dreams	2395	24	22	50.18084518
20	chestnut	433	10	10	49.43001633

Figure C1.11 Z scores

assumes that data is normally distributed (see Unit A6.3), an assumption which is not true in most cases of statistical text analysis unless either enormous corpora are used, or the analysis is restricted to only very common words (which are typically the ones least likely to be of interest). As a consequence, the z-score measure can substantially overestimate the significance of infrequent words (see Dunning 1993). As can be seen from Figure C1.11, rare words such as *nothings* (with an overall frequency of 36 in the BNC, ranks first), *afton* (11, ranks fourth) and *marjoram* (47, ranks eighth) are given on the top-ten collocate list.

The solution Dunning proposes for this problem is the log-likelihood (LL) score (see Unit A6.4). The LL measure does not assume the normal distribution of data. For text analysis and similar contexts, the use of log-likelihood scores leads to considerably improved statistical results. Using the LL test, textual analysis can be done effectively with much smaller amounts of text than is necessary for statistical measures which assume normal distributions. Furthermore, this measure allows comparisons to be made between the significance of the occurrences of both rare and common features (Dunning 1993: 67). Once again, we are fortunate in that BNCWeb provides this statistic, and hence users do not need to resort to statistics packages like SPSS to calculate the LL score. We can select 'Log-likelihood' from the pull-down menu for 'statistics' and press 'Go' in Figure C1.8 to get a collocate list sorted by the log-likelihood score. The results are given in Figure C1.12. As can be seen, the top-ten collocates based on LL scores include both frequent and infrequent words (but none of the infrequent words in the top 10 list are as rare as *nothings, afton* and *marjoram*).

A quite different approach to measuring collocation is mutual information (MI). The MI measure is not as statistically rigorous as the log-likelihood test, but it is certainly widely used as an alternative to the LL and z-scores in corpus linguistics. Readers can refer back to Unit A6.5 for a brief description of the MI statistic. To obtain a list of collocates for *sweet* sorted by the MI score, select 'Mutual information' from the pull-down menu for 'statistics' and press 'Go' in Figure C1.8. The results are shown in Figure C1.13. As shown in the figure, the top four collocates on the list (e.g. *Afton, nothings, marjoram* and *smelling*) are all rare words which occur less than 100 times (11, 36, 47 and 53 respectively). *Sweet Afton* is a phrase from the lyrics expressing the beauty of River Afton. *Sweet nothings* means 'romantic and loving talk'. *Sweet marjoram* is the name of a plant. For lexicographical purposes, these are interesting and should be treated in a general-purpose dictionary. However, for pedagogical purposes, these expressions are of secondary importance compared with more basic collocations. These examples show that the MI score, like the z-score, gives too much weight to rare words.

There is a way of rebalancing the MI score to address this problem by giving more weight to frequent words and less to infrequent words. The MI3 score was developed for just this purpose. MI3 achieves this effect by 'cubing' observed frequencies (see Oakes 1998: 171–172). The cubing of the frequencies gives a much bigger boost to high frequencies than low frequencies, thus achieving the desired effect. To obtain the collocation list sorted by the MI3 score, simply select 'MI3' from the pull-down menu for 'statistics' and press 'Go' in Figure C1.8. The results are shown in Figure C1.14. As can be seen, more frequent collocates such as *peas, smell, tooth* come to the top of the list when MI3 is used. This means that the cubic rebalancing pays off: these collocates are more useful for second language learners at beginning and intermediate levels.

There are 5197 different types in your collocation database for "sweet". (Your query "sweet" returned 3477 matches in 1088 different texts)

No.	Word	Total No. in the whole BNC	As collocate	In No. of texts	Log-likelihood value
1	smell	2537	71	61	826.830177
2	peas	612	49	30	675.906429
3	tooth	635	44	39	593.660739
4	shop	10066	50	35	408.432481
5	potatoes	1597	29	22	312.025103
6	tea	8025	38	33	306.656926
7	scent	904	26	25	303.883845
8	maxwell	1315	26	12	284.184120
9	taste	3395	30	29	279.402511
10	wine	6063	33	26	275.419870
11	nothings	36	15	13	262.364300
12	smile	6018	30	26	245.101917
13	dreams	2395	24	22	229.526641
14	pea	172	14	10	193.455248
15	potato	859	17	11	185.800871
16	foods	2085	17	7	155.527765
17	revenge	1030	14	14	142.413102
18	perfume	522	12	12	134.765054
19	sherry	568	12	11	132.718353
20	success	13242	20	19	116.084102

Figure C1.12 Log-likelihood scores

There are 5197 different types in your collocation database for "sweet". (Your query "sweet" returned 3477 matches in 1088 different texts)

No.	Word	Total No. in the whole BNC	As collocate	In No. of texts	Mutual information value
1	afton	11	5	3	12.24309519
2	nothings	36	15	13	12.11756527
3	marjoram	47	5	2	10.14793843
4	smelling	53	5	5	9.97460728
5	pea	172	14	10	9.76168918
6	peas	612	49	30	9.73792073
7	savoury	69	5	5	9.59400269
8	tooth	635	44	39	9.52941860
9	peppers	204	8	6	8.70817441
10	scent	904	26	25	8.26085960
11	smell	2537	71	61	8.22143844
12	dessert	302	8	7	8.14219505
13	fragrance	324	8	8	8.04074906
14	chestnut	433	10	10	7.94430425
15	perfume	522	12	12	7.93765567
16	chariot	225	5	5	7.88874580
17	sherry	568	12	11	7.81581431
18	aroma	337	7	6	7.79134980
19	potato	859	17	11	7.72154817

Figure C1.13 MI scores

The cubic approach to eliminating any bias in favour of low-frequency co-occurrences is not the only remedy to the problem, however. The log-log formula is yet another measure which reduces this undesirable effect of the MI score. The log-log test is basically an extension of the MI formula (see Oakes 1998: 234 for a description). To obtain the collocation list sorted by the log-log score, simply select 'Log-log' from the pull-down menu for 'statistics' and press 'Go' in Figure C1.8. The

There are 5197 different types in your collocation database for "sweet". (Your query "sweet" returned 3477 matches in 1088 different texts)

No.	Word	Total No. in the whole BNC	As collocate	In No. of texts	MI3 value
1	peas	612	49	30	20.96734082
2	smell	2537	71	61	20.52093269
3	tooth	635	44	39	20.44828121
4	nothings	36	15	13	19.93134592
5	scent	904	26	25	17.66173933
6	pea	172	14	10	17.37639914
7	potatoes	1597	29	22	17.31339352
8	maxwell	1315	26	12	17.12107120
9	shop	10066	50	35	17.01496482
10	afton	11	5	3	16.88695180
11	taste	3395	30	29	16.37207506
12	tea	8025	38	33	16.15409600
13	wine	6063	33	26	15.94796538
14	dreams	2395	24	22	15.90967669
15	potato	859	17	11	15.89647334
16	smile	6018	30	26	15.54620253
17	perfume	522	12	12	15.10758064
18	sherry	568	12	11	14.98573952
19	revenge	1030	14	14	14.79423528
20	marjoram	47	5	2	14.79179457

Figure C1.14 MI3 scores

There are 5197 different types in your collocation database for "sweet". (Your query "sweet" returned 3477 matches in 1088 different texts)

No.	Word	Total No. in the whole BNC	As collocate	In No. of texts	Log-log value
1	peas	612	49	30	54.67560166
2	tooth	635	44	39	52.02520577
3	smell	2537	71	61	50.55976742
4	nothings	36	15	13	47.34199968
5	scent	904	26	25	38.82967393
6	pea	172	14	10	37.16621581
7	potatoes	1597	29	22	36.90817799
8	maxwell	1315	26	12	36.28829602
9	shop	10066	50	35	32.32378914
10	taste	3395	30	29	32.18083051
11	potato	859	17	11	31.56153911
12	dreams	2395	24	22	30.90150878
13	tea	8025	38	33	29.69403846
14	wine	6063	33	26	29.55599874
15	perfume	522	12	12	28.45619780
16	afton	11	5	3	28.42758766
17	smile	6018	30	26	28.12836435
18	sherry	568	12	11	28.01940195
19	revenge	1030	14	14	27.33500150
20	chestnut	433	10	10	26.39040670

Figure C1.15 Log-log scores

results are given in Figure C1.15. The list looks quite similar to the one based on MI3. Both measures aim to reduce the undesirable effect of MI and produce a collocation list that shows more high-frequency words with a high rank. If you are interested in lexically unique collocations, however, MI-scores might be more useful.

A comparison of the various statistical measures provided by BNCWeb which we have reviewed so far shows that the raw frequency tends to overvalue frequent words whereas the observed/expected MI and z-scores tend to put too much emphasis on infrequent words. In contrast, the log-likelihood, log-log and MI3 tests appear to provide more realistic collocation information.

While the statistical measures reviewed in this section may appear demanding, we are fortunate in that we do not need to compute them manually. As can be seen, they can be computed automatically using corpus exploration tools or statistical packages. It is important, nevertheless, that readers understand the results of these statistical tests.

C1.3 USING CORPUS DATA FOR IMPROVING A DICTIONARY ENTRY

The previous section provided us with an overview of how we could exploit statistical information when selecting useful collocations. Let us now consider how we can improve the contents of a dictionary entry with corpus data. In doing this, we will compare how the first (1978) and fourth (2003) editions of the *Longman Dictionary of Contemporary English* (hereafter referred to as LDOCE1 and LDOCE4 respectively) treat *sweet*.

C1.3.1 Focusing on high-frequency words

Figure C1.16 is the entry for adjectival *sweet* from LDOCE1. If you compare this with the entry from LDOCE4 (see Figure C1.17), the first striking difference you will find is the amount of space allocated by LDOCE1 and LDOCE4 to the description of this word.

In LDOCE1, only twelve lines were used to describe *sweet* whereas LDOCE4 used forty-eight lines. It might be argued that this is because the coverage of all words became wider in LDOCE4. That is not the case, however. The entry *sweeten*, for example, has eight lines in LDOCE1 and nine lines in LDOCE4. There are many other entries which are similar in length in the two editions of the dictionary. The major difference between the two editions, in our view, lies in the way important words are treated. After corpus data were used in the third edition (1985) of the dictionary, one major change in the editing policy of LDOCE was to focus more on high-frequency words. Note that the entry *sweet* (as an adjective) has the frequency labels [S2] and [W3] in LDOCE4, which indicate that the adjectival use of *sweet* is ranked among the top 2,000 in the spoken corpus data and the top 3,000 in the written corpus data. Primary emphasis was put on these high-frequency words as the lexicographers revised the entries, and as a result more space was allocated to *sweet* as an adjective in the third and fourth editions. Providing quality examples is a further area where corpus data can play an important role in pedagogical lexicography.

sweet¹ /swiːt/ *adj* [Wa1] **1 a** having a taste like that of sugar: *sweet fruit* **b** containing sugar: *sweet tea* **2** having a pleasant taste and smell; fresh: *sweet water* **3** pleasing to see or hear: *sweet sounds| sweet music* **4** gentle or attractive in manner; lovable: *a very sweet person|to have a sweet temper* **5 a** having a light pleasant smell, like many garden flowers **b** (of wine) having a taste caused by the presence of sugar; not DRY¹ (9) **6** pleasant: *the sweet smell of success* **7 sweet on** /ˈ· ·/ *infml* in love with —see also SHORT¹ (13) **and sweet** —**~ly** *adv* —**~ness** *n* [U]

sweet² *n BrE* **1** [C] a small piece of sweet substance, mainly sugar or chocolate, eaten for pleasure —see also CANDY **2** [C;U] (a dish of) sweet food served at the end of a meal —see also PUDDING, DESSERT **3** [*my*+N] (a word used for addressing a loved one)

Figure C1.16 The entry *sweet* in LDOCE1 (1978)

sweet¹ S2 W3 /swiːt/ *adj comparative* **sweeter**, *superlative* **sweetest**
1 TASTE containing or having a taste like sugar; → **sour, bitter, dry**: *This tea is too sweet.* | *sweet juicy peaches* | *sweet wine*
2 CHARACTER kind, gentle, and friendly: *a sweet smile* | *How sweet of you to remember my birthday!* → SWEET-TEMPERED
3 CHILDREN/SMALL THINGS especially *BrE* looking pretty and attractive; ⊟ **cute**: *Your little boy looks very sweet in his new coat.*
4 THOUGHTS/EMOTIONS making you feel pleased, happy, and satisfied: *Revenge is sweet.* | *the sweet smell of success* | *the sweet taste of victory* | *Goodnight, Becky. Sweet dreams.*
5 SMELLS having a pleasant smell; ⊟ **fragrant**: *sweet-smelling flowers* | *the sickly sweet* (=unpleasantly sweet) *smell of rotting fruit*
6 SOUNDS pleasant to listen to; ⊟ **harsh**: *She has a very sweet singing voice.*
7 have a sweet tooth to like things that taste of sugar
8 WATER/AIR if you describe water or air as sweet, you mean that it is fresh and clean; ⊟ **stale**: *She hurried to the door and took great gulps of the sweet air.*
9 keep sb sweet *informal* to behave in a pleasant, friendly way towards someone, because you want them to help you later: *I'm trying to keep Mum sweet so that she'll lend me the car.*
10 in your own sweet way/time if you do something in your own sweet way, you do it in exactly the way that you want to or when you want to, without considering what other people say or think: *You can't just go on in your own sweet way; we have to do this together.*
11 a sweet deal *AmE* a business or financial deal in which you get an advantage, pay a low price etc: *I got a sweet deal on the car.*

Figure C1.17 The entry *sweet* in LDOCE4 (2003)

C1.3.2 Providing examples

Let us now compare the entry of *sweet* in LDOCE1 and LDOCE4 by examining the illustrative examples they provided. Illustrative examples are a crucial piece of lexical information given under a dictionary entry. They provide us with syntactic, semantic and pragmatic information about the headword. Let us first compare the number of examples provided in each dictionary, following the steps described below.

1. Count the number of examples in LDOCE1. Make a distinction between examples in complete sentences and in phrases.
2. Do the same with LDOCE4 and create a table to compare the numbers.

Table C1.1 shows the numbers of illustrative examples given in the two editions. As can be seen, LDOCE4 provides twelve full-sentence examples whereas LDOCE1 provides none of this type. Rather, LDOCE1 only gives eight short example phrases. Illustrative examples in complete sentences are clearly more useful for language learners as they show the contexts in which headwords are used.

Table C1.1 The number of illustrative examples in LDOCE1 and LDOCE4

Example type	LDOCE1	LDOCE4
Complete sentences	0	12
Phrases	8	8

C1.3.3 Providing collocation information

More important than focusing on frequent words and providing examples in context is the collocation information provided by corpus data. Let us now examine, by following the steps below, how corpus data have helped to enrich LDOCE4 with collocation data.

1. List all the examples of *sweet* from LDOCE4, one example per line.
2. Make sure you will put down the definition number for each example.
3. Look at the entry *sweet* in LDOCE1 and pick up examples that are equivalent in meaning to those in LDOCE4. Create a table to contrast how many and what types of examples are available for each definition, as shown in Table C1.2.

We can see immediately from the table that the two editions of the dictionary contrast markedly in the quality of their illustrative examples. In the table, the first column indicates the definition number in LDOCE4. The second column shows the examples from LDOCE4 while the third column gives LDOCE1 examples which have meaning/usage almost equivalent to those in LDOCE4. Clearly the example phrases in LDOCE1 are usually shorter, showing only the 'adjective + noun' pattern divorced from their contexts. In contrast, the illustrative examples in LDOCE4 are much longer and are given as complete sentences. This way of providing illustrative examples not only makes them sound more authentic in context, it provides the learner with much richer examples also. It is the use of corpus data that has enabled this. At this point, the table is already quite revealing in that it shows that LDOCE4 gives a much more comprehensive account of the uses of *sweet*. If we go on with this experiment following the procedures described below, we will be able to see an even more marked contrast between LDOCE1 and LDOCE4.

Table C1.2 Comparison of illustrative examples in LDOCE4 and LDOCE1

Def	Examples in LDOCE4	Examples in LDOCE1
1	This tea is too sweet.	sweet tea
1	sweet juicy peaches	
1	sweet wine	
1		sweet fruit
2	a sweet smile	a very sweet person
2	How sweet of you to remember my birthday!	to have a sweet temper
3	Your little boy looks very sweet in his new coat.	n/a
4	Revenge is sweet.	
4	the sweet smell of success	the sweet smell of success
4	the sweet taste of victory	
4	Goodnight, Becky. Sweet dreams.	
5	sweet-smelling flowers	n/a
5	the sickly sweet smell of rotting fruit	
6	She has a very sweet singing voice.	sweet sounds; sweet music
8	She hurried to the door and took great gulps of the sweet air.	sweet water
9	I'm trying to keep Mum sweet so that she'll lend me the car.	n/a
10	You can't just go on in your own sweet way; we have to do this together.	n/a
11	I got a sweet deal on the car.	n/a
12	'How much did they pay you for that job?' 'Sweet FA!'	n/a
13	a couple whispering sweet nothings to each other	n/a
14	'I got four tickets to the concert.' 'Sweet!'	n/a

4. Go back the collocation list derived from BNCWeb and sort the list by frequency rather than other collocation statistics this time (see Figure C1.8).

5. Set the window span as +/−3. This adjustment is necessary because we are now interested in the collocation patterns that appear either before or after the node word *sweet* (e.g. *This tea is too sweet* or *sweet tea*). The result is given in Table C1.3.

6. Now make a new table to record the nouns co-occurring with *sweet* in each example that LDOCE4 and LDOCE1 provide for the entry *sweet* in Table C1.2. For instance, the first example *This tea is too sweet* in LDOCE4 has a combination of *tea* and *sweet*. Simply write down *tea* in the column for LDOCE4. Do the same with the rest of the examples.

7. Insert the columns to show the frequency band of each noun you have recorded using the rank orders given in Table C1.3. If a noun appears on the top-ten list, mark it with three asterisks (***). If it ranks between top eleven and thirty, mark it with two asterisks (**). If it ranks between top thirty-one and fifty, mark it with one asterisk (*).

The results should look like those given in Table C1.4. We can now compare the results between LDOCE1 and LDOCE4 and discuss how corpus data can be used to augment a dictionary with collocation information. In the table, the second column shows whether the noun collocates used in illustrative examples in LDOCE4 actually appear among the top fifty collocates (based on raw frequency) in the BNC. Of 14 nouns, 11 are found on the top 30 list (78.57 per cent), and 6 are on the top 10 list (42.86 per cent). This indicates clearly that lexicographers have

Table C1.3 The top fifty noun collocates of *sweet* in a 3:3 window

Rank No.	Word	Rank No.	Word
1	smell	26	love
2	shop	27	foods
3	peas	28	way
4	air	29	heaven
5	tooth	30	nothings
6	taste	31	fruit
7	tea	32	jesus
8	wine	33	mouth
9	smile	34	bill
10	potatoes	35	biscuits
11	scent	36	pea
12	maxwell	37	music
13	voice	38	reason
14	home	39	tastes
15	dreams	40	baby
16	life	41	sherry
17	face	42	sauce
18	Mrs	43	water
19	things	44	lady
20	success	45	perfume
21	revenge	46	spot
22	girl	47	flavour
23	thing	48	wines
24	man	49	boy
25	potato	50	corn

Table C1.4 Noun collocates in LDOCE1 and LDOCE4

LDOCE4	Frequency band	LDOCE1	Frequency band
air	***	fruit	*
deal	–	music	*
dreams	**	person	–
FA	–	smell	***
nothings	**	sounds	–
peaches	–	tea	***
revenge	**	temper	–
smell	***	water	*
smile	***		
taste	***		
tea	***		
voice	**		
way	**		
wine	***		

Keys: *** = top 10; ** = top 11–30; * = top 31–50

chosen these words deliberately, and with confidence, as the examples of *sweet* in LDOCE4. In contrast, LDOCE1 is wanting in this regard with 33.33 per cent (2 words) on the top 10 list and 62.5 per cent (5 words) on the top 50 list (see the last column in Table C1.4). The contrast between LDOCE1 and LDOCE4 shows that collocation information would not have been readily available without corpus data.

As we do not have access to the corpus originally used by Longman dictionary-makers (the Longman Corpus Network), we have used BNCWeb instead. As both the BNC and the Longman corpus are large, balanced and represent the same type of English in roughly the same time frame they should provide similar collocation data. The different corpus that we have used might also explain why some collocates of *sweet* in LDOCE4 (e.g. *peaches* and *deal*) are not on the top 50 list in the second column of Table C1.4.

This case study explored corpus-based lexicography, primarily intended for language learners. This case study relates to the area of phraseology, i.e. the description of the behaviour of words in relation to the context in which they occur together. The focus of the study was on collocation analysis and the study sought to describe collocation patterns from corpus data and to relate that information to the description of a dictionary entry. The study has also demonstrated how to use BNCWeb for collocation analysis and reviewed the collocation statistics commonly used in corpus linguistics (e.g. the log-likelihood, log-log, MI and z-scores).

Summary

FURTHER STUDY

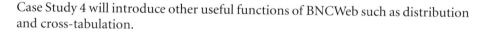

Case Study 4 will introduce other useful functions of BNCWeb such as distribution and cross-tabulation.

If you have become familiar with collocation analysis using BNCWeb, it would be a useful exercise for you to do a small survey of the validity of collocation information in major collocation dictionaries. For example, you can look at the collocation dictionaries that follow:

- *The BBI Combinatory Dictionary of English Word Combinations*, by Benson, Benson and Ilson, (1997, 2nd edition);
- *The LTP Dictionary of Selected Collocations*. Edited by Jimmie Hill and Michael Lewis, (1997);
- *Oxford Collocations Dictionary for Students of English*. Edited by Diana Lea, (2002).

A comparative study of these three dictionaries proves to be quite insightful. It is often the case with research in pedagogical lexicography that some empirical evidence should be provided in order to evaluate the quality of dictionaries in an objective way. However, it should be noted that we need to be careful not to over-emphasize the value of a particular dictionary over another. Since dictionaries contain different types of information and are designed for specific target users, each dictionary has its own advantages and disadvantages, depending on the type of information provided and the intended use of that information. One should use different dictionaries for different purposes. While it is important to clarify some problems with a dictionary in this type of exploration, we should keep in mind that any problems we identify may simply reflect a deliberate design decision made in the process of dictionary building which, in context, was quite justifiable.

Unit C2
HELP or *HELP to*: what do corpora have to say?

CASE STUDY 2

C2.1 INTRODUCTION

This unit further explores, via a case study of the type of infinitive following *HELP*, variations in language varieties as discussed in Units A10.5 and B4.4–B4.5, and the recent language change as discussed in Unit B5.5. This case study will use the tests of statistical significance introduced in Unit A6.4.

Help is one of the most frequent words in the English language, ranking as the 245th most frequent word in the word frequency list of the British National Corpus (BNC). When we look at the most frequent verbs (lemmatized) in the BNC, *HELP* rises to 72nd in the word frequency list, occurring 528.62 times per million words. Furthermore, *HELP* is a unique verb in that it can control either a full infinitive or a bare infinitive, either with or without an intervening noun phrase (NP), as in the following examples, cited from the BNC:

- (a) The pattern *help to V*
  Perhaps the book helped to prevent things from getting even worse.
- (b) The pattern *help NP to V*
  I thought I could help him to forget.
- (c) The pattern *help V*
  Savings can help finance other Community projects.
- (d) The pattern *help NP V*
  We helped him get to his feet and into a chair.

While most English grammars and dictionaries take it for granted that the omission of *to* following *HELP* is arbitrary (e.g. Chalker 1984: 106; Eastwood 1992: 106; Murphy 1985: 110; *Longman* 1986, 1993; *Collins* 1995), others do take into account some factors that are possibly relevant to the omission of *to*. For example, Biber *et al.* (1999: 73) observe that 'AmE [American English] has an especially strong preference for the pattern *verb + bare infinitives* although the bare infinitive is more common than the *to*-infinitive in both varieties'. This case study investigates some factors that may potentially influence a language user's choice of a full or bare infinitive following *HELP*, namely, varieties of English, language change over the three decades from 1961 to 1991, as well as the syntactic conditions of an inter-vening noun phrase (NP), the infinitive marker *to* preceding *help* and the passive construction. For a fuller account of this study, readers can refer to McEnery and Xiao (2005b), on which this case study is based.

In this case study, we will give you a step-by-step account of how to conduct the investigation using the corpus tool MonoConc Pro. We will also show you how to interpret the frequency data obtained from the concordancer by applying the statistics package SPSS for Windows.

 ## C2.2 CONCORDANCING

As the first step in this investigation, we will concordance each of the four corpora of the Brown family to get the frequencies of patterns (a–d) introduced in Unit C2.1. Note that the inflections of the controlling verb HELP (e.g. *help*, *helped*, *helps* and *helping*) will also be counted. We suppose that the four corpora to be used in this case study are located in individual directories on your local drive:

> LOB   c:\My corpora\LOB
> FLOB c:\My corpora\FLOB
> Brown c:\My corpora\Brown
> Frown c:\My corpora\Frown

C2.2.1 The pattern HELP to V

To get the frequency of the pattern HELP *to* V in LOB, do the following:

1. Start MonoConc Pro and you will see the interface of the concordancer as shown in Figure C2.1.
2. Select *File → Load corpus* from the menu (Figure C2.2).
3. You will see the *Select File(s) to Open* window (Figure C2.3).
4. Locate and open the directory for LOB. You will find fifteen files named LOB_A to LOB_R. Highlight the file named LOB_A by clicking on it with your mouse. Hold down the *SHIFT* key and the down arrow key on your keyboard until all of the fifteen corpus files are selected, as shown in Figure C2.4.
5. Press *Open*. In a few seconds, the corpus will be loaded into the concordancer. In the bottom left hand corner of the window, the program shows that there are fifteen files currently loaded into the concordancer (Figure C2.5).
6. Select Concordance → Advanced Search, as shown in Figure C2.6.
7. When a new window appears, check the box preceding *Sentence mode* to ensure that the search string occurs in the same sentence. The box preceding *Ignore case of letters* is checked by default. Enter your search pattern *help*_VV* to_TO *_V?I* exactly as shown in Figure C2.7 and press the OK button.

Figure C2.1 MonoConc Pro interface

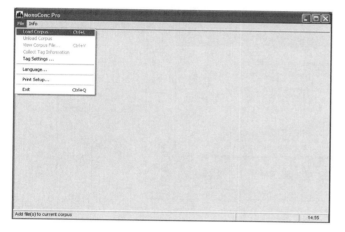

Figure C2.2 Loading corpus

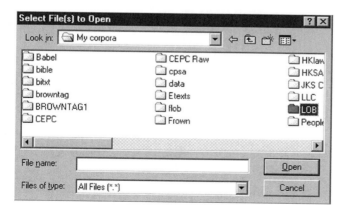

Figure C2.3 Selecting file(s) to open

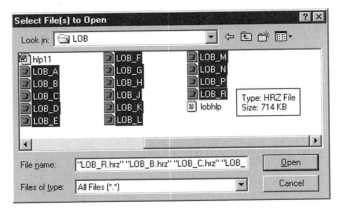

Figure C2.4 Selecting corpus files

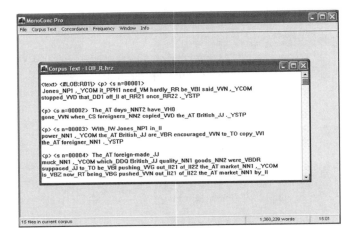

Figure C2.5 Fifteen files loaded

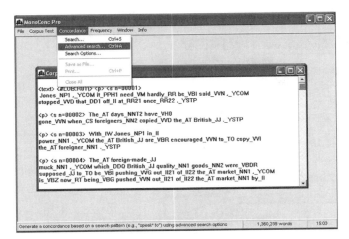

Figure C2.6 Activating the concordancer

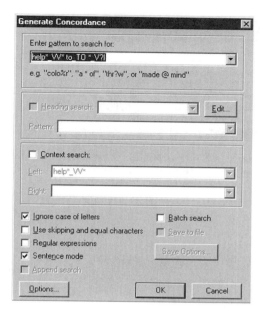

Figure C2.7 Entering the search string

Here, the special character ˟ allows the concordancer to match any number of characters so that the inflected forms of *HELP* are included. The special character ? stands for any single character. Therefore, the string *V?I* matches the infinitive form of any verb including *HAVE* and *BE*.

8. In a few seconds, you will see the concordancing result as shown in Figure C2.8. There are fifty-two matches of the search string. The lower part of the window shows the matched concordance lines in the KWIC (key-word-in-context) format, while the upper part of the window shows more context of a particular concordance line. If you want to have a better view of the concordance lines and their contexts, press the *Maximise* button in the upper right hand corner of the concordance window.

9. Record the frequency of the pattern *HELP to V* in LOB. Select *File → Unload corpus* to initialize the concordancer, as shown in Figure C2.9.

Repeat steps 1–9 for the other three corpora. The resulting frequencies should match those in Table C2.1. Note that the search patterns in this case study rely on part-of-speech (POS) tags. The concordance lines were not validated manually. Therefore, *You_PPY need_VV0 his_APPGE* **help_VVI** *to_TO cope_VVI ,_YCOM darling_NN1 ._YSTP* (<s n=00490>) is included as an instance for the pattern *help to V*. Readers are advised to refer to McEnery and Xiao (2005b) for a more accurate and complete account of factors contributing to the choice of a full or bare infinitive.

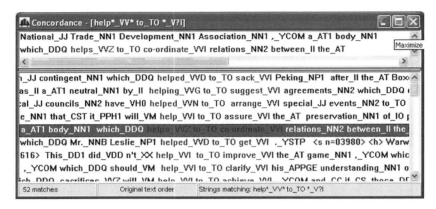

Figure C2.8 'help to V' pattern

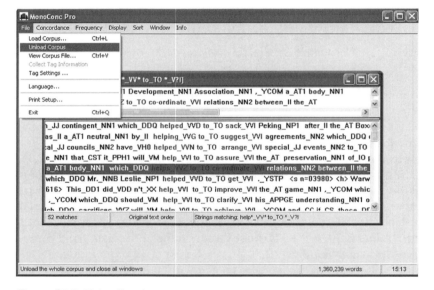

Figure C2.9 Unloading the corpus

C2.2.2 The pattern of *HELP V*

To get the frequency of the pattern *HELP V* in LOB, repeat steps 1–9 in Unit C2.2.1, replacing the search pattern in step 6 with *help*_VV* *_V?I*. Do the same for the other three corpora. The resulting frequencies should match those in Table C2.2.

C2.2.3 The pattern of *HELP NP to V*

An intervening noun phrase (NP) may vary in length. To simplify the concordancing process, we will only consider the case of a one-word intervening NP

Table C2.1 Frequencies of the pattern '*HELP to V*'

Corpus	Frequency
LOB	52
FLOB	48
Brown	38
Frown	32

Table C2.2 Frequencies of the pattern '*HELP V*'

Corpus	Frequency
LOB	11
FLOB	63
Brown	47
Frown	64

typically composed of a single noun or a pronoun. To get the frequency of the pattern *HELP NP to V* in LOB, do the following:

1. Repeat steps 1–6 from Unit C2.2.1.
2. Press the *Advanced* button. In the new window, select *Batch search*, as shown in Figure C2.10.
3. Press the *Edit search patterns* button. Enter the search patterns (*help*_VV**_N* to_TO*_V?I* and *help*_VV**_P* to_TO*_V?I*) on two separate lines as shown in Figure C2.11. Press the *OK* button to return to the previous window.
4. Press the *OK* button and in a few seconds you will see the resulting concordance window, as shown in Figure C2.12. There are twenty-one matches of the search strings. If you want to have a better view of the concordance lines and their contexts, press the *Maximise* button in the upper right hand corner of the concordance window.
5. Record the frequency of the pattern *HELP NP to V* in LOB. Select *File → Unload corpus* to reinitialize the concordancer, as shown in Figure C2.9.

Repeat steps 1–5 above for the other three corpora. The resulting frequencies are shown in Table C2.3.

C2.2.4 The pattern of *HELP NP V*

To get the frequency of the pattern *HELP NP V* in LOB, repeat steps 1–5 in Unit C2.2.3, replacing the search pattern in step 3 with *help*_VV**_N**_VVI* and *help*_VV**_P**_VVI*. Do the same for the other three corpora. The resulting frequencies are shown in Table C2.4.

Having obtained the necessary frequency data from the corpora, we are now ready to examine the possible influence of language variety, language change and an intervening NP on a language user's choice of infinitive variants. The frequencies themselves do not tell you whether a particular factor affects the choice. You must interpret the frequencies by conducting statistical tests to determine whether the difference in frequencies obtained from the relevant corpora is statistically significant (see Unit A6.4). If it is, you can conclude that the factor does influence the choice of a full or bare infinitive. Note, however, that frequency data must be interpreted with caution. As sample size may affect the level of statistical

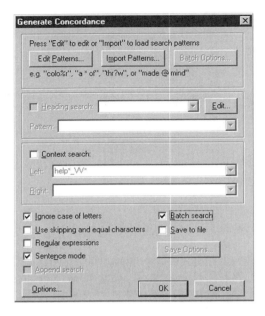

Figure C2.10 The Advanced search window

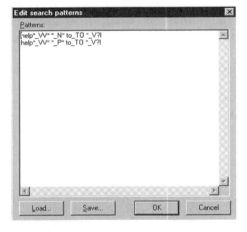

Figure C2.11 The Edit batch search patterns

Figure C2.12 The '*HELP NP to V*' pattern

Table C2.3 Frequencies of the pattern '*HELP* NP to V'

Corpus	Frequency
LOB	21
FLOB	21
Brown	12
Frown	10

Table C2.4 Frequencies of the pattern '*HELP* NP V'

Corpus	Frequency
LOB	6
FLOB	21
Brown	36
Frown	59

significance, frequencies obtained from corpora of different sizes must be normalized to a common base (usually the average size of the corpora used, see Unit A6.2). Since the four corpora used in this case study are of equal size, i.e., each containing roughly one million words, normalization is not necessary.

C2.3 LANGUAGE VARIETY

In this section, we will examine the two major varieties of English represented in the corpora studied, namely, American English (AmE) and British English (BrE). Onions (1965), Lind (1983: 264) and Biber *et al.* (1999: 73) observe that bare infinitives are more frequent in AmE than in BrE. To verify the validity of this observation, we will first rearrange the frequencies as shown in Table C2.5. As we are only interested in a comparison of language varieties in this section, the data gathered on intervening NPs will not be used; rather, the combined counts of infinitives with and without an intervening NP are used. We will use the frequencies in the column *Total* in Table C2.5 to compare LOB and Brown on the one hand, and FLOB and Frown on the other hand. The log-likelihood (LL) score is a reliable test for this purpose.

A convenient way to calculate the LL score is to use the statistics package SPSS for Windows by following the steps given below (assuming that SPSS for Windows Release 10.1):

1. Select *Start → Programs → SPSS for Windows → SPSS 10.1 for Windows*. You will see the interface for SPSS. Select *Type in data* and press the *OK* button as shown Figure C2.13.

Table C2.5 Full and bare infinitives in AmE and BrE

Variety	Corpus	Inf-type	No NP	With NP	Total
BrE	LOB	Full	52	21	73
		Bare	11	6	17
	FLOB	Full	48	21	69
		Bare	63	21	84
AmE	Brown	Full	38	12	50
		Bare	47	36	83
	Frown	Full	30	10	40
		Bare	64	59	123

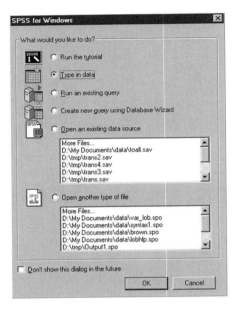

Figure C2.13 SPSS for Windows

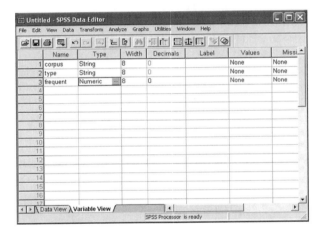

Figure C2.14 Defining variables

2. Select *Variable view* to define variables. In this case, we have three variables: corpus name (*corpus*), infinitive type (*type*), and frequency (*frequent*). The first two are string variables while the third is a numeric variable. As we are dealing with integers, the numerical is defined with no decimals (Figure C2.14).

3. Select *Data view* to type in data as shown in Figure C2.15.

4. As we type in the numerical value for the variable *frequent* directly, the value needs to be weighted. Select *Data* → *Weight cases* from the menu. You will see a window *Weight cases*. Select *Weight cases by* and highlight the variable *frequent* in the left panel, then click on the right arrow and press the *OK* button (Figure C2.16).

5. You will then return to the previous window. Select *Analyse* → *Descriptive*

	corpus	type	frequent
1	LOB	full-inf	73
2	LOB	bare-inf	17
3	Brown	full-inf	50
4	Brown	bare-inf	83

Figure C2.15 Typing in the data

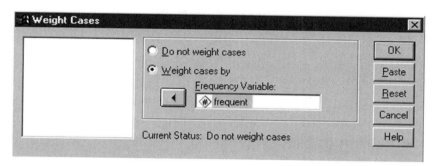

Figure C2.16 Weighting the cases

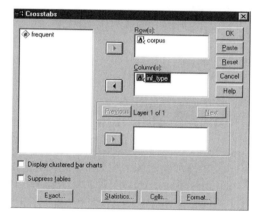

Figure C2.17 Defining row and column

statistics → *Crosstab* from the menu and you will come to the *Crosstab* window. Define the *Row(s)* with the variable *corpus* and the *Column(s)* with the variable *type* (Figure C2.17).

6. Press the *Statistics* button, select *Chi-square*, and then press *Continue* (Figure C2.18).

7. Press the *Cells* button, and select both *Observed* and *Expected* under the label of *Counts*. As the frequencies used are not normalized, also select *Unstandardized* under the label of *Residuals*. Press *Continue* (Figure C2.19).

8. Now you return to the *Crosstab* window. Press *OK* and in a few seconds you will be taken to the output window. You can ignore the first two tables and come to the table labelled *Chi-Square Tests*.

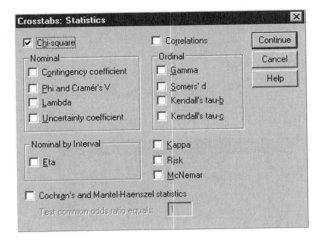

Figure C2.18 Selecting the statistical test

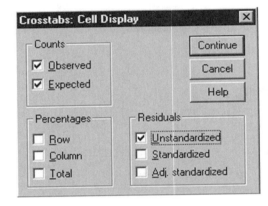

Figure C2.19 Selecting the cells

Note that the calculated log-likelihood ratio is 43.435 for 1 degree of freedom (d.f.), and the 2-sided significance level (0.000) is less than 0.001. If you consult an appendix table labelled the chi-square distribution in a textbook or reference book for statistics (e.g. Oakes 1998: 266), you will find the critical value for statistical significance at p<0.001 is 10.83 with 1 d.f. The calculated LL score is considerably greater than this critical value. Therefore, we can be more than 99.9 per cent confident that the difference in the frequencies of full and bare infinitives in BrE and AmE in the 1960s is statistically significant.

Before exiting SPSS, clear the data in step 3 (Figure C2.15) and enter the frequencies from FLOB and Frown to compare BrE and AmE in the 1990s. This time, you can skip steps 4, 6 and 7 and simply repeat steps 5 and 8. If you have exited SPSS and restarted the package, however, you will have to repeat the whole process. You will find the LL score calculated on the basis of frequencies from FLOB and Frown is 14.750 for 1 d.f., which is greater than the critical value 10.83. The two-sided significance level (0.000) is still less than 0.001. This means that the difference between BrE and AmE in the early 1990s is also statistically significant.

It is interesting to note that the contrast between BrE and AmE in the 1990s is not so marked as in the 1960s, as reflected by the much smaller LL score for the data in the 1990s. For the moment we will simply note this difference, though we will return to it in Unit C2.4.

HELP (NP) do is prevalent in AmE simply because this construction is of American provenance, though it has penetrated rapidly into BrE (see Onions 1965; Lind 1983: 264). As such, Zandvoort (1966) classifies this construction as an Americanism and claims that 'except in American English, however, to *help* usually takes an infinitive with *to*' (see Lind 1983: 264). However, if we take language change into account, which we will do in Unit C2.4, we find that Zandvoort's claim no longer holds.

C2.4 LANGUAGE CHANGE

Language change over time has affected the choice of a full or bare infinitive follow-ing *HELP* in both AmE and BrE. The bare infinitive after *HELP* is not mentioned in the *Concise Oxford Dictionary* (COD) but is now considered to be dialectal or vulgar in the *Oxford English Dictionary* (OED). The *Supplement to the OED* removes this label and judges it as being 'a common colloq. form' (see Kjellmer 1985: 264). Vallins (1951: 56) claims that 'the construction is not seriously questioned now (as it might have been twenty years ago) even in normal literary writing'. This section examines recent data to demonstrate the possible effect of language change on a language user's choice of alternative infinitive variants. We will use the frequency data in Table C2.5 to compare BrE in the 1960s and in the 1990s on the one hand, and AmE in the corresponding periods on the other hand.

Let us first compare LOB and FLOB using the same procedure as in Unit C2.3. Clear the data in step 3 (Figure C2.15) and enter the frequencies from LOB and FLOB. Repeat steps 5 and 8. You will find the LL score calculated on the basis of frequencies from the two corpora is 32.059 for 1 d.f., which is greater than the critical value 10.83. The two-sided significance level (0.000) is still less than 0.001.

Do the same with the frequencies from Brown and Frown. You will find the LL score calculated on the basis of frequencies from the two corpora is 5.884 for 1 d.f., which is greater than the critical value 3.84 for statistical significance at p<0.05. The two-sided exact significance level is 0.016.

Statistical tests show that in both BrE and in AmE, language change over the three decades has indeed exerted influence over the choice between infinitive variants. Figure C2.20 illustrates this point well. As can be seen in the figure, the proportions of bare infinitives in both BrE and AmE increased considerably from the 1960s to the 1990s. The contrast in BrE is even more marked than in AmE, as reflected by the much greater LL ratio and higher significance level for the BrE data. The reason

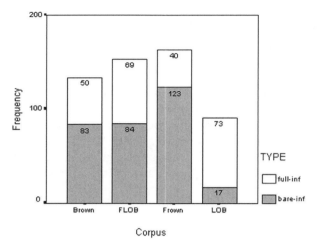

Figure C2.20 Frequencies of infinitives in the four corpora

for this apparent difference is that by 1961 AmE was already much more tolerant of bare infinitives than BrE (see Figure C2.20). Consequently a greater shift towards the use of the bare infinitives in the period 1961–1991 was possible for BrE, resulting in a more marked change.

C2.5 AN INTERVENING NP

Biber *et al.* (1999: 73), Lind (1983: 269) and Kjellmer (1985: 158) claim that bare infinitives occur more frequently after *HELP* with an intervening NP than where there is no intervening NP. To determine whether this argument is viable, we will first rearrange the frequencies as shown in Table C2.6. It can be seen from the table that an intervening NP typically contributes an increase of 18 per cent to the proportion of bare infinitives in the AmE data. In the BrE data, however, the effect of an intervening NP is unpredictable.

This finding is further supported by the LL tests, as shown in Table C2.7. For a difference to be statistically significant, the calculated LL score must be greater than the critical value for significance at p<0.05 (1 d.f.), 3.84. As can be seen from the table, in the BrE data, the increase or decrease in the proportion of bare infinitives contributed to by an intervening NP is not statistically significant, whereas in the AmE data, such increases are significant in both corpora. This provides further evidence that AmE behaves differently from BrE (see Unit C2.3). It is also of interest to note that the increase in the proportion of bare infinitives in AmE in the 1990s (significance level p=0.009) is more significant than that in the 1960s (significance level p=0.022). This finding is in line with our conclusion in Unit C2.4.

Table C2.6 The effect of an intervening NP (proportions)

Corpus	Inf-type	No NP		With NP		± %
		Fre.	%	Fre.	%	
LOB	Full	52	82.54	21	77.78	−4.76
	Bare	11	17.46	6	22.22	+4.76
FLOB	Full	48	43.24	21	50.00	+6.76
	Bare	63	56.76	21	50.00	−6.76
Brown	Full	38	44.71	12	25.00	−19.71
	Bare	47	55.29	36	75.00	+19.71
Frown	Full	30	31.91	10	14.49	−17.42
	Bare	64	68.09	59	85.51	+17.42

Table C2.7 The effect of an intervening NP (LL tests)

Corpus	Inf-type	No NP	With NP	LL ratio	Sig. level
LOB	Full	52	21	0.273	0.601
	Bare	11	6		
FLOB	Full	48	21	0.560	0.454
	Bare	63	21		
Brown	Full	38	12	5.239	0.022
	Bare	47	36		
Frown	Full	30	10	6.819	0.009
	Bare	64	59		

C2.6 THE INFINITIVE MARKER PRECEDING *HELP*

This section tests the claim, made by Biber *et al.* (1999: 737), Lind (1983: 269) and Kjellmer (1985: 159), that the infinitive marker *to* preceding the controlling verb *HELP* is a decisive syntactic condition encouraging the omission of *to* following *HELP*. As an intervening NP may influence the choice of a full or bare infinitive in AmE, we will exclude this factor. Considering that the pattern *to help* occurs only rarely in the individual corpora used, we will take our four corpora as a whole. MonoConc Pro allows one to load different corpora consecutively. In this section, we will also show you how to search corpora using regular expressions and how to sort concordance lines in a certain order. To obtain the relevant frequency data, do the following:

1. Activate MonoConc Pro and load the four corpora one at a time using the procedures in Unit C2.2.1. You will see, in the bottom left hand corner of the window, sixty files are selected.
2. Select *Concordance* → *Search* from the menu, a window will appear for you to enter a search pattern.

3. Press the *Advanced* button and check the boxes labelled *Regular expressions* and *Sentence mode*. The box labelled *Ignore case of letters* is checked by default. Enter the search string (*to_TO help_VVI .*_V.I*) exactly as shown in Figure C2.21. There are sixty-nine matches for this search pattern. Record the number of matches.

It should be noted that the special characters * and ? are used differently as wildcards and in regular expressions. Wildcards are common in a number of programs, including word processors and concordancers. Wildcards allow one to search words or expressions where one character is unspecified (with the unspecified character represented by a question mark) or many characters are unspecified (represented by an asterisk). Regular expressions also allow one to search for words or expressions where characters are unspecified. However, the symbols used in regular expressions, while at times similar to wildcards, have different meanings. The wildcard ? is equivalent to the regular expression . whereas the wildcard * is equivalent to the regular expression .*. When the box preceding *Regular expression* is unchecked (as in step 7 in Unit C2.2.1, see Figure C2.7), the asterisk matches any number (zero or more) of character(s). Note that when you use WordSmith tools, the special character * is used as a wildcard, as in step 7. When the option of regular expressions is selected, however, the syntax of regular expression must be followed, where the special character . stands for any single character. The asterisk is only a quantifier. The asterisk means 'equal to or more than zero' occurrence(s) of the preceding character. Therefore, if you forget to include the special character ., the concordancer will find no match at all, because there is no instance of *to help* followed by zero or more white spaces and an underscore (e.g. *to_TO help_VVI _VVI*). When a quantifier is absent, its default value is 1. As such, *V.I* matches *VVI*, *VHI*, *VDI* and *VBI*.

4. Repeat step 3 and enter the search string *to_TO help_VVI to_TO .*_V.?I*. There are only three matches. If you highlight the concordance lines, you will find that all of them occur in BrE (one in LOB and two in FLOB).

5. Repeat step 3 and enter the search string *help_VV[0I] .*_V.?I*. There are 115 matches for this search pattern. As this search string also matches *to help V*, we need to subtract the count of *to help V* from the total of 115. Select *Sort → 1 left → No Second Sort* from the menu, the concordance lines will be sorted alphabetically according to the first word on the left of the search term in ascending order (Figure C2.22).

6. Locate the first occurrence of *to help V* and move down to count until the last occurrence (Figure C2.23). You will find 69 such instances. The count is exactly what we find in step 3. Subtract 69 from 115, the result 46 is the frequency of the pattern *help V*.

7. Repeat step 3 and enter the search string *help_VV[0I] to_TO .*_V.?I*. The string *VV[0I]* matches both *VV0* and *VVI*. We need to include the latter because *help* can be preceded by a modal or auxiliary verb such as *can* and *did*. There are 52 matches for the search string. As three of these are of the pattern *to help to V*, there are 49 instances of the *help to V* type.

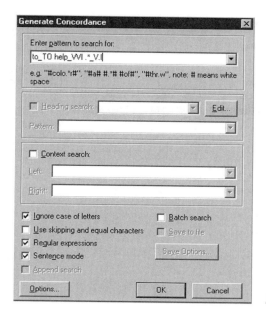

Figure C2.21 Using regular expression

Figure C2.22 Sorting the concordance lines

The frequency data obtained above are rearranged as shown in Table C2.8 and Figure C2.24.

As can be seen in Figure C2.24, there is a marked contrast between *help* and *to help*. While bare infinitives account for less than 50 per cent of the total number of infinitives following *help*, they make up more than 95 per cent when an infinitive marker precedes *help*. In the AmE data, the pattern *to help to V* is simply non-existent. The log-likelihood (LL) test shows that the difference as illustrated in Figure C2.24 is statistically significant. The calculated LL score is 50.601, which is

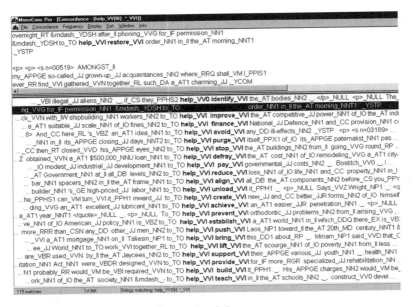

Figure C2.23 Sorted according to first left

Table C2.8 Frequencies of full and bare infinitives after *(to) help*

Inf-type	help	to help
Full	49	3
Bare	46	69

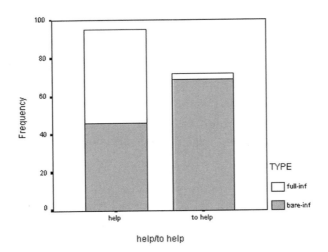

Figure C2.24 A contrast of *help* and *to help*

considerably greater than the critical value 10.83 for statistical significance at p<0.001. Therefore, we are more than 99.9 per cent confident that *to* preceding *help* encourages a language user to choose a bare infinitive after HELP.

C2.7 THE PASSIVE CONSTRUCTION

Palmer (1965: 169) claims that the 'passive occurs [. . .] only with to: They were helped to do it'. To test this claim, we will first find the frequencies of passive and non-passive constructions in our corpora. As the passive is an infrequent linguistic feature, we will not contrast the use of the passive synchronically or diachronically. Rather we will study all of the examples from the four corpora together. This section will show you how to interpret the frequency data for an infrequent linguistic feature.

Using the same concordancing procedure as in Unit C2.6, enter the search strings as shown in Table C2.9. The frequencies you gather will match those in the table. Search string No. 1 matches the pattern BE *helped to V* while No. 2 matches *be helped V*. In search string Nos. 3 and 4, *help. *_VV.* matches both the non-inflected form and all inflections of the controlling verb HELP, including passive constructions. Therefore, the counts of passive constructions should be subtracted from the frequencies for Nos. 3 and 4 to obtain the frequencies of non-passive constructions, as shown in Table C2.10.

To determine whether the difference between the passive and non-passive constructions is statistically significant, we will not use the log-likelihood test as at least one of four cells in the 2 × 2 contingency table has an expected value less than 5. Under such conditions the log-likelihood test is unreliable (see Howitt and Cramer 2001: 121–123). Rather, we will use Fisher's exact test to determine the exact significance level as it is more reliable in these circumstances.

Table C2.9 Search strings for (non-)passive constructions

No.	Search string	Frequency
1	. *_VB.* helped_VVN to_TO .*_V.?l	6
2	. *_VB.* helped_VVN .*_V.?l	0
3	help. *_VV.* to_TO .*_V.?l	170
4	help. *_VV.*.*_V.?l	185

Table C2.10 Frequencies of infinitives for (non-)passives

Pattern	Frequency
BE helped to V	6
BE helped V	0
help to V	164
help V	185

The Fisher's exact significance test is automatically calculated by SPSS if at least one of the cells of the contingency table has an expected value less than 5 when you select the chi-square test. Alternatively you may press the *Exact* button and then check the bullet point preceding *Exact.* You can find the two-sided exact significance level in the table labelled *Chi-square Tests* in the output window. In this case, Fisher's exact test shows an exact significance level of 0.012, meaning we can be 98.8 per cent sure that the passive prefers a full infinitive following *HELP*.

Summary

This case study used four *prêt-à-porter* corpora (LOB, Brown, FLOB, and Frown) to explore the potential factors that may influence a language user's choice of a full or bare infinitive after *HELP*. Our findings are summarized as follows.

AmE shows a stronger preference for bare infinitives after *HELP* than BrE. Language change over the three decades from 1961 to 1991 has produced a bias in favour of bare infinitives after *HELP* in both AmE and BrE. An intervening NP may increase the proportion of bare infinitives after *HELP* in AmE whereas in BrE, the effect of an intervening NP is unpredictable. The infinitive marker *to* preceding *help* encourages a language user to choose a bare infinitive. The passive construction exclusively selects bare infinitives.

In this case study, we gave a step-by-step demonstration of how to explore a corpus using MonoConc Pro, using its advanced features such as searching a corpus using regular expressions, sorting concordance lines and the batch search function. We also showed how to interpret frequency data with the SPSS statistics package.

★ FURTHER STUDY

In Unit C2.2.3, we only considered a single noun or pronoun as an intervening NP. Now use the batch search function of MonoConc Pro to include the cases of an article or determiner followed by a noun, e.g., *a/the boy* and *those students*. Do the above findings still hold?

Unit C3
L2 acquisition of grammatical morphemes

CASE STUDY 3

C3.1 INTRODUCTION

This unit returns to the issue of language learning as discussed in Units A10.8 and B6 via an interlanguage study on the basis of a learner corpus. We will also explore error tagging and problem-oriented annotation introduced in Units A4.4.8 and A4.4.9.

In this case study, we will use a corpus of learner English to investigate the data produced by L2 learners of English. The description of learner language is of particular interest to second language acquisition (SLA) research. The interest in learner language stems from the assumption that the researcher may gain insights into the process of second language acquisition by exploring the L2 productions of a language learner. If we have a better understanding of the second language acquisition process we can apply the findings to a variety of practical aspects of language teaching: syllabus design, materials development, task design, language testing, and so on.

A number of different approaches have been taken to the description of learner language. Ellis (1994: 44) identified four major approaches:

- the study of learners' errors;
- the study of developmental patterns;
- the study of variability;
- the study of pragmatic features.

The study of learners' errors was undertaken quite intensively in the late 1960s and 1970s after Corder (1967) made the significant claim that L2 learners, like L1 learners, were credited with a 'built-in-syllabus', which guided their language acquisition. Selinker (1969) coined the term *interlanguage* to refer to the special mental grammars which it was assumed that learners constructed during the course of their language acquisition. Interlanguage theory treated learner behaviour, including their errors, as rule-governed.

While initially associated strongly with error analysis, interlanguage analysis based upon error analysis went out of fashion in the 1980s as a number of methodological and theoretical problems with it were identified. Ellis (1994: 73), for example, pointed out that error analysis did not provide a complete picture of how learners acquire an L2 because it described learner language as a collection of errors. As a consequence of criticisms such as this, more and more attention was paid to the entirety of learner language. Central to this enterprise is the description of developmental patterns of interlanguage.

Dulay and Burt (1973) were among the first to conduct an empirical study of the acquisition order of the grammatical features of English. They studied the order of acquisition of grammatical morphemes (such as *-ing* and *the* that play a greater part in structure than content words such as *dog*), which was first investigated by Roger Brown in L1 acquisition (Brown 1973). Throughout their papers, Dulay and Burt claimed that L2 acquisition proceeds quite systematically and that the acquisition order is not rigidly invariant but is remarkably similar irrespective of the learners' L1 backgrounds, age and/or medium of production. Since then, more than fifty L2 morpheme studies have been reported, using data from a variety of L1 backgrounds and analysis procedures (see Larsen-Freeman and Long 1991; Ellis 1994 for a review).

Criticisms of the methodology utilized in the early morpheme studies are well known (see Long and Sato 1984). However, as Larsen-Freeman and Long (1991) noted, despite admitted limitations in some areas, the morpheme studies provide strong evidence that interlanguages exhibit common accuracy/acquisition orders. Contrary to what some critics have claimed, so many studies have been undertaken with sufficient methodological rigour which show sufficiently consistent general findings that the commonalities can no longer be ignored (*ibid*.: 92). The aim of this study is to verify some of their findings by using the corpus-based approach.

Recently there has been a growing awareness that it is necessary to investigate learner language by collecting a large amount of learner performance data on computer, so-called learner corpora (see Units A7.8 and A10.8). The term learner corpus was first used for Longman's learner dictionaries, in which the information on EFL learners' common mistakes was provided, based upon the Longman Learners' Corpus. Following from this, a project called the International Corpus of Learner English (ICLE) was launched as a part of the ICE (International Corpus of English) project (Granger 1998) in 1990 specifically to collect L2 data (see Unit A7.8). From these beginnings the interest in learner corpora has grown, and at the time of writing more than a dozen projects constructing learner corpora are under way around the world (see Unit A7.8).

In this case study, we will revisit a once popular topic of SLA research, acquisition studies of English grammatical morphemes and see how learner corpora can shed new light on this old area of study. There are a couple of reasons why we chose morpheme studies as our primary topic for this investigation. First, as Ellis (1990) noted, morpheme acquisition studies were a kind of performance analysis in the sense that they aimed to provide a description of the L2 learner's language development and looked not just at deviant but also at well-formed utterances (Ellis 1990: 46). Performance analysis provides a basis for investigating the following important questions:

- Is there any difference between the order of instruction and the order of acquisition?
- Is it possible to alter the 'natural' order of acquisition by means of instruction?
- Do instructed learners follow the same order of acquisition as untutored learners or a different order?

(Ellis 1990: 139)

Learner corpora, if used properly within a suitable research design, can prove to be an effective tool which can be used to answer these interrelated questions by providing the evidence of learner language in a more systematic and comprehensive way. Secondly, although there are many criticisms of morpheme studies (e.g. Hatch 1978; Long and Sato 1984), morpheme acquisition order studies are still a good starting point if one wishes to see how effective learner corpora can be in describing interlanguage.

C3.2 MORPHEME STUDIES: A SHORT REVIEW

In the early 1970s, it was discovered that English speaking children learn grammatical morphemes in a definite sequence (Brown 1973). Dulay and Burt (1973) decided to replicate the study with L2 learners. They asked Spanish-speaking children learning English to describe pictures, and checked how often the children used eight grammatical morphemes in the right places in a sentence. The results showed that L2 learners have a common order of difficulty for grammatical morphemes, as shown in Table C3.1:

Table C3.1 An accuracy order of grammatical morphemes (Dulay and Burt 1973)

Order	Morpheme	Example
1	plural *-s*	books
2	progressive *-ing*	John is go*ing*
3	copula BE	John *is* here
4	auxiliary BE	John *is* going
5	articles	*the* books
6	irregular past tense	John *went*
7	third person *-s*	John like*s* books
8	possessive *-s*	John*'s* book

One of the problems for the rank orders that Dulay and Burt observed is that they disguise the difference in accuracy in use between various morphemes. For instance, a morpheme with a one per cent lower accuracy of usage than another morpheme

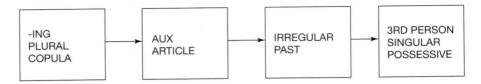

Figure C3.1 The natural order for L2 acquisition proposed by Krashen (1977)

is given a different ranking in just the same way as a morpheme that is used 25 per cent less accurately would be. To overcome this problem, Krashen (1977) proposed a grouping of morphemes (see Figure C3.1). He claimed that it was 'a natural order supported by the longitudinal and cross-sectional, individual and grouped SL findings. Items in the boxes higher in the order were regularly found (80–90%) accurately supplied in obligatory contexts before those in boxes lower in the order' (Krashen 1977: 151).

The results were used to claim that there was a more or less invariant order of acquisition which was independent of L1 background and age. Although this order was slightly different from that found for the same morphemes in L1 acquisition research, it provided evidence in favour of the existence of universal cognitive mechanisms which enabled learners to discover the structure of a particular language (see Ellis 1994 for a detailed review).

Although there were some stern critics of the morpheme studies as noted above, the interest in morpheme acquisition grew to the extent that different approaches to the study of morpheme acquisition emerged: target-like use analysis of morphemes, as opposed to obligatory context analysis only (Pica 1982; Lightbown 1983), morpheme acquisition in different L2 contexts (Fathman 1978; Makino 1980; Sajavaara 1981) and by learners with different L1 (Mace-Matluck 1977; Fuller 1978) and L2 backgrounds (Bye 1980; van Naerssen 1986). The different types of studies clearly made different contributions to the study of grammatical morpheme acquisition, though they were all focused on the same general question. Larsen-Freeman and Long (1991: 92), based on their review of this literature, concluded that those studies provided strong evidence of a developmental order for L2 grammatical morpheme acquisition.

Given that there is some merit in exploring the acquisition of such morphemes by learners, an obvious place to start such an investigation is in a learner corpus. That is what we will do now in this case study.

C3.3 THE LONGMAN LEARNERS' CORPUS

The learner corpus data used for this study are a subcorpus from the Longman Learners' Corpus (i.e. see Unit A7.8). We selected this corpus for our study because it is one of the few learner corpora which is publicly available for research and each of its components per L1 background is large enough to allow one to extract errors and provide data from learners at different proficiency levels.

In this study, we will use the subcorpus that is composed of the Japanese EFL learners' written composition data in order to see whether the acquisition order of grammatical morphemes is the same as the one found by previous studies. While this study examines the morpheme acquisition in Japanese learner data, the methodology and techniques described in the following sections should apply to other learner groups as well. Before we can undertake the interlanguage study, we will first need to annotate the corpus data for parts-of-speech and error types.

C3.4 PROBLEM-ORIENTED CORPUS ANNOTATION

Since we need to find all of the correct and incorrect instances of relevant morphemes in the learner data, this case study will involve a large amount of problem-oriented manual tagging work (see Unit A4.4.9). The basic procedure of data processing is as follows. First, the original corpus data will be pre-processed so that we can convert the header information into a format suitable for use with WordSmith (version 4). Second, the whole subcorpus will be tagged using a POS tagger. Third, we will manually tag morphological errors using the POS information as a guide. Then the accuracy rate of the usage of individual grammatical morphemes will be obtained based on the number of the error tags and relevant POS tags. Finally, the results will be compared with previous findings.

C3.4.1 Basic formatting of the texts

Since some of the corpus data were compiled in the 1980s, the header information was formatted in a way similar to the COCOA format (see Unit A3.3). In order to process this data properly for use with WordSmith, we need to convert the header section into the SGML format (see Unit A3.3), i.e. with the opening tag <head> and the ending tag </head>. This is necessary because by default WordSmith does not distinguish the header apart from the main text.

In this example, we will select the Japanese learner group (in the file folder 'J' in the Longman Learners' Corpus). The subcorpus contains approximately one million words in total. Table C3.2 shows the typical format of a corpus header, with glosses added by us to explain these header elements.

We will first show you how to convert the COCOA format into the SGML format. As each corpus file starts with the <RF> (i.e. reference number) tag, we can insert the <head> tag before <RF> and insert the </head> tag between the <TV> (target language variety) element and the first occurrence of <PA> (paragraph) tag. There are several different ways to do this. The simplest, yet most time-consuming way is to use the 'find and replace' function of a text editor. If you are using Microsoft

Table C3.2 The corpus header

Element	Example value	Gloss
<RF>	20522	Document reference number
<CO>	JAP	Source country code
<LA>	JAP	Student language & national variety code
<LE>	IN	Student level code (IN=intermediate)
<EN>	CLA	Environment code (CLA=classwork)
<TT>	2	Task type (2=free essay)
<TV>	AmE	Target language variety
<PA>	My friend and I went to . . .	The beginning of the essay

Word, go to *Edit – Replace* after opening a corpus file. Enter <RF> in the 'Find what' text box and <head>^p<RF> in the 'Replace with' text box (here ^p means a new line). Click on the 'Replace' button to insert the start tag <head>. Similarly, replace *the first occurrence* of <PA> with </head>^p<PA>. After these operations, save the file as a text file (i.e. 'Text only' rather than 'Word document'). The result should look like the example below:

```
<head>
<RF> 20522
<CO> JAP
<LA> JAP
<LE> IN
<EN> CLA
<TT> 2
<TV> AmE
</head>
<PA> My friend and I went to . . .
```

After creating the corpus header for all of the files, we will combine these files into eight large files, each for a proficiency level, as shown in Table C3.3. Note that in some subcorpora of the Longman corpus, there are a number of files in which the proficiency level is unknown or incorrectly coded. In these cases the proficiency level is labelled as 'XX' or 'ZZ'. If your study of a certain subcorpus contains such files, you can discard them. Since we have to add the corpus header to all of the files in the Japanese subcorpus (1,667 files), we need to find a more time and labour-saving way to do the task. One possible way is to write a so-called 'Word macro' for this purpose if you are good at programming (see the online help of Microsoft Word for a description of what a macro is or how to record a Word macro); alternatively you can download a tool such as PowerGREP from the Internet to help you. However, combining these small files into eight larger files according to their different proficiency levels presents yet another difficulty for most readers. As such, we have written a simple program that will help readers to add corpus headers and combine files at one go. The program also inserts the start tag <body> and the end tag </body> to indicate the corpus data proper. After you have downloaded the program from our companion website, simply place it in the file folder for the

Table C3.3 Proficiency levels encoded in the Longman Learners' Corpus

File name	Proficiency level	New group
llc_BE.txt	Beginning	Elementary
llc_EL.txt	Elementary	
llc_PI.txt	Pre-intermediate	Intermediate
llc_IN.txt	Intermediate	
llc_UI.txt	Upper-intermediate	Advanced
llc_AD.txt	Advanced	
llc_PR.txt	Proficient	Proficient
llc_AS.txt	Academic studies	
	Degree-course	

subcorpus you have selected (in the case of Japanese data, the file folder is J of the Longman Learners' Corpus) and double click the program file. You will have eight files named in Table C3.3, each containing marked-up corpus data for the relevant proficiency level (files of which the proficiency level is labelled as 'XX' or 'ZZ' are discarded automatically by the program). This tool can not only help you to pre-process the Japanese data used in this case study, it is also useful when you undertake your own mini-projects using the Longman Learners' Corpus.

With the SGML corpus header, tools such as WordSmith can be used to search the main body of text while excluding the data in the header. To facilitate our analysis of morpheme errors, we will put the eight files into four groups as indicated in Table C3.3 ('New group'): elementary, intermediate, advanced and proficient.

C3.4.2 Error tagging: a proper way and a dirty way

In this section, we will show you two different methods of extracting the error information on grammatical morphemes. One is to annotate the entire corpus and then extract error tag frequencies. The other way is to retrieve concordance lines using WordSmith and mark the lines with errors temporarily for counting. While both methods can yield the accuracy rate for each morpheme, each has its own advantages and disadvantages. The former will be more useful in terms of replicability and reusability, but it is quite time-consuming. The latter, on the other hand, is time-efficient, but the results are only valid as long as the processed data is stored on your computer – there is no way for the results to be used for secondary purposes. Both methods involve POS tagging. In this case study, we tagged the data with CLAWS (see Unit A4.4.1 and the Appendix). Note that the POS-tagged files were renamed as *llc_be.pos.hrz.txt*, etc.

Table C3.4 shows a tagset of grammatical morphemes with which we will annotate our data. We have chosen to study these grammatical morphemes because they were studied in Brown (1973), Dulay and Burt (1973) and Krashen (1977). By studying the same set of grammatical morphemes, we will be able see if their claims still hold in the light of corpus data.

Table C3.4 List of morpheme tags

Morpheme	Correct tag	Error tag
article	<ART>	<ER_ART>
possessive -*s*	<POS>	<ER_POS>
3rd person singular -*s*	<3PS>	<ER_3PS>
irregular past	<IRPST>	<ER_IRPST>
auxiliary *BE*	<AUXBE>	<ER_AUXBE>
plural -*s*	<PL>	<ER_PL>
copula *BE*	<COP>	<ER_COP>
progressive -*ing*	<PROG>	<ER_PROG>

To ensure the comparability between Dulay and Burt's study and ours, we will tag each text according to the criterion set for the Bilingual Syntax Measure proposed by Dulay and Burt. In other words, we will only look at the 'obligatory context', i.e. contexts that require the obligatory use of grammatical morphemes in samples of learner language. We will convert the relevant tags on the basis of the following rules:

(1) Tagging verb *BE* as <COP> or <AUXBE>:

   (a) Look for every occurrence of *BE* verb (*_VB*);
   (b) If those *BE* verbs are followed by either verbs with a progressive marker (*_VVG) or a past participle marker (*_VVN), then assign the tag <AUXBE>;
   (c) If those *BE* verbs are followed by adjectives (*_J*) or nouns (*_N*), then assign the tag <COP>.

(2) Assigning the tag <PL> to all the nouns with the tag NN2 (i.e. *_NN2);
(3) Assign the tag <POS> to all the items tagged as GE (i.e. *_GE);
(4) Assign the tag <PROG> to all the words tagged as VVG (i.e. *_VVG);
(5) Assign the tag <3PS> to the words tagged VVZ (*_VVZ);
(6) Assign the tag <ART> to *the*_AT, *a*_AT1 and *an*_AT1 (*_AT*);
(7) <IRPST> should be tagged by looking at each verb labelled VVD. Both regular and irregular verbs were labelled VVD, so there is no way of distinguishing them other than by a manual analysis.

The task of searching for and replacing relevant POS tags with the morpheme tags can be done semi-automatically (e.g. using WordPad) in cases (2)–(6) with the help of POS tags. For (1) and (7), you need to look at each case separately and manually correct the tags. For this, you can use a text editor with a search function (e.g. Notepad, Wordpad or Microsoft Word). We do not have space to illustrate this procedure step by step here. If you use MS Word, remember again to save the edited file as a text file.

After these tags are automatically assigned, errors can be manually tagged for each example retrieved using the above morpheme tags. Here we should remember at least three types of error notations:

254

1) *overuse error.* This is <ER_ART CF="">a</ER_ART> my dog.
2) *omission error.* This is <ER_ART CF="a"></ER_ART> dog.
3) *misformation error.* This is <ER_ART CF="a">an</ER_ART> dog.

Note that by specifying the value of the attribute CF ('correct form'), the morpheme error tags can specify types of target modification errors (overuse, omission or misformation) without creating extra tags. If one wants to extract overuse errors only, one can do so by extracting the lines that contain the string *CF=""*.

After tagging is done, we can calculate the accuracy rate with which the morphemes were actually used in our corpus data. We will again follow the measurement method adopted by Dulay and Burt, namely looking only at the obligatory context, so that the information on overuse of the forms will not be used even though the annotated corpus itself contains such information.

Readers may have already noted that the conventional 'proper way' of error tagging is extremely time and labour-consuming. However, the time and labour which you have invested will be repaid because the annotated data is reusable. For those who do not wish to invest a large amount of time in error-tagging their learner data, we will introduce a dirty yet quick way to complete the task, which takes advantage of the SET function of WordSmith version 4. As an example, we will give you a step-by-step demonstration of how to tag errors related to articles (*the, a* and *an*).

1. Open WordSmith 4 and choose texts (Figure C3.2).
2. In order to avoid searching the header section, we will need to limit our search to just the body of the text. To do this, choose *Settings – Adjust settings*. The *Tools Settings* window will open (Figure C3.3). Choose *Tags & Markup* and click on the *Only Part of File* button at the bottom. Then type in <head> and </head> in the blanks of *Sections to Cut Out*. Then press *OK* (Figure C3.4).
3. Also click on the *Text & Languages* tab, add the underscore (_) in the *Characters within word* field. This will ensure that the word plus POS information *the_AT*, for instance, is recognized as one word. If you do not add this information, the Concord function will not provide any information on collocations or clusters. So make sure you properly set this option (Figure C3.5).
4. Go back to the main window and choose *Concord* (Figure C3.6). Select *File – New*. The search window will then open. In order to find article errors, let us search for all the instances of singular nouns first. Type in *_NN1 in the search box and then press *OK* (Figure C3.7).
5. You will get the search results (Figure C3.8).
6. In order to check the missing articles, sort the concordance lines by the left context. Choose *Edit – Resort*. Then select L1 (the first word on the left of the node word) for the main sort, L2 and L3 for the second and the third sorts. Make sure you activate the sort by ticking the box on each tab menu (Figure C3.9).
7. The sorted concordance lines will appear (Figure C3.10).

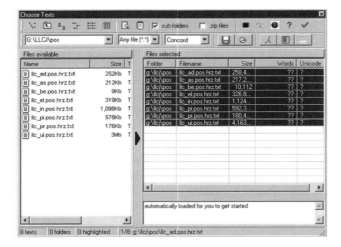

Figure C3.2 Choosing files

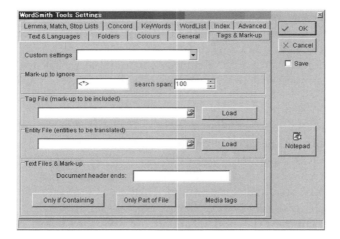

Figure C3.3 Adjusting settings

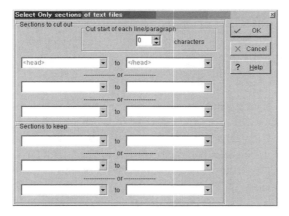

Figure C3.4 Choosing only part of file

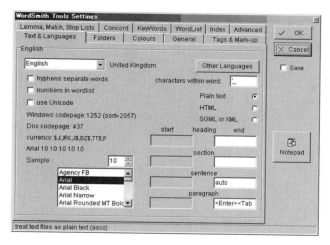

Figure C3.5 Defining a word

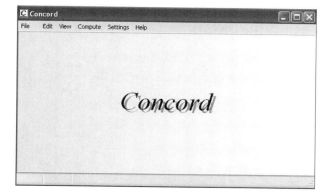

Figure C3.6 Concord

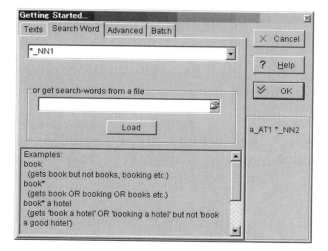

Figure C3.7 The search window

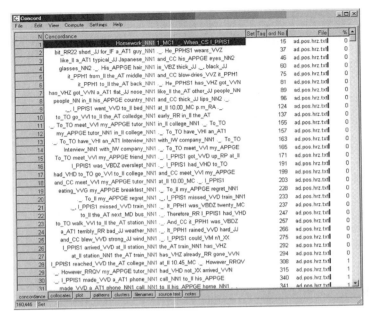

Figure C3.8 The search results

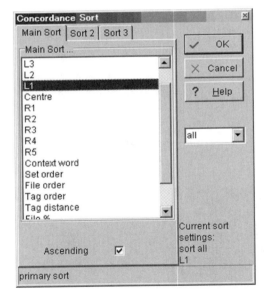

Figure C3.9 The sort window

8. Here you should check each concordance line to see if there is an article error. Move the cursor to the column *SET*. When you find an error, type 'E' in the same line on the *SET* column. By doing so, you can mark the concordance lines for errors (Figure C3.11).

You will have to make a realistic decision here. Since there are more than 160,000 concordance lines, it would be nearly as time-consuming as the 'proper way' to

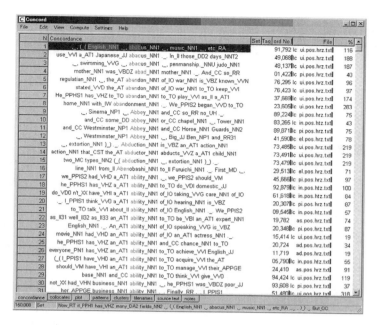

Figure C3.10
Sorted by the
left context

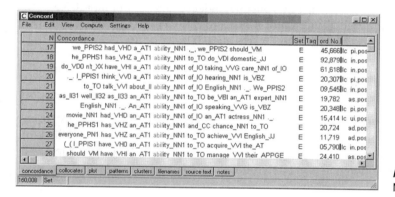

Figure C3.11
Marking errors

check every line. As such we would suggest that you error-tag concordances at random, for instance, every tenth line (make the adjustment in *WordSmith Settings – Concord*), if you wish to reduplicate this study as a warming-up exercise for your mini-project at the end of this case study. This random sampling will allow you to tag a few thousand examples in a reasonable time.

9. After the manual error tagging, you can re-sort the concordance lines by the *SET* order (Figure C3.12).

This will give you the number of article errors for singular nouns. You can do the same for plural nouns. Make sure that you will get both the number of correct cases and the number of incorrect cases.

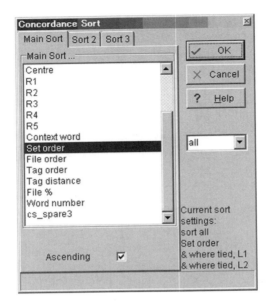

Figure C3.12 Sort by the *SET* order

Using the random sampling procedures, we have error-tagged 2,000 concordances for articles and each of the other morphemes under consideration. Table C3.5 shows what to search for each grammatical morpheme and Table C3.6 gives the overall frequencies of correct and incorrect forms of each morpheme.

C3.5 DISCUSSION

The accuracy rate can be easily computed by dividing the frequencies of correct forms by the total of frequencies of correct and incorrect forms shown in Table C3.6. The state of acquisition is defined as '90 per cent correct' in the same way as Dulay and Burt's Bilingual Syntax Measure.

Table C3.7 shows the results of the accuracy order of the eight grammatical morphemes, where the figures are expressed in proportions. According to this result, the Japanese-speaking learners of English have least difficulty with copula *BE*, which is basically the same as the order proposed in Dulay and Burt's (1973) and Krashen's (1977) studies. The most difficult item for them is the article (*the, a* and *an*). This late acquisition of the article system is similar to the findings with Polish learners reported by Botley and Uzar (1998). As neither Japanese nor Polish has an article system, it can be reasonably speculated that L1 knowledge can affect the acquisition process in both cases.

Among the eight morphemes, copula *BE*, auxiliary *BE*, possessive *-s* and progressive *-ing* reached a 90 per cent accuracy rate and can be regarded as 'acquired' items. However, the other four morphemes did not reach an accuracy rate high enough to be considered acquired, even in the proficient student group.

Table C3.5 POS tags for each morpheme

Morpheme	POS tags to search	Comments
copula BE	VB*	Right-sort, then delete all the cases in which the VVG and VVN tags follow BE verbs.
auxiliary BE	VB*	Right-sort, then retain the lines which have VVG and VVN tags after BE verbs
plural -s	NN*	NN1 for omission errors
progressive -ing	VVG; VB* + VV*	
3rd person singular -s	VVZ	
irregular past	VVD	

Table C3.6 Overall frequencies of morpheme errors

Grammatical morpheme	Data type	Elementary		Intermediate		Advanced		Proficient	
		Correct	Error	Correct	Error	Correct	Error	Correct	Error
Copula BE	Fre.	1885	115	1929	71	1908	92	1895	105
	%	94.25	5.75	96.45	3.55	95.40	4.60	94.75	5.25
Plural -s	Fre.	1598	402	1622	378	1630	370	1773	227
	%	79.90	20.10	81.10	18.90	81.50	18.5	88.65	11.35
3rd person -s	Fre.	1417	583	1394	606	1538	462	1760	240
	%	70.85	29.15	69.70	30.30	76.90	23.10	88.00	22.00
Possessive -s	Fre.	1538	462	1515	485	1879	121	1882	118
	%	76.90	23.10	75.75	24.25	93.95	6.05	94.10	5.90
Article	Fre.	1259	741	1404	596	1204	796	1590	410
	%	62.95	37.05	70.20	29.80	60.20	39.80	79.50	20.50
Irregular past	Fre.	1643	357	1590	410	1581	419	1671	329
	%	82.15	17.85	79.50	20.50	79.05	20.95	83.55	16.45
Auxiliary BE	Fre.	1773	227	1920	80	1737	263	1843	157
	%	88.65	11.35	96.00	4.00	86.85	13.15	92.15	7.85
Progressive -ing	Fre.	1444	556	1654	346	1796	204	1862	138
	%	72.20	27.80	82.70	17.30	89.80	10.20	93.10	6.90

Table C3.7 Accuracy order of eight grammatical morphemes

Grammatical morphemes	Elementary	Intermediate	Advanced	Proficient
Copula BE	94.2	96.3	95.5	94.7
Auxiliary BE	89	96.1	86.7	92.5
Possessive -s	76.7	76.2	94.8	95.2
Progressive -ing	72.1	82.3	89.8	94.3
Plural -s	80	81	81.4	88.5
3rd person -s	70.8	69.6	76.7	89.4
Irregular past	82.3	79.6	78.9	83.7
Article	63	70.2	60.2	79.6

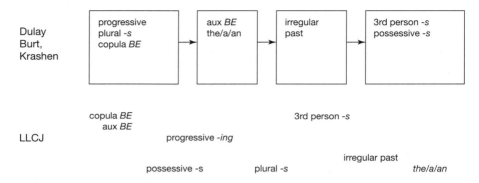

Figure C3.13 Comparison of morpheme acquisition orders

Figure C3.13 shows diagrammatically the comparison of our results with the order observed by Dulay and Burt (1973) and Krashen (1977). The noteworthy difference is that articles, which show the lowest accuracy rate in all of the morphemes, are the most difficult items for Japanese learners. Since the Japanese language does not have the notion of articles attached to nouns, the proper use of articles should be very difficult for them to acquire. Possessive *-s*, in contrast, is the item which is relatively easier for Japanese learners, as reflected by its higher rank order in relation to the order observed by Dulay and Burt, and Krashen. This is perhaps because Japanese has a particle *no*, which is similar to the English possessive *-s*, as in *John no hon* 'John's book'.

The results indicate that there are some differences between the order of acquisition of grammatical morphemes proposed previously and the order found on the basis of learner corpus data in this study. What is the implication of this finding? One possible implication is that one may argue that the concept of a universal order of acquisition needs to be reconsidered. A large-scale corpus-based analysis will shed more light on this issue. It would be interesting if one could compare the results for the Japanese learners with those of other L1 groups represented in the Longman Learners' Corpus (French, German, Spanish and so on). The other possible implication is that one may argue that the universal acquisition order should hold and the fact that it does not may lead us to examine carefully the quality of our learner corpus data. Since the Longman learner data were collected in an opportunistic way, the criteria for determining the subjects' proficiency level are sometimes subjective. Learners' proficiency levels as graded in the Longman Learners' Corpus do not always match the quality of actual compositions. If the corpus design had been better, the results might have been different. This is merely a possibility, but it is a timely reminder that the results derived from a corpus are, to some extent, only as good as the corpus itself (see Unit A10.15). A badly designed corpus, or indeed, even a well-designed corpus, when used for a purpose it is not designed for, may provide misleading results.

Summary

This study exploited a commercial learner corpus called the Longman Learners' Corpus by examining how Japanese learners acquire grammatical morphemes such as the ones investigated by Dulay and Burt (1973) and others in the 1970s. These influential studies claimed that L2 learners acquired grammatical morphemes in a universal order independent of the developmental path of learning. This study largely verified that claim using large learner-corpus data. It also introduced problem-oriented manual error tagging techniques and the newly released WordSmith 4.

FURTHER STUDY

As the Longman Learners' Corpus contains data from learners of English from various L1 backgrounds and at different proficiency levels, it has made it possible to investigate the features of interlanguage across different L1 backgrounds and developmental stages. Readers are advised to use the techniques introduced in this case study to analyse the order of acquisition of English grammatical morphemes on the basis of the components produced by learners with their L1 backgrounds.

Unit C4
Swearing in modern British English

CASE STUDY 4

C4.1 INTRODUCTION

We discussed language variation in Units A10.4 and B4 and sociolinguistics in Unit A10.11. This case study explores variations in spoken and written registers in modern British English and demonstrates how corpora can be used in sociolinguistic studies.

Swearing is a part of everyday language use. To date it has been infrequently studied, though some recent work on swearing in American English (e.g. Jay 1992), Australian English (e.g. Kidman 1993) and British English (e.g. McEnery, Baker and Hardie 2000) has addressed the topic. Nonetheless, there is still no systematic account of swear words in English (though McEnery 2005 seeks to provide a better historical explanation of attitudes to bad language in English). In terms of methodology, swearing has been approached from the points of view of history (e.g. Hughes 1991), psycholinguistics (e.g. Jay 1992) and semantics (Kidman 1993). There have been, to date, few studies of swearing based on sociolinguistic variables such as gender, age and social class (see McEnery, Baker and Hardie 2000 for an exception). Such a study has been difficult in the absence of appropriate corpus resources. With the production of the British National Corpus (see Unit A7.2), such a study became possible. In addition to parts of speech, the corpus is richly encoded with metadata pertaining to demographic features such as age, gender and social class, and textual features such as register, publication medium and domain. In this case study, we will explore such dimensions of variation to discover a general pattern of usage for one word, *FUCK*, in modern British English. While bad language may be related to religion (e.g. *Jesus, heaven, hell* and *DAMN*), sex (e.g. *FUCK* and *cunt*), racism (e.g. *nigger*), defecation (e.g. *SHIT* and *PISS*), homophobia (e.g. *queer*) or other matters, we decided to examine only the distribution pattern of *FUCK* (including its morphological variants), because *FUCK* is a typical swear word that occurs frequently in the BNC. *FUCK* is perhaps 'one of the most interesting and colourful words in the English language today' that can be used to describe pain, pleasure, hatred and even love (Andersson and Trudgill 1992: 60). As the word became more highly charged semantically, it has also acquired more grammatical flexibility so that *FUCK* 'has altered from being exclusively a verb to every part of speech' (Nurmi 1997).

For this study we will use BNCWeb. BNCWeb is a user-friendly interface to the BNC corpus. Note that the old BNCWeb query system is used in this study. Users of the BNCWeb World Edition query system (as used in Case Study 1) may obtain frequencies which are slightly different from those shown in the screenshots. This case study will introduce two other important features of BNCWeb, namely distribution and cross-tabulation, and show you how to explore language variation using the metadata encoded in the corpus. Readers interested in a more comprehensive account of the use of FUCK in the BNC can refer to McEnery and Xiao (2004), on which this case study is based.

This unit consists of four sections. Unit C4.2 compares spoken and written registers. Unit C4.3 explores the pattern of FUCK usage in the spoken register while Unit C4.4 explores the pattern of FUCK usage in the written register.

C4.2 SPOKEN vs. WRITTEN REGISTER

The spoken register is generally more informal than the written register, and one of the linguistic indicators of informality is swearing (see Collins and Hollo 2000). In the BNC corpus, the spoken section consists of around 10 per cent of the data while the other 90 per cent are written texts. This section compares the distribution patterns of FUCK in spoken and written registers. To get the frequencies needed in this investigation, do the following:

1. Start *Internet Explorer*, type in the URL of BNCWeb and press the *Enter* key. You will be led to the website of BNCWeb, as shown in Figure C4.1.
2. Click on the link *Log on the BNCWeb query system*, and you will be prompted to type in your user name and password (Figure C4.2).
3. Enter your user name and password as required and confirm by pressing the *OK* button. Now the BNCWeb query system is ready for use, as shown in Figure C4.3. You can explore the whole BNC corpus or select spoken or written texts alone.
4. As we are interested in comparing spoken and written registers, we will use the whole BNC corpus. But we will search for FUCK (including its morphological variants *fuck, fucked, fucks, fuckin(g)* and *fucker(s)*) separately so that we can have a clearer view of their distribution patterns across register. First type in *fuck* in the text box, select 1000 for the *Number of hits per page* and press the *Start query* button, as shown in Figure C4.4.
5. Now you can see the concordance window for *fuck*. Click on the down arrow near *Thin* and select *Distribution* from the pull-down menu. Press the *Go* button (Figure C4.5).
6. You will be taken to the *Distribution window* of *fuck* (Figure C4.6). Record the *Number of words, Number of hits* and *Frequency per million words* for the spoken and written registers.
7. Now press the *Back* button on *Internet Explorer* a couple of times until you return to the interface of the BNCWeb query system (Figure C4.3), and repeat

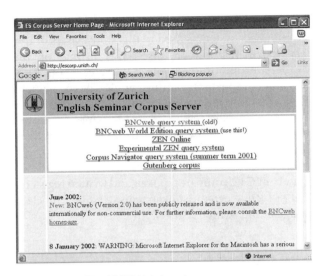

Figure C4.1 The BNCWeb interface

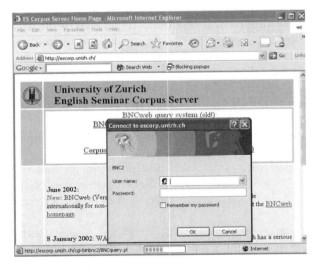

Figure C4.2 Log on to BNCWeb

steps 1–6 for the search strings *fucked*, *fucks*, *fucking\fuckin* and *fucker\fuckers* separately (the character I means *or*). Do the same for the search string *fuck\ fucked\fucks\fucking\fuckin\fucker\ fuckers* to find all of the instances of FUCK.

Your results should match those in Table C4.1. The normalized frequencies (NF) allow us to compare the distributions of individual word forms while word numbers and raw frequencies (RF) make it possible for us to calculate the log-likelihood score and significance level for the difference in frequencies by using SPSS statistics package (see Case Study 2).

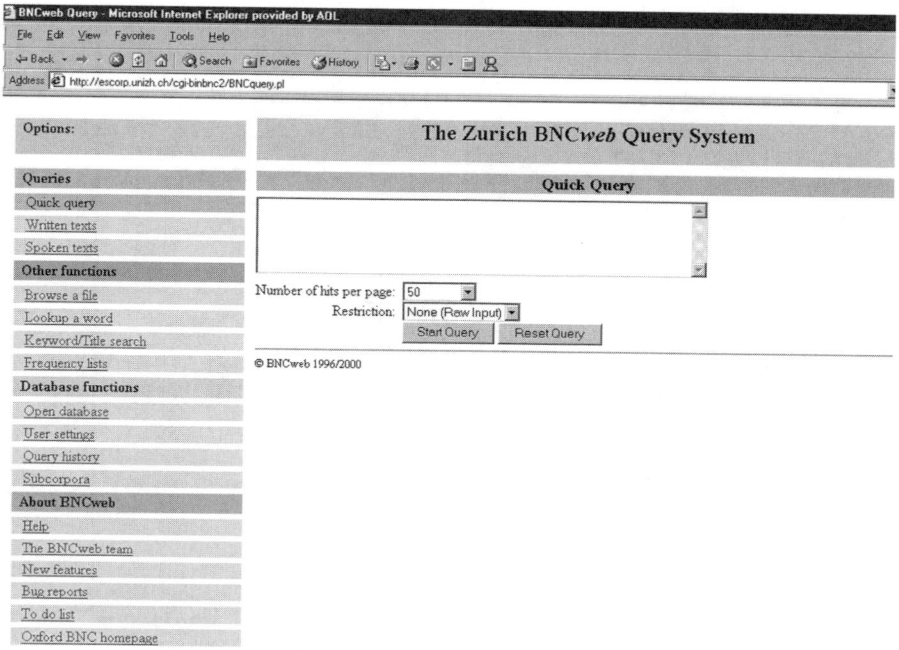

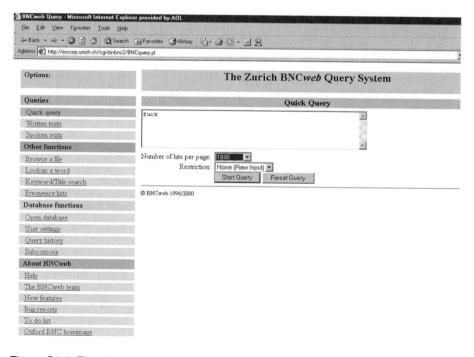

Figure C4.3 The BNCWeb query system

Figure C4.4 Enter the search string

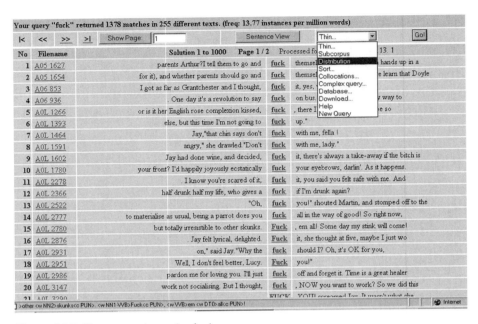

Figure C4.5 The concordance for *fuck*

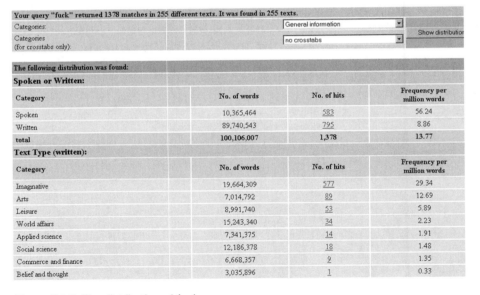

Figure C4.6 The distribution of *fuck*

Table C4.1 Spoken vs. written register

Form	Register	Words	RF	NF	LL ratio	Sig. level
fuck	Spoken	10365464	583	56.24	940.406	<0.001
	Written	89740543	795	8.86		
fucked	Spoken	10365464	62	5.98	68.066	<0.001
	Written	89740543	130	1.45		
fucks	Spoken	10365464	10	0.96	12.792	<0.001
	Written	89740543	18	0.2		
fucking	Spoken	10365464	2164	208.77	6150.587	<0.001
	Written	89740543	969	10.8		
fucker(s)	Spoken	10365464	25	2.41	28.841	<0.001
	Written	89740543	50	0.56		
All forms	Spoken	10365464	2844	274.37	6827.547	<0.001
	Written	89740543	1962	21.86		

As can be seen from the table, for all of the word forms under examination, the difference between spoken and written language is statistically significant at the level p<0.001. FUCK occurs twelve times more frequently in spoken language than in written language. The greatest contrast is found for *fuckin(g)*, which was used nearly twenty times as frequently in the spoken section as in the written section of the corpus. While it is not clear why people use FUCK considerably more frequently in spoken language than in written language, our speculation is that FUCK occurs more frequently in informal than formal contexts. The censorship of published written texts is another possible explanation for the relatively low frequency of FUCK in written language. In spite of this quantitative difference, different word forms distribute across the registers in the same descending order: *fuckin(g), fuck, fucked, fucker(s)* and *fucks*. However, the general difference between spoken and written uses of FUCK obscures a number of finer differences in usage both within the general discussions of speech and writing and between them. The rest of this unit is devoted to identifying these finer distinctions.

C4.3 VARIATIONS WITHIN SPOKEN ENGLISH

This section explores the pattern of FUCK usage in spoken British English using metadata pertaining to the different sociolinguistic variables encoded in the BNC. We will compare demographically sampled and context-governed spoken data. We will also examine the possible influence of speaker gender, age, social class and education level on the pattern of uses of FUCK.

C4.3.1 Demographically sampled vs. context-governed spoken language

As noted in Unit A2.4, the BNC contains orthographically transcribed spoken language using two different sampling regimes: demographically determined and context-governed. To get the word numbers and frequencies of *FUCK* for the two types of spoken language, click on the down arrow on the right side of *General information* in step 6, select *Overall: Type of text* and press the *Show distribution* button, as shown in Figure C4.7. You will be taken to the distribution window giving the word number, number of hits (RF) and frequency per million words (NF) for three types of text: spoken demographic, written and spoken context-governed (Figure C4.8). Record the word numbers and frequencies for the two types of spoken text. Do the same for search strings *fucked, fucks, fucking\fuckin, fucker\ fuckers*, and *fuck\fucked\fucks\fucking \fuckin\fucker\fuckers* as in step 7. Your results should match those in Table C4.2.

With regard to the frequency of *FUCK*, the two types of spoken language differ significantly at the level p<0.001. As can be seen in Table C4.2, demographically sampled spoken data contains 146 times as many instances of *FUCK* as context-governed spoken data. Some word forms, e.g. *fucks* and *fucker(s)*, are simply non-existent in context-governed spoken data, even though this part contains nearly one million more tokens than the first type of data.

Surprisingly, the contrast between the two types of spoken language is even more marked than the distinction between spoken and written registers. While context-governed spoken language is indeed more formal than demographically sampled

Your query "fuck" returned 1378 matches in 255 different texts. It was found in 255 texts.

Categories:			General information ▼	Show distribution
Categories (for crosstabs only):			Overall: Spoken or Written	
			Overall: Type of Text	
			Written: Text Type	
			Written: Date of Creation	
			Written: Medium of Text	
The following distribution was found:			Written: Text Sample	
Spoken or Written:			Written: Reception Status	
			Written: Age of Author	
Category	No. of words		Written: Gender of Author	frequency per million words
			Written: Domicile of Author	
			Written: Type of Author ▼	
Spoken	10,365,464		582	56.24
Written	89,740,543		795	8.86
total	100,106,007		1,378	13.77

Text Type (written):

Category	No. of words	No. of hits	Frequency per million words
Imaginative	19,664,309	577	29.34
Arts	7,014,792	89	12.69
Leisure	8,991,740	53	5.89
World affairs	15,243,340	34	2.23
Applied science	7,341,375	14	1.91
Social science	12,186,378	18	1.48
Commerce and finance	6,668,357	9	1.35
Belief and thought	3,035,896	1	0.33

Figure C4.7 Show distribution

Your query "fuck" returned 1378 matches in 255 different texts. It was found in 255 texts.		
Categories:		Overall: Type of Text
Categories (for crosstabs only):		no crosstabs — Show distribution

The following distribution was found:

Type of text:

Category	No. of words	No. of hits	Frequency per million words
spoken demographic	4,211,216	576	136.78
written	89,740,543	795	8.86
spoken context-governed	5,034,707	7	1.39
total	98,986,466	1,378	13.92

[Back to BNC Query Result] [New Query]

Ⓓ BNCweb 1996/2000

Figure C4.8 Distribution across text type

Table C4.2 Spoken demographically sampled vs. spoken context-governed

Form	Type	Words	RF	NF	LL ratio	Sig. level
fuck	Demographic	4211216	576	136.78	838.609	<0.001
	Context-governed	5034707	7	1.39		
fucked	Demographic	4211216	61	14.49	86.922	<0.001
	Context-governed	5034707	1	0.2		
fucks	Demographic	4211216	10	2.37	15.729	<0.001
	Context-governed	5034707	0	0		
fucking	Demographic	4211216	2149	510.3	3218.681	<0.001
	Context-governed	5034707	15	2.98		
fucker(s)	Demographic	4211216	25	5.94	39.321	<0.001
	Context-governed	5034707	0	0		
All forms	Demographic	4211216	2821	669.88	4196.573	<0.001
	Context-governed	5034707	23	4.57		

spoken language (see Aston and Burnard 1998: 31), the difference between the two types of spoken language cannot be explained by the formal/informal distinction alone: written language is basically more formal than spoken language, yet the contrast between them is not as marked as that between two types of spoken language. A reasonable explanation is that the social contexts from which the second type of spoken data was sampled militated in favour of considerably fewer forms of FUCK than in the demographically sampled spoken data.

C4.3.2 Gender of speaker

Men and women differ in their use of strong language (see Lakoff 1975: 5; Hughes 1991: 211; Holmes 1992: 171–176). For example, Stenström (1991) found from the London-Lund spoken corpus that male speakers prefer *hell*-related words like DAMN and *devil* while female speakers show a preference for *heaven*-related words like *heavens* and *gosh*. Consequently we decided to explore the hypothesis that the gender of speakers also influences the frequency of their use of FUCK.

To retrieve a range of word frequency data from the corpus related to male and female uses of FUCK, select *Speaker Gender* in the pull-down menu in the *Distribution* window in step 6.

Table C4.3 compares male and female speakers' use of FUCK. As can be seen from the normalized frequencies, when all word forms are taken as a whole, male speakers use FUCK more than twice as frequently as female speakers, a difference that is statistically significant at the level of $p<0.001$. When we consider word forms individually, we find that male speakers use *fuckin(g)*, *fuck* and *fucker(s)* significantly more frequently than female speakers. The difference in the frequencies of male and female speakers' use of *fucked* and *fucks* is, however, not statistically significant. One possible explanation is that the two word forms tend to denote the literal meaning of the word (see McEnery and Xiao 2004 for a discussion of the semantic categories of FUCK).

On the other hand, while the use of FUCK differs quantitatively by speaker gender, it does not differ qualitatively. For both males and females, the rank and proportion of different word forms show a very similar distribution pattern (Table C4.4). Both genders use *fuckin(g)* most frequently, followed by *fuck*. While proportions of different word forms may vary slightly across gender, this variation is not statistically significant, as shown in Table C4.5.

C4.3.3 Age of speaker

Speaker age is another sociolinguistic variable that influences the pattern of FUCK usage. As Holmes observes:

> The extensive swear word vocabulary which some teenagers use is likely to change over time [. . .] Though they continue to know these terms, the frequency with which they use them often diminishes, especially as they begin to have children and socialise with others with young families.
> (Holmes 1992: 183)

To test this hypothesis, we will first get the frequencies of FUCK used by speakers of different age groups by selecting *Speaker Age* in the *Distribution* window in step 6. Table C4.6 gives the frequencies of FUCK for different age groups. The table shows that for each of the forms of FUCK, and for all of word forms taken together, the difference in the distribution of FUCK across different age groups is statistically significant, though the significance level varies by word form, with the most marked contrast for *fuckin(g)*, followed by *fuck*. For all age groups, the most frequently used word form is *fuckin(g)*, followed by *fuck*, though the other word forms do not show a predictable pattern.

Table C4.3 Gender of speaker

Form	Gender	Words	RF	NF	LL ratio	Sig. level
fuck	Male	4918075	337	68.52	50.025	<0.001
	Female	3255533	106	32.56		
fucked	Male	4918075	25	5.08	0.510	0.475
	Female	3255533	13	3.99		
fucks	Male	4918075	5	1.02	0.386	0.534
	Female	3255533	2	0.61		
fucking	Male	4918075	1394	283.44	353.624	<0.001
	Female	3255533	321	98.6		
fucker(s)	Male	4918075	18	3.66	8.967	0.003
	Female	3255533	2	0.61		
All forms	Male	4918075	1779	361.73	401.668	<0.001
	Female	3255533	444	136.38		

Table C4.4 Proportion and rank of word forms by male and female speakers

Gender	Form	Proportion (%)	Rank
Male	fucking	78.36	1
	fuck	18.94	2
	fucked	1.41	3
	fucker(s)	1.01	4
	fucks	0.28	5
Female	fucking	72.30	1
	fuck	23.87	2
	fucked	2.93	3
	fucker(s)	0.45	4/5
	fucks	0.45	4/5

Table C4.5 Comparison of the normalized frequencies across gender

Form	Male	Female	LL ratio	Sig. level
fuck	68.52	32.56		
fucked	5.08	3.99		
fucks	1.02	0.61	4.17	0.35
fucking	283.44	98.6		
fucker(s)	3.66	0.61		

With respect to age group, young people and teenagers (age groups 15–24, 25–34) appear to use *FUCK* more frequently than people of other age groups (Table C4.7). While it is not surprising that young people use *FUCK* readily, children of the age group 0–14 appear to show an unexpectedly marked propensity to say *FUCK* whereas people aged 35–44 demonstrate an aversion for the word. One plausible reason, in line with Holmes' hypothesis, for the relatively low frequency for age

Table C4.6 Age of speaker

Form	Age	Words	RF	NF	LL ratio	Sig. level
fuck	0–14	460627	158	343.01		
	15–24	511858	126	246.16		
	25–34	1113709	93	83.50	622.580	<0.001
	35–44	1066857	8	7.50		
	45–59	1605978	46	28.64		
	60+	1122133	3	2.67		
fucked	0–14	460627	2	4.34		
	15–24	511858	10	19.54		
	25-34	1113709	5	4.49	29.912	<0.001
	35–44	1066857	1	0.94		
	45–59	1605978	2	1.25		
	60+	1122133	0	0		
fucks	0–14	460627	3	6.51		
	15–24	511858	1	1.95		
	25–34	1113709	1	0.90	11.097	0.015
	35–44	1066857	0	0		
	45–59	1605978	2	1.25		
	60+	1122133	0	0		
fucking	0–14	460627	217	471.10		
	15–24	511858	638	1246.44		
	25–34	1113709	582	522.58	1967.681	<0.001
	35–44	1066857	71	66.55		
	45–59	1605978	173	107.72		
	60+	1122133	18	16.04		
fucker(s)	0–14	460627	12	26.05		
	15–24	511858	18	35.17		
	25–34	1113709	8	7.18	88.829	<0.001
	35–44	1066857	0	0		
	45–59	1605978	0	0		
	60+	1122133	0	0		
All forms	0–14	460627	392	851.01		
	15–24	511858	793	1549.26		
	25–34	1113709	689	618.65	2613.071	<0.001
	35–44	1066857	80	74.99		
	45–59	1605978	223	138.86		
	60+	1122133	21	18.71		

Table C4.7 Frequencies of *FUCK* by age group

Age	NF	Rank by NF
15–24	1549.26	1
0–14	851.01	2
25–34	618.65	3
45–59	138.86	4
35–44	74.99	5
60+	18.71	6

group 35–44 is that parents with children and teenagers around them say *FUCK* less frequently than those who are yet to have children and those whose children have grown up and do not live with them. Children under the age of 15 use *FUCK* more frequently because they consciously want to shock adults and to behave in what they perceive to be an adult fashion. However, on the basis of corpus data alone, we cannot evaluate these explanations.

Yet if we cross-tabulate the variables speaker age and gender, a more distinct pattern can be observed. To do this, we need to select two variables in the *Distribution* window. Click on the first down arrow and select *Speaker Gender*. Click on the down arrow next to *no crosstabs* and select *Speaker Age*. Then press the *Show distribution* button, as shown in Figure C4.9. Table C4.8 shows the result of the cross-tabulation. As can be seen from the table, except for the age group 60+, the difference between male and female speakers is statistically significant. For all age groups, male speakers say *FUCK* more frequently than female speakers. The greatest contrast between male and female speakers is found in young people (age groups 25–34 and 15–24), as reflected by their much greater LL scores.

C4.3.4 Social class of speaker

The BNC classifies speakers into four social classes, namely AB, C1, C2 and DE. In this section, we will examine the possible influence of social class on the distribution pattern of *FUCK*. To get the frequencies of *FUCK*, select *Speaker: Social Class* from the pull-down menu in the *Distribution window* for each search string in step 6. Table C4.9 gives the frequencies of *FUCK* used by different social classes. As can be seen

Your query "fuck|fucked|fucks|fuckin|fucking|fucker|fuckers" returned 4806 matches in 334 different texts. It was found in 334 texts.

Categories:		Speaker: Gender		
Categories (for crosstabs only):		Speaker: Age		Show distribution

The following distribution was found:

Age / Gender: Male

Category	No. of words	No. of hits	Frequency per million words
15-24	215,310	657	3051.41
25-34	543,791	643	1182.44
0-14	237,530	248	1044.08
45-59	1,072,944	135	125.82
35-44	557,551	64	114.79
60+	590,441	7	11.86
total	3,217,567	1,754	545.13

Age / Gender: Female

Category	No. of words	No. of hits	Frequency per million words
0-14	223,092	144	645.47
15-24	296,548	136	458.61
45-59	531,429	88	165.59
25-34	569,709	46	80.74
35-44	509,306	16	31.42

Figure C4.9 The cross-tabulation of speaker gender and age

Table C4.8 Cross-tabulation of speaker age and gender

Age	Gender	Words	RF	NF	LL ratio	Sig. level
0–14	Male	237530	248	1044.08	21.77	<0.001
	Female	223092	144	645.47		
15–24	Male	215310	657	3051.41	558.717	<0.001
	Female	296548	136	458.61		
25–24	Male	543791	643	1182.44	645.124	<0.001
	Female	569709	46	80.74		
35–44	Male	557551	64	114.79	26.657	<0.001
	Female	509306	16	31.42		
45–59	Male	531429	88	165.59	3.93	0.047
	Female	1072944	135	125.82		
60+	Male	531692	14	26.33	3.17	0.84
	Female	590441	7	11.86		

Table C4.9 Speaker social class

Form	Class	Words	RF	NF	LL ratio	Sig. level
fuck	AB	696819	93	133.46	75.494	<0.001
	C1	427872	7	16.36		
	C2	485682	45	92.65		
	DE	267818	55	205.36		
fucked	AB	696819	18	25.83	15.993	0.001
	C1	427872	0	0		
	C2	485682	4	8.24		
	DE	267818	2	7.47		
fucks	AB	696819	3	4.31	1.987	0.583
	C1	427872	0	0		
	C2	485682	1	2.06		
	DE	267818	1	3.73		
fucking	AB	696819	187	268.36	297.527	<0.001
	C1	427872	39	91.15		
	C2	485682	305	627.98		
	DE	267818	198	739.31		
fucker(s)	AB	696819	1	1.44	8.087	0.012
	C1	427872	0	0		
	C2	485682	2	4.12		
	DE	267818	4	14.94		
All forms	AB	696819	302	433.4	339.734	<0.001
	C1	427872	46	107.51		
	C2	485682	357	735.05		
	DE	267818	260	970.81		

from the table, except for the word form *fucks* (there are only five instances of *fucks*, we doubt a statistical test based on such limited data can yield a reliable result), the difference in the distribution of all other word forms across social class is statistically significant. As with speaker gender and age, the greatest contrast is for *fuckin(g)*, followed by *fuck*, as indicated by their LL scores. The overall frequencies of FUCK also show that the distinction between social classes is quantitatively significant.

The normalized frequencies for all forms show such a distinction. People from classes DE and C2 are most frequent users of FUCK, followed by AB. Interestingly, those from the class AB do not say FUCK less frequently than C1, especially people from age group 60+ (see Table C4.11). One might speculate that the older people from AB use FUCK frequently because they want to flaunt their seniority, while those from C1 show a considerably lower rate of FUCK usage because they consciously or unconsciously pay special attention to their linguistic behaviour so as to appear closer to how they perceive the AB speech to be. This observation is further supported by the cross-tabulation of speaker gender and social class on the one hand, and of speaker age and social class on the other hand (see Figure C4.9 for cross-tabulation), as shown in Tables C4.10 and C4.11. Table C4.10 shows the result of cross-tabulation of gender and social class. As can be seen from the table, while the difference between male and female speakers is statistically significant for all social classes, the greatest contrast is found for the class C2. Male and female speakers of the class DE show a much less marked contrast because both sexes from this class use FUCK very frequently. However, non-corpus based research into the relationship between swearing and power is clearly needed to substantiate further the hypothesis that those in authority flaunt their seniority through the use of swear words.

C4.3.5 Education level of speaker

A common belief is that the better educated one is, the less likely one is to use bad language. A popular explanation for swearing is that people use swear words when they have few words at their disposal, i.e. their vocabulary is so impoverished that they have to use 'easy' and 'lazy' words in certain situations (see Andersson and Trudgill 1992: 65). This explanation is, in our view, unlikely to be true. The BNC encodes information pertaining to speaker's education level, thus enabling us to test the influence of education on the use of FUCK.

Select *Speak: Education* in step 6 for the frequencies of FUCK used by speakers of different education levels, which are given in Table C4.12. Note that the table does not include the group *Still in education*. We decided to leave this group out of our

Table C4.10 Cross-tabulation of speaker gender and social class

Class	Gender	Words	RF	NF	LL ratio	Sig. level
AB	Male	266857	175	655.78	42.934	<0.001
	Female	413150	127	307.39		
C1	Male	187946	43	228.79	52.035	<0.001
	Female	239926	3	12.5		
C2	Male	169737	348	2050.23	654.976	<0.001
	Female	315945	9	28.49		
DE	Male	126512	176	1391.17	64.701	<0.001
	Female	138247	84	607.61		

Table C4.11 Cross-tabulation of speaker age and social class

Age	Class	Words	RF	NF	LL ratio	Sig. level
0–14	AB	127228	209	1642.72	24.550	<0.001
	C1	5722	0	0		
	C2	4439	1	225.28		
	DE	2	0	0		
15–24	AB	78210	80	1022.89	99.486	<0.001
	C1	40544	1	24.66		
	C2	29072	29	977.52		
	DE	42303	81	1914.76		
25–34	AB	101503	0	0	312.701	<0.001
	C1	55654	26	467.17		
	C2	192484	317	1646.89		
	DE	23468	4	170.44		
35–44	AB	81002	2	24.69	4.813	0.090
	C1	201306	17	84.45		
	C2	97480	10	102.59		
	DE	0	0	0		
45–59	AB	132275	0	0	431.876	<0.001
	C1	106972	2	18.7		
	C2	84611	0	0		
	DE	115857	168	1450.06		
60+	AB	94332	7	74.21	7.835	0.023
	C1	17674	0	0		
	C2	77596	0	0		
	DE	48244	0	0		

Table C4.12 Speaker education level

Education	Words	RF	NF	LL ratio	Sig. level
Left school 15/16	639039	596	932.57	762.703	<0.001
Left school 17/18	217282	32	147.27		
Educ. until 19/over	318267	16	50.27		
Left school 14/under	378669	9	23.77		

discussion because this group may overlap with others. There are 807.74 instances of *FUCK* per million words (443 instances in 548,444 words) for those still in education. Interestingly, people of this group do not use *FUCK* less frequently because they are mostly of the age group 15–24. As can be seen, people who left school at 15/16 are most frequent users of *FUCK*. The general pattern of uses of *FUCK* is that people who have received less education say *FUCK* more frequently. People who left school at 14 or under show an unexpectedly low frequency of uses of *FUCK* because people from this group are mostly over 60 – young people are unlikely to leave school so early. Of the nine instances of *FUCK* for this group, only two are used by young people aged 15–24 while seven are used by people aged 60 or over. In terms

Table C4.13 Comparison of normalized frequencies across education level

Education level	Word form	NF	Rank
Left school 14/under	fucking	21.13	1
	fuck	2.64	2
	fucked	0	–
	fucker(s)	0	–
	fucks	0	–
Left school 15/16	fucking	772.97	1
	fuck	143.95	2
	fucked	6.26	3/4
	fucker(s)	6.26	3/4
	fucks	3.13	5
Left school 17/18	fucking	110.46	1
	fuck	36.82	2
	fucked	0	–
	fucker(s)	0	–
	fucks	0	–
Educ. until 19/over	fucking	31.42	1
	fuck	12.57	2
	fucked	6.28	3
	fucker(s)	0	–
	fucks	0	–

of word forms, the distinction across education level is quantitative rather than qualitative. For people of all levels of education, *fuckin(g)* is the most frequent word form, followed by *fuck* (see Table C4.13).

C4.4   VARIATIONS WITHIN WRITTEN ENGLISH

This section explores the distribution pattern of FUCK in written British English using metadata pertaining to the different sociolinguistic variables encoded in the BNC. We will examine the possible influence of gender and age of author and audience, as well as the reception status of writing on the distribution pattern of FUCK.

C4.4.1   Gender of author

We assume that author gender has a similar effect on the pattern of uses of FUCK to that of speaker gender. To test this assumption, we will first get the frequencies of FUCK used by male and female authors by selecting *Written: Gender of Author* in step 6. The results should match those given in Table C4.14. As can be seen from the table, male authors use FUCK more than twice as frequently as female authors. This difference is significant at the level p<0.001 (LL=162.124, 1 d.f.). The difference between the two genders is also quantitatively significant for each word form, though the significance level may vary, with *fuckin(g)* demonstrating the greatest contrast. In terms of word forms, while female authors appear to prefer *fuck* to

Table C4.14 Gender of author

Form	Gender	Words	RF	NF	LL ratio	Sig. level
fuck	Male	31586324	486	15.39	28.625	<0.001
	Female	15497994	147	9.49		
fucked	Male	31586324	78	2.47	7.549	0.007
	Female	15497994	20	1.29		
fucks	Male	31586324	14	0.44	6.503	0.029
	Female	15497994	1	0.06		
fucking	Male	31586324	709	22.45	128.474	<0.001
	Female	15497994	132	8.52		
fucker(s)	Male	31586324	35	1.11	7.142	0.012
	Female	15497994	6	0.39		
All forms	Male	31586324	1322	41.85	162.124	<0.001
	Female	15497994	306	19.74		

Table C4.15 Proportion and rank of word forms by male and female authors

Gender	Form	Proportion (%)	Rank
Male	fucking	53.63	1
	fuck	36.76	2
	fucked	5.90	3
	fucker(s)	2.65	4
	fucks	1.06	5
Female	fucking	43.14	2
	fuck	48.04	1
	fucked	6.54	3
	fucker(s)	1.96	4
	fucks	0.33	5

Table C4.16 Comparison of the normalized frequencies across gender

Form	Male	Female	LL ratio	Sig. level	LL ratio	Sig. level
fucking	22.45	8.52	0.439	0.570		
fuck	15.39	9.49				
fucked	2.47	1.29			1.162	0.867
fucker(s)	1.11	0.39	0.680	1.000		
fucks	0.44	0.06				

fuckin(g) more than male authors (see Table C4.16), the difference is not statistically significant (LL=0.439, 1 d.f.). The proportion and rank of word forms show a very similar distribution pattern across author gender (Table C4.15). The fluctuation of the normalized frequencies can be discarded (LL=1.162, 3 d.f.).

Table C4.17 Age of author

Form	Age	Words	RF	NF	LL ratio	Sig. level
fuck	0–14	581962	3	5.15		
	15–24	437149	3	6.86		
	25–34	1325516	97	73.18	178.234	<0.001
	35–44	2813226	32	11.37		
	45–59	2847335	36	12.64		
	60+	2451519	14	5.71		
fucked	0–14	581962	0	0]		
	15–24	437149	0	0		
	25–34	1325516	20	15.09	46.263	<0.001
	35–44	2813226	5	1.78		
	45–59	2847335	11	3.86		
	60+	2451519	0	0		
fucks	0–14	581962	0	0		
	15–24	437149	0	0		
	25–34	1325516	1	0.75	3.286	0.778
	35–44	2813226	1	0.36		
	45–59	2847335	1	0.35		
	60+	2451519	0	0		
fucking	0–14	581962	12	20.62		
	15–24	437149	5	11.44		
	25–34	1325516	87	65.63	121.236	<0.001
	35–44	2813226	36	12.8		
	45–59	2847335	41	14.4		
	60+	2451519	21	8.57		
fucker(s)	0–14	581962	2	3.44		
	15–24	437149	0	0		
	25–34	1325516	3	2.66	7.216	0.129
	35–44	2813226	1	0.36		
	45–59	2847335	4	1.4		
	60+	2451519	1	0.41		
All forms	0–14	581962	17	29.21		
	15–24	437149	8	18.3		
	25–34	1325516	208	156.92	336.394	<0.001
	35–44	2813226	75	26.66		
	45–59	2847335	93	32.66		
	60+	2451519	36	14.68		

C4.4.2 Age of author

Author age in written language is a sociolinguistic variable comparable to speaker age in spoken language and may, therefore, influence the distribution of FUCK. By selecting *Written: Age of Author* in the distribution window, you will get the word numbers and frequencies given in Table C4.17. As can be seen, the differences in the frequencies of FUCK between authors of different age groups are statistically significant when all word forms are taken together. A comparison by word form shows that except for the two very infrequent words *fucks* (three instances) and *fucker(s)* (nine instances), all of the other word forms demonstrate a significant variation between age groups.

Table C4.18 Comparison of spoken and written languages

Age group	Spoken		Written	
	NF	Rank	NF	Rank
0–14	851.01	2	29.21	3
15–24	1549.26	1	18.3	5
25–34	618.65	3	156.92	1
35–44	74.99	5	26.66	4
45–59	138.86	4	32.66	2
60+	18.71	6	14.68	6

While young people also use FUCK a lot in written language as they do in spoken language, the pattern of using FUCK in written language appears to be different from that in spoken language in spite of some similarities, as shown in Table C4.18. In written English, the age group 60+ uses FUCK least frequently. However, authors aged 25–34 use FUCK most frequently, followed by the age group 45–59. While authors aged 45–59 use FUCK slightly more often than those aged 35–44, the difference is not statistically significant (LL=1.721, p=0.217). Like speakers under 15, authors of this age group use FUCK more frequently than expected, though not as obtrusively as in spoken language. Surprisingly, people aged 15–24 use FUCK less frequently than expected in written English, though this age group is the most frequent user of FUCK in spoken English.

C4.4.3 Gender of audience

The BNC classifies the gender of the intended audience of writing contained in the corpus into four types: male, female, mixed and unknown. In this section, we will only consider the first three categories. Select *Written: Gender of Audience* in the distribution window. You will get the frequencies as given in Table C4.19. The table shows that when all word forms are considered together, the difference between audience genders is statistically significant. However, *fucked* is the only word form which, in itself, shows a significant difference of distribution across writing intended for males and writing intended for females. *Fucked* is frequently used as the past form of the word with its literal meaning (see McEnery and Xiao 2004). Writing with an intended female audience contains significantly fewer occurrences of *fucked* than writings for an intended male audience. Other word forms (especially *fuck* and *fuckin(g)*) used for emphasis do not show a significant contrast.

Interestingly, writing intended for a mixed audience is quite similar to writing intended for a male audience in terms of distribution patterns of FUCK (the difference is not statistically significant; LL=0.134, d.f.=1, p=0.714) when all word forms are taken together. The difference in distributions of FUCK in writing intended for females and that for a mixed audience is statistically significant at the level p<0.001 (LL=35.363, 1 d.f.). With respect to individual word forms, the difference between writing with an intended male audience and writing intended

Table C4.19 Gender of audience

Form	Gender	Words	RF	NF	LL ratio	Sig. level
fuck	Male	2451934	21	8.56	0.521	0.471
	Female	6235502	44	7.06		
	Mixed	54289029	591	10.89	–	–
fucked	Male	2451934	17	6.93	28.091	<0.001
	Female	6235502	3	0.48		
	Mixed	54289029	90	1.66	–	–
fucks	Male	2451934	0	0	–	–
	Female	6235502	0	0		
	Mixed	54289029	14	0.26	–	–
fucking	Male	2451934	24	9.79	1.405	0.236
	Female	6235502	45	7.22		
	Mixed	54289029	701	12.91	–	–
fucker(s)	Male	2451934	0	0	–	–
	Female	6235502	0	0		
	Mixed	54289029	43	0.79	–	–
All forms	Male	2451934	62	25.29	10.270	0.001
	Female	6235502	92	14.75		
	Mixed	54289029	1439	26.51	–	–

for a mixed audience is not statistically significant while the difference between writing with an intended female audience and writing intended for a mixed audience is significant for *fuck* and *fuckin(g)*. For *fucked*, the difference of writing for the three types of audience is significant, though writing intended for a mixed audience is more akin to writing with an intended female audience.

C4.4.4   Age of audience

This section examines the possible influence of audience age on the pattern of uses of FUCK in written English. There are four age groups for audience: adults, teenagers, children and unknown. We will consider the first three categories, the frequencies of which can be obtained by selecting *Written: Age of Audience* in the distribution window.

Table C4.20 gives the frequencies of FUCK across these age groups. As can be seen from the table, writing for adults contains nearly twice as many uses of FUCK as writing for teenagers. FUCK occurs in writing for adults over seven times as frequently as in writing for children. This difference is significant at the level $p<0.001$. In terms of word forms, the greatest contrast is in *fuckin(g)*, followed by *fuck* while *fucked*, *fucks* and *fucker(s)* do not show a significant contrast because of the low overall frequencies of these word forms (there are only 2.73, 0.22 and 1.76 instances of *fucked*, *fucks* and *fucker(s)* per million words). This finding is in line with the social convention that writing for children avoids bad language more than writing for adults.

Table C4.20 Age of audience

Form	Age	Words	RF	NF	LL ratio	Sig. level
fuck	Adult	82335639	784	9.52		
	Teenager	1697721	10	5.89	14.482	0.001
	Child	969382	1	1.03		
fucked	Adult	82335639	128	1.55		
	Teenager	1697721	2	1.18	0.755	0.712
	Child	969382	0	0		
fucks	Adult	82335639	18	0.22		
	Teenager	1697721	0	0	0.110	1.000
	Child	969382	0	0		
fucking	Adult	82335639	960	11.66		
	Teenager	1697721	7	4.12	22.217	<0.001
	Child	969382	2	2.06		
fucker(s)	Adult	82335639	48	0.58		
	Teenager	1697721	2	1.18	1.412	0.347
	Child	969382	0	0		
All forms	Adult	82335639	1938	23.54		
	Teenager	1697721	21	12.37	37.603	<0.001
	Child	969382	3	3.09		

C4.4.5 Reception status

In this section, we will examine the potential relationship between reception status and the pattern of usage of FUCK. The BNC classifies the reception statuses of written texts into four types: high, medium, low and unknown. We will discard cases where reception status is unknown. First select *Written: Reception Status* in the distribution window for each search string and get their frequencies. Your results should match those given in Table C4.21. As can be seen, whether we consider the word forms of FUCK separately or together, the difference in the distribution of FUCK across reception status is statistically significant. In this case, medium reception status appears to be closer to high than low status. In terms of word forms, the difference between high and medium reception statuses is only significant for *fucks* and *fuckin(g)*.

We can get a vague picture of the pattern of usage of FUCK across reception status by sorting by normalized frequencies, as shown in Table C4.22. The table by itself does not show a pattern of FUCK usage. However, if we combine Tables C4.21 and C4.22 and take statistical significance into consideration, we are able to see clearly the pattern of usage for FUCK across reception status.

Table C4.21 shows that the difference between high and medium reception statuses is not statistically significant for *fuck* (p=0.245), *fucked* (p=0.381) and *fucker(s)* (p=0.083), hence *High* and *Medium* in rows 1, 2 and 5 in Table C4.22 can be swapped, i.e. *High (1)*, *Medium (2)* and *Low (3)*. Note, however, that the ranks of *High* and *Medium* cannot be inverted for *fucks* and *fucking*, because the inverted

Table C4.21 Reception status

Form	Level	Words	RF	NF	LL ratio	Sig. level	LL ratio	Sig. level
fuck	High	24138350	278	11.52	1.353	0.245		
	Medium	31885282	402	12.61			73.179	<0.001
	Low	16488041	83	5.03	–	–		
fucked	High	24138350	40	1.66	0.776	0.381		
	Medium	31885282	63	1.98			8.456	0.015
	Low	16488041	15	0.91	–	–		
fucks	High	24138350	11	0.46	7.357	0.007		
	Medium	31885282	3	0.09			7.077	0.025
	Low	16488041	4	0.24	–	–		
fucking	High	24138350	402	16.65	6.252	0.012		
	Medium	31885282	447	14.02			179.914	<0.001
	Low	16488041	60	3.64	–	–		
fucker(s)	High	24138350	13	0.54	3.006	0.083		
	Medium	31885282	30	0.94			9.681	0.008
	Low	16488041	4	0.24	–	–		
All forms	High	24138350	744	30.82	0.639	0.424		
	Medium	31885282	945	29.64			245.785	<0.001
	Low	16488041	166	10.07	–	–		

Table C4.22 Distribution pattern of FUCK by reception status

Row	Form	High	Medium	Low
1	fuck	2	1	3
2	fucked	2	1	3
3	fucks	1	3	2
4	fucking	1	2	3
5	fucker(s)	2	1	3
6	All forms	1	2	3

order cannot explain the statistical significance as shown by *fucks* (p=0.007) and *fuckin(g)* (p=0.012). As the difference between high and medium reception statuses is significant for *fucks* and *fuckin(g)*, *High* and *Medium* cannot be swapped in rows 3 and 4. However, in row 3, *Medium* and *Low* can be swapped (i.e. *High (1)*, *Medium (2)* and *Low (3)*) because the difference between these two categories is not statistically significant (LL=1.551, 1 d.f., p=0.213). These rearrangements clearly present the pattern of usage of FUCK across reception status: *High>Medium>Low*. This format is in harmony with the pattern observed when all word forms are taken as a whole, as shown in row 6 in Table C4.22. This finding is unusual but true. As such, swear words are very common in popular books and movies. The explanation for this phenomenon, however, is beyond the corpus-based approach and would require, at the very least, substantial sociological study to explain.

In this unit, we used the metadata information encoded in the BNC to explore the distribution pattern of FUCK both within and across spoken and written registers.

Summary

Exploration

While the investigation presented in this unit is only possible with appropriate corpus resources, we feel that the corpus-based approach is not all-powerful (cf. Unit A10.15). Corpora are useful in formulating and testing linguistic hypotheses, but they cannot provide explanations to questions such as 'why do people from higher social classes use *FUCK* frequently?'. Nevertheless, the corpus methodology, in combination with other methodologies, is undoubtedly of use in providing descriptions that any purported explanations must account for. This unit gave you a step-by-step demonstration of how to use BNCWeb to explore language variation in the BNC.

 FURTHER STUDY

The BNC is extensively encoded with metadata. In addition to those factors encoded in the metadata explored in this unit, the distribution of *FUCK* may be influenced by many other factors encoded in the BNC. Among those you might care to examine are *domain* of context-governed speech in the spoken register, as well as *date of creation* and *level of audience* in the written register.

Unit C5
Conversation and speech in American English

CASE STUDY 5

C5.1 INTRODUCTION

This case study uses Biber's (1988) multifeature/multidimensional approach to genre analysis (see Units A10.4 and B4.2) to compare the genres of conversation and speech in American English. The terms *conversation* and *speech* as used in this case study correspond to the demographically sampled and context-governed spoken data in the British National Corpus (BNC, see Aston and Burnard 1998: 31). Conversation represents the type of communication we experience every day (Biber 1988: 10) whereas speech is produced in situations where there are few producers and many receivers (e.g. classroom lectures, sermons and political speeches). The result of this analysis will also be compared with the keyword analysis as discussed in Units A10.11–A10.12.

We noted in Case Study 4 that, in modern British English, informal conversation and formal speech differ considerably in terms of the frequency and distribution of swear words. While it is possible to simply describe conversation as informal and speech as formal, it would be more accurate to consider the formal/informal or oral/literate distinction as a continuous dimension of variation distinguishing the two (see Biber 1988: 9). This however, requires the undertaking of a Biber-style analysis in order to explore how these two varieties of spoken language vary in these dimensions. It is this analysis that we will undertake in this unit. While our previous study of spoken English focused on modern British English, in this unit we will switch our focus slightly and look instead at spoken American English, using the multifeature/multidimensional (MF/MD) analytic framework established in Biber (1985, 1988) (see Units A10.4 and B4.2).

In this case study, we will also show you some advanced features of WordSmith (version 3), including concordance using file-based search patterns, wordlist and keyword. As Biber's original framework involves sophisticated statistical analyses and is very time-consuming, the wordlist and keyword functions of WordSmith (referring to version 3 in this study) will be used to achieve an approximate effect of Biber's multidimensional analysis (see Tribble 1999). For a fuller comparison of the two approaches to genre analysis, see Xiao and McEnery (2005).

The major corpus resources used in this unit consist of the Santa Barbara Corpus of Spoken American English (SBCSAE) and two files (comm797.txt and comr797. txt) from the Corpus of Professional Spoken American English (CPSA) (see Units A7.3 and A7.5 for a description of the two corpora). In order to contrast spoken data and written data, the section of academic prose (category J) from the Frown corpus (Frownj) is also included in this case study. Table C5.1 shows the data used in this unit.

This unit consists of five sections. Unit C5.2 explains the functions of fifty-eight linguistic features and designs a set of search algorithms for extracting their frequencies; Unit C5.3 calculates the basic statistics for each linguistic feature, including minimum/maximum frequency, range, mean and standard deviation (see Unit A6.3); Unit C5.4 compares the three genres alongside seven dimensions while unit C5.5 presents a keyword analysis using WordSmith.

Table C5.1 Corpus data

Genre	Corpus	Sampling date	No. of texts	No. of tokens	No. of tokens by genre
Conversation	SBCSAE	1988–1993	31	135834	135834
Speech	SBCSAE	1988–1993	12	46312	203810
	CPSA	1997	2	157498	
Academic prose	Frownj	1991–1992	80	166169	166169
Total			125	505813	

C5.2 SALIENT LINGUISTIC FEATURES

The sixty-seven linguistic features Biber (1988) used are all functionally related and have been studied extensively. Biber (1998: 223–245) provides a good review of the functions of each of these linguistic features. The salient linguistic features associated with each of the seven factors (Biber 1988: 102–103) are given in Table C5.2. Note that in the table (Factor +3), WH relative clauses on object and subject positions are kept together to make presentation easier. For the same reason, THAT relative clauses (Factor +6) refer to those in either object or subject positions. Combinations of similar features like these reduce the number of linguistic features under consideration to fifty-eight.

As can be seen from the table, some factorial structures include factors with negative loadings. Biber observes that features with positive loadings on a dimension co-occur frequently whereas features with negative loadings occur together. The dimension score of a text is computed by adding together the factor score of each feature with a positive loading, and then subtracting the factor score of each feature, if any, with a negative loading. The dimension score of a genre is the mean of the factor scores of the texts within the genre. We will show you how to compute

Table C5.2 Factorial structures of seven dimensions

Factor	Linguistic features
+1	(1) private verbs, (2) THAT deletion, (3) contraction, (4) present tense verbs, (5) 2nd person pronouns, (6) DO as pro-verb, (7) analytic negation, (8) demonstrative pronouns, (9) general emphatics, (10) 1st person pronouns, (11) pronoun IT, (12) BE as main verb, (13) causative subordination, (14) discourse markers, (15) indefinite pronouns, (16) general hedges, (17) amplifiers, (18) sentence relatives, (19) WH questions, (20) possibility modals, (21) non-phrasal coordination, (22) WH clauses, (23) final prepositions
−1	(24) other nouns, (25) word length, (26) prepositions, (27) type/token ratio, (28) attributive adjectives
+2	(29) past tense verbs, (30) 3rd person pronouns, (31) perfect aspect verbs, (32) public verbs, (33) synthetic negation, (34) present participial clauses
+3	(35) WH relative clauses, (36) pied-piping constructions, (37) phrasal coordination, (38) nominalizations
−3	(39) time adverbials, (40) place adverbials, (41) other adverbs
+4	(42) infinitives, (43) prediction modals, (44) suasive verbs, (45) conditional subordination, (46) necessity modals, (47) split auxiliaries
+5	(48) conjuncts, (49) agentless passives, (50) past participial clauses, (51) BY-passives, (52) past participial WHIZ deletions, (53) other adverbial subordinators
+6	(54) THAT clauses as verb complements, (55) demonstratives, (56) THAT relative clauses, (57) THAT clauses as adjective complements
+7	(58) SEEM/APPEAR

the factor score in Unit C5.4. But first we need to explain the functions of salient linguistic features and find a way to extract their frequency counts in the corpus.

The features with positive loadings on Factor 1, which are 'characterized as verbal, interactive, affective, fragmented, reduced in form, and generalized in content', 'can be associated in one way or another with an involved, non-informational focus' (Biber 1988: 105). Conversely, high frequencies of features with negative weights are associated with a high informational focus and a careful integration of infor-mation in a text. The features with salient positive weights on Factor 2 can all be used for narrative purposes (Biber 1988: 92), though narrative discourse depends heavily on the past tense and perfect aspect verbs (Biber 1988: 109). Alongside Factor 3, features with positive loadings include WH relative clauses, phrasal coordination and nominalization. Relativization specifies 'the identity of referents within a text in an explicit and elaborated manner, so that the addressee will have no doubt as to the intended referent' while 'the co-occurrence of phrasal coordi-nation and nominalizations with these relativization features indicates that referentially explicit discourse also tends to be integrated and informational' (Biber 1988: 110). The two features with negative weights, time and place adverbials, on the other hand, depend crucially on the addressee for text-internal references. The features associated with Factor 4 function together to mark persuasion, whether overt marking of the addresser's own viewpoint, or an assessment of the advisability or likelihood of an event presented to persuade the addressee (see Biber 1988: 111).

The features associated with Factor 5 are conjuncts, main/subordinate passive constructions and adverbial subordinators. Discourse with a high frequency of passives is typically abstract and technical in content, as well as formal in style. This type of discourse is generally characterized by complex logical relations, which are achieved by conjuncts and adverbial subordinators (see Biber 1988: 112). Features with salient positive weights on Factor 6 function to mark informational elaboration in discourse that is informational but produced under real-time conditions (Biber 1988: 113–114). Factor 7 only has one salient positive feature, *SEEM*/*APPEAR*. *SEEM* and *APPEAR* mark perception rather than assertion of fact and thus mark an assertion as uncertain. They are typically used in academic discourse as a downtoner to qualify the extent to which an assertion is known (Biber 1988: 114).

Biber (1988: 211–245) proposed a set of algorithms for the automatic identification of the sixty-seven linguistic features he used. As the data he used were annotated differently from ours, Biber's algorithms do not apply to our data. We have designed search patterns suitable for corpora POS tagged by CLAWS using the BNC C7 tagset (see Unit A4.4.1). As the normal concordance function of WordSmith allows only fifteen search phrases as long as they are limited to eighty characters, including the symbol / ('or'), some of our search phrases are file-based, i.e., saved as a text file. This approach allows up to 500 search patterns. You will need to download the file-based search patterns from our companion website. We assume that you have placed these files in the same file folder as WordSmith. In the remainder of this section, we will show you, through corpus examples, what we are looking for with regard to each of the linguistic features listed in Table C5.2. You will find all of the search patterns on our companion website.

C5.2.1 Dimension 1 Informational versus involved production

This entails twenty-three features with positive loadings and five with negative loadings.

C5.2.1.1 Features with positive loadings

These include the following:

(1) private verbs: all morphological forms of the following verbs: *anticipate, assume, believe, conclude, decide, demonstrate, determine, discover, doubt, estimate, fear, feel, find, forget, guess, hear, hope, imagine, imply, indicate, infer, know, learn, mean, notice, prove, realize, recognize, remember, reveal, see, show, suppose, think, understand*;

(2) THAT deletion: e.g., *I think [that] it's so funny*;

(3) contraction: *n't, 'll, 'd, 'm, 're, 've, 's* (excluding possessive form);

(4) present tense verbs: all base forms and third person singular present verb forms;

(5) second person pronouns: *you, your, yourself, yourselves, yours*;
(6) DO as a pro-verb: e.g., *You did that?*;
(7) analytic negation: *not, n't*;
(8) demonstrative pronouns: *this, that, these* and *those* (not followed by a noun);
(9) general emphatics: *for sure, a lot, such a, real, so, just, really, most, more* and DO + *verb*;
(10) first person pronouns: *I, my, our, myself, ourselves, mine* and *ours*;
(11) pronoun IT: *it*;
(12) BE as a main verb (excluding BE as an auxiliary): e.g., *You are right*;
(13) causative subordination: *because*;
(14) discourse markers: *well, anyway, anyways, anyhow*;
(15) indefinite pronouns: e.g., *none, one, anyone, someone, somebody, anybody, nobody, everything, nothing*;
(16) general hedges: *about* (not as a preposition), *something like, more or less, almost, maybe, sort of* and *kind of* (excluding *sort* and *kind* as true nouns);
(17) amplifiers: *absolutely, altogether, completely, enormously, entirely, extremely, fully, greatly, highly, intensely, perfectly, strongly, thoroughly, totally, utterly* and *very*;
(18) sentence relatives: e.g., *The present book, which is the first* . . . ;
(19) WH questions: e.g., *What is it?*;
(20) possibility modals: *can, could, may* and *might* (including contracted forms);
(21) non-phrasal coordination: e.g., *Yeah, and it has*;
(22) WH clauses: e.g., *You know what I mean*;
(23) final prepositions: e.g., *Where did you get it from?*

C5.2.1.2 *Features with negative loadings*

These include the following:

(24) other nouns: all noun forms excluding nominalizations (see 38 below);
(25) word length: (WordSmith wordlist function: average word length);
(26) prepositions: all prepositions like *at, by, in* and *of*;
(27) type/token ratio: (WordSmith wordlist function: standardized type/token ratio);
(28) attributive adjectives: e.g., *young girl* and *new regulatory requirements*.

C5.2.2 Dimension 2 Narrative versus non-narrative concerns

This entails six linguistic features, all with positive loadings.

(29) past tense verbs: all past tense verbs;
(30) third person pronouns: *she, he, they, her, him, them, his, its, hers, their, theirs, himself, herself* and *themselves* (including contractions);
(31) perfect aspect verbs: e.g., *That hasn't finished*;

(32) public verbs: all morphological forms of the following verbs: *acknowledge, admit, agree, assert, claim, complain, declare, deny, explain, hint, insist, mention, proclaim, promise, protest, remark, reply, report, say, suggest, swear* and *write*;

(33) synthetic negation: *neither, nor* and *no* (excluding *no* as a response);

(34) present participial clauses: e.g., *So, you got this Oscar there, swimming there in the tank.*

C5.2.3 Dimension 3 Explicit versus situation-dependent reference

This entails four features with positive loadings and three with negative loadings.

C5.2.3.1 *Features with positive loadings*

These include the following:

(35) WH relative clauses: e.g., *You know the little folks who live above me*;

(36) pied-piping constructions: e.g., *the problems with which he is concerned*;

(37) phrasal coordination: e.g., *economic and social conditions, racism and sexism, pick and choose*;

(38) nominalizations: all nouns ending in *-tion, -ment, -ness, -ity* (including plural forms).

C5.2.3.2 *Features with negative loadings*

(39) time adverbials: all adverbs of time;

(40) place adverbials: all adverbs of place;

(41) other adverbs: all adverbs minus all totals of hedges, amplifiers, downtoners, place adverbials and time adverbials.

C5.2.4 Dimension 4 Overt expression of persuasion

This entails six linguistic features, all with positive loadings.

(42) infinitives: *to* + base form of a verb (may be separated by one or two adverbs);

(43) prediction modals: *will, shall* and *would* (including contractions);

(44) suasive verbs, including all morphological forms of the following verbs: *agree, arrange, ask, beg, command, decide, demand, grant, insist, instruct, ordain, pledge, pronounce, propose, recommend, request, stipulate, suggest* and *urge*;

(45) conditional subordination: *if* and *unless*;

(46) necessity modals: *ought, should* and *must*;

(47) split auxiliaries: e.g., *You're just saying that.*

C5.2.5 Dimension 5 Abstract versus non-abstract information

This entails six linguistic features, all with positive loadings.

(48) conjuncts: *alternatively, altogether, consequently, conversely, eg, e.g., else, furthermore, hence, however, i.e., instead, likewise, moreover, namely, nevertheless, nonetheless, notwithstanding, otherwise, rather, similarly, that is, therefore, thus, viz, in (comparison, contrast, particular, addition, conclusion, consequence, sum, summary, any event, any case, other words), for example (instance), by contrast (comparison), as a result (consequence), on the contrary (other hand)*;

(49) agentless passives: e.g., *And this book was written in nineteen ten*;

(50) past participial clauses: e.g., *This problem, combined with administrative failure to meet . . .* ;

(51) BY-passives: e.g., *It is shared by preacher and audience*;

(52) past participial WHIZ deletions: e.g. *tests designed for old age groups*;

(53) other adverbial subordinators: *since, while, whilst, whereupon, whereas, whereby, such that, so that, inasmuch as, forasmuch as, insofar as, insomuch as, as long as* and *as soon as*.

C5.2.6 Dimension 6 Online informational elaboration

This entails four linguistic features, all with positive loadings.

(54) THAT clauses as verb complements: e.g., *So he knew that the oil was leaking?*

(55) demonstratives: *this, that, these* and *those* followed by a noun;

(56) THAT relative clauses: e.g., *In fact, I eat stuff that he doesn't eat*;

(57) THAT clauses as adjective complements: e.g., *I'm just happy that I beat you.*

C.5.2.7 Dimension 7 Academic hedging

(58) *SEEM/APPEAR*: all morphological forms of *SEEM* and *APPEAR*.

While some of the patterns we have devised may only extract typical instances and some of them may even generate false matches due to tagging errors, the same patterns are applied to all corpus files. Hence we consider the results for the different genres to be comparable and sufficiently reliable, in spite of the small margin of error associated with our pattern matching procedure, as it is assumed that the errors are distributed evenly across the files.

C5.3 BASIC STATISTICAL DATA FROM THE CORPUS

This section demonstrates how to extract the frequencies of salient linguistic features and compute the mean, range and standard deviation of each of the features in the whole corpus (see Unit A6.3 for a discussion of these statistics). We will use the mean and standard deviation to compute the factor scores of linguistic features.

To begin the computation of the factor scores, we need to extract the frequencies of each feature from the corpus using WordSmith and the search patterns established in Unit C5.2. Note that in this section, all frequencies are normalized to a common 1,000-word basis to ensure comparability between files of different sizes.

We have formatted our corpus data to place metadata in angled brackets so that it can be ignored in concordancing by activating *Tags to ignore <*>* in WordSmith Settings. Ensure that you have made this change to settings before proceeding. Then load WordSmith with all of the 125 corpus files by selection *File – Choose texts* in the main menu.

To find out the minimum/maximum frequencies, mean, range and standard deviation for private verbs in the corpus, do the following:

1. Start the concordance function of WordSmith, type in the path of the file containing search patterns of private verbs, and press *Go Now*, as shown in Figure C5.1.
2. You will be led to the concordance window as shown in Figure C5.2. Press on the toolbar to show the distribution of private verbs across files (Figure C5.3).

The left panel of the dispersion window shows the number of files containing private verbs, filenames, file sizes in tokens, raw frequencies and normalized frequencies (per 1,000 words) while the right panel shows the location of the matches in each file. Note that if a linguistic feature is absent in some files, the number of files shown here may be fewer than the number of files you loaded. Of these we are only interested in the normalized frequencies. The files are arranged in descending order on the basis of normalized frequencies. You can click your mouse on the ⚙ icon in the toolbar or press F6 on your keyboard to re-sort the files into the order you wish. As we will see later, it is a good idea to re-sort filenames in alphabetical order.

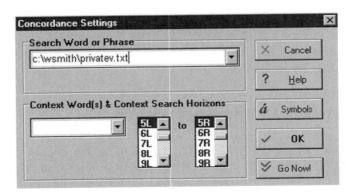

Figure C5.1 The file-based search pattern

Figure C5.2 A concordance of private verbs

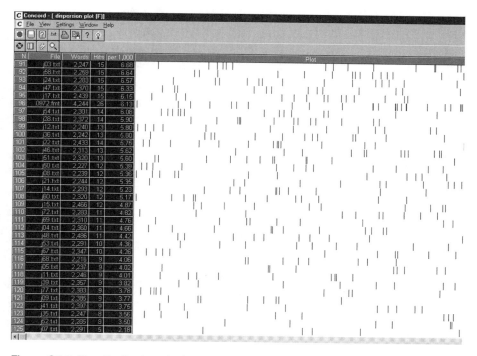

Figure C5.3 The distribution of private verbs

While you can type the normalized frequencies into the data editor of SPSS one by one manually, you can also use the copy and paste function provided by Windows. To select the data needed, click your mouse on the filename of the first file, hold down the *SHIFT* key on your keyboard, and move the right arrow key until *File*, *Words*, *Hits* and *per 1,000* are highlighted. Then while still holding down the *SHIFT* key, move the down arrow key until the whole left panel is highlighted. Press *Ctrl+C* to make a copy.

3. Start the SPSS statistics package (see Case Study 2) and define five variables as shown in Figure C5.4.
4. Select the *Data View* label in the bottom left corner of the window, select the first field under the variable *file_no* by clicking your mouse on it, and press *Ctrl+V* to paste the data into the SPSS data editor, as shown in Figure C5.5.

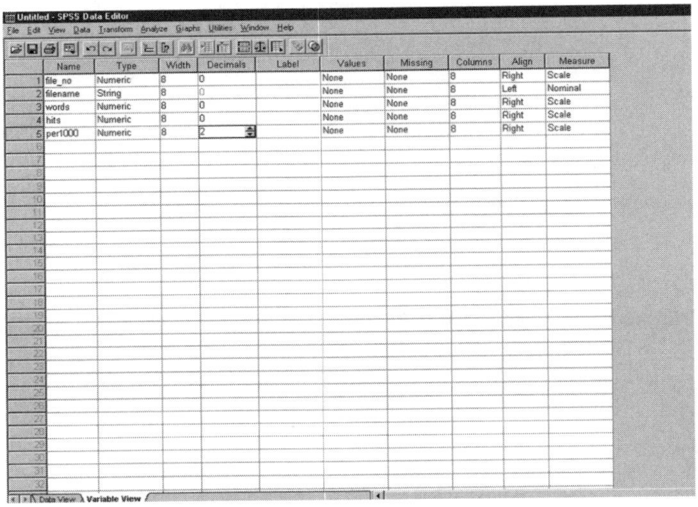

	Name	Type	Width	Decimals	Label	Values	Missing	Columns	Align	Measure
1	file_no	Numeric	8	0		None	None	8	Right	Scale
2	filename	String	8	0		None	None	8	Left	Nominal
3	words	Numeric	8	0		None	None	8	Right	Scale
4	hits	Numeric	8	0		None	None	8	Right	Scale
5	per1000	Numeric	8	2		None	None	8	Right	Scale

Figure C5.4 Defining variables with SPSS

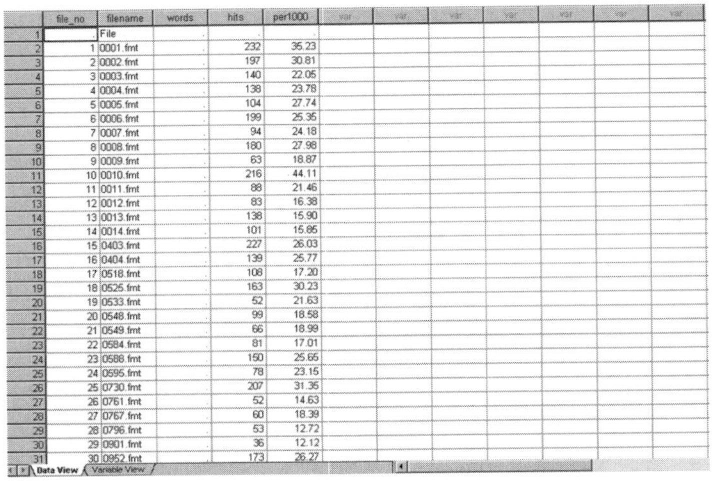

	file_no	filename	words	hits	per1000
1	.	File	.	.	.
2	1	0001.fmt	.	232	35.23
3	2	0002.fmt	.	197	30.81
4	3	0003.fmt	.	140	22.05
5	4	0004.fmt	.	138	23.78
6	5	0005.fmt	.	104	27.74
7	6	0006.fmt	.	199	25.35
8	7	0007.fmt	.	94	24.18
9	8	0008.fmt	.	180	27.98
10	9	0009.fmt	.	63	18.87
11	10	0010.fmt	.	216	44.11
12	11	0011.fmt	.	88	21.46
13	12	0012.fmt	.	83	16.38
14	13	0013.fmt	.	138	15.90
15	14	0014.fmt	.	101	15.86
16	15	0403.fmt	.	227	26.03
17	16	0404.fmt	.	139	25.77
18	17	0518.fmt	.	108	17.20
19	18	0525.fmt	.	163	30.23
20	19	0533.fmt	.	52	21.63
21	20	0548.fmt	.	99	18.58
22	21	0549.fmt	.	66	18.99
23	22	0584.fmt	.	81	17.01
24	23	0588.fmt	.	150	25.65
25	24	0595.fmt	.	78	23.15
26	25	0730.fmt	.	207	31.36
27	26	0761.fmt	.	52	14.63
28	27	0767.fmt	.	60	18.39
29	28	0796.fmt	.	53	12.72
30	29	0801.fmt	.	36	12.12
31	30	0952.fmt	.	173	26.27

Figure C5.5 Pasting data into SPSS

Note that the numbers of words, as well as the counts of hits that contain a comma, are not shown in the data editor because we have defined these variables as numerical, which cannot include commas. But this is not a problem. All we need are the frequencies *per 1,000* tokens.

5.   Select Analyse → Descriptive Statistics → Descriptives as shown in Figure C5.6.
6.   Select the variable *per1000* as shown in Figure C5.7.
7.   Press *Options* and select *Range* (*Mean, Std deviation, minimum* and *maximum* are selected by default). Press *Continue* to return to the previous window (Figure C5.8). Press *OK*.
8.   You will be taken to the output window as shown in Figure C5.9. Here you can find the basic descriptive statistics of private verbs in the corpus.

The above steps provide a standard procedure for computing the basic statistics of linguistic features. However, some features may require more complicated operations. For example, to extract the instances of THAT deletion, you will need

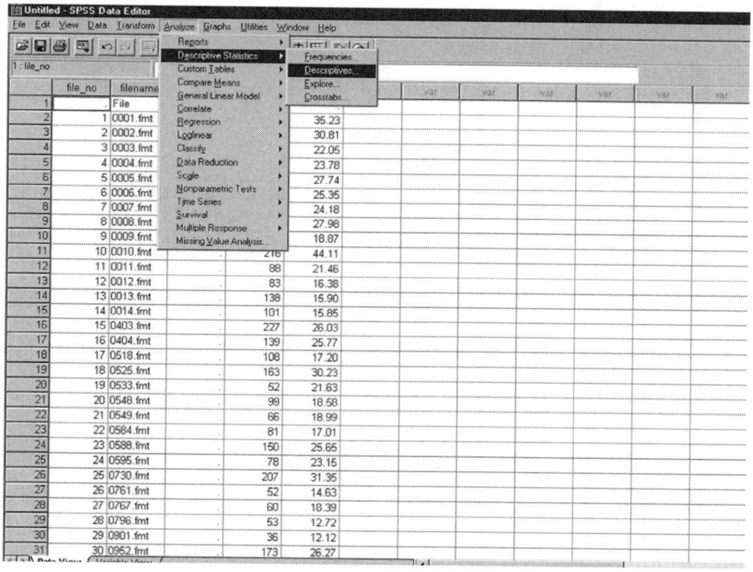

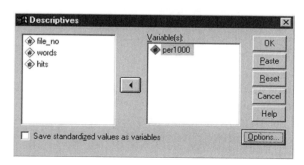

Figure C5.6 Computing basic statistics using SPSS

Figure C5.7 Selecting variable(s)

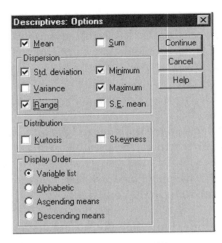

Figure C5.8 Selecting the parameters

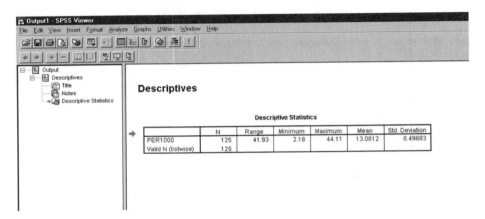

Figure C5.9 Basic statistics relating to private verbs

to search the corpus eight times and save each concordance as a separate file, and merge two files at one time (by selecting *File → Merge* from the menu of *Concord*) until all of the eight files are combined into one concordance list.

As some of the linguistic features are very frequent (e.g. *first person pronouns, present tense verbs, attributive adjectives, other nouns, other adverbs, prepositions*), WordSmith ignores all matches beyond a ceiling of 16,368. If the program shows 16,368 matches, the actual number of matches may be greater. If you have not yet done so, select the *Concord* label in WordSmith Settings and define *Entities wanted* to be 16,368. In order to extract all examples in such cases, you will need to load part of the corpus files and copy the data from the dispersion window to the SPSS data editor several times. For example, the single file *comr797.txt* (speech) needs to be split into two halves to extract the frequencies of *other nouns*. Note, however, that it is essential that you *clear previous files* whenever you choose fresh texts, otherwise the new texts will simply be added to the old.

To extract the frequency of *other adverbs*, it is necessary to discover the count of *_R*, and then subtract the counts of hedges, amplifiers, downtoners, place adverbials and time adverbials. Note that as the search pattern for hedges includes *something like*, which is not tagged as adverbial (R*), the count of this expression should not be included. You can use *c:\wsmith\hedge1.txt* as the search pattern for hedges in this case. When you copy and paste data from the concordance dispersion window to the SPSS data editor, it is necessary to re-sort filenames alphabetically and make adjustments in the SPSS data editor so that the frequencies from each file appear on the same row before doing the subtractions.

The word length and type/token ratio can be obtained by using the wordlist function of WordSmith. As the program by default treats the underscore linked part-of-speech tag (e.g. *and_CC*) as the suffix (i.e. *ANDCC*) as well as a separate token (i.e. *CC*), we need to adjust the settings to allow the program to treat the tagged corpus files appropriately. *Make sure, however, that you restore the tag setting after you make a wordlist for the corpus; otherwise, the search algorithms will not work.*

9. Select the *Tags* label in WordSmith Settings and define the tag to ignore as _*, as shown in Figure C5.10.
10. Click on *Only Part of File*, activate *Sections to Cut* and define the start mark as the opening bracket < and the end mark as the closing bracket > (Figure C5.11). This definition achieves the same effect as ignoring tag <*>. Press *OK* twice.
11. Load all of the 125 files (again, remember to clear previous files before this operation).
12. Select *Tools → Wordlist*. Press the start button ⦿ on the toolbar, and you will see the *Getting started* window. Make sure that the number of files chosen is 125. Press *Make a wordlist now* (Figure C5.12).

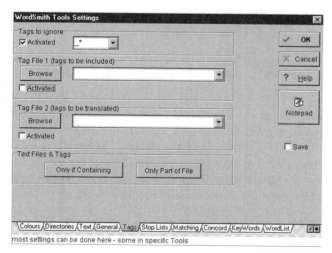

Figure C5.10 Adjusting tag setting

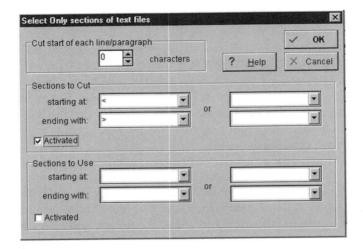

Figure C5.11
Defining sections to
cut

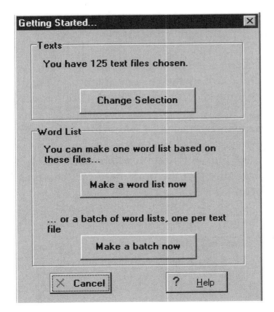

Figure C5.12 Making a wordlist

13. You will see three wordlists are made. Wordlist (A) is an alphabetically ordered list, wordlist (F) is a frequency ordered list and wordlist (S) shows the basic statistics such as type/token ratio and average word length (Figure C5.13).
14. Select wordlist (S), and type the *Ave word length* for 125 files into the SPSS data editor to compute the minimum/maximum frequency, mean, range and standard deviation. Do the same for *Standardised Type/Token Ratio*.

Following the above procedures, the statistics you obtain should match those given in Table C5.3. As can be seen from the table, some features distribute rather evenly

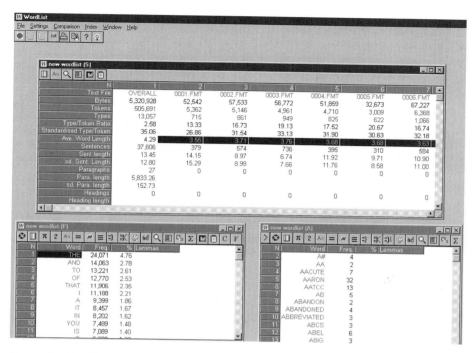

Figure C5.13 Wordlists of the corpus

across the corpus (e.g. sentence relatives, WH clauses, present and past participial clauses) while others show appreciable differences in dispersion (e.g. present tense verbs, prepositions, first person pronouns and other nouns). Using these statistics, we will be able to compute the factor score for each file and compare the three genres alongside seven dimensions.

Table C5.3 Basic statistics of linguistic features (per 1,000 tokens)

Dimension	Features	Min.	Max.	Range	Mean	Std dev.
+1	(1) private verbs	2.19	44.11	41.92	13.08	8.50
	(2) THAT deletion	0	64.05	64.05	2.72	6.14
	(3) contraction	0	47.92	47.92	11.04	15.72
	(4) present tense verbs	3.15	91.08	87.93	41.86	20.53
	(5) 2nd person pronouns	0	48.98	48.98	8.69	12.54
	(6) DO as pro-verb	0	7.79	7.79	1.28	1.40
	(7) analytic negation	0	18.08	18.08	7.10	4.83
	(8) demonstrative pronouns	0	30.22	30.22	6.50	6.06
	(9) general emphatics	0	20.49	20.49	5.20	3.89
	(10) 1st person pronouns	0	76.11	76.11	18.42	20.26
	(11) pronoun IT	0	33.93	33.93	9.60	8.14
	(12) BE as main verb	5.07	34.26	29.19	18.04	6.91
	(13) causative subordination	0	5.95	5.95	1.35	1.41
	(14) discourse markers	0	12.19	12.19	2.10	2.78
	(15) indefinite pronouns	0	10.75	10.75	2.85	2.61

continued

Table C5.3 continued

Dimension	Features	Min.	Max.	Range	Mean	Std dev.
	(16) general hedges	0	10.55	10.55	1.24	1.46
	(17) amplifiers	0	8.85	8.85	1.58	1.54
	(18) sentence relatives	0	3.22	3.22	0.71	0.80
	(19) WH questions	0	6.31	6.31	0.78	1.11
	(20) possibility modals	0.41	15.88	15.47	5.11	2.62
	(21) non-phrasal coordination	0	9.33	9.33	1.44	2.08
	(22) WH clauses	0	3.45	3.45	0.45	0.60
	(23) final prepositions	0	4.64	4.64	0.83	1.09
−1	(24) other nouns	78.27	365.15	277.88	209.61	71.20
	(25) word length	3.41	5.76	2.35	4.58	0.69
	(26) prepositions	28.14	153.17	125.03	95.02	31.70
	(27) type/token ratio	21.50	51.65	30.15	36.87	6.36
	(28) attributive adjectives	7.96	104.89	96.93	49.05	26.26
+2	(29) past tense verbs	0.81	77.75	76.94	21.53	16.82
	(30) 3rd person pronouns	0	55.29	55.29	16.51	14.42
	(31) perfect aspect verbs	0	11.49	11.49	4.15	2.65
	(32) public verbs	0	19.19	19.19	3.39	2.81
	(33) synthetic negation	0	6.04	6.04	1.60	0.90
	(34) present participial clauses	0	1.37	1.37	0.33	0.35
+3	(35) WH relative clauses	0.15	11.73	11.58	3.02	2.11
	(36) pied-piping constructions	0	5.45	5.45	0.93	1.11
	(37) phrasal coordination	0	10.05	18.05	5.74	4.18
	(38) nominalizations	0.28	66.58	66.30	23.77	16.80
−3	(39) time adverbials	0	13.38	13.38	3.56	3.00
	(40) place adverbials	0	15.31	15.31	3.11	2.92
	(41) other adverbs	14.38	90.24	75.86	44.71	16.10
+4	(42) infinitives	1.68	24.33	22.65	11.04	4.82
	(43) prediction modals	0	15.53	15.53	4.66	3.32
	(44) suasive verbs	0	7.59	7.59	1.10	1.07
	(45) conditional subordination	0	9.22	9.22	2.18	1.88
	(46) necessity modals	0	7.30	7.30	1.35	1.30
	(47) split auxiliaries	0.39	7.59	7.20	2.97	1.41
+5	(48) conjuncts	0	15.04	15.04	3.01	3.18
	(49) agentless passives	0.29	23.62	23.33	7.61	5.18
	(50) past participial clauses	0	3.46	3.46	0.46	0.64
	(51) BY-passives	0	4.46	4.46	1.24	1.24
	(52) past participial WHIZ deletions	0	8.41	8.41	2.01	2.02
	(53) other adverbial subordinators	0	6.43	6.43	1.39	1.28
+6	(54) THAT clauses as verb complements	0.25	11.32	11.07	2.66	1.93
	(55) demonstratives	1.28	22.38	21.10	7.46	3.01
	(56) THAT relative clauses	0	7.80	7.80	2.14	1.63
	(57) THAT clauses as adjective complements	0	1.71	1.71	0.34	0.42
+7	(58) SEEM/APPEAR	0	6.44	6.44	0.72	1.00

C5.4 THE DIMENSION SCORES OF THREE GENRES

In Unit C5.3, we explored the whole corpus of 125 files. In this section, we will search the files by genre applying the same search algorithms and procedures. This operation will provide you with the frequency of each linguistic feature in each file in the three genres. This data, together with the mean score and standard deviation in Table C5.3, will be used to compute the factor score of each feature in each text, and the mean factor score for each genre.

The factor score (κ) of a feature in a text can be formulated as

$$\kappa = \frac{F - \mu}{\sigma}$$

In the formula, F is the normalized frequency of the feature in the text, σ stands for standard deviation and μ is the mean frequency of the feature in the whole genre. The mean score and standard deviation of each linguistic feature are listed in Table C5.3.

The factor score of a feature in a genre ϖ equals the mean score of the feature in the genre, that is, the sum of factor scores of the feature in each text of the genre divided by the number of text N even if some files do not contain such a feature (N equals 31 for the genre of conversation, 14 for speech and 80 for academic prose):

$$\varpi = \frac{\sum \kappa}{N}$$

The dimension score of a genre can be obtained by adding together the mean factor scores of all features with positive weights on a factor and then subtracting the mean factor scores of all features with negative weights on the same factor:

$$\omega = \sum \varpi$$

For example, the factor score of Dimension 1 equals the sum of mean factor scores of all features that appear under the label +1 less the total of mean factor scores of the features that appear under the label −1. Note that the positive or negative sign preceding a value should be retained so that − (−1) means +1. For example, suppose for the genre of academic prose the mean factor scores of the four features with positive weights on Factor 3 are −0.57, +0.53, +0.51 and +0.60 while those for features with negative weights are −0.44, −0.43 and −0.51, the dimension score of Factor 3 for academic prose should be +2.45 rather than −0.31.

The three formulae presented above may involve thousands of arithmetic operations. We wrote a simple program to do the boring calculations using the output of WordSmith. If you do not wish to do the calculations by yourself, you can download the program from our companion website (see the *readme* file accompanying the program for details of how to use it). The dimension scores for Factors 1–7 computed for the genres of conversation, speech and academic prose are given in Tables C5.4–C5.10.

As can be seen in Table C5.4, with the exception of *THAT deletion, amplifiers* and *sentence relatives*, the features with positive loadings on Factor 1 have greater scores in conversation than in speech. Similarly, the absolute values of the scores of features with negative weights on Factor 1 are greater in conversation than in speech. The contrast between academic prose and conversation is even more marked. Dimension 1 is a fundamental parameter to mark the relative 'oralness' or 'literateness' of a genre (Biber 1988: 108). Therefore, conversation, which has an involved, interactive focus and is subject to real-time production constraints, is the most 'oral' of the three genres in this study. In contrast, academic prose is the most 'literate' of the three in that it is characterized by careful editing possibilities and informational density.

Table C5.5 shows that alongside Dimension 2, speech is more narrative than academic prose and conversation. This is unsurprising when one considers that academic prose has its focus on exposition rather than narration whereas conversation, while it may involve narration, has an interactive and affective focus.

Alongside Dimension 3, conversation and speech are quite similar in that both genres make explicit context-independent references, though to varying degrees (Table C5.6). In contrast, academic prose tends to make context dependent references. This feature is explicable in terms of the greater number of opportunities that writing affords to undertake careful editing. Such opportunities are atypical of spontaneous speech.

As can be seen in Table C5.7, all of the three genres under consideration are related to persuasion. Speech is the most persuasive while academic prose is the least persuasive. Conversation may involve persuasion, but to a lesser extent than speech.

In terms of Dimension 5, academic prose is much more technical and abstract than speech and conversation. Surprisingly, our data shows that conversation is more abstract than speech, which runs contrary to one's intuition (Table C5.8).

Table C5.9 shows that speech has the greatest score for Dimension 6, which marks the degree of online informational elaboration under strict real-time conditions. As conversation does not have an informational focus, it does not need stylistic elaboration. While academic prose is an informationally dense genre that needs elaboration, it is not subject to strict real-time conditions. Rather it is produced under circumstances that allow precise lexical choice and careful structural elaboration. Only the genre of speech, which is informationally dense but produced under real-time conditions, needs more online informational elaboration.

Table C5.4 Dimension 1 (Informational versus involved production)

Dimension	Linguistic feature	Private conversation	Public speech	Academic prose
+1	private verbs	+1.36	+0.37	−0.59
	THAT deletion	+0.19	+0.27	+0.03
	contractions	+1.54	+0.68	−0.14
	present tense verbs	+1.20	+0.67	−0.58
	2nd person pronouns	+1.44	+0.60	−0.10
	DO as pro-verb	+1.06	+0.59	−0.15
	analytic negation	+1.32	+0.61	−0.60
	demonstr. pronoun	+1.28	+0.80	−0.58
	emphatics	+1.26	+0.19	−0.49
	1st person pronoun	+1.30	+0.90	−0.51
	pronoun IT	+1.40	+0.47	−0.60
	BE as main verb	+0.94	+0.69	−0.49
	caus. subordination	+0.73	+0.78	−0.05
	discourse markers	+1.36	+0.45	−0.61
	indefinite pronouns	+1.25	+0.43	−0.38
	hedges	+1.08	+0.41	−0.14
	amplifiers	−0.20	+0.84	+0.11
	sentence relative	−0.22	+0.04	+0.49
	WH questions	+0.92	+0.88	−0.004
	possibility modals	+0.35	+0.03	−0.14
	non-phrasal coordination	+1.03	+0.49	−0.19
	WH clauses	+1.09	−0.83	−0.33
	final prepositions	+1.09	+0.76	−0.05
−1	other nouns	−1.12	−0.72	+0.66
	word length	−1.35	−0.71	+0.66
	prepositions	−1.43	−0.64	+0.67
	type/token ratio	−1.05	−0.60	+0.53
	attributive adjectives	−1.24	−0.84	+0.63
Dimension 1 factor score: +1− (−1)		+28.96	+14.63	−9.24

Table C5.5 Dimension 2 (Narrative versus non-narrative concerns)

Linguistic feature	Private conversation	Public speech	Academic prose
past tense verbs	+0.58	+0.49	−0.31
3rd person pronouns	+0.86	+0.75	−0.44
perfect aspect verbs	−0.04	+0.12	+0.05
public verbs	+0.39	+1.13	−0.26
synthetic negation	−0.80	−0.90	−0.09
present participle clause	+0.21	+0.41	+0.44
mean factor score	+1.20	+2.00	−0.61

Though Dimension 7, academic hedging, is only tentatively proposed as a dimension in Biber (1988), it is supported by our data. As can be seen in Table C5.10, academic prose demonstrates the greatest score for Dimension 7. Speech and conversation do not show significant difference in this respect.

Table C5.6 Dimension 3 (Explicit versus situation-dependent reference)

Dimension	Linguistic feature	Private conversation	Public speech	Academic prose
+3	WH relative clause	−0.99	−0.84	−0.57
	pied-piping constructs	−0.13	−0.33	+0.53
	phrasal coordination	−0.98	−0.64	+0.51
	nominalization	−1.25	−0.66	+0.60
−3	time adverbials	+1.06	+0.90	−0.44
	place adverbials	+1.12	+0.84	−0.43
	adverbs	+1.10	+0.50	−0.51
Dimension 3 mean factor score: +3−(−3)		−6.63	−4.71	+2.45

Table C5.7 Dimension 4 (Overt expressions of persuasion)

Linguistic feature	Private conversation	Public speech	Academic prose
infinitives	−0.14	+0.39	+0.10
predication modals	+0.82	+0.74	−0.38
suasive verbs	−0.21	+0.22	+0.30
conditional sub.	+0.59	+0.53	−0.15
necessity modals	−0.14	−0.15	+0.31
split auxiliaries	−0.18	−0.40	+0.14
mean factor score	+0.74	+1.33	+0.32

Table C5.8 Dimension 5 (Abstract versus non-abstract information)

Linguistic feature	Private conversation	Public speech	Academic prose
conjuncts	−0.48	−0.52	+0.48
agentless passives	−0.11	−0.42	+0.50
past participial clause	−0.11	−0.26	+0.52
BY-passives	−0.13	−0.46	+0.52
past participial WHIZ deletion	−0.41	−0.59	+0.51
other adverbial subordination	−0.52	−0.52	+0.37
mean factor score	−1.76	−2.77	+2.9

Table C5.9 Dimension 6 (Online informational elaboration)

Linguistic feature	Private conversation	Public speech	Academic prose
THAT clause as verb complements	−0.64	−0.14	+0.23
Demonstratives	+0.06	+0.74	−0.15
THAT relative clauses	−0.62	+0.44	+0.23
THAT clauses as adj. complements	+0.01	+0.19	+0.53
mean factor score	−1.19	+1.23	+0.84

Table C5.10 Dimension 7 (Academic hedging)

Linguistic feature	Private conversation	Public speech	Academic prose
SEEM/APPEAR	−0.05	+0.03	+0.40
mean factor score	−0.05	+0.03	+0.40

Table C5.11 Dimension scores of the three genres

Dimension	Conversation	Speech	Academic prose	F–E value	Sig. level
1	+28.96	+14.63	−9.24		
2	+1.20	+2.00	−0.61		
3	+1.10	−4.47	+2.45		
4	+0.74	+1.33	+0.32	32.47	<0.001
5	−1.76	−2.77	+2.90		
6	−1.19	+1.23	+0.84		
7	−0.05	+0.03	+0.40		

For ease of comparison, the dimension scores of the three genres are shown in Table C5.11. Fisher's exact test (F–E test; see Case Study 2) shows that the difference between genres is statistically significant (F–E score=32.47, p<0.001). Plotting these dimension scores allows a clearer view of the difference, as shown in Figure C5.14. As can be seen in the figure, the most marked contrast between these genres lies in Dimension 1, though conversation, speech and academic prose also show noticeable differences in Dimensions 3, 5 and 6.

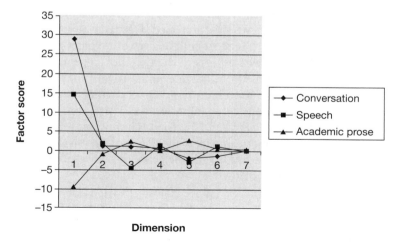

Figure C5.14 The comparison of three genres

C5.5 THE KEYWORD APPROACH TO GENRE ANALYSIS

As can be seen from the previous sections, Biber's MF/MD approach involves very sophisticated statistical analyses and is extremely time-consuming. Tribble (1999) shows that the wordlist and keyword functions of WordSmith Tools can be used to achieve an approximate effect of Biber's MF/MD approach. Specifically, a keyword analysis not only indicates the 'aboutness' (Scott 1999) of a particular genre, it can also reveal the salient features which are functionally related to that genre. In this section, we will show you how to do that step by step.

The first step is to make a wordlist of the corpus files by genre. In Unit C5.3 (steps 9–13), we made a wordlist for the whole corpus used in that section. What is needed here is to make a wordlist for each of the three genres and save the wordlists as *conv.lst*, *speech.lst* and *acadp.lst*.

The second step is to make a list of keywords for files of each genre using the keyword function of WordSmith. Keywords are those words whose frequency is unusually high (positive keywords) or low (negative keywords) in comparison with a reference corpus. As part of the Frown corpus is already used as the target of this study, we cannot use it as our reference corpus. We could use the Brown corpus, but that corpus sampled texts in the early 1960s, well before the data used in this study. Consequently we decide to use a corpus of British English as a reference. It is far from ideal to use a British English corpus to provide a reference wordlist for American English data. Using a British English corpus may give prominence to Americanisms in our data. However, given that the three genres will be compared against the same reference corpus, using British English as a reference will not affect our observations notably if the assumption holds that the genres studied here use Americanisms with roughly similar frequency.

One further issue related to the reference corpus is that it is clearly much larger than the corpora that are contrasted with it. Tribble (1999: 171) claims that the size of the corpus from which the reference wordlist is created is relatively unimportant. Before we undertake a keyword analysis, we will first carry out a baseline test to verify this claim by comparing the keyword lists of the two spoken genres, which were created using a reference wordlist from the one-million-word FLOB corpus and a reference wordlist from the 100-million-word BNC corpus. Both of the reference wordlists are available on our companion website. We assume that you have downloaded and saved them as *flob.lst* and *bnc.lst*. It is important to note that keywords are extracted from our American data while FLOB or the BNC only act as a reference corpus. To make a keyword list for the genre of conversation using *flob.lst*, carry out the process as listed below.

1. The keyword function of WordSmith allows you to set the program to restrict the number of keywords identified so as to find, for example, the top 10 keywords. As negative keywords appear at the end of a keyword list, they will be thrown away in this case. In this study, we will examine both positive and

negative keywords. To include the negative keywords, the program will be set to create a list that allows a maximum of 16,000 keywords, as shown in Figure C5.15, which is large enough to include all keywords.

2. Selecting *Tools → Keywords* from the main menu of WordSmith Tools Controller leads you to the keyword function (Figure C5.16).
3. Press the start button ● on the toolbar, the program will be ready to create a keyword list (Figure C5.17).
4. Press *Find keywords in a text*, select *conv.lst* in the left panel and *flob.lst* in the right panel, and then press *OK* (Figure C5.18).
5. In a few seconds, you will see the keyword list of conversation (using FLOB as reference corpus), as shown in Figure C5.19. The list is sorted by *keyness*. You can re-sort the list according to other parameters by clicking on the ● icon if you wish. Positive keywords are at the top of the list. Moving down to the end of the list, you will see negative keywords. Make a note of the top 10 positive and top 10 negative keywords and save the list as *conv_fl.kws*.

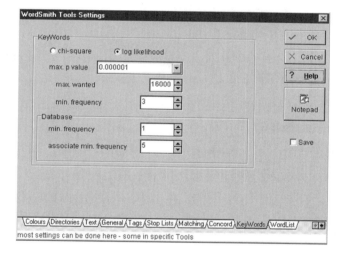

Figure C5.15 The keyword settings

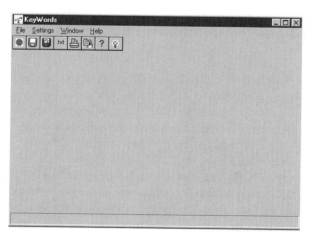

Figure C5.16 The keyword function

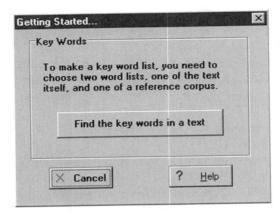

Figure C5.17 Starting the keyword function

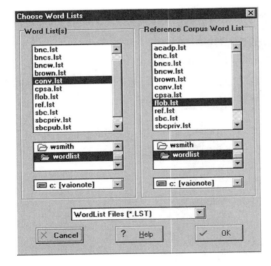

Figure C5.18 Selecting wordlists

Repeat steps 1–5 in this section to make a keyword list of conversation using the BNC as the reference corpus and save it as *conv_bnc.kws*. Do the same for the genres of speech and academic prose and save the keyword lists as *spch_fl.kws, spchbnc.kws, acadp_fl.kws* and *acadpbnc.kws*.

Let us now compare keyword lists created using two different reference corpora. Tables C5.12 and C5.13 list the top 10 positive and negative keywords from the genres of conversation and speech. As can be seen in Table C5.12, nine out of the top 10 positive keywords extracted from the American conversation corpus appear in both the FLOB and BNC-based keyword lists. Only one item from the FLOB/ BNC-based list does not appear amongst the top 10 in the BNC/FLOB-based list. The contracted negation (*n't*) from the FLOB-based list ranks thirteenth in the BNC-based list while *hm* from the BNC-based list ranks twenty-first in the FLOB-based list. The top 10 negative keyword lists also show similarities, though not as marked as the positive keywords. A similar pattern is found for the American speech corpus.

```
KeyWords - [key words (keyness)]
File  Settings  Window  Help
```

N	WORD	FREQ	CONV.LST %	FREQ	FLOB LST %	KEYNESS	P
1		5,440	4.00	7,079	0.69	8,163.8	0.000000
2	YOU	4,077	3.00	4,116	0.40	7,293.7	0.000000
3	YEAH	1,489	1.10	12		6,288.0	0.000000
4	KNOW	1,714	1.26	767	0.07	4,517.0	0.000000
5	UH	915	0.67	4		3,894.2	0.000000
6	OH	1,001	0.74	162	0.02	3,416.8	0.000000
7	MHM	698	0.51	0		3,008.2	0.000000
8	UM	629	0.46	0		2,710.5	0.000000
9	OKAY	608	0.45	14		2,489.5	0.000000
10	NT	1,755	1.29	2,476	0.24	2,438.6	0.000000
11	IT	3,574	2.63	9,666	0.94	2,366.3	0.000000
12	DO	1,448	1.07	1,986	0.19	2,057.8	0.000000
13	LIKE	1,238	0.91	1,423	0.14	2,012.5	0.000000
14	S	2,862	2.11	7,607	0.74	1,941.2	0.000000
15	NA	405	0.30	12		1,638.8	0.000000
16	JUST	940	0.69	1,108	0.11	1,499.3	0.000000
17	RE	642	0.47	517	0.05	1,300.6	0.000000
18	THAT	3,082	2.27	10,797	1.04	1,255.8	0.000000
19	GON	300	0.22	4		1,250.5	0.000000
20	RIGHT	670	0.49	631	0.06	1,240.2	0.000000
21	HM	282	0.21	0		1,214.6	0.000000
22	SO	1,132	0.83	2,223	0.22	1,137.5	0.000000
23	WELL	790	0.58	1,118	0.11	1,091.6	0.000000
24	REALLY	459	0.34	299	0.03	1,034.3	0.000000
25	WHAT	1,021	0.75	2,120	0.21	961.3	0.000000
26	MEAN	393	0.29	235	0.02	920.4	0.000000
27	THEY	1,387	1.02	3,755	0.36	908.5	0.000000
28	M	581	0.43	776	0.08	841.4	0.000000
29	GOT	450	0.33	444	0.04	808.7	0.000000
30	THINK	489	0.36	604	0.06	752.4	0.000000
31	GET	494	0.36	654	0.06	720.3	0.000000
32	LL	391	0.29	401	0.04	685.3	0.000000
33	GO	470	0.35	674	0.07	641.5	0.000000

Figure C5.19 The keyword list of conversation (FLOB as reference)

Table C5.13 compares the two keyword lists of the genre of speech. Eight positive keywords are the same whether one-million-word FLOB or the 100-million-word BNC is used as a reference corpus. The two items of the top 10 positive keywords from the FLOB-based list, *you* and *do*, appear as eleventh and thirteenth in the BNC-based list. The two items of the top 10 positive keywords from the BNC-based list, *uh* and *NAEP (the National Assessment for Education Progress)*, appear as eleventh and twentieth in the FLOB-based list. The top 10 negative keywords from the two lists are exactly the same, though they appear in a slightly different order. The top 10 positive and negative keywords created for academic prose (not shown in the tables) using a reference wordlist from FLOB and the BNC are also very similar. The above test provides evidence to show that the size of a reference corpus is not very important in making a keyword list. With Tribble's (1999) claim supported, we are now ready to compare the keyword lists of the three genres. We will examine positive keywords that were extracted from the American data using the BNC as a reference corpus.

When we made adjustments to the settings of the keyword function (step 1 in this section, see Figure C5.15), we defined the minimum frequency as 3 (the default value). This allows the program to exclude very unusual and infrequent words from the resulting keyword list. Another safeguard WordSmith provides to ensure that keywords are representative of the genre under examination is the *key keyword*

Table C5.12 Top 10 positive and negative keywords from conversation

| | Positive keywords | | |
No.	FLOB as reference corpus	No.	BNC as reference corpus
1*	I	1*	uh
2*	you	2*	I
3*	yeah	3*	um
4*	know	4*	you
5*	uh	5*	know
6*	oh	6*	yeah
7*	mhm	7*	mhm
8*	um	8*	okay
9*	okay	9*	oh
10	n't	10	hm
	Negative keywords		
No.	FLOB as reference corpus	No.	BNC as reference corpus
1*	the	1	yes
2*	of	2	mm
3*	in	3*	the
4*	as	4*	as
5	by	5*	of
6	his	6	've
7	which	7*	in
8	its	8	quite
9	for	9	terms
10	their	10	very

Note: Keywords marked with an asterisk appear among the top 10 of both FLOB and BNC-based lists.

function. In genre analysis, a key keyword list may prove more useful than a keyword list, because it excludes keywords that occur frequently in only a few texts of a genre. For example, with reference to the BNC, the keywords *test* and *NAEP* only occur frequently in two texts in our American speech corpus, namely, comm797.txt and comr797.txt, which were taken from the CPSA corpus. These files contain frequent uses of the two keywords simply because they are transcripts of a national meeting on reading tests (hence the word *test*) and a national meeting on mathematics tests (hence the mentions of the NAEP – the National Assessment of Educational Progress, a US government education watchdog). As WordSmith can create a key keyword database automatically, key keywords are as simple to extract as keywords. Note, however, that as negative keywords are omitted automatically from a key keyword list, we will compare negative keywords from the keyword lists rather than key keyword lists.

To make a key keyword list of the conversation genre, carry out the steps as listed below.

1. If you have not yet done so, adjust WordSmith settings to ignore CLAWS POS tags (steps 9–10 in Unit C5.3).

Table C5.13 Top 10 positive and negative keywords from speech

	Positive keywords			
No.	FLOB as reference corpus	No.	BNC as reference corpus	
1*	we	1*	we	
2*	I	2*	that	
3*	that	3	uh	
4	you	4*	I	
5*	think	5*	test	
6*	're	6*	think	
7*	okay	7	NAEP	
8*	what	8*	okay	
9*	test	9*	're	
10	do	10*	what	
	Negative keywords			
No.	FLOB as reference corpus	No.	BNC as reference corpus	
1*	his	1*	the	
2*	the	2*	his	
3*	he	3*	her	
4*	her	4*	by	
5*	of	5*	he	
6*	by	6*	of	
7*	she	7*	she	
8*	had	8*	had	
9*	was	9*	its	
10*	its	10*	was	

2. Load the 31 files of the conversation genre. Select *Tools → Wordlist* from the menu of WordSmith Tools Controller. Press the *Start* button and select *Make a batch now* (see Figure C5.12 in Unit C5.3).

3. A dialogue box will appear that allows you to specify the directory and filenames for the resulting wordlists. Select *use mask*, type in *conv* (the typing space allows up to four characters), and press *OK* as shown in Figure C5.20.

4. As the program progresses, a window shows that the resulting wordlists are named *conv0001.lst . . . conv0031.lst* and saved in the directory *c:\wsmith\wordlist* (Figure C5.21). Press *OK*.

5. Select *Tools → Keywords* from the menu of *WordSmith Tools Controller* (see Figure C5.16).

6. Select *File → New Database* from the menu (Figure C5.22).

7. Select *conv0001.lst . . . conv0031.lst* from the left panel and *bnc.lst* from the right panel. Press *OK* (Figure C5.23).

8. In the dialogue box, specify the directory for the database of key keywords, select *use mask* and type in *conv*, and then press *OK* (Figure C5.24).

9. You will see a window showing that a new database of key keywords has been created and saved as *conv0001.kdb* in the directory of *c:\wsmith\keywords*. Press *OK* as shown in Figure C5.25.

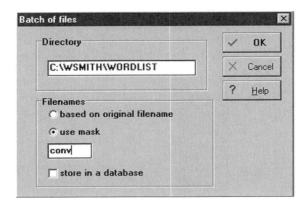

Figure C5.20 Making a batch of wordlists

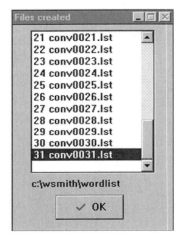

Figure C5.21 The result of the batch command

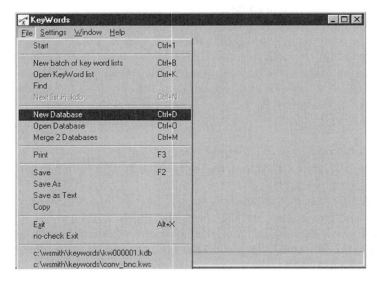

Figure C5.22 Creating a key keyword list

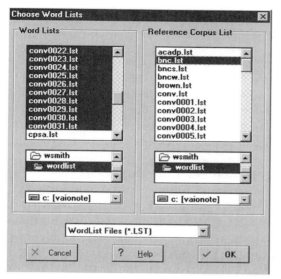

Figure C5.23 Selecting wordlists and reference list

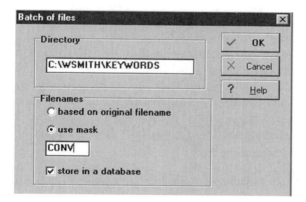

Figure C5.24 Making a key keyword list

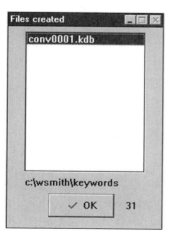

Figure C5.25 The resulting key keyword list

10. To view the key keyword list, select *File → Open Database* from the menu (see Figure C5.22), select *conv0001.kdb*, and press *OK*.

Table C5.14 lists the top 10 key keywords from conversation and speech. It also shows as a percentage the frequency of the keyword in terms of how often it occurs in the genre (you can find this data by opening the relevant wordlist, pressing the function key F12 on your keyboard or clicking on 🔍 in the toolbar, and typing a search word) as well as the coverage of the keywords. As can be seen from the table, over 50 per cent of the texts in each genre contain these keywords.

Table C5.15 compares the top 10 key keywords from conversation and speech. The table is revealing in that it suggests the difference between conversation and speech in four dimensions, though Dimensions 3 and 5 are not as clearly reflected as Dimensions 1 and 6. Note that in this table, as in other similar tables in this section, we are talking about the top 10 keywords. As such we cannot assume, for example, that there is no instance of a present tense verb or of questions in speech simply because DO does not appear on the top 10 key keyword list of the speech genre. As noted in Unit C5.4, constructions such as private verbs, second person pronouns and the pronoun IT all carry an interactive and affective focus. While the two genres share eight key keywords, two key keywords, DO and IT, appear among the top 10 of the conversation list but not among the top 10 of the speech list. Concordances of DO from the thirty-one texts of the conversation genre show that DO appears in the following structures: (a) analytic negation (i.e. *do not, don't*); (b) special and general questions; and (c) pro-verb *do* in the present tense. As all of these are Factor +1 features which have an interactive focus, we will not make a distinction between them; rather the gross percentage will be used for all of these features. Similarly, *n't* is both a contraction and an analytic negation, so we will not draw a distinction between the two.

Another feature of note in Table C5.15 is *interjections*. Interjections are of note for two reasons. First, they are more common in conversation than speech. Second,

Table C5.14 Top 10 BNC-based key keywords from conversation and speech

Conversation				Speech			
No.	Keyword	Fre. %	Coverage (%)	No.	Keyword	Fre. %	Coverage (%)
1	I	4.00	100	1	uh	0.26	85.71
2	you	3.00	96.77	2	that	3.35	85.71
3	yeah	1.10	96.77	3	um	0.11	78.57
4	n't	1.29	93.55	4	I	2.67	64.29
5	um	0.46	93.55	5	you	1.65	64.29
6	uh	0.67	90.32	6	n't	0.78	50.00
7	know	1.26	87.10	7	we	1.82	50.00
8	it	2.63	87.10	8	so	0.71	50.00
9	do	1.07	87.10	9	okay	0.30	50.00
10	oh	0.74	74.19	10	know	0.35	50.00

Table C5.15 Comparison of top 10 key keywords from conversation and speech

Factor	Linguistic feature	Conversation		Speech	
		Keyword	Freq. %	Keyword	Freq. %
+1	private verb	know	1.26%	know	0.35%
	2nd person pron.	you	3.00%	you	1.65%
	DO as pro-verb	do	1.07%	–	–
	present tense verb				
	questions				
	emphatic	–	–	so (9%*0.71%)	0.06%
	contraction	n't	1.29%	n't	0.78%
	analytic negation				
	1st person pron.	I	4.00%	I, we	4.49%
	pronoun IT	it	2.63%	–	–
	interjections	yeah, um, uh, oh	2.93%	uh, um, okay	0.67%
	demonstr. pron.	–	–	that (35.8%*3.35%)	1.20%
Total of factors +1			16.18%		9.20%
–3	other adverbs	–	–	that (0.5%*3.35%),	0.02%
				so (77%*0.71%)	0.55%
Total of factors –3			–		0.57%
+5	conjuncts	–	–	that (0.2%*3.35%)	0.01%
	other adv. sub.	–	–	so (14%*0.71%)	0.10%
Total of factors +5			–		0.11%
+6	demonstrative	–	–	that (10.1%*3.35%)	0.34%
	THAT clause	–	–	that (53.4%*3.35%)	1.79%
Total of factors +6			–		2.13%

interjections were not considered as discourse markers by Biber (1988), though they are actually used in the same way as discourse particles to maintain conversational coherence (Schiffrin 1982) and are typical of spoken language (see Aijmer 1987: 61–86 for an interesting account of the functions of *oh* and *ah* in the London–Lund corpus). Hence, while interjections are not included as a relevant linguistic feature in the MF/MD approach, they are an important feature in a keyword analysis. Two key keywords that are found among the top 10 of the speech list but not among the top 10 of the conversation list are THAT and SO. As CLAWS makes a distinction between the different uses of these words, it is easy to determine their proportions. Concordances of *that_** from the fourteen texts of the speech genre show that THAT is used in the following contexts: (a) THAT-clause (*that_CS**): 53.4 per cent. We will not differentiate between the three types of THAT clause because they are all features with positive weights on Factor 6; (b) demonstrative pronoun (*that_DD1 context 0L 2R = ~*_NN**): 35.8 per cent; (c) demonstrative (*that_DD1 context 0L 2R = *_NN**): 10.1 per cent; (d) emphatic (*that_RG*): 0.5 per cent; and (e) other adverbial subordination (*that_REX21*): 0.2 per cent. The keyword SO is used in the following contexts: (a) *other adverbs* (*so_RR**): 77 per cent; (b) *other adverbial subordination* (*so_CS**): 14 per cent; and (c) emphatics (*so_RG**): 9 per cent. The overall percentages of the two keywords are allocated to appropriate features accordingly. It can be seen in Table C5.15 that the total of Factor +1 for the conversation genre (16.18 per cent) is considerably greater than the total for the speech genre 9.20 per cent. Conversely, in relation to Factors +3 and +5, the total of Factor +6 for the speech genre is significantly greater than that for conversation, suggesting a possibly significant difference between the two spoken genres along Dimension 6, which indicates the level of online elaboration. These observations of the two spoken genres are in line with the MF/MD results in Unit C5.4.

In contrast, the top 10 key keywords from the genre of academic prose include: *of, the, is, formula, system, American, B, G, C* and *program*. The first two key keywords are *of* and *the. Of* as a preposition adds a negative weight to the dimension of informational vs. involved production. Tribble (1999: 175–177) observes that *of* and *the* are typically associated with nouns. In academic prose, for example, *of* is typically used as a post-modifier in the N1 + *of* + N2 structure (e.g. *center of mass, clusters of galaxies*). The definite article *the* is also associated with nouns. In an MD/MF analysis, nouns of the nominalization type are a feature with a positive loading for Dimension 3 (explicit vs. situation-dependent reference) while nouns of other types are a feature with a negative loading for Dimension 1 (informational vs. involved focus). *Is* as a main verb is typically used in academic prose to make a statement or claim (e.g. *it is an excellent example of . . . , it is the user's responsibility to . . .*). The four content words (*formula, system, American* and *program*) indicate the 'aboutness' of academic prose. The three letters are used mainly as part of a list of variable labels, which are typical of academic prose. These key keywords enable us to get a general view of the content and style of academic prose.

Let us now consider the top 10 negative keywords from the two spoken genres. Note that because negative keywords are omitted automatically from a key keyword list, we will compare negative keywords from the keyword lists. As negative keywords are relatively infrequent words in relation to a reference corpus, we cannot take the same approach as when studying positive keywords. We need to refer back to the reference corpus to find an explanation for the relatively low frequency of negative keywords in our American data. There is little advantage in using a relatively large reference corpus (Tribble 1999:171). Furthermore, as WordSmith (version 3) only allows a maximum of 16,368 concordances at a time, it would be very inconvenient to use the BNC as the reference corpus. As such, we will use the FLOB-based keyword lists to study negative keywords in conversation and speech. We will also include negative keywords from academic prose for a contrast.

Table C5.16 lists the top 10 negative keywords from the three genres. As can be seen, negative keywords are as revealing as positive keywords. The four linguistic features with positive weights on Factor 1, which are associated with interactive and affective discourse, are only found amongst the top 10 negative keywords of academic prose. Conversely, the two features with negative weights on Factor 1 are only found among the top 10 negative keywords of conversation and speech. It is also interesting to note the contrast between the two spoken genres: six out of 10 negative keywords from conversation are associated with Factor –1 features while only three

Table C5.16 Top 10 FLOB-based negative keywords of three genres

Factor	Linguistic feature	Conversation	Speech	Academic prose
+1	2nd person pronouns	–	–	you
	1st person pronouns	–	–	I
	contraction	–	–	n't
	analytic negation	–	–	n't
–1	nouns	the, of	the, of	–
	prepositions	in, as, by, for	by	–
+2	3rd person pronouns	his, its, their	his, he, her, she, its	he, she, her, his
	past tense verbs	–	had, was	had, was, (said)
	public verbs	–	–	said
+3	WH relative clauses	which	–	–
	pied-piping	which	–	–

negative keywords from speech are associated with Factor –1 features. Similarly, seven negative keywords and three linguistic features from academic prose are associated with Factor 2, which supports our previous observation that academic prose has a less narrative focus than the two spoken genres. While the difference between the three genres alongside Dimension 2 is not statistically significant, academic prose has the lowest score for this dimension. It is more difficult to interpret *which*, which is found only in the top 10 negative keywords from the conversation genre. Concordances of *which* from the reference corpus (FLOB) show that *which* is primarily used in WH relative clauses and pied-piping constructions (67.7 per cent, with the remaining 32.3 per cent being mainly sentence relatives and WH clauses), which are salient features associated with Factor 3. The unusually low frequency of these features indicates that conversation relies heavily upon context-dependent reference. The relatively low frequency of WH relative clauses in conversation is conformant with its lowest score for Factor 3 (see Figure C5.14).

The above analysis demonstrates that both positive and negative keywords can be good indicators of genre features. While it would seem that a keyword analysis can reflect only some MF/MD dimensions, the results obtained by both approaches are consistent across the three different genres under consideration; keywords can be used to achieve an approximation to an MF/MD analysis.

Summary

In this unit, we compared the genres of conversation and speech in American English alongside seven dimensions, using Biber's MF/MD approach and Tribble's keyword approach using WordSmith. The results obtained by the two approaches are similar. The most significant difference between conversation and speech lies in Dimension 1, a measure of the informational vs. involved distinction. They also differ marginally alongside Dimension 6, which indicates the level of online elaboration. This means that conversation is considerably more interactive and affective than speech. While speech is informationally dense, it is subject to real-time production conditions and thus speech needs online informational elaboration. The two spoken genres differ significantly from academic prose along Dimensions 1, 3, and 5. This means that, on the one hand, academic prose is the most 'literate', technical, and abstract of the three genres under consideration while on the other hand, this written genre tends to make explicit in-text reference whereas the two spoken genres make context-dependent references.

Methodologically, the MF/MD approach, while providing a powerful and comprehensive tool for genre analysis, requires considerable expertise in data extraction and statistical analysis. The keyword approach, in contrast, provides a less demanding approach to genre analysis. But since this approach provides a less comprehensive contrast of genres and may not work for some fine-grained types of genre analysis, it is not simply a substitute for MF/MD analysis. Nevertheless, as the keyword approach requires little technical expertise and can be undertaken swiftly, it provides a quick and simple means of evaluating a genre against Biber's dimensions. The keyword approach to genre analysis provides linguists with a powerful and easily used tool.

 FURTHER STUDY

Biber (1987) compared nine written genres from British and American English, and Biber (1988) compared twenty-one genres in British English. In this unit we were concerned with conversation and speech in American English. This unit might motivate you to pursue genre analysis from a diachronic viewpoint by comparing genres in the LOB and FLOB corpora. Alternatively, you might wish to compare the five types of imaginative texts (text categories K, L, M, N and P) in the Brown corpus to see whether its sampling frame (see Unit A7.4), which has, to date, rarely been questioned, is justified.

Unit C6
Domains, text types, aspect marking and English–Chinese translation

CASE STUDY 6

C6.1 INTRODUCTION

This unit uses comparable and aligned parallel corpora (see Unit A5) to approach contrastive and translation studies as discussed in Units A10.6 and B5.2–B5.3. In Unit A10.6, we noted that while aligned parallel corpora are well suited for translation studies, they provide a poor basis for contrastive language study if used as the sole source of data. They should most often be used in conjunction with comparable L1 language corpora. This unit extends this argument via a case study of aspect marking in English and Chinese. But before presenting the case study in detail, it is appropriate to provide background knowledge of aspect markers in Chinese.

Both English and Chinese mark aspect grammatically, but the aspect systems in the two languages differ considerably. As far as grammatical aspect (also known as *viewpoint aspect* as opposed to *situation aspect*; see Unit A10.9) is concerned, English marks the progressive, the perfect, the perfect progressive and the simple aspect (see Biber *et al.* 1999: 461). In contrast, Chinese is more aspectual in that it has four perfective viewpoints (marked by -*le*, -*guo*, verb reduplication and resultative verb complements (RVCs)) and four imperfective viewpoints (marked by -*zhe*, *zai*, -*qilai* and -*xiaqu*) in addition to a number of complex viewpoints (see Unit B5.3 for a discussion of aspect marking in Chinese). Aspectual meanings in Chinese can be realized in three ways: (i) marked explicitly by aspect markers, for example -*le*, highlighted in (1a), (ii) marked adverbially, for example *zheng*, highlighted in (1b), and (iii) marked covertly (1c), i.e., taking the lack-viewpoint-morpheme (LVM) form (see Xiao 2002), as illustrated in the following examples from the CEPC parallel corpus (see Unit C6.2 for a description of the corpora used in this work). Note that the Chinese examples are Romanized using Pinyin. They are followed by literal glosses and their English translations as they appear in the parallel corpus. The following abbreviations are used to gloss grammatical categories in Chinese examples: CLF (classifier), GEN (genitive), PSV (passive), PFV (perfective), PROG (progressive) and RVC (resultative verb complement).

(1) (a) *zhe ben cezi   liechu-le   wuyong dupin de   zhongzhong*
        this CLF booklet point-out-PFV misuse drug GEN various
        qianzai wenti
        potential problems
        'This booklet points out the potential problems from misusing drugs.'
    (b) *ruguo ni **zheng** bei   chouqu xiueye yangben . . .*
        if   you PROG PSV take   blood sample
        'If a blood sample is being taken . . .'
    (c) *zai   chuxian aizibing zhengzhuang zhiqian, henduo ren   dou bu*
        when appear AIDS   symptom   before many   people all not
        zhidao ziji yi   shoudao aizibing du   de   ganran
        know self already get   AIDS   virus GEN infection
        'Many people do not realize that they have been infected with HIV until
        they develop symptoms of AIDS.'

In (1a) perfectivity is marked by the aspect marker -*le*; in (1b) the adverb *zheng*
indicates progressiveness. While Chinese is rich in aspect markers, it is interesting
to note that covert marking of the LVM form is a frequent and important strategy
used to express aspectual meanings in Chinese discourse, as shown in (1c). In this
example, the verb phrase *shoudao . . . ganran* 'be infected by' shows a perfective
meaning but is not marked overtly, even though the aspect marker -*le* can be used
optionally in this context (i.e. *shoudao-le . . . ganran*). Such LVM forms typically
occur in three situations. Stative situations normally take the LVM form because
statives do not have to be marked aspectually (see Xiao 2002). For dynamic
situations, there are two types of LVM sentences in discourse. They are imperfective
as *irrealis* (e.g. future, habitual or conditional) or as having a perfective aspect
marker deleted for discourse reasons (Chu 1987). In a discourse segment that
presents a series of events, -*le* is 'used as an explicit marker for the peak event', i.e.
the most important – and typically the last – event in a series (Chang 1986: 265),
even though -*le* applies to the whole series of events rather than just the peak event
as shown in (2a). Events other than the peak event can also be marked explicitly if
the speaker chooses to regard them as separate events or wants any of them to stand
out as separate events, as shown in (2b) (see Yang 1995: 138). For example (verbs
in bold typeface, peak event underlined):

(2) (a) *houlai, ta kaishi dui saiche   **fasheng** xingqu, bingqie <u>you</u>-le*
        then   he start in banger-racing happen interest and   have-PFV
        yi-ge   wengu de   nüpengyou (CEPC-health)
        one-CLF steady GEN girlfriend
        'Then, he started getting interested in banger-racing and got a steady
        girlfriend.'
    (b) *ta zhujian **jianshao**-le xiuxi rongji, tongshi   ta de j iankang ye*
        he gradually reduce-PFV sniff solvent meanwhile he GEN health   also
        <u>*you*</u>-le   *gaishan* (CEPC-health)
        have-PFV improvement
        'Gradually he sniffed less and less, and his health improved.'

In this case study we will first use ParaConc (version 1.0) to explore an English–Chinese parallel corpus and examine how aspectual meanings in English are translated into Chinese. We will then compare the translated Chinese texts with L1 Chinese texts to study the translation effect, followed by a contrast of texts from different domains and text types to see what effect, if any, domains and text types have on aspect marking. For a further discussion of this research question, readers can refer to McEnery and Xiao (2002), on which this case study is based.

While this study is focused on a non-European language, it should be apparent that the techniques and findings of this case study are also applicable to European languages. Since the corpus has been properly annotated, even if you do not understand Chinese, you will be able to understand the points raised in this case study and should be able to reduplicate the work presented in the following sections.

C6.2 THE CORPUS DATA

We will use three corpora for this work. The first corpus, the English–Chinese Parallel Health Corpus (CEPC-health), is aligned at the sentence level (see Unit A5.3 for a discussion of alignment). It was constructed using a collection of English–Chinese bilingual pamphlets and leaflets issued from 1992 to 1994 by the Department of Health and the Central Office of Information of the British government. The corpus covers one domain, public health, and two text types, exposition and narration. The English texts in the parallel corpus were annotated for parts of speech using the CLAWS tagger (see Unit A4.4.1). The Chinese data was tokenized and POS tagged manually following a tagging scheme which was developed by Piao (2000) on the basis of the CKIP (Chinese Knowledge Information Processing) tagset (see Chen *et al.* 1994).

As the frequency of aspect markers is exceptionally low in translated Chinese (see Unit C6.3), we constructed a comparable L1 Chinese corpus, the Chinese Health Corpus (C-health), to compare the translated texts with L1 Chinese data (see Unit C6.4). The corpus contains texts from current official websites for public health in China. As we hypothesize that the distribution of aspect markers may vary across domain and text type (see Units C6.5 and C6.6), C-health matches the CEPC-health corpus in the domain and text types. To ensure the maximum comparability between the L1 Chinese corpus and the parallel corpus, this comparable corpus was POS tagged using the CKIP tagger. In addition to POS tagging, these two corpora have also been annotated semantically using a problem-oriented annotation scheme (see Unit C6.3). They will also be used to study the effect of text types on aspect marking.

A third corpus, the Weekly corpus, will be used to explore the possible effects of domains and text types on the distribution of aspect markers in Chinese. This is an L1 Chinese corpus built with texts sampled from the *Southern Weekly*, a weekly newspaper with a sales volume of 1.3 million copies, published in China (see Xiao

Table C6.1 Corpora used in this study

Corpus	Language	Domain	Tokens	Text type
CEPC-health	L1 English	public health	31,638	⅔ exposition
	L2 Chinese		35,877	⅓ narration
C-health	L1 Chinese	public health	34,174	⅔ exposition
				⅓ narration
weekly training	L1 Chinese	mixed	96,897	mixed
weekly test	L1 Chinese	mixed	10,054	mixed

and McEnery 2004b for a description). This newspaper corpus contains a mix of domains and text types. It was also tagged using the CKIP tagger. Table C6.1 compares the corpora used in this case study.

While the original versions of the Chinese corpora contain Chinese characters, we have converted these into the Roman alphabet using a system called Pinyin as we assume that most readers of this book will be unable to read Chinese characters. By using Pinyin, one can read Chinese without having to learn thousands of Chinese characters.

We assume that you have downloaded the three corpora used in this case study from our companion website and decompressed them into the following directories on your computer:

      CEPC-health   c:\My corpora\CEPC-health
      C-health   c:\My corpora\C-health
      Weekly   c:\My corpora\Weekly

 ## C6.3 TRANSLATION OF ASPECT MARKERS

In this section, we will examine how aspectual meanings in English are translated into Chinese. Unit C6.3.1 explores the translation of the progressive; Units C6.3.2 and C6.3.3 are concerned with the perfect and the perfect progressive; Unit C6.3.4 discusses the simple aspect.

C6.3.1 The progressive

This section examines how the progressive in English is translated into Chinese. To find the progressive forms in the English texts and their Chinese expressions in CEPC-health, conduct the steps as set out below.

1.   Activate ParaConc. You will see the interface of the concordancer, which is ready to load corpus files. The default number of parallel texts is two and English is selected by default. If you are running ParaConc for the first time and you have not already done so, a second language is undefined, as shown in Figure C6.1.

2. Define the second language as Chinese (PRC) by clicking on the button next to <undefined> and selecting the language from the list, as shown in Figure C6.2.
3. Click on the *Add* button on the left panel (for English). The *Select file(s) to open* window will appear (Figure C6.3).
4. Locate the directory in which the CEPC-health corpus is stored and select the twenty files the filenames of which start with *hlthe* in the subdirectory named *English*. Press *Open* and the English texts of CEPC-health will be loaded into the concordancer. Do the same for the Chinese texts in the subdirectory named *Chinese* (Figure C6.4).
5. Now ParaConc has loaded the English–Chinese parallel corpus and is ready for concordancing. Select *Search* → *Search* from the main menu. A new window

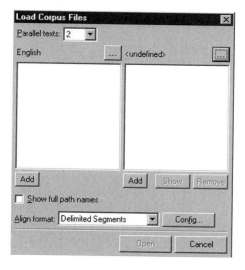

Figure C6.1 The ParaConc interface

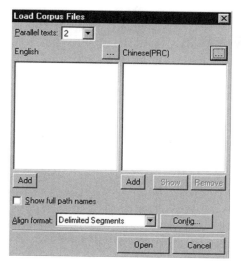

Figure C6.2 Selecting the languages

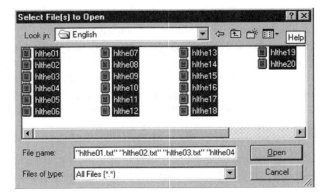

Figure C6.3 Selecting files

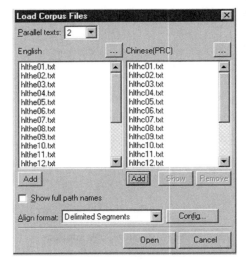

Figure C6.4 Loading corpus files

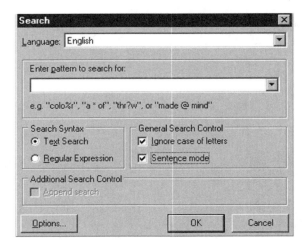

Figure C6.5 The search window

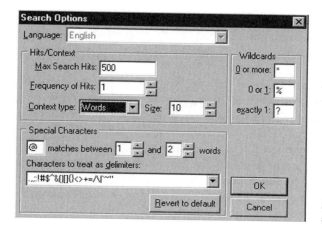

Figure C6.6 Defining search context

will appear for you to type in a search pattern. Make sure that English is selected as the language option. Select *text search* for *Search Syntax*, and *Ignore case of letters* and *Sentence mode* for *General Search Control*, as shown in Figure C6.5.

6. The default context is forty characters on both sides of the search string. If you want to read more context, you can change this default setting by clicking on the *Option* button and defining *Context type* as *words* and the *size* as 10, as shown in Figure C6.6.

7. In this case study, we are only interested in the progressive form in which the verb *BE* and present participles are separated by 0–2 words. First you need to press the *Option* button to define the special character @ as matching 1 and 2 words (see Figure C6.6). Then type in *_VB* *_V?G* to get the concordance lines for the pattern *BE verbing*, and *_VB* @ *_V?G* to get the concordance lines where *BE* is separated by one or two words.

While in this step, we should have been able to define the special character @ as 0–2 words, which enables us to extract the structure of *BE* separated by 0–2 words from the present participle at one go but ParaConc version 1.0 does not work in this way. In the new version of the package, though, the special character @ can be defined as 0.

Here the special characters * and ? are used as wildcards (see Case Study 2). You will get eighty-four concordances for the first search string and thirty-eight for the second search string. But these concordance lines need to be evaluated manually because there are eight instances of the perfect progressive, which will be discussed separately in Unit C6.3.3. The concordances also include thirty invalid matches, as exemplified in (3). Alternatively, you may wish to take advantage of the semantic annotation in the corpus, which we will discuss shortly, to avoid the time-consuming manual evaluation.

(3) (a) [. . .] make sure you heat it until it **is piping hot** . . .
    (b) [. . .] the experience may **be damaging** for someone with mental illness . . .

(c)   A specific danger with mushrooms **is picking** the wrong ones . . .

(d)   Be fun, be consistent, **be caring**, but don't give the impression you approve of what they are doing.

In addition to its canonical use to signal the ongoing nature of a situation, the English progressive can refer to a habitual situation or an anticipated happening (see Leech 1971; see Unit A10.6). The three types of progressives are annotated in the corpus respectively as <+PROG>, <+HABIT> and <+FUTURE>. As an alternative to extracting all progressive forms and evaluating them manually, readers can use this annotation scheme to extract English progressives of different types. To find the frequency and concordance lines of the progressive forms that denote ongoing situations, simply type in *PROG* as the search string. There are seventy-nine matches, as shown in Figure C6.7. The upper window shows the matched concordance lines in the English texts while the lower window shows their Chinese translations. Type in the search strings *HABIT* and *FUTURE* respectively to get the frequencies and concordance lines of progressive forms that denote the habitual (four matches) and future meaning (one match).

When you click on a concordance line in the upper window, the corresponding translation will be highlighted in the lower window. In this way, you can examine how a progressive form in English is translated into Chinese. To help readers who do not understand Chinese, we have annotated the Chinese texts in the parallel corpus with both part-of-speech and semantic information. The progressive meaning in Chinese texts is marked by the progressive *zai* (tagged as PROGZ), *zai* functioning both as a progressive marker and as a locative preposition (PROGZ2), the adverb *zheng* (ZHENG) and the durative *-zhe* (DURZ). The non-progressive

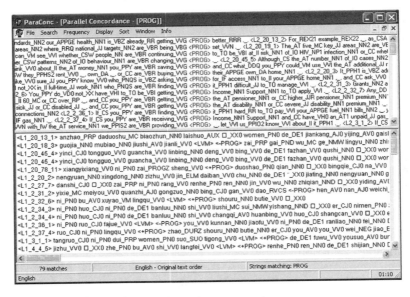

Figure C6.7 Concordances of ongoing progressives

meaning is marked by the actual -*le* (ACTL), the experiential -*guo* (EXPG), resultative verb complements (RVCC, RVCS, RVCD) or negation (NEG). In addition to the part-of-speech tags, there is an extra semantic tag in Chinese translations indicating whether an English progressive form is translated as progressive, non-progressive, or is paraphrased, i.e., an English progressive form is paraphrased with a noun phrase that is irrelevant to aspect marking. This semantic tag also shows how the aspectual meaning in the English source texts is marked in translations. For example, the tag <+PROG_ZAI> means that a progressive form in English is translated as progressive and is marked with the progressive marker *zai*. The tag <–PROG_LVM> indicates that a progressive form in English is translated as non-progressive and is covertly marked, and <0PROG_PARA> means that a progressive form in English is paraphrased in translation and is irrelevant to progressiveness.

8. Now you can examine the Chinese translations and classify each concordance line with the help of the tags described above. The results of your classification should match those in Table C6.2.

Table C6.3 shows that if a progressive in the English source text refers to a habitual situation, the progressive aspect marker is not used in the Chinese translation, as shown in (4a) below. Similarly, when the progressive form in the English source text

Table C6.2 The translation of the progressive

Progressive translated as	Aspect marking in Chinese		Freq.	Marked/LVM
progressive (56%)		(zheng)zai	14	
	marked	(zheng . . .)-zhe	3	
		zheng	5	0.88:1
	LVM		25	
non-progressive (35.7%)		-le	3	
	marked	RVC	4	0.36:1
		negation	1	
	LVM		22	
paraphrase (8.3%)			7	
total (100%)			84	

Table C6.3 Types of English progressives and their translations

Aspectual meaning in English	Translated in Chinese as	Freq.
Progressive	progressive	47
	non-progressive	25
	paraphrase	7
Habitual	non-progressive	4
Future	non-progressive	1
Total		84

refers to an anticipated event, the progressive *zai* is not used in the Chinese translation, as shown in (4b) below. We hypothesize that this is because the progressive
in Chinese only corresponds to the canonical use of the English progressive. While
the progressive meaning is necessarily marked by the progressive form in English,
it can be marked overtly or take the LVM form in Chinese. Our finding is in line
with Comrie's (1976: 33) observation that 'in some languages the distinction
between progressive and nonprogressive meaning by means of progressive and
nonprogressive forms is obligatory whereas in others the use of the specifically
progressive forms is optional'. It is clear that English belongs to the first type while
Chinese belongs to the second type.

(4) (a) If your child's health or behaviour shows that they **are taking drugs
          regularly**, you must take further action. (CEPC-health)
          ruguo ni   de   haizi de   jiankang huo xingwei   xianshi tamen
          if   you GEN child GEN health   or   behaviour show   they
          ***jingchang shiyong dupin,** na   ni   jiu   bixu caiqu jinyibu de*
          regularly use   drug   then you just must take   further GEN
          xingdong
          action
     (b) Graham (aged 12) seemed to be sniffing to relieve the tension he felt
          because his parents' marriage **was breaking up**. (CEPC-health)
          Amote   (shier sui) xiuxi rongji sihu   shi weile   jietuo
          Graham (12   year) sniff solvent apparently is   in-order-to relieve
          *youyu   ta fumu hunyin **polie**   er   ganshou-dao de*
          because-of he parent marriage break-up then feel-RVC   GEN
          jinzhang
          tension

C6.3.2 The perfect

The English perfect relates a previous situation to the present. Note that as non-
finite verb constructions with *having* plus a past participle and perfect forms taking
modals like *must, would, could*, and *may/might* do not denote perfect meaning (see
Comrie 1976: 55; Brinton 1988: 248), they are not discussed in this study. According
to Comrie (1976: 56–62), the current relevance of a situation in the past can be
manifested in four different ways: the perfect of result (5a), of experience (5b), of
recent past (5c) and of persistent situation (5d).

(5)   (a) John has arrived. (Comrie 1976: 56)
         (b) Bill has been to America. (*ibid.*: 59)
         (c) I have recently learned that the match is to be postponed. (*ibid.*:
              60)
         (d) I've shopped there for years. (*ibid.*: 60)

It is clear that the perfect is not simply concerned with perfectivity. While the
first three types of perfect are perfective, the last is imperfective in nature (see

Mourelatos 1981: 195). Unlike English, Chinese does not have a grammatical marker for the perfect. While the sentence-final *le* in Chinese also indicates current relevant state (see Li and Thompson 1981), it is clearly different from the English perfect. First, the Chinese *le* is not restricted to the present. Rather it can indicate current relevance relative to a past, present or future time reference. A further contrast between the English perfect and the Chinese *le* lies in the fact that, on the one hand, the perfect can carry the experiential meaning whereas *le* cannot, while on the other hand, *le* can refer to an imminent change of state whereas the perfect cannot (see Xiao 2002). When a Chinese sentence takes both the perfective *-le* and the sentence-final *le*, it is translatable by the English perfect of persistent situation (see also Henne *et al.* 1977: 113), because the sentence-final *le* in combination with the actual *-le* denotes a previous situation continuing into the present.

The four types of perfect in the English texts are tagged respectively as <PERFECT1>, <PERFECT2>, <PERFECT3> and <PERFECT4>. In the Chinese translations, there are also tags that show how a particular type of perfect is translated, e.g., <PERFECT1_LE>, <PERFECT2_GUO>, <PERFECT3_RVC>, <PERFECT4_LVM> and <PERFECT1_PARA>, which respectively indicate that the Chinese translation is overtly marked by the actual *-le*, the experiential *-guo*, an RVC or is covertly marked as LVM or paraphrased as a noun phrase.

If you have unloaded corpus files or exited ParaConc, you will need to repeat steps 1 and 3–6 in Unit C6.3.1, though there is no need to define languages in step 2 again. Otherwise, simply select *Search → Search* from the menu and type in *PERFECT1*. There are seventy-one matches. Now you can examine how the perfect of result is translated into Chinese by looking in the corresponding Chinese translations for the tag listed above. You will find that sixteen translations take *-le*, five take negative adverbs, eight take RVCs, thirty-seven take the LVM tag, and five are paraphrased. Do the same with the search strings *PERFECT2, PERFECT3* and *PERFECT4*. Your results will match those in Table C6.4. The table shows the frequencies of the four types of perfect in the English texts and their translations. It can be seen that the perfect of result is the most common of the four types of perfect. When perfect constructions are translated into Chinese, they tend to depend on context to indicate perfect meanings rather than mark it explicitly, though aspect markers such as *-le, -guo*, RVCs and the sentence-final *le* could be used where appropriate. Whether the translations take aspect markers or contextually imply the perfect depends largely on the type of perfect in the English source texts. While the LVM forms are dominant in all of the four categories, aspect markers are more frequent in translations of the perfect of result and the perfect of experience than the latter two categories. This difference is statistically significant at p<0.01 (the critical value for which is 6.64 with 1 d.f.), as shown in Table C6.5.

C6.3.3 The perfect progressive

The perfect progressive is an interaction between the perfect and the progressive, indicating the immediacy of an effect. It takes the form of HAVE *been* verb*ing*.

Table C6.4 Translation of the perfect

Type of perfect	Freq.	Translated as	Freq.	Marked/LVM
result	71 (65.74%)	-le	16	0.78:1
		negation	5	
		RVC	8	
		LVM	37	
		paraphrase	5	
experience	17 (15.74%)	-guo	7	0.7:1
		LVM	10	
recency	6 (5.56%)	RVC	1	0.2:1
		LVM	5	
persistency	14 (12.96%)	negation	1	0.09:1
		LVM	11	
		paraphrase	2	
total	108 (100%)			

Table C6.5 Comparison of four types of perfect

Type of perfect	Translated as	Freq.	Marked	LVM	LL (1 d.f.)
result	-le	16	36	47	
	negation	5			
	RVC	8			
	LVM	37			
experience	-guo	7			7.61
	LVM	10			
recency	RVC	1	2	16	
	LVM	5			
persistency	negation	1			
	LVM	11			

Therefore, it is easy to find this structure in the parallel corpus. Simply type in the search string *_VH* been_VBN *_V?G, where the special character ? matches any single character so that VVN, VDN, VHN and VBN are included. In Chinese translations, there are also semantic tags that indicate whether the perfect progressive is translated as progressive or non-progressive. These tags also show how the aspectual meaning is marked in translated texts. For example, the tag <–PROG_LE> means that the perfect progressive is translated as non-progressive and is marked by the aspect marker -le, and <?PROG_LVM> indicates that the translation is covertly marked as LVM and is ambiguous between a progressive and non-progressive reading. There are only eight instances of the perfect progressive in the English texts of the CEPC-health corpus. Of these seven are translated as non-progressive and one instance (i.e. 'If you find that your child has been using drugs what can you do' translated as *ruguo ni fajue ni de haizi shiyong dupin ni ruhe yingfu*) is ambiguous between a progressive and a non-progressive reading in the Chinese translation. Surprisingly, while Chinese has a well-established progressive marker *zai*, translation of the English perfect progressive normally preserve its perfect meaning and discard its progressive meaning.

This observation is contrary to what Zhang (1995: 181) would have us expect. Zhang uses the example in (6a) to assert that translations of the perfect progressive only render the progressive part of meaning. But the translation in (6b) is not as accurate as (6c) which does not support Zhang's claim. In this alternative translation, the addition of the temporal adverb *gang* 'just a while ago, just now' renders the immediacy effect expressed by the perfect progressive in the source text (i.e., the paint is still wet). Zhang's assertion, however, is clearly ungrounded, as the corpus example in (7) illustrates:

(6) (a) They have been painting on my staircase. (Zhang 1995: 181)
   (b) *wo jia   de   louti   zhengzai youqi* (*ibid.*)
       my home GEN staircase PROG   paint
   (c) *wo jia   de   louti   gang youqi-guo* (Our translation)
       my home GEN staircase   just paint-PFV
(7)   In most cases, your complaint can probably be handled by the member of staff you've been dealing with. (CEPC-health)
       zai daduoshu de   shijian zhong, ni de   tousu   keneng hui you
       in most   GEN time   during you GEN complaint probably can by
       yi wei cengjing he   ni jiechu de   zhiyuan   lai   chuli
       one CLF once   with you contact GEN staff-member come deal-with

Like the perfect and the progressive, translations of the perfect progressive primarily take the LVM form. In the data, only two instances are explicitly marked by *-le* (tagged as <LE>) while aspectual meanings are marked covertly (tagged as <LVM>) in all of the other translations, registering a marked/LVM ratio of 0.33:1.

C6.3.4 The simple aspect

According to Hatcher (1951: 259–260), the simple form in English has no aspectual meaning and it is indifferent to aspect. As such, the simple aspect may express a perfective, habitual or timeless situation. When aspect interacts with tense, we have the simple past, the simple present and the simple future. The simple present prototypically refers to states, i.e., statements made for all time (8a) and habitual situations (8b).

(8) (a) Flu is more common in the winter months. (CEPC-health)
   (b) Septicaemia often occurs with meningococcal meningitis. (CEPC-health)

As stative situations do not have to be marked aspectually in Chinese to have a closed reading, translations of the simple present tend to take the LVM form. The simple future refers to a future time reference. Chinese does not mark tense grammatically (see Wang 1943: 151; Norman 1988: 163). Future time references in

Chinese are most frequently expressed by modal auxiliaries (see Xiao and McEnery 2004b). As a predicate can only be marked for either mode or tense and aspect (Biber *et al.* 1999), Chinese translations of the simple future do not take aspect markers. As the canonical use of the simple past is to locate a situation prior to the present moment, it is natural that perfectivity in English is most commonly expressed by the simple past, less often by the simple present (Brinton 1988: 52). Therefore, in this case study, we will investigate how the simple past and the simple present are translated into Chinese.

In this section, we will only include lexical verbs (tagged by CLAWS as *VVD* for the simple past and *VV0* and *VVZ* for the simple present in the English corpus) while excluding the verbs BE (*was/were/is/am/are*), HAVE (*had/have/has*) and DO (*did/do/does*), because these verbs can also function as auxiliaries and are likely to make the concordancing procedure too complicated for the purpose of this study. A further reason for this decision is that the verbs BE and HAVE are stative verbs when they have lexical meanings (see discussion in Unit C6.4).

C6.3.4.1 *The simple past*

To get the frequencies and concordances of the simple past form of lexical verbs, type in the search pattern *_VVD. There are eighty-four matches. You can examine the translation pattern of the simple past by looking at the semantic tags in angled brackets in the Chinese translations. For example, <*PAST_+PERFECTIVE_GUO*> indicates that a simple past form in English is translated as perfective and is marked by the aspect marker -*guo*. <*PAST_–PERFECTIVE_ZAI*> means that a simple past form is translated as imperfective and is marked by the aspect marker *zai*, while <*PAST_0PERFECTIVE_PARA*> shows that the Chinese translation is a paraphrase to which an aspectual analysis does not apply. By examining these tags in the Chinese translation of a corresponding concordance, you will be able to establish a translation pattern of the simple past. Here you will notice that verbs taking the simple past form are found primarily in texts numbers 15 and 18, as shown in Figure C6.8. For the moment, we will simply note this phenomenon, though we will return to consider this observation in Unit C6.6.

Table C6.6 shows the translation pattern of the simple past. It is clear that verbs taking the simple past form are translated primarily as perfective (95 per cent), either marked overtly or taking the LVM form. This is as expected, because the English simple past normally marks situations that were completed or terminated in the past. In Chinese, situations of this type are most frequently expressed by the actual aspect (either marked by -*le* or taking the LVM form) and the completive aspect (marked by RVCs), because the former indicates the actualization while the latter indicates the completiveness of a situation. It is also interesting to note that aspectual meanings are frequently marked covertly in Chinese discourse, even though Chinese is rich in aspect markers. If we discount the three instances of paraphrase, the translated texts register a marked/LVM ratio of 0.222:1.

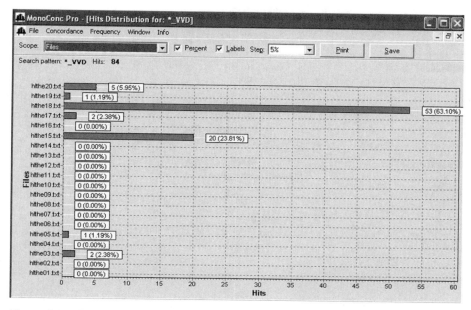

Figure C6.8 The distribution of the simple past in CEPC

Table C6.6 Translation pattern of the simple past

Simple past translated as	Aspect marker in Chinese	Freq.
Perfective	-le	10
	Negation	1
	RVC	4
	-le + RVC	2
	LVM	63
Imperfective	-xiaqu	1
Paraphrase		3
Total		84

C6.3.4.2 The simple present

As the simple present form of a lexical verb is tagged as *VV0* or *VVZ*, you will need to search for the corpus twice using the search patterns *_VV0* and *_VVZ*. There are 735 matches for the first search pattern and 212 matches for the second. In the Chinese translations, the annotation scheme for the simple present is the same as that used for the simple past with the exception that *PAST* is replaced by *PRESENT*. The annotation indicates whether the simple present is translated as perfective (+PERFECTIVE), imperfective (−PERFECTIVE), or is paraphrased or omitted in translations and is thus irrelevant to perfectivity (0PERFECTIVE). It also shows how the aspectual meaning denoted by the simple present is marked in Chinese translations, e.g., taking -*le*, -*guo*, RVC, or paraphrased or omitted. With the help of

Table C6.7 Translation pattern of the simple present

Simple present translated as		Translated into Chinese as	Freq.
Perfective		-le	9
		-guo	1
	Marked	RVC	61
		Negation	2
		-le + RVC	3
		Negation + RVC	1
	LVM		810
Imperfective		(zheng . . .)-zhe	10
	Marked	(zheng)zai	7
		zheng	1
		-qilai	1
Others		Paraphrase	35
		Omission	5
		As original	1
Total			947

this annotation scheme, you will be able to see the general pattern of how the English simple present is translated into Chinese, as shown in Table C6.7. It can be seen from the table that, as with the simple past, when situations referred to by the English simple present are overtly marked in Chinese translations, they most frequently take RVCs and the actual -le. Since states do not have to be marked aspectually, the majority of situations expressed by the simple present take the LVM form in Chinese translations. If we discount the frequencies in the *Others* category, a much lower marked/LVM ratio (0.106:1) than that for the simple past is found in Chinese translations.

C6.4 TRANSLATION AND ASPECT MARKING

The discussion in Unit C6.3 showed that the marked/LVM ratios in Chinese translations for English aspect markers are exceptionally low. We hypothesize that the relatively low frequency of aspect markers in translated texts is a result of translation choices and is atypical in L1 Chinese. In this section, we will test this hypothesis using a comparable corpus of L1 Chinese, C-health. As the distribution of aspect markers may vary across domain and text type (see Units C6.5 and C6.6), C-health was constructed using roughly the same sampling frame as that used for the CEPC-health corpus. Like the CEPC parallel corpus, the comparable L1 Chinese corpus is also semantically annotated in addition to POS tagging.

To test the above hypothesis, we will experiment with two well-established perfective aspect markers in Chinese, -*le* and -*guo*, which are tagged in the C-health corpus respectively as *ACTL* and *EXPG*. Two additional tags were added to simplify the concordancing process. Verbs marked by -*le* or -*guo* were labelled as <MARKED> while the others are labelled as <LVM> unless they take a modal auxiliary.

It is a straightforward process to get the frequencies of marked cases in C-health using MonoConc Pro. Simply load the two corpus files named *narrative.txt* and *expository.txt* in the directory for the C-health corpus and type in the search string *MARKED* (see Case Study 2 for the use of MonoConc Pro). There are 213 matches. The frequencies of marked cases (i.e., verbs taking -*le* or -*guo*) in the translated texts in the CEPC parallel corpus can be obtained by loading the twenty corpus files whose filenames start with *hlthc* in the subdirectory *Chinese* (but remember to unload the C-health corpus first) and use the batch search function of MonoConc Pro, typing in the search patterns *_ACTL and *_EXPG. There are 98 concordances for the search strings.

Table C6.8 shows the frequencies of the two perfective markers in both corpora. As can be seen from the table, the normalized frequency of perfective markers is twice as high in the L1 Chinese comparable corpus as in the translated texts. The calculated log-likelihood (LL) score 49.113 is much greater than 10.83, the critical value for significance at p<0.001 (1 d.f.). In other words, the difference in the distribution of perfective aspect markers in L1 Chinese texts and in the translated texts is statistically significant.

A closer examination of the marked/LVM ratio in the Chinese translations of the tensed verbs in CEPC-health English texts illustrates this point well. Table C6.9 shows the distribution of tensed verbs in CEPC-health English texts. In the table the column *Marked* only includes the counts of -*le* and -*guo*, and the column *Others* includes the instances of paraphrase, omission and imperfective viewpoints in the Chinese translations. If we discount the instances in the *Others* column, the marked cases account for only 4.79 per cent of the total instances of perfectives, registering a marked/LVM ratio of 0.05:1. This is in sharp contrast with L1 Chinese data in the C-health corpus, as shown in Table C6.10.

Table C6.8 Perfective markers in CEPC-health Chinese texts and C-health

Corpus	Tokens	Perfective markers	Freq. per 10k tokens	LL (1 d.f.)
C-health	34,174	213	62.33	
				49.113
CEPC-health	35,877	98	27.32	

Table C6.9 Translations of tensed verbs in CEPC-health

Aspect	Marked	LVM	Others	Total
Simple present	13	874	60	947
Simple past	12	68	4	84
Perfect	23	78	7	108
Progressive	3	27	54	84
Perf. progressive	2	6	0	8
Total	53	1,053	125	1,231

Table C6.10 Predicates in L1 Chinese texts

Corpus	Marked	LVM	Marked/LVM	Marked %	LL value
CEPC-health	53	1,053	0.05:1	4.79%	15.792
C-health	213	2,329	0.09:1	8.38%	

To match the counting procedure applied to CEPC-health English texts, verbs that take a modal auxiliary or do not function as predicates are not annotated and thus not counted. It can be seen from the table that the marked/LVM ratio in L1 Chinese texts is nearly twice as high as that in the translated texts. This difference is statistically significant, as indicated by the calculated log-likelihood score 15.792, which is considerably greater than the critical value 10.83 for significance at $p<0.001$.

Note that the frequencies obtained from C-health include all predicates, whether they are stative or dynamic. The frequencies from the CEPC-health corpus, however, include only lexical verbs. If we include verbs BE and HAVE, a more marked contrast between translated texts and L1 Chinese texts is expected, because the two verbs are most frequently translated as statives and take the LVM form in translations. Furthermore, verbs taking the LVM form in translations for the progressive fall under the category of *Others* in Tables C6.9 and C6.10, whereas the frequency of LVM cases from C-health includes all verbs taking the LVM form, irrespective of whether an LVM form denotes a perfective or imperfective meaning, because such information is not annotated in the corpus. If we classified LVM verbs that are used imperfectively as *Others*, the contrast between translations and L1 texts would have been even more marked.

C6.5 DOMAIN AND ASPECT MARKING

Table C6.10 shows that the frequencies of perfective aspect markers in both C-health and the translated texts in CEPC-health are rather low. Even if we discount the effect of translation on the distribution of aspect markers and consider L1 Chinese data alone, there are only 62.33 occurrences of -*le* and -*guo* per 10,000 tokens (see Table C6.11). As Chinese is an aspect language and hence aspect markers are supposed to occur more frequently, we hypothesize that the distribution of aspect markers varies across domain.

In this section, we will test this hypothesis by comparing the distribution of -*le* and -*guo* in the C-health corpus and the Weekly corpus. C-health is confined to only one domain, i.e. public health, while the Weekly corpus covers mixed domains. We already have the frequency of the marked cases in the C-health corpus. To get the frequencies of -*le* and -*guo* in the Weekly training and test corpora, simply load the two corpora separately (but again, remember to unload the previous texts first) and type in *_ACTL, *_DUAL, and *_EXPG, where *DUAL* is the POS tag for -*le*

Table C6.11 Frequencies of perfective aspect markers

Corpus	Tokens	Raw freq.	Freq. per 10k tokens
Weekly training	96,897	1,117	115.28
Weekly test	10,054	132	123.29
C-health	34,174	213	62.33

functioning as both a perfective marker and a change-of-state (COS) or sentence-final *le*. There are 1,019 matches of *ACTL*, 23 matches of *DUAL* and 75 matches of *EXPG* in the training corpus, and 119 instances of *ACTL*, 4 instances of *DUAL* and 9 instances of *EXPG* in the test corpus. Table C6.11 gives the frequencies of -*le* and -*guo* in the corpora.

As Tables C6.12 and C6.13 show, while the two perfective markers are slightly more frequent in the test corpus than in the training corpus, the difference is not statistically significant (the LL value is 1.907, less than 3.84, the critical value for significance at $p<0.05$). In contrast, the difference between Weekly as a whole and C-health is statistically significant (the LL value is 82.087) at $p<0.001$, the critical value for which is 10.83. Perfective aspect markers appear in the Weekly corpus nearly three times as frequently as in the C-health corpus.

Table C6.12 The Weekly training vs. the Weekly test corpus

			Size_marker		Total
			Freq. of markers	Corpus size	
Corpus	Test	Count	132	10054	10186
		Expected Count	117.6	10068.4	10186.0
	Training	Count	1117	96897	98014
		Expected count	1131.4	96882.6	98014.0
Total		Count	1249	106951	108200
		Expected Count	1249.0	106951.0	108200.0
Pearson chi-square		1.975	Log-likelihood (LL)		1.907

Table C6.13 The Weekly corpus vs. the C-health corpus

			Size_marker		Total
			Freq. of markers	Corpus size	
Corpus	C-health	Count	213	34174	34387
		Expected count	352.6	34034.4	34387.0
	Weekly	Count	1249	106951	108200
		Expected count	1109.4	107090.6	108200.0
Total		Count	1462	141125	142587
		Expected count	1462.0	141125.0	142587.0
Pearson chi-square		73.576	Log-likelihood (LL)		82.087

C6.6   TEXT TYPE AND ASPECT MARKING

The perfective aspect is expressed most commonly by the simple past in English (see Brinton 1988: 52). As you may have noticed in Unit C6.3.4.1, the majority of the verbs taking the simple past form were found in only two texts: *Drugs – a Parent's Guide* (*hlthe15.txt*) and *Solvents – a Parent's Guide* (*hlthe18.txt*). These two texts constitute around one third of the English data in the parallel corpus and are primarily narrative in nature, showing what certain parents did to help their children stop their drug and solvent abuse. The other two thirds of the English texts in the corpus are expository writings and only contain a dozen instances of *VVD*. As such, we hypothesize that different text types may have an influence on aspect marking. In this section, we will test this hypothesis by examining the relation between the frequency of simple past forms and the number of tokens in the two text types in the English data and the relation between verbs taking -*le* or -*guo* in the two text types in the C-health corpus.

To discover the frequency of verbs taking the simple past form in the narratives in the parallel corpus, you need to initialize the concordancer by unloading previous corpus files, and then load files named *hlthe15.txt* and *hlthe18.txt* in the subdirectory *English* in the file folder containing the CEPC-health parallel corpus. Type in the search pattern *_VVD. There are seventy-three matches. Do the same with the other files in that subdirectory. You will find only eleven matches. This means that the narrative texts that make up one third of the English texts in the parallel corpus account for 86.9 per cent of the total frequency of *VVD* while the expository texts that make up two thirds of the English data account for only 13.1 per cent.

It can be seen from Table C6.14 that the simple past occurs more than 12 times as frequently in narrative texts as in expository texts. The calculated log-likelihood score 65.216 is considerably greater than the critical value of 10.83 for significance at the level p<0.001, indicating that the two text types are indeed different (see Unit B5.3).

As perfectives in English are all marked, the marked/LVM distinction is irrelevant. In Chinese, however, perfectives can be overtly marked or take the LVM form in discourse. To find out if the above finding also applies to the Chinese data, we will first search the two components of the C-health corpus to get the frequencies of marked cases and LVM cases. Load the corpus file named *narrative.txt* in the directory for C-health and type in *MARKED* and *LVM* respectively. There are 94 instances of marked cases and 526 instances of LVM. Do the same for *expository.txt* in the same directory. There are 119 marked cases and 1,803 instances of LVM.

Table C6.15 shows the frequency of perfective aspect markers -*le* and -*guo* in the C-health corpus and other relevant statistics. In spite of the overall low frequencies of perfective markers in the domain of public health, there is a marked contrast between the two text types in the domain. Perfective markers occur 2.97 times as frequently in the narrative texts as in the expository texts (per 10,000 tokens). Both

Table C6.14 Text type vs. aspect marking in English (simple past)

Text type	Tokens	Raw freq.	Freq. per 10k tokens	LL value (1 d.f.)
Narrative texts	11,226	73	65.03	65.216
Expository texts	20,512	11	5.36	

Table C6.15 Text type vs. aspect marking in Chinese (*-le* and *-guo*)

Text type	Narrative texts	Expository texts
Number of tokens	7,167	27,007
Number of predicates	620	1,922
Raw frequency of markers	94	119
Frequency per 10k tokens	131.16	44.06
Marked per cent	15.16%	6.19%
Marked/LVM ratio	0.179:1	0.066:1

Table C6.16 Text type vs. aspect marking (LL test)

Text type	Marked	LVM	LL ratio (1 d.f.)	Sig. level
Narrative	94	526	43.656	p<0.001
Expository	119	1,803		

the proportion of marked cases and the marked/LVM ratio are more than twice as high in the narrative texts as in the expository texts. The LL test in Table C6.16 shows that the difference in the distribution of aspect markers in the two text types is indeed statistically significant.

In this section, we only experimented with two text types. However, our finding, that the distribution of aspect markers varies across text type, appears to be generalizable to other text types. Li, Thompson and Thompson (1982: 26–27), for example, also observe that the 'perfect' particle *le* is 'very rare in expository and scientific writing and practically non-existent in news-reporting, speeches, lectures, and proclamations'. Hence, we can claim that text types do indeed have an effect on aspect marking (see Unit B5.3).

Summary

In this unit, we investigated how aspectual meanings in English are translated into Chinese and explored the effects of translation, domains and text types on aspect marking. We used one English–Chinese parallel corpus and two L1 Chinese corpora (one comparable corpus and one reference corpus) in this unit to produce a number of findings based upon this data.

It was found that the English progressive can be translated into Chinese either as ongoing or as perfective. If a progressive form in an English source text refers to a habitual situation or an anticipated happening, the progressive aspect marker is not used in Chinese translation. We hypothesize that this is because the progressive in Chinese only corresponds to the canonical use of the English progressive.

Also, in English, the perfect of result is the most common of the four types of perfect identified by Comrie (1976). When perfect constructions are translated into Chinese, they more often than not depend on context to indicate the perfect meaning. This is because Chinese does not have a grammatical aspect marker for the perfect. In this case, however, aspect markers such as -*le* and -*guo* could be used to mark the perfective. Whether the translations take overt aspect markers or imply the perfect meaning contextually depends largely on the type of perfect in the English source text.

With reference to the simple aspect, we found that situations marked by the English simple aspect are mainly presented perfectively and most of them take the LVM form in Chinese translations. The high frequency of perfectives in translations of the simple aspect can be accounted for by the fact that the simple forms in English, the simple past in particular, are basically perfective in nature (see Brinton 1988). Translations of the simple past show a marked/LVM ratio twice as high as that in translations of the simple present. A natural explanation for this contrast is that the simple present typically denotes states, which do not have to be marked aspectually.

The use of translated data allowed us to discover that translated Chinese texts differ markedly from L1 Chinese texts with regard to aspect marking. The frequency of the perfective markers -*le* and -*guo* is nearly twice as high in L1 Chinese data as in translated Chinese texts. We hypothesize that this difference is a consequence of the potential influence of the translation process, since translators cannot rid themselves of the influence of the source language when translating.

Considering the L1 Chinese health corpus data in contrast to the other forms of data, it is apparent that in Chinese the frequency of aspect markers in the domain of public health is considerably lower than in the mixed domains. The perfective aspect markers -*le* and -*guo* distribute nearly three times as frequently in general domain as in the domain of public health. This can be explained by the fact that the domain of public health primarily contains texts of an expository nature and is concerned with general truth.

Finally, the distribution of aspect markers varies significantly between different text types even in the same domain. Perfective markers are more frequent in narratives than in expository writings. This is because narrative texts typically present situations that are actualized, experienced or completed in relation to a particular reference time whereas expository writings are primarily concerned with timeless states.

The above findings demonstrate the potential values of aligned parallel corpora and comparable L1 corpora in translation and contrastive language studies.

Methodologically, this unit also showed you how to explore parallel corpora using ParaConc and provided you with an opportunity to practise using MonoConc Pro with monolingual corpus data.

FURTHER STUDY

At this point you might wish to explore the CEPC-health parallel corpus to find out how the English simple future is translated into Chinese. The simple future in English is marked by *will, shall, be going to* and *be (about) to*. Will your observations support our findings concerning the effect of translation, domain and text type on aspect marking?

Glossary

AAVE	African American Vernacular English
ACE	the Australian Corpus of English, also known as the Macquarie Corpus
ACH	the Association for Computers and the Humanities
ACL	the Association for Computational Linguistics
alignment	establishing a link between the source text and the translation, usually at the sentence, phrase or word level
ALLC	the Association for Literary and Linguistic Computing
ANC	the American National Corpus
annotation	the process of encoding interpretative linguistic information in a corpus
ARCHER	a Representative Corpus of Historical English Registers
ASCII	American Standard Code for Information Interchange
authenticity	a feature that characterizes naturally occurring corpus data
BNC	the British National Corpus
BNCweb	the web interface of the BNC, developed at Zurich University
BoE	the Bank of English
Brown	the Brown University Standard Corpus of Present-day American English
CA	contrastive analysis
CANCODE	the Cambridge and Nottingham Corpus of Discourse in English
CDA	critical discourse analysis
CED	the Corpus of English Dialects

CEPC	Chinese–English Parallel Corpus
CES	the Corpus Encoding Standard
character encoding	a system of using numeric values to represent characters
CHILDES	the Child Language Data Exchange System
chi-square test	a measure of statistical significance
CIA	Contrastive Interlanguage Analysis
CKIP	the Chinese Knowledge Information Processing group at Academia Sinica, Taipei
CLC	Cambridge Learner Corpus
CLEC	Chinese Learner English Corpus
COCOA	one of the earliest mark-up schemes that uses a set of attribute names and values enclosed in angled brackets
colligation	the collocation of a node word with a particular grammatical class of words
collocation	the characteristic co-occurrence of patterns of words
comparable corpus	a corpus which is composed of L1 data collected from different languages using the same sampling techniques
comparative corpus	a corpus containing components of varieties of the same language
concordance	an alphabetical index of a search pattern in a corpus, showing every contextual occurrence of the search pattern
concordancer	a software package that extracts concordances from a corpus
corpora	the widely accepted plural form of corpus
corpus	a collection of sampled texts, written or spoken, in machine readable form which may be annotated with various forms of linguistic information
corpus balance	the range of different types of language that a corpus claims to cover
corpuses	a less commonly used plural form of corpus
corpus header	the part of a corpus that provides necessary bibliographical information, taxonomies used and other metadata relating to a corpus
CPE	the Corpus of Professional English
CPSA	the Corpus of Professional Spoken American English

cross-tabulation	a table showing the frequencies for each variable across each sample
CSAE	the Corpus of South African English
DCMI	the Dublin Core Metadata Initiative
DDL	data-driven learning
dispersion	a term in descriptive statistics which refers to a quantifiable variation of measurements of differing members of a population within the scale on which they are measured
ditto tag	in corpus annotation assigning the same part-of-speech code to each word in an idiomatic expression
DTD	Document Type Definitions in mark-up languages such as HTML, SGML and XML
EAGLES	Expert Advisory Group on Language Engineering Standards
EAP	English for academic purposes
EBMT	example-based machine translation
EFL	English as a foreign language
EMILLE	the Enabling Minority Language Engineering [project and corpora]
ENPC	the English–Norwegian Parallel Corpus
error-tagging	assigning codes indicating the types of errors occurring in a learner corpus
factor analysis	a statistical analysis commonly used in the social and behavioural sciences to summarize the interrelationships among a large group of variables in a concise fashion
Fisher's exact test	an alternative to the chi-square or log-likelihood test that measures exact statistical significance level
FLOB	the Freiburg–LOB Corpus of British English, an update of the LOB corpus in the early 1990s
frequency	also called raw frequency, the actual count of a linguistic feature in a corpus
Frown	the Freiburg–Brown Corpus of American English, an update of the BROWN corpus in the early 1990s
HKUST	the HKUST Computer Science Corpus
HTML	Hypertext Mark-up Language
ICE	the International Corpus of English

ICLE	the International Corpus of Learner English
IMDI	the ISLE Metadata Initiative
interlanguage	the learner's knowledge of the L2 which is independent of both the L1 and the actual L2
JEFLL	the Japanese EFL Learner Corpus
keyword	words in a corpus whose frequency is unusually high (positive keywords) or low (negative keywords) in comparison with a reference corpus
KWIC	keyword-in-context concordance
LCA	the Lancaster Corpus of Abuse
LCMC	the Lancaster Corpus of Mandarin Chinese
lemmatization	grouping together all of the different inflected forms of the same word
lexicon	an inventory of word forms in a given language
LGSWE	the *Longman Grammar of Spoken and Written English*
LIVAC	Linguistic Variations in Chinese Speech Communities, a synchronous corpus of Mandarin Chinese
LLC	the London–Lund Corpus; also found to refer to the Longman Learners' Corpus in the literature
LOB	the Lancaster–Oslo–Bergen Corpus of British English
LOCNESS	the Louvain Corpus of Native English Essays
log-likelihood test	also known as an LL test, an alternative to the chi-square test
LPC	the Lancaster Parsed Corpus
LSAC	the Longman Spoken American Corpus
LSP	language for specific purposes
mark-up	a system of standard codes inserted into a document stored in electronic form to provide information *about* the text itself and govern formatting, printing or other processing
MATE	the Multilevel Annotation Tools Engineering [project]
mean	the arithmetic average, which can be calculated by adding all of the scores together and then dividing the sum by the number of scores
merger	combination of two or more words (e.g. *can't* and *gonna*)

metadata	a term used to describe data about data, typically the contextual information of corpus samples
MI	mutual information, a statistical formula borrowed from information theory
MICASE	the Michigan Corpus of Academic Spoken English
Microconcord	a concordance package published by Oxford University Press
ML	machine learning
MLCT	the Multilingual Corpus Tool package developed by Scott Songlin Piao
monitor corpus	a corpus that is constantly supplemented with fresh material and keeps increasing in size
MonoConc	a concordancer package published by Athelstan
MUC	Message Understanding Conference
Multiconcord	a multilingual parallel concordancer developed at the University of Birmingham
MWU	multiword unit
NLP	natural-language processing
normalization	a process which makes frequencies from samples of markedly different sizes comparable by bringing them to a common base
OCR	optical character recognition
OLAC	the Open Language Archives Community
ParaConc	a bilingual or multilingual concordancer published by Athelstan
parallel corpus	a corpus which is composed of source texts and their translations in one or more different languages; sometimes referred to as translation corpus
parsing	also called treebanking or bracketing, a process that analyses the sentences in a corpus into their constituents
PERC	the Professional English Research Consortium
PNC	the Polish National Corpus
population	the entire set of items from which samples can be drawn
POS	part of speech
post-editing	human correction of automatically processed data

range	the difference between the highest and lowest frequencies
reference corpus	a balanced representative corpus for general usage; in keyword analysis, a corpus that is used to provide a reference wordlist
representativeness	a corpus is thought to be representative of the language variety it is supposed to represent if the findings based on its contents can be generalized to the said language variety
RP	Received Pronunciation, the notional standard form of spoken British English
sample	elements that are selected intentionally as a representation of the population being studied
sample corpus	as opposed to a monitor corpus, a sample corpus is of finite size and consists of text segments selected to provide a static snapshot of language
SARA	SGML Aware Retrieval Application for the BNC
SBCSAE	the Santa Barbara Corpus of Spoken American English
SEC	the Lancaster/IBM Spoken English Corpus
SED	the Survey of English Dialects corpus
semantic prosody	the collocational meaning arising from the interaction between a given node word and its collocates
SEU	Survey of English Usage
SGML	the Standard Generalized Mark-up Language
skeleton parsing	also called shallow parsing, a parsing technique that uses less fine-grained constituent types than would be present in a full parse
SLA	second language acquisition
sort	arrange concordances or a wordlist in a certain order
SPAAC	the Speech Act Annotated Corpus developed at UCREL Lancaster
specialized corpus	a corpus that is domain or genre specific and is designed to represent a sub-language
SPSS	Statistical Package for the Social Sciences
SST	the Standard Speaking Test corpus consisting of spoken data produced by Japanese learners of English
standardized type-token ratio	similar to TYPE-TOKEN RATIO, but computed every n (e.g. 1,000) words as the WordSmith Wordlist goes through each text file

subcorpus	a component of a corpus, usually defined using certain criteria such as text types and domains
tagging	an alternative term for annotation, especially word-level annotation such as POS tagging and semantic tagging
tagset	a scheme of codes for corpus annotation, especially POS tagging
TEI	the Text Encoding Initiative
token	an occurrence of any given word form
tokenization	also called segmentation, a process that divides running text into legitimate word tokens, especially important for languages such as Chinese that do not delimit words with white spaces
transcription	converting spoken data into a written form
translationese	a version of L1 language that has been influenced by the translation process
treebank	an alternative term for a parsed corpus
t-test	an alternative statistical test to the chi-square test
type	a word form
type-token ratio	the ratio between types and tokens, useful when comparing samples of roughly equal length
UCL	University College London
UCLES	the University of Cambridge Local Examinations Syndicate
UCREL	the University Centre for Computer Corpus Research on Language, Lancaster
Unicode	a character-encoding system designed to support the interchange, processing and display of all of the written texts of the diverse languages of the world
URL	uniform resource locator, i.e. an Internet address
USAS	the UCREL Semantic Analysis System
UTF	Unicode Transformation Format
wildcard	a special character such as an asterisk (*) or a question mark (?) that can be used to represent one or more characters in pattern matching
wordlist	a list of words occurring in a corpus, possibly with frequency information

WordSmith	a corpus exploration package with sophisticated statistical analysis, published by Oxford University Press
WSC	the Wellington Corpus of Spoken New Zealand English
WWC	the Wellington Corpus of Written New Zealand English
Xaira	XML Aware Indexing and Retrieval Architecture, a new XML-aware version of SARA that can work with different corpora
Xanadu	an X-windows interactive editor for anaphoric annotation, developed at Lancaster UCREL
XCES	XML Corpus Encoding Standard
XML	the Extensive Mark-up Language
z-test:	an alternative statistical test to the CHI-SQUARE TEST

Bibliography

Aarts, B. 2001. 'Corpus linguistics, Chomsky and fuzzy tree fragments' in C. Mair and M. Hundt (eds) *Corpus Linguistics and Linguistic Theory*, pp. 5–13. Amsterdam: Rodopi.

Aarts, J. 1998. 'Introduction' in S. Johansson and S. Oksefjell (eds) *Corpora and Cross-linguistic Research*, pp. ix–xiv. Amsterdam: Rodopi.

Aarts, J. 2002. 'Review of *Corpus Linguistics at Work*'. *International Journal of Corpus Linguistics* 7/1: 118–123.

Aarts, J. and Meijs, W. (eds) 1984. *Corpus Linguistics*. Amsterdam: Rodopi.

Aijmer, K. 1987. '*Oh* and *ah* in English conversation' in W. Meijs (ed.) *Corpus Linguistics and Beyond*, pp. 61–86. Amsterdam: Rodopi.

Aijmer, K., Altenberg, B. and Johansson, M. (eds) 1996. *Language in Contrast: Papers from a Symposium on Text-based Cross-linguistic Studies, Lund, March 1994*. Lund: Lund University Press.

Alderson, C. 1996. 'Do corpora have a role in language assessment?' in J. Thomas and M. Short (eds) *Using Corpora for Language Research*, pp. 248–259. London: Longman.

Alexandersson, J., Buschbeck-Wolf, B., Fujinami, T., Maier, E., Reithinger, N., Schmitz, B. and Siegel, M. 1997. 'Dialogue acts in VERBMOBIL-2'. VM-Report 204, DFKI GmbH, Stuhlsatzenhausweg 3, 66123 Saarbrücken.

Allan, Q. 1999. 'Enhancing the language awareness of Hong Kong teachers through corpus data'. *Journal of Technology and Teacher Education* 7/1: 57–74.

Allan, Q. 2002. 'The TELEC secondary learner corpus: a resource for teacher development' in S. Granger, J. Hung and S. Petch-Tyson (eds) *Computer Learner Corpora, Second Language Acquisition and Foreign Language Teaching*, pp. 195–212. Philadelphia: John Benjamins.

Allen, J., Bradford, W., Ringger, E. and Sikorshi, T. 1996. 'A robust system for natural spoken dialogue' in Association for Computational Linguistics (ed.) *Proceedings of the Annual Meeting*, pp. 62–70.

Altenberg, B. and Granger, S. 2001. 'The grammatical and lexical patterning of MAKE in native and non-native student writing'. *Applied Linguistics* 22/2: 173–195.

Altenberg, B. and Granger, S. 2002. 'Recent trends in cross-linguistic lexical studies' in B. Altenberg and S. Granger (eds) *Lexis in Contrast*, pp. 3–48. Amsterdam: John Benjamins.

Amsler, R. 2002. In Corpora List Archive 'Legal aspects of corpora compiling'. URL: http://helmer.hit.uib.no/corpora/2002–3/0256.html

Anderson, A., Bader, M., Bard, E., Boyle, E., Doherty, G., Garrod, S., Isard, S., Kowtko, J., McAllister, J., Miller, J., Sotillo, C., Thompson, H. and Weinert, R. 1991. 'The HCRC Map Task Corpus'. *Language and Speech* 34/4: 351–366.

Andersson, L. and Trudgill, P. 1992. *Bad Language*. London: Penguin.

Archer, D. and Culpeper, J. 2001. 'Sociopragmatic annotation: new directions and possibilities in historical corpus linguistics' in P. Rayson, A. Wilson, A. McEnery, A.

Hardie and S. Khoja (eds) *Proceedings of Corpus Linguistics 2001*. Lancaster: Lancaster University.

Arnovick, L. 2000. *Diachronic Pragmatics*. Amsterdam: John Benjamins.

Aston, G. (ed.) 2001. *Learning with Corpora*. Houston, TX: Athelstan.

Aston, G. 1995. 'Corpora in language pedagogy: matching theory and practice' in G. Cook and B. Seidlhofer (eds) *Principle and Practice in Applied Linguistics: Studies in Honour of H. G. Widdowson*, pp. 257–270. Oxford: Oxford University Press.

Aston, G. 1999. 'Corpus use and learning to translate'. *Textus* 12: 289–314. URL: http://home.sslmit.unibo.it/~guy/textus.htm

Aston, G., Bernardini, S. and Stewart, D. (eds) 2004. *Corpora and Language Learners*. Amsterdam: John Benjamins.

Aston, G. and Burnard, L. 1998. *The BNC Handbook*. Edinburgh: Edinburgh University Press.

Atkins, B. and Levin, B. 1995. 'Building on a corpus: a linguistics and lexicographical look at some near synonyms'. *International Journal of Corpus Linguistics* 8/2: 85–114.

Atkins, S., Clear, J. and Ostler, N. 1992. 'Corpus design criteria'. *Literary and Linguistic Computing* 7/1: 1–16.

Atkinson, D. 1992. 'The evolution of medical research writing from 1735 to 1985: the case of the *Edinburgh Medical Journal*'. *Applied Linguistics* 13: 337–374.

Atkinson, D. 1993. 'A historical discourse analysis of scientific research writing from 1675 to 1975: the case of the philosophical transactions of the Royal Society of London'. Ph.D. thesis. University of Southern California.

Bahns, J. 1993. 'Lexical collocations: a contrastive view'. *ELT Journal* 47/1: 56–63.

Baker, M. 1993. 'Corpus linguistics and translation studies: implications and applications' in M. Baker, G. Francis and E. Tognini-Bonelli (eds) *Text and Technology: in Honour of John Sinclair*, pp. 233–352. Amsterdam: Benjamins.

Baker, M. 1995. 'Corpora in translation studies: an overview and some suggestions for future research'. *Target* 7: 223–243.

Baker, M. 1999. 'The role of corpora in investigating the linguistic behaviour of professional translators'. *International Journal of Corpus Linguistics* 4: 281–298.

Baker, P. 2004. '"Unnatural acts": discourses of homosexuality within the House of Lords debate gay male law reform'. *Journal of Sociolinguistics* 8/1: 88–106.

Baker, P., Hardie, A., McEnery, A., Xiao, R., Bontcheva, K., Cunningham, H., Gaizauskas, R., Hamza, O., Maynard, D., Tablan, V., Ursu, C., Jayaram B. and Leisher, M. 2004. 'Corpus linguistics and South Asian languages: corpus creation and tool development'. *Literary and Linguistic Computing* 19/4: 509–524.

Baldauf, C. 1999. 'Forensic linguistics in Germany'. Paper presented at IAFL Conference '99. University of Birmingham, 28 June–1 July 1999.

Ball, F. 2001. 'Using corpora in language testing'. *Research Notes* 6: 6–8.

Ball, F. 2002. 'Developing wordlists for BEC'. *Research Notes* 8: 10–13.

Ball, F. and Wilson, J. 2002. 'Research projects relating to YLE Speaking Tests'. *Research Notes* 7: 8–10.

Banjo, A. 1996. 'The sociolinguistics of English in Nigeria and the ICE project' in S. Greenbaum (ed.) *Comparing English Worldwide: The International Corpus of English*, pp. 239–248. Oxford: Clarendon Press.

Baranowski, M. 2002. 'Current usage of the epicene pronoun in written English'. *Journal of Sociolinguistics* 6/3: 378–397.

Barlow, M. 1995. *A Guide to ParaConc*. Houston, TX: Athelstan.

Barlow, M. 1998. *A Corpus of Spoken Professional American English*. Houston, TX: Athelstan.

Barlow, M. 2000. 'Parallel texts and language teaching' in S. Botley, A. McEnery and A. Wilson (eds) *Multilingual Corpora in Teaching and Research*, pp. 106–115. Amsterdam: Rodopi.

Barnbrook, G. 1996. *Language and Computers*. Edinburgh: Edinburgh University Press.

Bauer, L. 2002. 'Inferring variation and change from public corpora' in J. Chambers, P. Trudgill and N. Schilling-Estes (eds) *Handbook of Language Variation and Change*, pp. 97–114. Oxford: Blackwell.

Beare, J. and Scott, B. 1999. 'The spoken corpus of the Survey of English Dialects: language variation and oral history'. Paper presented ar ACH-ALLC '99 International Humanities Computing Conference, June 1999. Charlottesville, Virginia. URL: http://www.iath.virginia.edu/ach-allc.99/proceedings/scott.html

Belica, C. 1996. 'Analysis of temporal change in corpora'. *International Journal of Corpus Linguistics* 1/1: 61–74.

Benson, M., Benson, E. and Ilson, R. 1986. *The BBI Combinatory Dictionary of English: A Guide to Word Combinations*. Amsterdam: John Benjamins.

Berber-Sardinha, T. 1998. 'Size of a representative corpus'. URL: http://nora.hd.uib.no/corpora/1998–3/0107.html

Berglund, Y. 2000. 'Utilising present-day English corpora: a case study concerning expressions of future'. *ICAME Journal* 24: 25–63.

Bernardini, S. 1997. 'A "trainee" translator's perspective on corpora'. Paper presented at the Conference on Corpus Use and Learning to Translate. Bertinoro, November 1997.

Berry-Rogghe, G. 1972. 'The computation of collocations and their relevance in lexical studies' in J. Aarts and W. Meijs (eds) *Theory and Practice in Corpus Linguistics*. Amsterdam: Rodopi.

Besnier, N. 1988. 'The linguistic relationships of spoken and written Nukulaelae registers'. *Language* 64: 707–736.

Biber, D. 1985. 'Investigating macroscopic textual variation through multifeature /multidimensional analysis'. *Linguistics* 23: 337–360.

Biber, D. 1987. 'A textual comparison of British and American writing'. *American Speech* 62: 99–119.

Biber, D. 1988. *Variation Across Speech and Writing*. Cambridge: Cambridge University Press.

Biber, D. 1989. 'A typology of English texts'. *Linguistics* 27: 3–43.

Biber, D. 1990. 'Methodological issues regarding corpus based analyses of linguistic variation'. *Literary and Linguistic Computing* 5/4: 257–269.

Biber, D. 1991. 'Oral and literate characteristics of selected primary school reading materials'. *Text* 11: 73–96.

Biber, D. 1993. 'Representativeness in corpus design'. *Literary and Linguistic Computing* 8/4: 243–257.

Biber, D. 1995a. 'On the role of computational, statistical, and interpretive techniques in multidimensional analysis of register variation: a reply to Watson'. *Text* 15/3: 341–370.

Biber, D. 1995b. *Dimensions of Register Variation: A Cross-Linguistic Comparison*. Cambridge: Cambridge University Press.

Biber, D. 2003. 'Lexical bundles in academic speech and writing' in B. Lewandowska-Tomaszczyk (ed.) *Practical Applications in Language and Computers*, pp. 165–178. Frankfurt: Peter Lang.

Biber, D. 2004. 'Historical patterns for the grammatical marking of stance: a cross-register comparison'. *Journal of Historical Pragmatics* 5/1: 107–136.

Biber, D. and Conrad, S. 1999. 'Lexical bundles in conversation and academic prose' in

H. Hasselgard and S. Oksefjell (eds) *Out of Corpora: Studies in Honour of Stig. Johansson*, pp. 181–189. Amsterdam: Rodopi.

Biber, D., Conrad, S. and Reppen, R. 1998. *Corpus Linguistics: Investigating Language Structure and Use*. Cambridge: Cambridge University Press.

Biber, D. and Finegan, E. 1989. 'Drift and evolution of English style: a history of three genres'. *Language* 65: 487–517.

Biber, D. and Finegan, E. 1991. 'On the exploitation of computerized corpora in variation studies' in K. Aijmer and B. Altenberg (eds) *English Corpus Linguistics*, pp. 204–220. London: Longman.

Biber, D. and Finegan, E. 1992. 'The linguistic evolution of five written and speech-based English genres from the 17th to the 20th centuries' in M. Rissanen, O. Ihalainen and T. Nevalainen (eds) *History of Englishes: New Methods and Interpretations in Historical Linguistics*, pp. 688–704. Berlin: Mouton.

Biber, D. and Finegan, E. (eds) 1994a. *Sociolinguistic Perspectives on Register*. New York: Oxford University Press.

Biber, D. and Finegan, E. 1994b. 'Multi-dimensional analyses of authors' style: some case studies from the eighteenth century' in D. Ross and D. Brink (eds) *Research in Humanities Computing 3*, pp. 3–17. Oxford: Oxford University Press.

Biber, D. and Hared, M. 1992. 'Dimensions of register variation in Somali'. *Language Variation and Change* 4: 41–75.

Biber, D. and Hared, M. 1994. 'Linguistic correlates of the transition to literary in Somali: language adaptation in six press registers' in D. Biber and E. Finegan (eds) *Sociolinguistic Perspectives on Register*, pp. 182–216. New York: Oxford University Press.

Biber, D., Johansson S., Leech G., Conrad S. and Finegan, E. 1999. *Longman Grammar of Spoken and Written English*. London: Longman.

Binongo, J. and Smith, M. 1999a. 'The application of principal component analysis to stylometry'. *Literary and Linguistic Computing* 14/4: 445–465.

Binongo, J. and Smith, M. 1999b. 'A bridge between statistics and literature: the graphs of Oscar Wilde's literary genres'. *Journal of Applied Linguistics* 26/7: 781–787.

Bird, S. and Simons, G. 2000. *White Paper on Establishing an Infrastructure for Open Language Archiving*. URL: http://www.language-archives.org/docs/white-paper.html

Boas, F. 1940. *Race, Language and Culture*. New York: Macmillan.

Bolinger, D. 1974. 'Concept and percept: two infinitive constructions and their vicissitudes' in Phonetic Society of Japan (ed.) *World Papers in Phonetics: Festschrift for Dr Onishi Kijer*, pp. 65–91. Tokyo: Phonetic Society of Japan.

Botley, S., McEnery, A. and Wilson, A. 2000. *Multilingual Corpora in Teaching and Research*. Amsterdam: Rodopi.

Botley, S. and McEnery, A. 2001. 'Demonstratives in English: a corpus-based study'. *Journal of English Linguistics* 29: 7–33.

Botley, S. and Uzar, R. 1998. 'Higher quality data-driven learning through the testing of definite and indefinite articles' in *TALC '98. Teaching and Language Corpora*. Oxford: Oxford University Press.

Bowker, L. 1998. 'Using specialized native-language corpora as a translation resource: a pilot study'. *Meta* 43/4. URL: http://www.erudit.org/revue/meta/1998/v43/n4/003425ar.pdf

Bowker, L. 2000. 'Towards a methodology for exploiting specialized target language corpora as translation resources'. *International Journal of Corpus Linguistics* 5/1: 17–52.

Bowker, L. 2001. 'Towards a methodology for a corpus-based approach to translation evaluation'. *Meta* 46/2: 345–364.

Brems, L. 2003. 'Measure noun constructions: an instance of semantically-driven gram-maticalization'. *International Journal of Corpus Linguistics* 8/2: 283–312.

Brinton, L. 1988. *The Development of English Aspectual Systems*. Cambridge: Cambridge University Press.

Brown, P., Lai, J. and Mercer, R. 1991. 'Aligning sentences in parallel corpora' in *Proceedings of the 29th Annual Meeting of the Association for Computational Linguistics*, pp. 169–176. Berkeley, CA.

Brown, R. 1973. *A First Language: The Early Stages*. Cambridge, MA: Harvard University Press.

Bryman, A. and Cramer, D. 2001. *Quantitative Data Analysis with SPSS Release 10 for Windows*. London: Routledge.

Burnard, L. 2002. *Validation Manual for Written Language Resources*. URL: http://www. oucs.ox.ac.uk/rts/elra/D1.xml

Burnard, L. and McEnery, A. (eds) 2000. *Rethinking Language Pedagogy from a Corpus Perspective*. New York: Peter Lang.

Burnard, L. and Todd, T. 2003. 'Xara: an XML aware tool for corpus searching' in D. Archer, P. Rayson, A. Wilson and A. McEnery (eds) *Proceedings of Corpus Linguistics 2003*, pp. 142–144. Lancaster University.

Butler, C. 1992. *Computers and Written Texts*. Oxford: Blackwell.

Butterfield, J. and Krishnamurthy, R. 2000. 'Beyond the dictionary: on-line learning in the classroom'. *TESOL Spain Newsletter* 23:3–5.

Buyse, K. 1997. 'The study of multi- and unilingual corpora as a tool for the development of translation studies: a case study'. Paper presented at the conference on Corpus Use and Learning to Translate. Bertinoro, November 1997.

Bye, C. 1980. 'The acquisition of grammatical morphemes in Quiche Mayan'. Ph.D. thesis. University of Pittsburgh.

Caldas-Coulthard, C. and Moon, R. 1999. 'Curvy, hunky, kinky: using corpora as tools in critical analysis'. Paper presented at the Critical Discourse Analysis Meeting. University of Birmingham, April 1999.

Carletta, J. and Isard, A. 1999. 'The MATE annotation workbench: user requirements' in *Proceedings of the ACL Workshop: Towards Standards and Tools for Discourse Tagging*, pp. 11–17. University of Maryland, June 1999.

Carter, R. 1999. 'Common language: corpus, creativity and cognition'. *Language and Literature* 8/3: 195–216.

Carter, R. and McCarthy, M. 1988. *Vocabulary and Language Teaching*. London: Longman.

Carter, R. and McCarthy, M. 1995. 'Grammar and the spoken language'. *Applied Linguistics* 16/2: 141–158.

Carter, R. and McCarthy, M. 1997. *Exploring Spoken English*. Cambridge: Cambridge University Press.

Carter, R. and McCarthy, M. 1999. 'The English *get*-passive in spoken discourse: description and implication for an interpersonal grammar'. *English Language and Literature* 3/1: 41–58.

Carter, R. and McCarthy, M. 2004. 'Talking, creating: interactional language, creativity, and context'. *Applied Linguistics* 25/1: 62–88.

Chalker, S. 1984. *Current English grammar*. London: Macmillan.

Chambers, J., Trudgill, P. and Schilling-Estes, N. (eds) 2002. *Handbook of Language Variation and Change*. Oxford: Blackwell.

Chang, C. and Chen, C. 1993. 'HMM-based part-of-speech tagging for Chinese corpora' in *Proceedings of the Workshop on Very Large Corpora, WVLC-1*, pp. 40–47. Ohio State University.

Chang, V. 1986. 'The particle LE in Chinese narrative discourse: an investigative description'. Ph.D. thesis. University of Florida.

Chen, K., Liu, S., Chang, L. and Chin, Y. 1994. 'Practical tagger for Chinese corpora' in *Proceedings of ROCLING VII*, pp. 111–126.

Chief, L., Huang, C., Chen, K., Tsai, M. and Chang, L. 2000. 'What can near synonyms tell us?' *Computational Linguistics and Chinese Language Processing* 5/1: 47–60.

Choi, I., Kim, K. and Boo, J. 2003. 'Comparability of a paper-based language test and a computer-based language test'. *Language Testing* 20/3: 295–320.

Chomsky, N. 1962. Paper given at the University of Texas 1958, 3rd Texas Conference on Problems of Linguistic Analysis in English. University of Texas.

Christensen, M. 1994. 'Variation in spoken and written Mandarin narrative discourse'. Ph.D. thesis. Ohio State University.

Chu, C. 1987. 'The semantics, syntax, and pragmatics of the verbal suffix *zhe*'. *Journal of Chinese Language Teachers Association* 22/1: 1–41.

Church, K. and Hanks, P. 1990. 'Word association norms, mutual information and lexicography'. *Computational Linguistics* 16/1: 22–29.

Church, K., Hanks, P. and Moon, R. 1994. 'Lexical substitutability' in B. Atkins and A. Zampolli (eds) *Computational Approaches to the Lexicon*, pp. 153–177. Oxford: Oxford University Press.

Close, R. 1988. *A Reference Grammar for Students of English*. London: Longman.

Coates, J. 1999. 'Women behaving badly: female speakers backstage'. *Journal of Sociolinguistics* 3/1: 65–80.

Collins, M. 1997. 'Three generative, lexicalized models for statistical parsing' in *Proceedings of the 34th Annual Meeting of the ACL (ACL '97)*, pp. 16–23. Madrid.

Collins, P. and Hollo, C. 2000. *English Grammar: An Introduction*. London: Macmillan.

Comrie, B. 1976. *Aspect*. Cambridge: Cambridge University Press.

Comrie, B. 1985. *Tense*. Cambridge: Cambridge University Press.

Coniam, D. 1997. 'A preliminary inquiry into using corpus word frequency data in the automatic generation of English language cloze tests'. *CALICO Journal* 16/2–4: 15–33.

Connor-Linton, J. 1988. 'Author's style and world-view in nuclear discourse: a quantitative analysis'. *Multilingua* 7: 95–132.

Conrad, S. 1994. 'Variation in academic writing: textbooks and research articles across disciplines'. Paper presented at the annual conference of the American Association of Applied Linguistics. Baltimore.

Conrad, S. 1999. 'The importance of corpus-based research for language teachers'. *System* 27: 1–18.

Conrad, S. 2000. 'Will corpus linguistics revolutionize grammar teaching in the 21st century?' *TESOL Quarterly* 34: 548–560.

Cook, G. 1998. 'The uses of reality: a reply to Ronald Carter'. *ELT Journal* 52/1: 57–64.

Cooper, D. 2003. In Corpora List Archive 'Legal aspects of corpora compiling'. URL: http://helmer.aksis.uib.no/corpora/2003–1/0596.html

Corder, S. 1967. 'The significance of learners' errors'. *International Review of Applied Linguistics* 5: 161–169.

Cornish, G. P. 1999. *Copyright: Interpreting the Law for Libraries, Archives and Information Services* (3rd edn). Library Association Publishing.

Cotterill, J. 2001. 'Domestic discord, rocky relationships: semantic prosodies in representations of marital violence in the O. J. Simpson trial'. *Discourse and Society* 12/3: 291–312.

Coulthard, M. 1993. 'On beginning the study of forensic texts: corpus concordance collocation' in M. Hoey. (ed.) *Data Description and Discourse*. London: HarperCollins.

Coulthard, M. 1994. 'On the use of corpora in the analysis of forensic texts'. *Forensic Linguistics* 1/1: 27–44.

Cowie, A. (ed.) 1998. *Phraseology: Theory, Analysis and Applications*. Oxford: Oxford University Press.

Cowie, A. 1994. 'Phraseology' in R. Asher (ed.) *The Encyclopaedia of Language and Linguistics* Vol. 6, pp. 3168–3171. Oxford: Pergamon Press Ltd.

Culpeper, J. and Kytö, M. 2000. 'Data in historical pragmatics: spoken interaction (re)cast as writing'. *Journal of Historical Pragmatics* 1/2: 175–199.

Cutting, D. 1994. 'Porting a stochastic part-of-speech tagger to Swedish' in R. Eklund (ed.) *Proceedings of the 9th Scandinavian Conference on Computational Linguistics*, pp. 65–70, Stockholm University.

Dagneaux, E., Denness, S. and Granger, S. 1998. 'Computer-aided error analysis'. *System* 26/2: 163–174.

Dailey-O'Cain, J. 2000. 'The sociolinguistic distribution of and attitudes toward focuser *like* and quotative *like*'. *Journal of Sociolinguistics* 4/1: 60–80.

de Beaugrande, R. 1998. 'Linguistics, sociolinguistics, and corpus linguistics: ideal language versus real language'. *Journal of Sociolinguistics* 3/1: 128–139.

de Beaugrande, R. 1999. 'Discourse studies and the ideology of "liberalism"'. *Discourse Studies* 1/3: 259–295.

de Beaugrande, R. 2001. 'Interpreting the discourse of H. G. Widdowson: a corpus-based critical discourse analysis'. *Applied Linguistics* 22/1: 104–121.

de Beaugrande, R. [date unknown] 'Large corpora and applied linguistics: H. G. Widdowson versus J. McH. Sinclair'. URL: http://beaugrande.bizland.com/Widdow SincS.htm

Deignan, A. 1999. 'Linguistic metaphors and collocation in non-literary corpus data'. *Metaphor and Symbol* 14/1: 19–36.

Dekkers, M. and Weibel, S. 2003. 'State of the Dublin Core Metadata Initiative'. *D-Lib Magazine* 9/4. URL: http://www.dlib.org/dlib/april03/weibel/04weibel.html

Dixon, R. 1991. *A New Approach to English Grammar on Semantic Principles*. Oxford: Oxford University Press.

Downs, D. 2002. 'Representing gun owners: frame identification as social responsibility in news media discourse'. *Written Communication* 19/1: 44–75.

Drave, N. 2002. 'Vaguely speaking: a corpus approach to vague language in intercultural conversations' in P. Peters, P. Collins and A. Smith (eds) *New Frontiers of Corpus Research*, pp. 25–40. Amsterdam: Rodopi.

Duffley, P. 1992. *The English Infinitive*. London: Longman.

Dulay, H. and Burt, M. 1973. 'Creative construction in second language learning and teaching' in M. Burt and H. Dulay (eds) *On TESOL '75: New Directions in Second Language Learning, Teaching and Bilingual Education*, pp. 21–32 Washington, DC: TESOL.

Dulay, H., Burt, M. and Krashen, S. 1982. *Language Two*. New York: Oxford University Press.

Dunning, T. 1993. 'Accurate methods for statistics of surprise and coincidence'. *Computational Linguistics* 19/1: 61–74.

Eastwood, J. 1992. *Oxford Practical Grammar*. Oxford: Oxford University Press.

Ebeling, J. 1998. 'Contrastive linguistics, translation, and parallel corpora'. *Meta* 43/4. URL: http://www.erudit.org/revue/meta/1998/v43/n4/002692ar.pdf

Ellis, R. 1990. *Instructed Second Language Acquisition*. Oxford: Blackwell.

Ellis, R. 1994. *The Study of Second Language Acquisition*. Oxford: Oxford University Press.

Emi I., Saiga, T., Supnithi, T., Uchimoto, K. and Isahara, H. 2003. 'The development of the spoken corpus of Japanese learner English and the applications in collaboration with NLP techniques' in D. Archer, P. Rayson, A. Wilson and A. McEnery (eds) *Proceedings of Corpus Linguistics 2003*, pp. 359–566. Lancaster University.

English Language Institute. 2003. *MICASE Manual: The Michigan Corpus of Academic Spoken English* (version 1.1). University of Michigan. URL: http://www.lsa.umich.edu/eli/micase/MICASE_MANUAL.pdf

Faber, D. and Lauridsen, K. 1991. 'The compilation of a Danish–English–French corpus in contract law' in S. Johansson and A. Stenström (eds) *English Computer Corpora. Selected Papers and Research Guide*, pp. 235–43. Berlin: Mouton de Gruyter.

Fairclough, N. 1992. *Discourse and Social Change*. Cambridge: Policy Press.

Fairclough, N. 1995. *Critical Discourse Analysis*. London: Longman.

Fairclough, N. 2000. *New Labour, New Language*. London: Routledge.

Farwell, D., Helmreich, S. and Casper, M. 1995. 'SPOST: a Spanish part-of-speech tagger' in *Procesamiento del Lenguaje Natural* 17: 42–56.

Fathman, A. 1978. 'ESL and EFL learning: similar or dissimilar?' in C. Blatchford and J. Schachter (eds) *On TESOL'78: EFL Policies, Programs, Practices*, pp. 213–23. Washington: TESOL.

Feng, Z. 2001. 'Hybrid approaches for automatic segmentation and annotation of Chinese text corpus'. *International Journal of Corpus Linguistics* 6: 35–42.

Firth, J. 1957. *Papers in Linguistics*. Oxford: Oxford University Press.

Firth, J. 1968. 'A synopsis of linguistic theory' in F. Palmer (ed.) *Selected Papers of J. R. Firth 1952–59*. London: Longmans. 168–205.

Fligelstone, S. 1991. *A Description of the Conventions Used in the Lancaster Anaphoric Treebank Scheme* (2nd edn). UCREL Technical report. Lancaster University.

Fligelstone, S. 1992. 'Developing a scheme for annotating text to show anaphoric relations' in G. Leitner (ed.) *New Directions in English Language Corpora*, pp. 153–170. Berlin: Mouton de Gruyter.

Florey, M. 1998. 'Alune incantations: continuity or discontinuity in verbal arts'. *Journal of Sociolinguistics* 2/2: 204–231.

Flowerdew, J. 1993. 'Concordancing as a tool in course design'. *System* 21/3: 231–243.

Fox, G. 1987. 'The case for examples' in J. Sinclair (ed.) *Looking Up: An Account of the COBUILD Project*, pp. 137–149. London: HarperCollins.

Francis, G., Hunston, S. and Manning, E. 1996. *Collins COBUILD Grammar Patterns 1: Verbs*. London: HarperCollins.

Francis, G., Hunston, S. and Manning, E. 1998. *Collins COBUILD Grammar Patterns 2: Nouns and Adjectives*. London: HarperCollins.

Francis, G., Manning, E. and Hunston, S. 1997. *Verbs: Patterns and Practice*. London: HarperCollins.

Francis, N. 1992. 'Language corpora B. C.' in J. Svartvik (ed.) *Directions in Linguistics: Proceedings of Nobel Symposium 82*. Stockholm, 4–8 August 1991. Berlin: Mouton de Gruyter.

Frawley, W. 1984. 'Prolegomenon to a theory of translation' in W. Frawley (ed.) *Translation: Literary, Linguistic and Philosophical Perspectives*, pp. 159–75. London: Associated University Press.

Friedbichler, I. and Friedbichler, M. 1997. 'The potential of domain-specific target-language corpora for the translator's workbench'. Paper presented at the Conference on Corpus Use and Learning to Translate. Bertinoro, November 1997.

Fries, C. 1945. *Teaching and Learning English as a Foreign Language*. Ann Arbor: University of Michigan Press.

Fuller, J. 1978. 'Natural and monitored sequences by adult learners of English as a second language'. Ph.D. thesis. Florida State University.

Gaizauskas, R. and Humphreys, K. 1996. 'Quantitative evaluation of coreference algorithms in an information extraction system'. Paper presented at the DAARC-1 Conference, Lancaster University. Reprinted in S. Botley and A. McEnery (eds) (2000) *Corpus-Based and Computational Approaches to Discourse Anaphora*, pp. 143–167. Amsterdam: John Benjamins.

Gale, W. and Church, K. 1993. 'A program for aligning sentences in bilingual corpora'. *Computational Linguistics* 19/1: 75–102.

Garside, R. 1993. 'The marking of cohesive relationships: tools for the construction of a large bank of anaphoric data'. *ICAME Journal* 17: 5–27.

Garside, R. and Smith, N. 1997. 'A hybrid grammatical tagger: CLAWS4' in R. Garside, G. Leech and A. McEnery (eds) *Corpus Annotation*, pp.102–121. London: Longman.

Garside, R., Fligelstone, S. and Botley, S. 1997. 'Discourse annotation: anaphoric relations in corpora' in R. Garside, G. Leech and A. McEnery (eds) *Corpus Annotation*, pp. 66–84. London: Longman.

Garside, R., Leech, G. and McEnery, A. (eds) 1997. *Corpus Annotation*. London: Longman.

Garside, R., Leech, G. and Sampson, G. 1987. *The Computational Analysis of English*. London: Longman.

Gavioli, L. and Aston, G. 2001. 'Enriching reality: language corpora in language pedagogy'. *ELT Journal* 55/3: 238–246.

Gavioli, L. and Zanettin, F. 1997. 'Comparable corpora and translation: a pedagogic perspective'. Paper presented at the Conference on Corpus Use and Learning to Translate. Bertinoro, November 1997.

Ge, N. 1998. 'Annotating the Penn Treebank with coreference information'. Internal report. Brown University.

Gellerstam, M. 1996. 'Translations as a source for cross-linguistic studies' in K. Aijmer, B. Altenberg and M. Johansson (eds) *Language in Contrast: Papers from a Symposium on Text-based Cross-linguistic Studies, Lund, March 1994*, pp. 53–62. Lund: Lund University Press.

Gendner, V. 2002. 'Comparative study of oral and written French automatically tagged with morpho-syntactic information' in *Proceedings of LREC 2002*, pp. 774–778. Las Palmas, Gran Canaria, Spain, 29–31 May 2002.

Gilquin, G. 2003. 'Causative *get* and *have*'. *Journal of English Linguistics* 31/2: 125–148.

Givon, T. 1995. *Functionalism and Grammar*. Amsterdam: John Benjamins.

Goethals, M. 2003. 'EET: the European English Teaching vocabulary-list' in B. Lewandowska-Tomaszczyk (ed.) *Practical Applications in Language and Computers*, pp. 417–427. Frankfurt: Peter Lang.

Graham, P. 2001. 'Space: irrealis objects in technology policy and their role in a new political economy'. *Discourse and Society* 12/6: 761–788.

Granger, S. 1994. 'The learner corpus: a revolution in applied linguistics'. *English Today* 10/3: 25–29.

Granger, S. 1996. 'From CA to CIA and back: an integrated approach to computerized bilingual and learner corpora' in K. Aijmer, B. Altenberg and M. Johansson (eds) *Language in Contrast: Papers from a Symposium on Text-Based Cross-Linguistic Studies, Lund, March 1994*, pp. 38–51. Lund: Lund University Press.

Granger, S. (ed.) 1998. *Learner English on Computer*. London: Longman.

Granger, S. 2002. 'A bird's-eye view of learner corpus research' in S. Granger, J. Hung and S. Petch-Tyson (eds) *Computer Learner Corpora, Second Language Acquisition and Foreign Language Teaching*, pp. 3–33. Philadelphia: John Benjamins.

Granger, S. 2003a. 'The International Corpus of Learner English: a new resource for foreign language learning and teaching and second language acquisition research'. *TESOL Quarterly* 37/3: 538–546.

Granger, S. 2003b. 'Practical applications of learner corpora' in B. Lewandowska-Tomaszczyk (ed.) *Practical Applications in Language and Computers*, pp. 291–302. Frankfurt: Peter Lang.

Granger, S., Hung, J. and Petch-Tyson, S. (eds) 2002. *Computer Learner Corpora, Second Language Acquisition, and Foreign Language Teaching*. Philadelphia: John Benjamins.

Greenbaum, S. 1974. 'Some verb-intensifier collocations in American and British English'. *American Speech* 49: 79–89.

Gries, S. 2003. 'Testing the sub-test: an analysis of English *-ic* and *-ical* adjectives'. *International Journal of Corpus Linguistics* 8/1: 31–61.

Grönqvist, L. 2004. 'Literature review of representativeness of linguistic resources'. Paper presented at the 7th Annual CLUK Research Colloquium. University of Birmingham, 6–7 January 2004.

Gross, M. 1993. 'Local grammars and their representation by finite automata' in M. Hoey (ed.) *Data, Description, Discourse*, pp. 26–28. London: HarperCollins.

Gui, S. and Yang, H. 2001. 'Computer analysis of Chinese learner English'. Keynote lecture given at the Conference on Technology in Language Education, Hong Kong, June 2001.

Guthrie, L. 2003. 'Semantic annotation of nouns'. Paper presented at the Prague Workshop on Lexico-semantic Classification and Tagging. Prague, 8–9 December 2003.

Haenlein, H. 1999. *Studies in Authorship Recognition – A Corpus-Based Approach*. Frankfurt: Peter Lang.

Hakulinen, A., Karlsson, F. and Vilkuna, M. 1980. *Suomen tekstilauseiden piirteitä: kvantitatiivinen tutkimus*. Department of General Linguistics, University of Helsinki. Publications No. 6.

Halliday, M. 1966. 'Lexis as a linguistic level' in C. Bazell, J. Catford, M. Halliday and R. Robins (eds) *In Memory of J. R. Firth*, pp. 148–162. London: Longman.

Halliday, M. and Hasan, R. 1976. *Cohesion in English*. London: Longman.

Hartmann, R. 1995. 'Contrastive textology'. *Language and Communication* 5: 25–37.

Haruno, M., Ikehara, S. and Yamazaki, T. 1996. 'High performance bilingual text alignment using statistical and dictionary information' in *Proceedings of the 34th ACL*, pp. 131–138. Santa Cruz: University of California.

Hatch, E. 1978. 'Acquisition of syntax in a second language' in J. Richards (ed.) *Understanding Second and Foreign Language Learning: Issues and Approaches*, pp. 34–71. Rowley, MA: Newbury House.

Hatcher, A. 1951. 'The use of the progressive form in English: a new approach'. *Language* 27: 258–280.

Hausser, H. 1999. *Functions of Computational Linguistics*. Berlin: Springer-Verlag.

Hawkey, R. 2001. 'Towards a common scale to describe L2 writing performance'. *Research Notes* 5: 9–10.

Heffer, C. 1999. 'Courtroom corpora and data deception: change in forensic linguistic analysis'. Paper presented at the BAAL 32nd Annual Meeting (Colloquium on New Applications of Linguistics to Legal Issues). University of Edinburgh, 16–18 September 1999.

Henne, H., Rongen, O. and Hansen, L. 1977. *A Handbook on Chinese Language Structure*. Oslo: Universitetsforlaget.

Herbst, T. 1996. 'What are collocations: sandy beaches or false teeth?' *English Studies* 77/4: 379–393.

Higgins, J. and Johns, T. 1984. *Computers in Language Learning*. Oxford: Oxford University Press.

Hinkel, E. 2004. 'Tense, aspect the passive voice in L1 and L2 academic texts'. *Language Teaching Research* 8/1: 5–29.

Hinrichs, E., Kübler, S., Müller, F. and Ule, T. 2002. 'A hybrid architecture for robust parsing of German' in *Proceedings of the Third International Conference on Language Resources and Evaluation (LREC 2002)*, pp. 1505–1512. Las Palmas, May 2002.

Hirschman, L. 1997. *MUC-7 Coreference Task Definition* (Version 3.0). URL: www.itl.nist. gov/iaui/894.02/related_projects/muc/proceedings/co_task.html

Hoey, M. 1991. *Pattern of Lexis in Text*. Oxford: Oxford University Press.

Hoey, M. 1997. 'From concordance to text structure: new uses for computer corpora' in J. Melia and B. Lewandowska (eds) *PALC '97: Proceedings of Practical Applications of Linguistic Corpora Conference*, pp. 2–23. University of Lodz.

Hoey, M. 2000. 'A world beyond collocation: new perspectives on vocabulary teaching' in M. Lewis (ed.) *Teaching Collocations*, pp. 224–245. Hove: Language Teaching Publications.

Hoey, M. 2004. 'Lexical priming and the properties of text' in A. Partington, J. Morley and L. Haarman (eds) *Corpora and Discourse*, pp. 385–412. Bern: Peter Lang. URL: www. monabaker.com/ tsresources/LexicalPrimingandthePropertiesofText.htm

Hoffman, S. 2002. 'In hot pursuit of data: complex prepositions in late modern English' in P. Peters, P. Collins and A. Smith (eds) *New Frontiers in Corpus Linguistics*, pp.127–146. Amsterdam: Rodopi.

Hofland, K. 1996. 'A program for aligning English and Norwegian sentences' in S. Hockey, N. Ide and G. Perissinotto (eds) *Research in Humanities Computing*, pp. 165–178. Oxford: Oxford University Press.

Holmes, D. 1998. 'The evolution of stylometry in humanities scholarship'. *Literary and Linguistic Computing* 13/3: 111–117.

Holmes, J. 1992. *An Introduction to Sociolinguistics*. London: Longman.

Holmes, J. 1993a. 'Charpersons, chairpersons and goddesses: sexist usages in New Zealand English'. *Te Reo* 36: 99–113.

Holmes, J. 1993b. 'Sex-marking suffixes in written New Zealand English'. *American Speech* 68/4: 357–370.

Holmes, J. 1993c. 'He-man beings, poetesses, and tramps: sexist language in New Zealand' in L. Bauer and C. Franzen (eds) *Of Pavlova, Poetry and Paradigms: Essays in Honour of Harry Orsman*, pp. 34–49. Wellington: Victoria University Press.

Holmes, J. 1994. 'Inferring language change from computer corpora: some methodological problems'. *ICAME Journal* 18: 27–40.

Holmes, J. 1997. 'Generic pronouns in the Wellington Corpus of Spoken New Zealand English'. *Kotare* 1: 32–40.

Holmes, J. and Marra, M. 2002. 'Having a laugh at work: how humour contributes to workplace culture'. *Journal of Pragmatics* 34: 1683–1710.

Holmes, J. and Sigley, R. 2002. 'What's a word like *girl* doing in a place like this? Occasional labels, sexist usage and corpus research' in P. Peters, P. Collins and A. Smith (eds) *New Frontiers of Corpus Research*, pp. 247–264. Amsterdam: Rodopi.

Hoover, D. 2001. 'Statistical stylistics and authorship attribution: an empirical investigation'. *Literary and Linguistic Computing* 16/4: 421–444.

Hoover, D. 2002. 'Frequent word sequences and statistical stylistics'. *Literary and Linguistic Computing* 17/2: 157–180.

Hoover, D. 2003a. 'Frequent collocations and authorial style'. *Literary and Linguistic Computing* 18/3: 261–286.

Hoover, D. 2003b. 'Multivariate analysis and the study of style variation'. *Literary and Linguistic Computing* 18/4: 341–360.

Hornby, A., Gatenby, E. and Wakefield, H. 1942. *Idiomatic and Syntactic English Dictionary.* Tokyo: Kaitakusha.

Horner, D. and Strutt, P. 2004. 'Analysing domain-specific lexical categories: evidence from the BEC written corpus'. *Research Notes* 15: 6–8.

Horvath, J. 1999. 'Advanced writing in English as a foreign language, a corpus-based study of processes and products'. Ph.D. thesis. Janus Pannonius University. URL: http://www.geocities.com/writing_site/thesis/

Howitt, D. and Cramer D. 2001. *A Guide to Computing Statistics with SPSS for Windows.* Edinburgh: Prentice Hall.

Huang, C., Chen, K., Chen, F. and Chang, L. 1997. 'Segmentation standard for Chinese natural language processing'. *Computational Linguistics and Chinese Language Processing* 2/2: 47–62.

Huddleston, R. and Pullum, G. 2000. *The Cambridge Grammar of the English Language.* Cambridge: Cambridge University Press.

Hughes, G. 1991. *Swearing: A Social History of Foul Language, Oaths and Profanity in English.* London: Blackwell.

Hughes, R. and McCarthy, M. 1998. 'From sentence to discourse: discourse grammar and English language teaching'. *TESOL Quarterly* 32/2: 263–287.

Hundt, M. 1998. *New Zealand English Grammar: Fact or Fiction?* Amsterdam: John Benjamins.

Hundt, M., Sand, A. and Siemund, R. 1998. *Manual of Information to Accompany the Freiburg–LOB Corpus of British English (FLOB).* URL: http://khnt.hit.uib.no/icame/manuals/flob/INDEX.HTM

Hundt, M., Sand, A. and Skandera, P. 1999. *Manual of Information to Accompany the Freiburg–Brown Corpus of American English (Frown).* URL: http://khnt.hit.uib.no/icame/manuals/frown/INDEX.HTM

Hunston, S. 1999a. 'Local grammars: the future of corpus-driven grammar?' Paper presented at the 32nd BAAL Annual Meeting. University of Edinburgh, September 1999.

Hunston, S. 1999b. 'Corpus evidence for disadvantage: issues in critical interpretation'. Paper presented at the BAAL/CUP seminar Investigating Discourse Practices through Corpus Research: Methods, Findings and Applications. University of Reading, May 1999.

Hunston, S. 2002. *Corpora in Applied Linguistics.* Cambridge: Cambridge University Press.

Hunston, S. 2004. 'Counting the uncountable: problems of identifying evaluation in a text and in a corpus' in A. Partington, J. Morley and L. Haarman (eds) *Corpora and Discourse*, pp. 157–188. Bern: Peter Lang.

Hunston, S. and Francis, G. 2002. *Pattern Grammar.* Amsterdam: John Benjamins.

Hunston, S. and Sinclair, J. 2000. 'A local grammar of evaluation' in S. Hunston and G. Thomas (eds) *Evaluation in Text: Authorial Stance and the Construction of Discourse,* pp. 75–101. Oxford: Oxford University Press.

Hutchins, J. 2003. 'Machine translation: general overview' in R. Mitkov (ed.) *Oxford Handbook of Computational Linguistics*, pp. 501–511. Oxford: Oxford University Press.

Hyland, K. 1999. 'Talking to students: metadiscourse in introductory coursebooks'. *English for Specific Purposes* 18/1: 3–26.

Ide, N. 1998. 'Corpus Encoding Standard: SGML guidelines for encoding linguistic corpora' in *LREC-1998 Proceedings*, pp. 463–470.

Ide, N. and Priest-Dorman, G. 2000. *Corpus Encoding Standard – Document CES 1.* URL: http://www.cs.vassar.edu/CES/

Ide, N., Patrice, B. and Laurent, R. 2000. 'XCES: an XML-based encoding standard for linguistic corpora' in *LREC-2000 Proceedings*, pp. 825–830.

Jackson, H. 1997. 'Corpus and concordance: finding out about style' in A. Wichmann, S. Fligelstone, A. McEnery and G. Knowles (eds) *Teaching and Language Corpora*, pp. 224–239. London: Longman.

Jacobsson, M. 2002. '*Thank you* and *thanks* in Early Modern English'. *ICAME* 26: 63–80.

James, C. 1980. *Contrastive Analysis*. London: Longman.

Jay, T. 1992. *Cursing in America: A Psycholinguistic Study of Dirty Language in the Courts, in the Movies, in the Schoolyards and on the Streets*. Philadelphia: John Benjamins.

Jefferson, G. 1978. 'Sequential aspects of storytelling in conversation' in K. Schenkein (ed.) *Studies in the Organization of Conversational Interaction*. New York: Academic Press.

Jesperson, O. 1909–1949. *A Modern English Grammar on Historical Principles*. London: Allen & Unwin.

Johansson S. and Oksefjell S. (eds) 1998. *Corpora and Cross-Linguistics Research*. Amsterdam: Rodopi.

Johansson, S. 1991. 'Times change, and so do corpora' in K. Aijmer and B. Altenberg (eds) *English Corpus Linguistics*, pp. 305–314. London: Longman.

Johansson, S. 1998. 'On the role of corpora in cross-linguistic research' in S. Johansson and S. Oksefjell (eds) *Corpora and Cross-Linguistics Research*, pp. 3–24. Amsterdam: Rodopi.

Johansson, S. and Hofland, K. 1994. 'Towards an English–Norwegian parallel corpus' in U. Fries, G. Tottie and P. Schneider (eds) *Creating and Using English Language Corpora*, pp. 25–37. Amsterdam: Rodopi.

Johansson, S. and Oksefjell, S. (eds) 1998. *Corpora and Cross-Linguistic Research*. Amsterdam: Rodopi.

Johansson, S., Leech, G. and Goodluck, H. 1978. *Manual of Information to Accompany the Lancaster–Oslo/Bergen Corpus of British English, for Use with Digital Computers*. University of Oslo.

Johns, T. 1991. '"Should you be persuaded": two samples of data-driven learning materials' in T. Johns and P. King (eds) *Classroom Concordancing ELR Journal 4*. University of Birmingham.

Johns, T. 1993. 'Data-driven learning: an update'. *TELL & CALL* 3: 4–10.

Johnson, A. 1997. 'Textual kidnapping: a case of plagiarism among three student texts?' *Forensic Linguistics* 4: 210–225.

Johnson, S., Culpeper, J. and Suhr, S. 2003. 'From "politically correct councillors" to "Blairite nonsense": discourses of "political correctness" in three British newspapers'. *Discourse and Society* 14/1: 29–47.

Jucker, A., Smith, S. and Lüdge, T. 2003. 'Interactive aspects of vagueness in conversation'. *Journal of Pragmatics* 35: 1737–1769.

Jucker, A. and Taavitsainen, I. 2000. 'Diachronic speech act analysis: insults from flyting to flaming'. *Journal of Historical Pragmatics* 1/1: 67–95.

Kachru, Y. 2003. 'On definite reference in world Englishes'. *World Englishes* 22/4: 497–510.

Kaltenböck, G. 2003. 'On the syntactic and semantic status of anticipatory *it*'. *English Language and Linguistics* 7/2: 235–255.

Karlsson, F., Voutilainen, A., Heikkilä, J. and Anttila, A. (eds) 1995. *Constraint Grammar*. Berlin: Mouton de Gruyter.

Karpati, I. 1995. *Concordance in Language Learning and Teaching*. Pecs: University of Pecs.

Kaszubski, P. and Wojnowska, A. 2003. 'Corpus-informed exercises for learners of English: the TestBuilder program' in E. Oleksy and B. Lewandowska-Tomaszczyk (eds) *Research and Scholarship in Integration Processes: Poland – USA – EU*, pp. 337–354. Łódź: Łódź University Press.

Keck, C. 2004. 'Corpus linguistics and language teaching research: bridging the gap'. *Language Teaching Research* 8/1: 83–109.

Kennedy, G. 1998. *An Introduction to Corpus Linguistics*. London: Longman.

Kennedy, G. 2003. 'Amplifier collocations in the British National Corpus: implications for English language teaching'. *TESOL Quarterly* 37/3: 467–487.

Kenny, D. 1998. 'Creatures of habit? What translators usually do with words?' *Meta* 43/4. URL: http://www.erudit.org/revue/meta/1998/v43/n4/003302ar.pdf

Kettemann, B. 1995. 'On the use of concordancing in ELT'. *TELL & CALL* 4: 4–15.

Kettemann, B. 1996. 'Concordancing in English language teaching' in S. Botley, J. Glass, A. McEnery and A. Wilson (eds) *Proceedings of Teaching and Language Corpora*, pp. 4–16. Lancaster University.

Kettemann, B. and Marko, G. 2002. *Teaching and Learning by Doing Corpus Analysis*. Amsterdam: Rodopi.

Kidman, A. 1993. 'How to do things with four-letter words: a study of the semantics of swearing in Australia'. BA thesis. University of New England.

Kilgariff, A. 2002. In Corpora List Archive 'Legal aspects of corpora compiling'. URL: http://helmer.hit.uib.no/corpora/2002–3/0253.html

Kilpiö, M. 1997. 'On the forms and functions of the verb *be* from Old to Modern English' in M. Rissanen, M. Kytö and K. Heikkonen (eds) *English in Transition: Corpus-based Studies in Linguistic Variation and Genre Styles*, pp. 101–120. Berlin: Mouton de Gruyter.

Kim, Y. and Biber, D. 1994. 'A corpus-based analysis of register variation in Korean' in D. Biber and E. Finegan (eds) *Sociolinguistic Perspectives on Register*, pp. 157–181. New York: Oxford University Press.

Kinsbury, P., Palmer, M. and Marcus, M. 2002. 'Adding semantic annotation to the Penn Treebank' in *Proceedings of the Human Language Technology Conference*, San Diego, CA.

Kita, K. and Ogata, H. 1997. 'Collocations in language learning: corpus-based automatic compilation of collocations and bilingual collocation concordancer'. *Computer Assisted Language Learning* 10/3: 229–238.

Kjellmer, G. 1985. 'Help to/help θ revisited'. *English Studies* 66/2: 156–61.

Kjellmer, G. 1986. '"The lesser man": observations on the role of women in modern English writings' in J. Aarts and W. Meijs (eds) *Corpus Linguistics II*, pp. 163–176. Amsterdam: Rodopi.

Kjellmer, G. 1991. 'A mint of phrases' in K. Aijmer and B. Altenberg (eds) *English Corpus Linguistics: Studies in Honour of Jan Svartvik*. London: Longman.

Koester, A. 2002. 'The performance of speech acts in workplace conversations and the teaching of communicative functions'. *System* 30: 167–184.

Koller, V. 2004. 'Businesswomen and war metaphors: "possessive, jealous and pugnacious"?' *Journal of Sociolinguistics* 8/1: 3–22.

Krashen, S. 1977. 'Some issues relating to the Monitor Model' in H. Brown, C. Yorio, and R. Crymes (eds) *On TESOL'77*, pp. 144–158. Washington, DC: TESOL.

Kreyer. R. 2003. 'Genitive and *of*-construction in modern written English: processability and human involvement'. *International Journal of Corpus Linguistics* 8/2: 169–207.

Krishnamurthy, R. 2000. 'Collocation: from *silly ass* to lexical sets' in C. Heffer, H. Sauntson and G. Fox (eds) *Words in Context: A Tribute to John Sinclair on his Retirement*. Birmingham: University of Birmingham.

Krishnamurthy, R. (ed.) 2004. *English Collocation Studies: The OSTI Report by John Sinclair, Susan Jones and Robert Daley*. London: Continuum.

Krueger, R. 1994. *Focus Group: A Practical Guide for Applied Research* (2nd edn). Thousand Oakes, CA: Sage.

Kucĕra, H. and Francis, W. 1967. *Computational Analysis of Present-Day English*. Providence: Brown University Press.

Kupiek, J. 1993. 'An algorithm for finding noun–phrase correspondences in bilingual corpora' in *Proceedings of the 31st ACL*, pp. 17–22.

Kurtböke, P. and Potter, L. 2000. 'Co-occurrence tendencies of loanwords in corpora'. *International Journal of Corpus Linguistics* 5/1: 83–100.

Labbé, C. and Labbé, D. 2001. 'Intertextual distance and authorship attribution. Corneille and Molière'. *Journal of Quantitative Linguistics* 8/3: 213–231.

Laforest, M. 2002. 'Scenes of family life: complaining in everyday conversation'. *Journal of Pragmatics* 34: 1595–1620.

Lakoff, R. 1975. *Language and Woman's Place*. New York: Harper & Row.

Langford, I. 1999. 'The semantics of key words of the law'. Paper presented at the IAFL Conference '99. University of Birmingham, 28 June–1 July 1999.

Larsen-Freeman, D. and Long, M. 1991. *An Introduction to Second Language Acquisition Research*. London: Longman.

Laviosa, S. 1997. 'How comparable can "comparable corpora" be?' *Target* 9: 289–319.

Laviosa, S. 1998a. 'The corpus-based approach: a new paradigm in translation studies'. *Meta* 43/4. URL: http://www.erudit.org/revue/meta/1998/v43/n4/003424ar.html

Laviosa, S. 1998b. 'Core patterns of lexical use in a comparable corpus of English narrative prose'. *Meta* 43/4. URL: http://www.erudit.org/revue/meta/1998/v43/n4/003425ar.html

Leech, G. 1971. *Meaning and the English Verb* (2nd edn 1987; 3rd edn 2004). London: Longman.

Leech, G. 1991. 'The state of art in corpus linguistics' in K. Aijmer and B. Altenberg (eds) *English Corpus Linguistics*, pp. 8–29. London: Longman.

Leech, G. 1992. 'Corpora and theories of linguistic performance' in J. Svartvik (ed.) *Directions in Corpus Linguistics*, pp. 105–122. Berlin: Mouton de Gruyter.

Leech, G. 1997a. 'Introducing corpus annotation' in R. Garside, G. Leech and A. McEnery (eds) *Corpus Annotation*, pp. 1–18. London: Longman.

Leech, G. 1997b. 'Teaching and language corpora: a convergence' in A. Wichmann, S. Fligelstone, A. McEnery and G. Knowles (eds) *Teaching and Language Corpora*, pp. 1–23. London: Longman.

Leech, G. 2000. 'Grammar of spoken English: new outcomes of corpus-oriented research'. *Language Learning* 50/4: 675–724.

Leech, G. 2002. 'Recent grammatical changes in British English'. Paper presented at *ICAME 2002*. Göteborg. 22–26 May 2002.

Leech, G. and Fligelstone, S. 1992. 'Computers and corpus analysis' in C. Bulter (ed.) *Computers and Written Texts*, pp. 115–140. Oxford: Blackwell.

Leech, G. and Short, M. 1981. *Style in Fiction*. London: Longman.

Leech, G. and Weisser, M. 2003. 'Generic speech act annotation for task-oriented dialogues' in D. Archer, P. Rayson, A. Wilson and A. McEnery (eds) *Proceedings of Corpus Linguistics 2003*, pp. 441–446. Lancaster University.

Leech, G. and Weisser, M., Grice, M. and Wilson, A. 2000. 'Representation and annotation of dialogue' in D. Gibbon, I. Mertins and R. Moore (eds) *The Handbook of Multimodal and Spoken Dialogue Systems*, pp. 1–101. Berlin: Mouton de Gruyter.

Leech, G., McEnery, A. and Wynne, M. 1997. 'Further levels of annotation' in R. Garside, G. Leech and A. McEnery (eds) *Corpus Annotation*, pp. 85–101. London: Longman.

Lehmann, H. 2002. 'Zero subject relative constructions in American and British English' in P. Peters, P. Collins and A. Smith (eds) *New Frontiers in Corpus Research*, pp. 163–177. Amsterdam: Rodopi.

Lenk, U. 1995. 'Discourse markers and conversational coherence'. *Anglicana Turkuensia 14* (special issue: Organisation in Discourse): 341–352.

Lenk, U. 1998a. *Marking Discourse Coherence: Functions of Discourse Markers in Spoken English.* Tübingen: Narr.

Lenk, U. 1998b. 'Discourse markers and global coherence in conversation'. *Journal of Pragmatics* 30: 245–257.

Lewandowska-Tomaszczyk, B. 2003. 'The PELCRA project – state of art' in B. Lewandowska-Tomaszczyk (ed.) *Practical Applications in Language and Computers,* pp. 105–121. Frankfurt: Peter Lang.

Lewis, M. 1993. *The Lexical Approach: The State of ELT and the Way Forward.* Hove: Language Teaching Publications.

Lewis, M. 1997a. *Implementing the Lexical Approach: Putting Theory into Practice.* Hove: Language Teaching Publications.

Lewis, M. 1997b. 'Pedagogical implications of the lexical approach' in J. Coady and T. Huckin (eds) *Second Language Vocabulary Acquisition: A Rationale for Pedagogy,* pp. 255–270. Cambridge: Cambridge University Press.

Lewis, M. (ed.) 2000. *Teaching Collocation: Further Developments in the Lexical Approach.* Hove: Language Teaching Publications.

Li, N. and Thompson, S. 1981. *Mandarin Chinese.* Berkeley: University of California Press.

Li, N., Thompson, S. and Thompson, R. 1982. 'The discourse motivation for the perfect aspect: the Mandarin particle *le*' in P. Hopper (ed.) *Tense–Aspect: Between Semantics and Pragmatics,* pp. 19–43. Amsterdam: John Benjamins.

Lightbown, P. 1983. 'Exploring relationships between developmental and instructional sequences in L2 acquisition' in H. Seliger and M. Long (eds) *Classroom Oriented Research in Second Language Acquisition,* pp. 217–243. Rowley, MA: Newbury House.

Lind, A. 1983. 'The variant forms of help to/help θ'. *English Studies* 64/3: 263–275.

Ling, X. 1999. *Cihui Yuyi he Jisuan Yuyanxue* [*Lexical Semantics and Computational Linguistics*]. Beijing: Lingua Publishing House.

Long, M. and Sato, C. 1984. 'Methodological issues in interlanguage studies: an interactionist perspective' in A. Davies, C. Criper and A. Howatt (eds) *Interlanguage,* pp. 253–279. Edinburgh: Edinburgh University Press.

Longman. 1993. *Longman Language Activator.* London: Longman.

Louw, W. 1991. 'Classroom concordancing of delexical forms and the case for integrating language and literature' in T. Johns and P. King (eds) *Classroom Concordancing, ELR Journal 4,* pp. 151–178. CELS University of Birmingham.

Louw, B. 1993. 'Irony in the text or insincerity in the writer? The diagnostic potential of semantic prosodies' in M. Baker, G. Francis and E. Tognini-Bonelli (eds) *Text and Technology: In Honour of John Sinclair,* pp. 157–176. Amsterdam: John Benjamins.

Louw, B. 1997. 'The role of corpora in critical literary appreciation' in A. Wichmann, S. Fligelstone, A. McEnery and G. Knowles (eds) *Teaching and Language Corpora,* pp. 240–251. London: Longman.

Louw, B. 2000. 'Contextual prosodic theory: bringing semantic prosodies to life' in C. Heffer, H. Sauntson and G. Fox (eds) *Words in Context: A Tribute to John Sinclair on his Retirement.* Birmingham: University of Birmingham.

Lu, G. 1996. *The English–Chinese Dictionary.* Shanghai: Shanghai Translation Press.

Mace-Matluck, B. 1977. 'The order of acquisition of certain oral English structures by native-speaking children of Spanish, Cantonese, Tagalog and Ilokano learning English as a second language between the ages of five and ten'. Ph.D. thesis. University of Texas at Austin.

MacWhinney, B. 1992. *The CHILDES Database* (2nd edn). Dublin, OH: Discovery Systems.

Maia, B. 1998. 'Word order and the first person singular in Portuguese and English'. *Meta* 43/4. URL: www.erudit.org/revue/meta/1998/v43/n4/003539ar.pdf

Mair, C. 1995. 'Changing patterns of complementation, and concomitant grammaticalization of the verb *help* in present-day British English' in B. Aarts and C. Meyer (eds) *The Verb in Contemporary English*, pp. 258–272. Cambridge: Cambridge University Press.

Mair, C. 2002. 'Three changing patterns of verb complementation in late modern English'. *English Language and Linguistics* 6/1: 105–131.

Mair, C., Hundt, M., Leech, G. and Smith, N. 2002. 'Short-term diachronic shifts in part-of-speech frequencies'. *International Journal of Corpus Linguistics* 7/2: 245–264.

Makino, T. 1980. 'Acquisition order of English morphemes by Japanese secondary school students'. *Journal of Hokkaido University of Education* 30/2: 101–148.

Malmkjær, K. 1998. 'Love thy neighbour: will parallel corpora endear linguists to translators?' *Meta* 43/4. URL: www.erudit.org/revue/meta/1998/v43/n4/003545ar.pdf

Manning, C. and Schütze, H. 1999. *Foundations of Statistical Natural Language Processing.* Cambridge, MA: The MIT Press.

Marcus, M., Santorini, B. and Marcinkiewicz, M. 1993. 'Building a large annotated corpus of English'. *Computational Linguistics* 19/2: 313–330.

Martin, J. 1999. 'Grace: the logogenesis of freedom'. *Discourse Studies* 1/1: 29–56.

Mason, O. and Uzar, R. 2000. 'NLP meets TEFL: tracing the zero article' in B. Lewandowska-Tomaszczyk and J. Melia (eds) *'99 Practical Applications in Language Corpora*, pp. 105–116. Frankfurt: Peter Lang.

Mauranen, A. 2002. 'Will "translationese" ruin a contrastive study?' *Languages in Contrast* 2/2: 161–186.

McAlpine, J. and Myles, J. 2003. 'Capturing phraseology in an online dictionary for advanced users of English as a second language: a response to user needs'. *System* 31: 71–84.

McCarthy, D. and Sampson, G. (eds) 2004. *Corpus Linguistics: Readings in a Widening Discipline.* New York: Continuum.

McCarthy, M. 1998. *Spoken Language and Applied Linguistics.* Cambridge: Cambridge University Press.

McCarthy, M. and Carter, R. 1997. 'Grammar, tails and affect: constructing expressive choices in discourse'. *Text* 17/3: 406–429.

McCarthy, M. and Carter, R. 2001. 'Size isn't everything: spoken English, corpus and the classroom'. *TESOL Quarterly* 35/2: 337–340.

McEnery, A. 2003. 'Corpus linguistics' in R. Mitkov (ed.) *The Oxford Handbook of Computational Linguistics*, pp. 448–463. Oxford: Oxford University Press.

McEnery, A. 2005. *Swearing in English.* London: Routledge.

McEnery, A., Baker, P. and Cheepen, C. 2001. 'Lexis, indirectness and politeness in operator calls' in C. Meyer and P. Leistyna (eds) *Corpus Analysis: Language Structure and Language Use.* Amsterdam: Rodopi.

McEnery, A., Baker, P. and Cheepen, C. 2002. 'Lexis, indirectness and politeness in operator calls' in P. Peters, P. Collins and A. Smith (eds) *New Frontiers of Corpus Research*, pp. 53–70. Amsterdam: Rodopi.

McEnery, A., Baker, P. and Hardie, A. 2000. 'Swearing and abuse in modern British English' in B. Lewandowska-Tomaszczyk and P. Melia (eds) *PALC '99: Practical Applications in Language Corpora*, pp. 37–48. Berlin: Peter Lang.

McEnery, A., Baker, P. and Hutchinson, J. 1997. 'A corpus-based grammar tutor' in R. Garside, G. Leech and A. McEnery (eds) *Corpus Annotation*, pp. 209–219. London: Longman.

McEnery, A., Baker, P., Gaizauskas, R. and Cunningham, H. 2000. 'EMILLE: towards a corpus of South Asian languages'. *British Computing Society Machine Translation Specialist Group* 11: 1–9.

McEnery, A. and Oakes, M. 1995. 'Sentence and word alignment in the Crater project: methods and assessment' in S. Warwick-Armstrong (ed.) *Proceedings of the Association for Computational Linguistics Workshop SIG–DAT Workshop*, pp. 77–86. Dublin.

McEnery, A. and Oakes, M. 1996. 'Sentence and word alignment in the Crater project' in J. Thomas and M. Short (eds) *Using Corpora for Language Research*, pp. 211–231. London: Longman.

McEnery, A. and Wilson, A. 2001. *Corpus Linguistics* (1st edn 1996). Edinburgh: Edinburgh University Press.

McEnery, A., Wilson, A., Sanchez-Leon, F. and Nieto-Serano, A. 1997. 'Multilingual resources for European languages: contributions of the Crater project'. *Literary and Linguistic Computing* 12/4: 219–226.

McEnery, A. and Xiao, Z. 2002. 'Domains, text types, aspect marking and English–Chinese translation'. *Languages in Contrast* 2/2: 211–229.

McEnery, A. and Xiao, Z. 2004. 'Swearing in modern British English: the case of FUCK in the BNC'. *Language and Literature* 13/3: 235–268.

McEnery, A. and Xiao, Z. 2005a. 'Character encoding in corpus construction' in M. Wynne (ed.) *Guide to Good Practice*. Oxford: AHDS.

McEnery, A. and Xiao, Z. 2005b. 'HELP or HELP to: what do corpora have to say?' *English Studies* 86/2: 161–187.

McEnery, A. and Xiao, Z. 2005c. 'A corpus-based approach to tense and aspect in English–Chinese translation' in J. Schwitalla and W. Wegstein (Hg.) *Korpuslinguistik deutsch: synchron–diachron–kontrastiv*, pp. 27–50. Niemeyer: Tübingen.

McEnery, A., Xiao Z. and Mo L. 2003. 'Aspect marking in English and Chinese: using the Lancaster Corpus of Mandarin Chinese for contrastive language study'. *Literary and Linguistic Computing* 18/4: 361–378.

McIntyre, D., Bellard-Thomson, C., Heywood, J., McEnery, A., Semino, E. and Short, M. 2003. 'The construction of a corpus to investigate the presentation of speech, thought and writing in written and spoken British English' in D. Archer, P. Rayson, A. Wilson and A. McEnery (eds) *Proceedings of Corpus Linguistics 2003*, pp. 513–522. Lancaster University.

McKenzie, M. 1987. 'Free indirect speech in a fettered insecure society'. *Language and Communication* 7/2: 153–159.

Meijs, W. 1996. 'Linguistic corpora and lexicography'. *Annual Review of Applied Linguistics* 16: 99–114 .

Merriam, T. 2003. 'Intertextual distances, three authors'. *Literary and Linguistic Computing* 18/4: 379–388.

Meunier, F. 2002. 'The pedagogical value of native and learner corpora in EFL grammar teaching' in S. Granger, J. Hung and S. Petch-Tyson (eds) *Computer Learner Corpora, Second Language Acquisition and Foreign Language Teaching*, pp. 119–142. Philadelphia: John Benjamins.

Meyer, C. and Tenny, R. 1993. 'Tagger: an interactive tagging program' in C. Souter and E. Atwell (eds) *Corpus-Based Computational Linguistics*, pp. 25–36. Amsterdam: Rodopi.

Meyers, M. 1994. 'Various perspectives on educational linguistics gleaned from a collaborative project on the use of dictionaries'. *Language Awareness* 3/3–4: 193–200.

Milton, J. 1998. 'WORDPILOT: enabling learners to navigate lexical universes' in S. Granger and J. Hung (eds) *First International Symposium on Computer Learner*

Corpora, Second Language Acquisition and Foreign Language Teaching, pp. 97–98. Chinese University of Hong Kong, 14–16 December 1998.

Mindt, D. 1991. 'Syntactic evidence for semantic distinctions in English' in K. Aijmer and B. Altenberg (eds) *English Corpus Linguistics: Studies in Honour of Jan Svartvik*, pp. 182–196. London: Longman.

Mindt, D. 1996. 'English corpus linguistics and the foreign language teaching syllabus' in J. Thomas and M. Short (eds) *Using Corpora for Language Research*, pp. 232–247. London: Longman.

Mitkov, R. 2002. *Anaphora Resolution*. London: Longman.

Mitkov R. (ed.) 2003. *Oxford Handbook of Computational Linguistics*. Oxford: Oxford University Press.

Mitkov, R., Evans, R., Orasan, C., Barbu, C., Jones, L. and Sotirova, V. 2000. 'Coreference and anaphor: developing annotating tools, annotated resources and annotation strategies' in *Proceedings of the Discourse, Anaphor and Reference Resolution Conference (DAARC2000)*, pp. 49–58. Lancaster University.

Mitkov, R., Orasan, C. and Evans, R. 1999. 'The importance of annotated corpora for natural language processing' in *Proceedings of the TALN '99 Workshop on Corpora and NLP*, pp. 60–69. Cargese, France.

Montagu, A. 1967. *The Anatomy of Swearing* (2nd edn 1973). London: Macmillan.

Mooney, R. 2003. 'Machine learning' in R. Mitkov (ed.) *Oxford Handbook of Computational Linguistics*, pp. 448–463. Oxford: Oxford University Press.

Moore, S. 2002. 'Disinterring ideology from a corpus of obituaries: a critical post mortem'. *Discourse and Society* 13/4: 495–536.

Mourelatos, A. 1981. 'Events, processes, and states' in P. Tedeschi and A. Zaenen (eds) *Tense and Aspect (Syntax and Semantics 14)*, pp. 191–212. New York: Academic Press.

Murison-Bowie, S. 1996. 'Linguistic corpora and language teaching'. *Annual Review of Applied Linguistics* 16: 182–199.

Murphy, R. 1985. *English Grammar in Use*. Cambridge: Cambridge University Press.

Nattinger, J. and DeCarrico, J. 1992. *Lexical Phrases and Language Teaching*. Oxford: Oxford University Press.

Nelson, G. 1996. 'The design of the corpus'. In S. Greenbaum (ed.) *Comparing English Worldwide: The International Corpus of English*, pp. 27–35. Oxford: Clarendon Press.

Nelson, M. 2000. 'A corpus-based study of business English and business English teaching materials'. Ph.D. thesis. University of Manchester. URL: www.kielikanava.com/thesis.html

Nesselhauf, N. 2003. 'The use of collocations by advanced learners of English and some implications for teaching'. *Applied Linguistics* 24/2: 223–42.

Nevalainen, T. 2000. 'Gender differences in the evolution of standard English'. *Journal of English Linguistics* 28: 38–59.

Nevalainen, T. and Rissanen. M. 2002. 'Fairly pretty or pretty fair? On the development and grammaticalization of English downtoners'. *Language Sciences* 24: 359–380.

Nicholls, D. 2003. 'The Cambridge Learner Corpus – error coding and analysis for lexicography and ELT' in D. Archer, P. Rayson, A. Wilson and A. McEnery (eds) *Proceedings of Corpus Linguistics 2003*, pp. 572–581. Lancaster University.

Norman, J. 1988. *Chinese*. Cambridge: Cambridge University Press.

Nurmi, M. 1997. 'Swearing in America'. URL: www.uta.fi/FAST/US1/P1/GEN/swear.html

O'Keeffe, A. and Farr, F. 2003. 'Using language corpora in initial teacher education: pedagogic issues and practical applications'. *TESOL Quarterly* 37/3: 389–418.

Oakes, M. 1998. *Statistics for Corpus Linguistics*. Edinburgh: Edinburgh University Press.

Oakes, M. and McEnery, A. 2000. 'Bilingual text alignment – an overview' in S. Botley, A. McEnery and A. Wilson (eds) *Multilingual Corpora in Teaching and Research*, pp. 1–37. Amsterdam: Rodopi.

Ogden, C. 1930. *Basic English: A General Introduction with Rules and Grammar*. London: Kegan Paul, Trench, Trubner & Co.

Oh, S. 2000. '*Actually* and *in fact* in American English: a data-based analysis'. *English Language and Linguistics* 4/2: 243–268.

Onions, C. 1965. *An Advanced English Syntax*. London: Routledge.

Orasan, C. 2000. 'CLinkA – a coreferential links annotator' in *Proceedings of the 2nd International Conference on Language Resources and Evaluation (LREC '2000)*, pp. 491–496. Athens.

Osborne, O. 2001. 'Integrating corpora into a language-learning syllabus' in B. Lewandowska-Tomaszczyk (ed.) *PALC 2001: Practical Applications in Language Corpora*, pp. 479–492. Frankfurt: Peter Lang.

Otlogetswe, T. 2004. 'The BNC design as a model for a Setswana language corpus'. Paper presented at the 7th Annual CLUK Research Colloquium. University of Birmingham, 6–7 January 2004. URL: http://www.cs.bham.ac.uk/~mgl/cluk/titles.html

Øverås, S. 1998. 'In search of the third code: an investigation of norms in literary translation'. *Meta* 43/4. URL: www.erudit.org/revue/meta/1998/v43/n4/003775ar.pdf

Page, R. 2003. '"Cherie: lawyer, wife, mum": contradictory patterns of representation in media reports of Cherie Booth/Blair'. *Discourse and Society* 14/5: 559–579.

Palmer, F. 1965. *A Linguistic Study of the English Verb*. London: Longman.

Pan, X. 2002. 'Consensus behind disputes: a critical discourse analysis of the media coverage of the right-of-abode issue in postcolonial Hong Kong'. *Media, Culture and Society* 24: 49–68.

Paolillo, J. 2000. 'Formalizing formality: an analysis of register variation in Sinhala'. *Journal of Linguistics* 36: 215–259.

Pardo, M. 2001. 'Linguistic persuasion as an essential political factor in current democracies: critical analysis of the globalization discourse in Argentina at the turn and at the end of the century'. *Discourse and Society* 12/1: 91–118.

Park, B. 2001. 'Introducing Korean National Corpus'. Talk given at the Corpus Research Group, Lancaster University, 19 November 2001.

Partington, A. 1998. *Patterns and Meanings*. Amsterdam: John Benjamins.

Partington, A. 2003. *The Linguistics of Political Argument*. London: Routledge.

Partington, A. 2004. '"Utterly content in each other's company": semantic prosody and semantic preference'. *International Journal of Corpus Linguistics* 9/1: 131–156.

Peitsara, K. 1993. 'On the development of the *by*-agent in English' in M. Rissanen, M. Kytö and M. Palander-Collin (eds) *Early English in the Computer Age: Exploration through the Helsinki Corpus*, pp. 217–233. Berlin: Mouton de Gruyter.

Peitsara, K. and Vasko, A. 2002. 'The Helsinki Dialect Corpus: characteristics of speech and aspects of variation'. *Helsinki English Studies* 2. URL: www.eng.helsinki.fi/hes/Corpora/helsinki_dialect_corpus2.htm

Peters, P. 1998. 'In quest of international English: mapping the levels of regional divergence' in A. Renouf (ed.) *Explorations in Corpus Linguistics*, pp. 281–291. Amsterdam: Rodopi.

Philip, G. 1999. 'Computer corpora and the law: a new approach to translation of legal terms'. Paper presented at the IAFL Conference '99. University of Birmingham, 28 June–1 July 1999.

Piao, S. 2000. 'Sentence and word alignment between Chinese and English'. Ph.D. thesis. Lancaster University.

Piao, S. 2002. 'Word alignment in English–Chinese parallel corpora'. *Literary and Linguistic Computing* 17/2: 207–230.

Piao, S., Wilson, A. and McEnery, A. 2002. 'A multilingual corpus toolkit'. Paper presented at the Fourth North American Symposium on Corpus Linguistics, 1–3 November 2002, Indianapolis, Indiana.

Pica, T. 1982. 'Second language acquisition in different language contexts'. Ph.D. thesis. University of Pennsylvania.

Piper, A. 2000. 'Some have credit cards and others have giro cheques: "individuals" and "people" as lifelong learners in late modernity'. *Discourse and Society* 11/3: 515–542.

Podhakecka, M. and Piotrowski, T. 2003. 'Russianisms in English (OED–BNC–LDOCE)' in B. Lewandowska-Tomaszczyk (ed.) *Practical Applications in Language and Computers*, pp. 241–252. Frankfurt: Peter Lang.

Popov, B., Kiryakov, A., Kirilov, A., Manov, D., Ognyanoff, D. and Goranov, M. 2003. 'KIM–Semantic Annotation Platform' in the *Proceedings of the 2nd International Semantic Web Conference (ISWC2003)*, pp. 834–849. Berlin: Springer-Verlag.

Poutsma, H. 1923. *The Infinitival, the Gerund and the Participle of the English Verb*. Groningen: P. Noordhoff.

Pravec, N. 2002. 'Survey of learner corpora'. *ICAME Journal* 26: 81–114.

Puchta, C. and Potter, J. 1999. 'Asking elaborate questions: focus groups and the management of spontaneity'. *Journal of Sociolinguistics* 3/3: 314–335.

Quirk, R., Greenbaum, S., Leech, G. and Svartvik, J. 1972. *A Contemporary English Grammar*. London: Longman.

Quirk, R., Greenbaum, S., Leech, G. and Svartvik, J. 1985. *A Comprehensive Grammar of the English Language*. London: Longman.

Rayson, P. 2001. 'Wmatrix: a web-based corpus processing environment'. Software demonstration presented at ICAME 2001 conference. Université Catholique de Louvain.

Rayson, P. and Wilson, A. 1996. 'The ACAMRIT semantic tagging system: progress report' in L. Evett, and T. Rose (eds) *Language Engineering for Document Analysis and Recognition*, pp. 13–20. LEDAR, AISB96 Workshop proceedings.

Renouf, A. 1987. 'Moving on' in J. Sinclair (ed.) *Looking Up: An Account of the COBUILD Project*. London: HarperCollins.

Reppen, R. 1994. 'Variation in elementary student writing'. Ph.D. thesis. Northern Arizona University.

Rissanen, M., Kytö, M. and Heikkonen, K. (eds) 1997a. *English in Transition: Corpus-based Studies in Linguistic Variation and Genre Styles*. Berlin: Mouton de Gruyter.

Rissanen, M., Kytö, M. and Heikkonen, K. (eds) 1997b. *Grammaticalization at Work: Studies of Long-term Developments in English*. Berlin: Mouton de Gruyter.

Rissanen, M., Kytö, M. and Palander-Collin, M. (eds) 1993. *Early English in the Computer Age: Exploration through the Helsinki Corpus*. Berlin: Mouton de Gruyter.

Roeh, I. and Nir, R. 1990. 'Speech presentation in the Israeli radio news: ideological constraints and rhetorical strategies'. *Text* 10/3: 225–244.

Rutherford, W. 1987. *Second Language Grammar: Learning and Teaching*. New York: Longman.

Sajavaara, K. 1981. 'The nature of first language transfer: English as L2 in a foreign language setting'. Paper presented at the 1st European–North American Workshop on Cross-Linguistics Second Language Acquisition Research. Lake Arrowhead, Calif.

Salager-Meyer, F., Ariza, A. and Zambrano, N. 2003. 'The scimitar, the dagger and the glove: intercultural differences in the rhetoric of criticism in Spanish, French and English medical discourse (1930–1995)'. *English for Specific Purposes* 22: 223–247.

Sampson, G. 2001. *Empirical Linguistics.* London: Continuum.

Santorini, B. 1991. *Bracketing Guidelines for the Penn Treebank Project* (draft version). URL: http://www.cis.upenn.edu/~treebank

Santos, D. 1996. 'Tense and aspect in English and Portuguese: a contrastive semantical study'. Ph.D. thesis. Universidade Tecnica de Lisboa.

Saraceni, M. 2003. 'The strange case of Dr Blair and Mr Bush: counting their words to solve a mystery'. *English Today* 19/3: 3–13.

Schiffrin, D. 1982. 'Discourse markers: semantic resource for the construction of conversation'. Ph.D. thesis. University of Pennsylvania.

Schilling-Estes, N. 2002. 'Investigating stylistic variation' in J. Chambers, P. Trudgill and N. Schilling-Estes (eds) *Handbook of Language Variation and Change*, pp. 375–401. Oxford: Blackwell.

Schmitt, N. (ed.) 2004. *Formulaic Sequences.* Amsterdam: John Benjamins.

Schmitt, N. and Carter, R. 2004. 'Formulaic sequences in action: an introduction' in N. Schmitt (ed.) *Formulaic Sequences*, pp. 1–22. Amsterdam: John Benjamins.

Scott, M. 1999. *WordSmith Tools.* Oxford: Oxford University Press.

Scott, M. 2003. *WordSmith Tools Manual.* URL: www.lexically.net/wordsmith/version4/

Seidlhofer, B. 2000. 'Operationalizing intertextuality: using learner corpora for learning' in L. Burnard and A. McEnery (eds) *Rethinking Language Pedagogy from a Corpus Perspective*, pp. 207–224. New York: Peter Lang.

Seidlhofer, B. 2002. 'Pedagogy and local learner corpora: working with learning driven data' in S. Granger, J. Hung and S. Petch-Tyson (eds) *Computer Learner Corpora, Second Language Acquisition and Foreign Language Teaching*, pp. 213–234. Philadelphia: John Benjamins.

Seidlhofer, B. (ed.) 2003. *Controversies in Applied Linguistics.* Oxford: Oxford University Press.

Selinker, L. 1969. 'Language transfer'. *General Linguistics* 9: 67–92.

Semino, E. and Short, M. 2004. *Corpus Stylistics: Speech, Writing and Thought Presentation in a Corpus of English Writing.* London: Routledge.

Semino, E., Short, M. and Culpeper, J. 1997. 'Using a corpus to test and refine a model of speech and thought presentation'. *Poetics* 25: 17–43.

Semino, E., Short, M. and Wynne, M. 1999. 'Hypothetical words and thoughts in contemporary British narratives'. *Narrative* 73: 307–334.

Seuren, P. 1998. *Western Linguistics: A Historical Introduction.* Oxford: Blackwell.

Sharoff, S. 2003. 'Methods and tools for development of the Russian Reference Corpus' in D. Archer, P. Rayson, A. Wilson and A. McEnery (eds) *Corpus Linguistics Around the World.* Amsterdam: Rodopi.

Shei, C. and Pain, H. 2000. 'An ESL writer's collocational aid'. *Computer Assisted Language Learning* 13/2: 167–182.

Sheidlower, J. 1995. *The F word.* New York: Random House.

Shimazumi, M. and Berber-Sardinha, A. 1996. 'Approaching the Assessment of Performance Unit (APU) archive of schoolchildren's writing from the point of view of corpus linguistics'. Paper presented at the *TALC '96 Conference.* Lancaster University, 11 August 1996.

Short, M., Semino, E. and Culpeper, J. 1996. 'Using a corpus for stylistics research: speech and thought presentation' in M. Short and J. Thomas (eds) *Using Corpora in Language Research.* London, pp. 110–131. London: Longman.

Short, M., Semino, E. and Wynne, M. 2002. 'Revisiting the notion of faithfulness in discourse presentation using a corpus approach'. *Language and Literature* 114: 325–355.

Short, M., Wynne, M. and Semino, E. 1999. 'Reading reports: discourse presentation in a corpus of narratives, with special reference to news reports' in H. Diller and E. Gert-Stratmann (eds) *English via Various Media*, pp. 39–66. Heidelberg: Universitatsverlag C Winter.

Sigley, R. 1997. 'Choosing your relatives: relative clauses in New Zealand English'. Ph.D. thesis. Victoria University of Wellington.

Simard, M., Foster, G., Hannan, M., Macklovitch E. and Plamondon, P. 2000. 'Bilingual text alignment: where do we draw the line?' in S. Botley, A. McEnery and A. Wilson (eds) *Multilingual Corpora in Teaching and Research*, pp. 38–64. Amsterdam: Rodopi.

Simpson, P. 1993. *Language, Ideology and Point of View*. London: Routledge.

Sinclair, J. (ed.) 1987. *Looking Up: An Account of the COBUILD Project in Lexical Computing*. London: Collins.

Sinclair, J. 1991a. *Corpus Concordance Collocation*. Oxford: Oxford University Press.

Sinclair, J. 1991b. 'Shared knowledge' in J. Alatis (ed.) *Georgetown University Round Table on Languages and Linguistics 1991*, pp. 489–500. Washington, DC: Georgetown University Press.

Sinclair, J. 1992. 'The automatic analysis of text corpora' in J. Svartvik (ed.) *Directions in Corpus Linguistics: Proceedings of the Nobel Symposium 82, Stockholm*, pp. 379–397. The Hague: Mouton.

Sinclair, J. 1995. Paper presented at *XI Encontro da Associação Portuguesa de Linguística*. Lisbon. 2–4 October 1995.

Sinclair, J. 1996. 'EAGLES preliminary recommendations on corpus typology'. *EAG-TCWG-CTYP/P*. Pisa: ILC-CNR.

Sinclair, J. 2000. 'Lexical grammar'. *Naujoji Metodologija* 24: 191–203.

Sinclair, J. 2003. 'Preface' in B. Lewandowska-Tomaszczyk (ed.) *Practical Applications in Language and Computers*, pp. 7–11. Frankfurt: Peter Lang.

Sinclair, J. 2004a. *Trust the Text: Language, Corpus and Discourse*. London: Routledge.

Sinclair, J. (ed.) 2004b. *How to Use Corpora in Language Teaching*. Amsterdam: John Benjamins.

Sinclair, J. and Renouf, A. 1988. 'A lexical syllabus for language learning' in R. Carter and M. McCarthy (eds) *Vocabulary and Language Teaching*. London: Longman.

Sinclair, J., Bullon, S., Krishnamurthy, R., Manning, E. and Todd, J. 1990. *Collins COBUILD English Grammar*. London: HarperCollins.

Smadja, F. and McKeown, K. 1990. 'Automatically extracting and representing collocations for language generation' in *Proceedings of the 28th Annual Meeting of Association for Computational Linguistics*, pp. 252–259.

Smith, C. 1997. *The Parameter of Aspect* (2nd edn; 1st edn 1991). Dordrecht: Kluwer.

Somers, H. 2003. 'Machine translation: latest developments' in R. Mitkov (ed.) *Oxford Handbook of Computational Linguistics*, pp. 512–528. Oxford: Oxford University Press.

Sotillo, S. and Starace-Nastasi, D. 1999. 'Political discourse of a working-class town'. *Discourse and Society* 10/2: 249–276.

Souter, C. 1993. 'Towards a standard format for parsed corpora' in J. Aarts, P. Haan and N. Oostdijk (eds) *English Language Corpora: Design, Analysis and Exploitation*, pp. 197–214. Amsterdam: Rodopi.

Sperberg-McQueen, C. M. and Burnard, L. (eds) 2002. *TEI P4: Guidelines for Electronic Text Encoding and Interchange* (XML Version). Oxford: Text Encoding Initiative Consortium.

Spoor, J. 1996. 'The copyright approach to copying on the Internet: (over)stretching the reproduction right?' in H. Hugenholtz (ed.) *The Future of Copyright in a Digital Environment*. Dordrecht: Kluwer Law International.

Sripicharn, P. 2000. 'Data-driven learning materials as a way to teach lexis in context' in C. Heffer, H. Sauntson and G. Fox (eds) *Words in Context: A Tribute to John Sinclair on his Retirement.* Birmingham: University of Birmingham.

Stenström, A. 1991. 'Expletives in the London–Lund corpus' in K. Aijmer and B. Altenberg (eds) *English Corpus Linguistics,* pp. 230–253. London: Longman.

Stevenson, M. and Wilks, Y. 2003. 'Word–sense disambiguation' in R. Mitkov (ed.) *The Oxford Handbook of Computational Linguistics,* pp. 448–463. Oxford: Oxford University Press.

Stubbs, M. 1995. 'Collocations and semantic profiles: on the cause of the trouble with quantitative methods'. *Function of Language* 2/1: 1–33.

Stubbs, M. 1996. *Text and Corpus Analysis.* Oxford: Blackwell.

Stubbs, M. 1997. 'Whorf's children: critical comments on critical discourse analysis' in A. Ryan and A. Wray (eds) *Evolving Models of Language,* pp. 100–116. Clevedon: Multilingual Matters.

Stubbs, M. 1999. 'Society, education and language: the last 2,000 (and the next 20?) years of language teaching'. Plenary lecture given at the 32nd Annual Meeting of the British Association for Applied Linguistics. University of Edinburgh. September 1999.

Stubbs, M. 2001a. 'On inference theories and code theories: corpus evidence for semantic schemas'. *Text* 21/3: 437–465.

Stubbs, M. 2001b. 'Texts, corpora, and problems of interpretation: a response to Widdowson'. *Applied Linguistics* 22/2: 149–172.

Stubbs, M. 2001c. *Words and Phrases.* Oxford: Blackwell.

Stubbs, M. 2002. 'Two quantitative methods of studying phraseology in English'. *International Journal of Corpus Linguistics* 7/2: 215–244.

Sun, M., Shen, D. and Tsou, B. 1998. 'Chinese word segmentation without using lexicon and hand-crafted training data' in S. Kahane and A. Polguere (eds) *Proceedings of COLING-ACL '98,* pp. 1265–1271. URL: http://acl.ldc.upenn.edu/P/P98/P98-2206.pdf

Svartvik, J. 1980. '*Well* in conversation' in S. Greenbaum, G. Leech and J. Svartvik (eds) *Studies in English Linguistics for Randolph Quirk,* pp. 167–177. London: Longman.

Svartvik, J. 1992. 'Introduction' in J. Svartvik (ed.) *Directions in Corpus Linguistics.* Berlin: Mouton de Gruyter.

Swen, B. and Yu, S. 1999. 'A graded approach for efficient resolution of Chinese word segmentation ambiguity' in *Proceedings of NLPPRS 99.* Beijing.

Szakos, J. and Wang, Y. 1999. 'Language in a Taiwanese court: how does the study of coherence contribute to fair trials?' Paper presented at the IAFL Conference '99. University of Birmingham, 28 June–1 July 1999.

Taavitsainen, I. 1997. 'Genre conventions: personal affect in fiction and non-fiction in early Modern English' in M. Rissanen, M. Kytö and K. Heikkonen (eds) *English in Transition,* pp. 185–266. Berlin: Mouton de Gruyter.

Tagnin, S. and Teixeira, E. 2003. 'British vs. American English, Brazilian vs. European Portuguese: how close or how far apart?' in B. Lewandowska-Tomaszczyk (ed.) *Practical Applications in Language and Computers,* pp. 193–208. Frankfurt: Peter Lang.

Tan, M. (ed.) 2002. *Corpus Studies in Language Education.* Bangkok: IELE Press.

Taylor, L. 2003. 'The Cambridge approach to speaking assessment'. *Research Notes* 13: 2–4.

Teich, E. 2002. 'System-oriented and text-oriented comparative linguistic research: cross-linguistic variation in translation'. *Languages in Contrast* 2/2: 187–210.

Teubert, W. 1996. 'Comparable or parallel corpora?' *International Journal of Lexicography* 9/3: 238–64.

Teubert, W. 1999. 'Corpus linguistics – a partisan view'. *TELRI Newsletter* No. 8.

Teubert, W. 2000. 'A province of a federal superstate, ruled by an unelected bureaucracy: keywords of the Eurosceptic discourse in Britain' in A. Musolff, C. Good, P. Points and R. Wittlinger (eds) *Attitudes Towards Europe: Language in the Unification Process*, pp. 45–86. Aldershot: Ashgate.

Thomas, J. and Short, M. (eds) 1996. *Using Corpora for Language Research*. London: Longman.

Thomas, J. and Wilson, A. 1996. 'Methodologies for studying a corpus of doctor–patient interaction' in J. Thomas and M. Short (eds) *Using Corpora for Language Research*, pp. 92–109. London: Longman.

Thompson, P. and Tribble, C. 2001. 'Looking at citations: using corpora in English for academic purposes'. *Language Learning and Technology* 5/3: 91–105.

Thorndike, E. 1935. *The Thorndike Century Junior Dictionary*. Chicago: Scott, Foresman.

Thorne, A. and Coupland, J. 1998. 'Articulation of the same-sex desire: lesbian and gay male dating advertisements'. *Journal of Sociolinguistics* 2/2: 233–257.

Thurstun, J. and Candlin, C. 1997. *Exploring Academic English: A Workbook for Student Essay Writing*. Sydney: NCELTR.

Thurstun, J. and Candlin, C. 1998. 'Concordancing and the teaching of the vocabulary of academic English'. *English for Specific Purposes* 17: 267–280.

Tognini-Bonelli, E. 2000. 'Corpus classroom currency'. *Naujoji Metodologija* 24: 205–244.

Tognini-Bonelli, E. 2001. *Corpus Linguistics at Work*. Amsterdam: John Benjamins.

Tono, Y. 2003. 'Learner corpora: design, development and applications' in D. Archer, P. Rayson, A. Wilson and A. McEnery (eds) *Proceedings of Corpus Linguistics 2003*, pp. 800–809. Lancaster University.

Tono, Y., Kaneko, T., Isahara, H., Saiga, T. and Izumi, E. 2001. 'The Standard Speaking Test (SST) Corpus: a 1 million-word spoken corpus of Japanese learners of English and its implications for L2 lexicography' in S. Lee (ed.) *ASIALEX 2001 Proceedings: Asian Bilingualism and the Dictionary*, pp. 257–262. The 2nd Asialex International Congress. Yonsei University, Korea, 8–10 August 2001.

Tottie, G. 1991. 'Conversational style in British and American English: the case of backchannels' in K. Aijmer and B. Altenberg (eds) *English Corpus Linguistics: Studies in Honour of Jan Svartvik*, pp. 254–271. London: Longman.

Tracey, M. and Morrison, D. 1979. *Whitehouse*. London: Macmillan.

Tribble, C. 1991. 'Concordancing and an EAP writing program'. *CAELL Journal* 1/2: 10–15.

Tribble C. 1997a. 'Corpora, concordances and ELT' in T. Boswood (ed.) *New Ways of Using Computers in Language Teaching*. Alexandria VA: TESOL.

Tribble C. 1997b. 'Improving corpora for ELT: quick and dirty ways of developing corpora for language teaching' in B. Lewandowska-Tomaszczyk and P. Melia (eds) *Practical Applications in Language Corpora – Proceedings of PALC '97*, pp. 107–117. Łódź: Łódź University Press.

Tribble, C. 1999. 'Writing difficult texts'. Ph.D. thesis. Lancaster University.

Tribble, C. 2000. 'Practical uses for language corpora in ELT' in P. Brett and G. Motteram (eds) *A Special Interest in Computers: Learning and Teaching with Information and Communications Technologies*, pp. 31–41. Kent: IATEFL.

Tribble, C. 2003. 'The text, the whole text . . . or why large published corpora aren't much use to language learners and teachers' in B. Lewandowska-Tomaszczyk (ed.) *Practical Applications in Language and Computers*, pp. 303–318. Frankfurt: Peter Lang.

Tribble, C. and Jones, G. 1990. *Concordances in the Classroom: A Resource Book for Teachers*. London: Longman.

Tribble, C. and Jones, G. 1997. *Concordances in the Classroom: Using Corpora in Language Education*. Houston TX: Athelstan.

Tutin, A., Trouilleux, F., Clouzot, C., Gaussier, E., Zaenen, A., Rayot, S. and Antoniadis, D. 2000. 'Annotating a large corpus with anaphoric links' in *Proceedings of the Discourse, Anaphor and Reference Resolution Conference (DAARC2000)*, pp. 28–38. Lancaster University.

Upton, T. and Connor, U. 2001. 'Using computerized corpus analysis to investigate the textlinguistic discourse move of a genre'. *English for Specific Purposes* 20: 313–329.

Vallins, G. 1951. *Good English: How to Write It*. London: Andre Deutsch.

van Naerssen, M. 1986. 'Hipotesis sobre la adquisición de una segunda lengua, consideraciones interlenguaje: comprobación en el español' in J. Meisel (ed.) *Adquisición de Lenguaje*. Vervuert, Frankfurt.

Váradi, T. 2000. 'Corpus linguistics – linguistics or language engineering?' in T. Erjavec and J. Gross (eds) *Information Society Multi-Conference Proceedings Language Technologies*, pp.1–5. Ljubljana, 17–18 October 2000. URL: http://nl.ijs.si/isjt00/zbornik/sdjt00-Varadi01.pdf

Wang, L. 1943. *Zhongguo Xiandai Yufa* [*Modern Chinese Grammar*] (Reprinted in 1985). Beijing: Commercial Printing House.

Wang, M. and Hirschberg J. 1992. 'Automatic classification of intonational phrase boundaries'. *Computer Speech and Language* 6: 175–196.

Watson, G. 1994. 'A multidimensional analysis of style in Mudrooroo Nyoongah's prose works'. *Text* 14: 239–285.

Watson, G. 1999. 'Evidentiality and affect: a quantitative approach'. *Language and Literature* 8/3: 217–240.

Weisser, M. 2003. 'SPAACy – a semi-automated tool for annotating dialogue acts'. *International Journal of Corpus Linguistics* 8/1: 63–74.

Wichmann, A. 1995. 'Using concordances for the teaching of modern languages in higher education'. *Language Learning Journal* 11: 61–63.

Wichmann, A. 1997. 'General introduction' in A. Wichmann, S. Fligelstone, A. McEnery and G. Knowles (eds) *Teaching and Language Corpora*, pp. xvi–xvii. London: Longman.

Wichmann, A., Fligelstone, S., McEnery A. and Knowles, G. (eds) 1997. *Teaching and Language Corpora*. London: Longman.

Widdowson, H. 1990. *Aspects of Language Teaching*. Oxford: Oxford University Press.

Widdowson, H. 1991. 'The description and prescription of language' in J. Alatis (ed.) *Georgetown University Round Table on Languages and Linguistics 1991*, pp. 11–24. Washington, DC: Georgetown University Press.

Widdowson, H. 2000. 'The limitations of linguistics applied'. *Applied Linguistics* 21/1: 3–25.

Widdowson, H. 2003. *Defining Issues in English Language Teaching*. Oxford: Oxford University Press.

Widdowson, H. 2004. *Text, Context, Pretext: Critical Issues in Discourse Analysis*. Oxford: Blackwell.

Wilks, Y. 2003. 'Semantic annotation and word–sense disambiguation'. Paper presented at the Prague Workshop on Lexico–semantic Classification and Tagging. Prague, 8–9 December 2003.

Williams, A. 1996. 'A translator's reference needs: dictionaries or parallel texts?' *Target* 8/2: 277–99.

Willis, D. 1990. *The Lexical Syllabus: A New Approach to Language Teaching*. London: HarperCollins.

Wittenburg, P., Peters, W. and Broeder, D. 2002. 'Metadata proposals for corpora and lexica' in *LREC 2002 Proceedings*, pp. 1321–1326.

Wood, F. 1962. *Current English Usage*. London: Macmillan.

Woolls, D. 1998. 'Multilingual parallel concordancing for pedagogical use' in *Proceedings of Teaching and Language Corpora*, pp. 222–227. Keble College, Oxford, 24–27 July 1998.

Woolls, D. 2000. 'From purity to pragmatism; user-driven development of a multilingual parallel concordancer' in S. Botley, A. McEnery and A. Wilson (eds) *Multilingual Corpora in Teaching and Research*, pp. 116–133. Amsterdam: Rodopi.

Woolls, D. and Coulthard, M. 1998. 'Tools for the trade'. *Forensic Linguistics* 5: 33–57.

Wu, D. 2002. 'Conception and application of computer-assisted translation'. Paper presented at the 1st International Symposium on Contrastive and Translation Studies between Chinese and English. Shanghai, 8–11 August 2002.

Wu, D. and Fung, P. 1994. 'Improving Chinese tokenization with linguistic filter on statistical lexical acquisition' in S. Schmid and S. Laderer (eds) *ANLP-94*. URL: http://acl.ldc.upenn.edu/A/A94/A94–1030.pdf

Xiao, Z. 2002. 'A corpus-based study of aspect in Mandarin Chinese'. Ph.D. thesis. Lancaster University.

Xiao, Z. and McEnery, A. 2002a. 'A corpus-based approach to tense and aspect in English–Chinese translation'. Paper presented at the 1st International Symposium on contrastive and translation studies between Chinese and English. Shanghai, 8–11 August 2002. Later published as McEnery and Xiao (2005c).

Xiao, Z. and McEnery A. 2002b. 'Situation aspect as a universal aspect: implications for artificial languages'. *Journal of Universal Language* 3/2: 139–177.

Xiao, Z. and McEnery, A. 2004a. 'A corpus-based two-level model of situation aspect'. *Journal of Linguistics* 40/2: 325–363.

Xiao, Z. and McEnery, A. 2004b. *Aspect in Mandarin Chinese: A Corpus-Based Study*. Amsterdam: John Benjamins.

Xiao, Z. and McEnery, A. 2005. 'Two approaches to genre analysis: three genres in modern American English'. *Journal of English Linguistics* 33/1: 62–82.

Yang, R. and Allison, D. 2003. 'Research articles in applied linguistics: moving from results to conclusions'. *English for Specific Purposes* 22: 365–385.

Yang, S. 1995. 'The aspectual system of Chinese'. Ph.D. thesis. University of Victoria.

Yates, F. 1965. *Sampling Methods for Censuses and Surveys* (3rd edn). London: Charles Griffin & Company Limited.

Zandvoort, R. 1966. *A Handbook of English Grammar*. London: Longman.

Zanettin, F. 1998. 'Bilingual comparable corpora and the training of translators'. *Meta* 43/4. URL: www.erudit.org/revue/meta/1998/v43/n4/004638ar.pdf

Zhang, H. and Liu, Q. 2002. 'Model of Chinese words rough segmentation based on N-shortest-paths method'. *Journal of Chinese Information Processing* 16/5: 1–7.

Zhang, L. 1995. *A Contrastive Study of Aspectuality in German, English and Chinese*. Frankfurt: Peter Lang.

Zhang, X. 1993. 'English collocations and their effect on the writing of native and non-native college freshmen'. Ph.D. thesis. Indiana University of Pennsylvania.

Zhou, Q. and Yu, S. 1997. 'Annotating the contemporary Chinese corpus'. *International Journal of Corpus Linguistics* 2/2: 239–258.

Appendix of useful Internet links

THE COMPANION WEBSITES FOR THIS BOOK

The publisher's companion website:
http://www.routledge.com/rcenters/linguistics/series/ral.htm

The authors' companion website:
http://www.ling.lancs.ac.uk/corplang/cbls/

CORPUS RESOURCES

BNC home: http://info.ox.ac.uk/bnc
BNC online: http://thetis.bl.uk/
BNCWeb: http://escorp.unizh.ch
Bank of English: http://www.collins.co.uk/books.aspx?group=153
LDC: http://www.ldc.upenn.edu
ELRA: http://www.elra.info/
OTA: http://ota.ahds.ac.uk
TRACTOR: http://www.tractor.de/
SNLR: http://crl.nmsu.edu/Resources/clr.htm
W3C: http://www.essex.ac.uk/linguistics/clmt/w3c/corpus_ling/content/corpora/
     list/
MICASE: http://www.hti.umich.edu/m/micase
ICLE: http://www.fltr.ucl.ac.be/fltr/germ/etan/cecl/cecl.html
CHILDES: http://childes.psy.cmu.edu/

CORPUS TOOLS

CLAWS tagger:
http://www.comp.lancs.ac.uk/computing/research/ucrel/claws/tagservice.html
http://www.comp.lancs.ac.uk/computing/research/ucrel/claws/ (for licensed user)

AMALGAM tagger:
http://www.scs.leeds.ac.uk/ccalas/amalgam/amalgtag3.html

Brill's tagger:
http://www.cs.jhu.edu/~brill/code.html

WordSmith concordancer:
http://www.lexically.net/wordsmith/ (versions 3 and 4)

MonoConc and ParaConc:
http://www.ruf.rice.edu/~barlow/#sof
http://www.athel.com/mono.html

Xaira concordancer:
http://www.xaira.org

PERSONAL WEBSITES

David Lee: (corpus resources and tools)
http://devoted.to/corpora

Yukio Tono: (learner corpora and language acquisition)
http://leo.meikai.ac.jp/~tono/

Tim Johns: (data-driven learning)
http://www.ecml/at/projects/voll/our_resources/graz_2002/ddrivenlrning/
whatisddl/resources/tim_ddl_learning_page.htm

Index